Unit 10

Drafting Financial Statements

Study Pack

Technician (NVQ Level 4)

Published August 1999 by Financial Training, 10–14 White Lion Street, London N1 9PE

Copyright © 1999 The Financial Training Co Ltd

ISBN 1 85179 781 5

This pack has been published by Financial Training, one of the leading providers of training in accountancy and finance. Although it is aimed at students on the Education and Training Scheme of the Association of Accounting Technicians (AAT) it is not published or approved directly by the AAT. Any queries on the Education and Training Scheme and AAT administration should be addressed to Student Services at AAT, 154 Clerkenwell Road, London EC1R 5AD (0207 837 8600), or emailed to student.services@aat.org.uk

Publisher's note

Financial Training Study Packs are distributed in the UK and overseas by Stanley Thornes (Publishers) Limited. They are another company within the Wolters Kluwer group. They can be contacted at: Stanley Thornes, Ellenborough House, Wellington Street, Cheltenham GL50 1YD. Telephone: (01242) 228888. Fax: (01242) 221914.

We are grateful to the Association of Accounting Technicians for their kind permission to reproduce tasks from the central assessments.

All business entities referred to in this publication are fictitious. Any resemblance to any actual organisation, past or present, is purely coincidental.

All rights reserved. No part of this book may be reproduced or transmitted in any form or by any means, electronic or mechanical, including photocopying, recording, or by any information storage and retrieval system, without prior permission from the publisher.

Contents

Introduction ix

Unit 10 Study Pack

Chapter 1   The Legal and Professional Framework

Objectives	1
Introduction	1
Companies Act 1985	2
Companies Act 1989	3
Accounting standards	3
Management accounts	5
Other professional requirements	6
Summary	7

Chapter 2   The Conceptual Framework

Objectives	9
Accounting concepts	9
The Statement of Principles	13
Questions	19
Summary	20

Chapter 3   Introduction to Final Accounts

Objectives	21
Types of business organisation	21
Non–profit making entities	24
Preparing final accounts	27
The accounts of a sole trader	29
Making adjustments	32
The extended trial balance	35
Further points	41
Questions	43
Summary	44

Chapter 4   The Accounts of Partnerships

Objectives	45
Introduction	45
Rights of partners	46
Appropriation of profit	47
Goodwill	50
Admission of new partners	54
Retirement of partners	59
Dissolution	63
Drafting partnership accounts	67
Questions	67
Summary	69

Chapter 5 Introduction to Limited Company Accounts

Objectives	71
Introduction	71
Pro forma company profit and loss account	72
Analysis of expenses	72
Corporation tax	73
Dividends	73
Pro forma company balance sheet	74
Share capital	74
Reserves	76
Share premium account	76
Bonus issues	77
Rights issues	78
Debentures	79
Capital instruments	79
Types of company	80
The duties of companies regarding accounting records	80
Annual accounts	80
Questions	82
Summary	84

Chapter 6 Manufacturing Accounts

Objectives	85
Introduction	85
The pro forma	86
Preparation of the manufacturing account	87
Questions	89
Summary	91

Chapter 7 Limited Company Accounts: the Balance Sheet

Objectives	93
Introduction	93
Form of accounts	94
Balance sheet – formats	94
Balance sheet – disclosures	97
Questions	104
Summary	105

Chapter 8 Limited Company Accounts: the Profit and Loss Account

Objectives	107
Profit and loss account – formats	108
Profit and loss account – disclosures	108
Sundry matters	112
The directors' report	112
FRS 14 *Earnings per share*	113
Accounts for small and medium–sized companies	115
Other exemptions for small companies	117
Financial Reporting Standard for Smaller Entities (FRSSE)	117
Summary financial statements	117
Questions	119
Summary	120

Chapter 9 Reporting Financial Performance

Objectives	121
Introduction	121
Continuing operations, acquisitions and discontinued operations	121
Exceptional items	123
Extraordinary items	125
Prior–period adjustments	125
Statement of total recognised gains and losses	127
Note of historical cost profit and lossses	129
Reconciliation of movements in shareholders' funds and statement of reserves	130
Comprehensive example	131
Questions	134
Summary	135

Chapter 10 Fixed Assets: Tangible Assets

Objectives	137
FRS 15 *Tangible fixed assets*	137
SSAP 19 *Accounting for investment properties*	146
SSAP 4 *Accounting for government grants*	148
Questions	150
Summary	152

Chapter 11 Fixed Assets: Intangible Assets

Objectives	153
SSAP 13 *Accounting for research and development*	153
FRS 10 *Goodwill and intangible assets*	157
FRS 11 *Impairment of fixed assets and goodwill*	162
Questions	165
Summary	166

Chapter 12 Stocks and Long–term Contracts

Objectives	167
Stock	167
Long–term contract work in progress	170
Disclosure requirements	174
Questions	175
Summary	176

Chapter 13 Accounting for Leases and Hire Purchase Contracts

Objectives	177
Types of transaction	177
Types of lease	178
Finance lease	178
Operating lease	179
Summary	179

Chapter 14 Taxation in Company Accounts

Objectives	181
Corporation tax	181
Accounting for value added tax	183
Accounting for deferred tax	184
Summary	186

Chapter 15 Post Balance Sheet Events, Provisions and Contingencies

Objectives	187
SSAP 17 *Accounting for post balance sheet events*	187
FRS 12 *Provisions, contingent liabilities and contingent assets*	190
Questions	193
Summary	194

Chapter 16 Cash Flow Statements

Objectives	195
The purpose of the cash flow statement	195
Basic illustration	195
Cash	197
Cash inflows and outflows	197
Format of the cash flow statement	199
Preparation of the cash flow statement	202
Interpreting a cash flow statement	206
Further points	208
Questions	211
Summary	212

Chapter 17 Interpretation of Accounts

Objectives	213
Introduction	213
Calculations	214
Answers	217
Interpretation	218
Further points	222
SSAP 25 *Segmental reporting*	224
Questions	226
Summary	228

Chapter 18 Sundry Accounting Problems

Objectives	229
Foreign currency translation	229
Accounting for pension costs	231
Reporting the substance of transactions	233
Related party transactions	234
Summary	235

Chapter 19 Group Accounts – Basic Principles

Objectives	237
Introduction	237
Groups and group accounts	237
Single entity concept	238
Basic principles: consolidated balance sheet	239
Control and ownership	243
Goodwill	245
Basic principles: consolidated profit and loss account	252
Questions	253
Summary	254

Chapter 20 Group Accounts – Consolidated Balance Sheet

Objectives	255
Summary of basic technique	255
Cancellation of intra-group balances	258
Dividends	263
Unrealised intra-group profit	265
Fair values	266
Other considerations	269
Pro forma consolidation workings	270
Questions	272
Summary	273

Chapter 21 Group Accounts – Consolidated Profit and Loss Account

Objectives	275
Introduction	275
Basic principles	275
Detailed requirements	276
Intra-group profit and provision for unrealised profit	281
Treatment of goodwill	283
Link between balance sheet and profit and loss account	283
Questions	285
Summary	286

Chapter 22 Group Accounts – Legal and Professional Requirements

Objectives	287
Introduction	287
Companies Act 1985 requirements	287
FRS 2 *Accounting for subsidiary undertakings*	289
Other types of investment	290
Associates and the Companies Act 1985	296
FRS 9 *Associates and joint ventures*	297
Other methods of consolidation	298
Merger accounting method	298
Summary	300

Chapter 23 Answers to Chapter Questions		301
Chapter 2		301
Chapter 3		302
Chapter 4		303
Chapter 5		306
Chapter 6		308
Chapter 7		312
Chapter 8		315
Chapter 9		318
Chapter 10		320
Chapter 11		322
Chapter 12		325
Chapter 15		326
Chapter 16		327
Chapter 17		329
Chapter 19		331
Chapter 20		333
Chapter 21		335

	Data & Tasks	Answer Book	Answers
Chapter 24 Practice Central Assessment	337	347	355

Unit 10 Central Assessment Pack

		Questions	Answers
Chapter 1	The Accounts of Partnerships and Sole Traders	365	380
Chapter 2	Manufacturing Accounts	395	397
Chapter 3	Limited Company Accounts	401	417
Chapter 4	Reporting Financial Performance	431	434
Chapter 5	Fixed Assets: Tangible Assets	439	441
Chapter 6	Fixed Assets: Intangible Assets	445	447
Chapter 7	Stocks and Long-term Contracts	451	452
Chapter 8	Accounting for Leases and Hire Purchase Contracts	453	454
Chapter 9	Post Balance Sheet Events, Provisions and Contingencies	455	456
Chapter 10	Cash Flow Statements	457	465
Chapter 11	Interpretation of Accounts	469	474
Chapter 12	Group Accounts – Consolidated Balance Sheet	479	485
Chapter 13	Group Accounts – Consolidated Profit and Loss Account	493	495
Chapter 14	Group Accounts – Legal and Professional Requirements	499	500

		Data & Tasks	Answer Book	Answers
Chapter 15	Mock Central Assessment	503	511	527

Index	537
Review Form	541

Introduction

1 What is Unit 10 about?

Unit 10 covers the preparation and analysis of full financial statements, primarily of organisations in the private sector. The ETB, manufacturing accounts, profit and loss accounts, balance sheets and cash flow statements are frequently assessed as are ratio analysis and consolidation.

2 Elements of study for Unit 10

Unit 10 contains two separate elements of competence, each of which is divided into performance criteria and a range statement. It is necessary to demonstrate competence in each performance criterion across the range statement. Each performance criterion is cross-referenced below to the chapter(s) in the Study Pack in which it is covered.

Element 10: Interpret financial statements

Performance criteria

		Chapter(s)
10.1.1	The general purpose of financial statements used in various organisations is identified	1–3
10.1.2	Elements in financial statements used in various organisations are identified	2
10.1.3	The relationship of elements within financial statements is identified	2
10.1.4	The relationship between elements of limited company financial statements is interpreted	17
10.1.5	Unusual features or significant issues are identified within financial statements	17
10.1.6	Valid conclusions are drawn from the information contained within financial statements	17
10.1.7	Conclusions and interpretations are clearly presented	17

Range statement

1. **Financial statements:** Balance sheet, income statements

2. **Elements:** Assets, liabilities, ownership interest, income, expenditure contribution from owners, distribution to owners, gains and losses

3. **Relationship between elements:** Profitability, liquidity, efficient use of resources, financial position

Element 10.2 Draft limited company, sole trader and partnership year end financial statements

Performance criteria

		Chapter(s)
10.2.1	Financial statements are accurately drafted from the appropriate information	3–16, 18–22
10.2.2	Subsequent adjustments are correctly implemented	3–6, 10–15, 19–22
10.2.3	Draft accounts comply with domestic standards and legislation and, where relevant, partnership agreement	4, 5, 7–16, 18–22
10.2.4	A cash flow statement is correctly prepared and interpreted where required	16
10.2.5	Year end financial statements are presented for approval to the appropriate person in a clear form	3–8
10.2.6	Confidentiality procedures are followed at all times	1
10.2.7	The organisation's policies, regulations, procedures and timescales relating to financial statements are observed at all times	1
10.2.8	Discrepancies, unusual features or queries are identified and either resolved or referred to the appropriate person	1

Range statement

1   **Financial statements:** Profit and loss account, balance sheet, owners capital and current account, cash flow statement, statement of total recognised gains and losses, the supplementary notes required by statute, SSAPs, FRSs or other relevant pronouncements

2   **Domestic standards:** Relevant SSAPs, relevant FRSs, other relevant pronouncements

3   **Limited company financial statements:** Unitary, consolidated

3 Assessment

Unit 10 *Drafting financial statements* is assessed by a Central Assessment. The central assessment lasts for three hours, plus fifteen minutes reading time. During the reading time, you will be allowed to read and write notes on the assessment paper itself but you will not be allowed to write in the answer booklet.

3.1 Format of the central assessment

The assessment will be in a number of sections, typically three or four. Marks for each section are not given but candidates are advised how long they should spend on each section.

Overall, the assessor will expect candidates to:

♦   display basic competence in the preparation of limited company accounts;
♦   be familiar with basic statutory requirements and the main relevant accounting standards

Sections 1 and 2 of the central assessment will *normally* involve:

- preparation of a profit and loss account and balance sheet from an extended trial balance with some adjustments;

- further questions on, for example,

    - interpretation of accounts;
    - the significance of transactions;
    - journal entries for adjustments;
    - the understanding of key accounting terms/concepts;
    - knowledge of relevant FRSs.

Remaining sections *may* involve, for limited companies or partnerships:

- cash flow statements;
- reconciliation of cash flow statements and operating profit statements;
- partnership appropriation accounts;
- test of candidates' knowledge of law, accounting principles and concepts.

Candidates will be expected to write brief reports or memos to managers or directors explaining, for example, accounting concepts.

3.2 Contents of past central assessments

June 1997

Section 1

- Preparation of limited company balance sheet.
- Permitted use of share premium account.
- Post balance sheet events.
- Associated undertakings.

Section 2

- Interpretation of accounts.
- Preparation of reconciliation between cash flows from operating activities and operating profit.

Section 3

- Preparation of accounts for sole trader from extended trial balance.
- Differences between legal status of sole traders and limited companies.

Section 4

- Preparation of partners' capital accounts, including admission and revaluation.

December 1997

Section 1

- Preparation of limited company profit and loss account and balance sheet from an extended trial balance.

Section 2

- Preparation of a cash flow statement.
- Calculation and accounting treatment of goodwill on consolidation.
- Calculation of ratios.

Section 3

- Adjustments to net profit of a partnership.
- Preparation of appropriation account, partners' capital accounts and partners' current accounts, including admission.

June 1998

Section 1

- Preparation of limited company profit and loss account and balance sheet from an extended trial balance.
- Revaluation of fixed assets.
- Accruals concept.
- Definition of a subsidiary undertaking.
- Calculation of minority interest.

Section 2

- Preparation of a cash flow statement.
- Interpretation of accounts.

Section 3

- Preparation of appropriation account, partners' capital accounts and partners' current accounts, including admission and treatment of bad debts.

December 1998

This forms the Mock Central Assessment at the end of the Central Assessment Pack and is not further analysed here.

3.3 Common problems with the central assessment

These are highlighted by the assessor's reports on past assessments. The overall impression given by the assessor's comments is that candidates perform the computational tasks relatively well, but have problems with the written tasks.

The assessor has made the following general criticisms:

- failure to show workings or give sufficient explanation;
- failure to answer the question set;
- failure to demonstrate understanding.

3.4 How to tackle the Central Assessment

- Always read all the instructions carefully before starting.
- Work through the paper in the order set.
- Read the questions. Answer the question that has been set.
- Allocate your time sensibly as instructed between the tasks, although time–pressure should not be a problem if you are well prepared.
- Work methodically through each section. Make sure that you deal with every item of information. Consider ticking each figure in the question as you use it.
- You must aim to get all of the exercise correct if you are to be assessed as competent.
- Plan your approach to the written questions and read all the information carefully. Make sure you understand what you are required to do and what the aim of the communication is. Remember that, in some cases, you may be writing to someone with limited or no knowledge of financial accounting, so you must adapt your approach accordingly.

Remember that your objective is to prove that you are competent in the unit being assessed. You must therefore aim for 100% accuracy and an extremely high standard of presentation. The actual pass mark is likely to be around 80%, so you cannot afford to ignore any tasks within the assessment.

You must aim to achieve the following.

- *Good presentation skills:* All work should be net and well presented, as if it were real work. You should use black ink or biro. Pencil is not acceptable, neither is correcting fluid (such as Tipp–Ex). Cross out any errors neatly and clearly. Always use a ruler for underlining. Use the proformas provided. Remember that you are being assessed on your knowledge of disclosure requirements as well as on your knowledge of accounting techniques.

- *Completeness:* All tasks should be complete (for example, columns totalled). You cannot decide to leave out part of an exercise and still hope to be successful.

- *Good communication skills:* Communication skills are fundamentally important in all the assessments for all stages. You are expected to show a good standard of English, including correct spelling and correct use of accounting terms.

- *Accuracy:* All calculations must be completed accurately, such as the calculation of depreciation or minority interest.

- *Technical knowledge:* Any explanations given – for example, the reasons for adopting a particular accounting treatment, etc – must be accurate. Remember that you are being assessed on your *understanding* of accounting principles.

4 Using this Study Pack

Whatever your previous experience, you are encouraged to work through this Study Pack as completely and as methodically as you can, paying particular attention to the areas which are most relevant to you. Here is a short explanation of the aim of each area of the Study Pack.

- **Study Pack Chapters 1-22.** These contain study material, examples and questions (with answers in Chapter 23) on a particular topic to help you to learn the required techniques. Performance criteria covered are identified at the beginning of each chapter, as is a list of what you should actually be able to do once you have completed your studies of the chapter. There is also a summary at the end.

- **Study Pack Chapter 24 Practice Central Assessment.** This formed the Specimen Central Assessment distributed by the AAT when the Standards were last revised in 1998, and so represents a fair example of what you will have to face.

- **Central Assessment Pack Chapters 1–14.** These contain additional questions, most of which come from recent Central Assessments set by the AAT. All have full answers.

- **Central Assessment Pack Chapter 15 Mock Central Assessment.** This is the December 1998 actual paper, for you to try as far as possible under timed conditions. It has a full answer.

You should try to make sure that you attempt all questions and central assessments in this Study Pack without looking at the answers. It is only by doing this that you get full value from the Pack. By peeking the only person you are cheating is yourself!

FTC Training Centres

Birmingham	*Leicester*	*Manchester*	*Wokingham*
1st floor Centre City Tower 7 Hill Street Birmingham B5 4UA Tel: 0121 644 4747	3rd Floor Beckville House 66 London Road Leicester LE2 0QD Tel: 0116 285 6767	6th Floor St James Building Oxford Street Manchester M1 6FQ Tel: 0161 233 2018	Swift House Market Place Wokingham RG40 1AP Tel: 0118 977 4922
Cardiff	*Liverpool*	*Newcastle*	*Hong Kong*
5th floor Market Chambers 5-7 St Mary's Street Cardiff CF1 2AT Tel: 01222 388 067	3rd Floor Coopers Building Church Street Liverpool L1 3AA Tel: 0151 708 8839	Provincial House Northumberland St Newcastle upon Tyne NE1 7DQ Tel: 0191 232 9365	24th Fl Wyndham Place 44 Wyndham Street Central Hong Kong Tel: (852) 2526 3686
Glasgow	*London (AAT/ACCA/CIMA)*	*Nottingham*	*Kuala Lumpur*
91 Mitchell Street Glasgow G1 3LN Tel: 0141 248 8080	7-13 Melior Street London SE1 3QP Tel: 0171 407 5000	3rd Floor Alan House 5 Clumber Street Nottingham NG1 3ED Tel: 0115 853 3600	1st Floor Wisma Alma 2-4 Jalan Manau 50460 Kuala Lumpur Malaysia Tel: (603) 274 8884
Hull	*London – ACA*	*Sheffield*	*Mauritius*
Suite R The Shirethorn Centre Prospect Street Hull HU2 8PX Tel: 01482 620578	10-14 White Lion Street London N1 9PD Tel: 0171 837 0700	Pegasus House 463a Glossop Road Sheffield S10 2QD Tel: 0114 266 9265	Coopers & Lybrand Training Centre 3rd Floor, Astor Court George Guidert Port Louis Mauritius Tel: (230) 208 7945
Leeds	*London – Financial Markets*	*Southampton*	*Singapore*
49 St Paul's Street Leeds LS1 2TE Tel: 0113 388 9320	New London House 6 London Street London EC3R 7LQ Tel: 0171 265 1011	32 Castle Way Southampton SO14 2AW Tel: 01703 220852	107A Sophia Road Singapore 228 172 Tel: (65) 333 1877

THE FINANCIAL TRAINING COMPANY

AAT DIVISION

E Mail: aat@financial-training.com

http:\\www.financial-training.com

A MEMBER OF THE WOLTERS KLUWER PROFESSIONAL TRAINING GROUP

CHAPTER 1

The Legal and Professional Framework

Objectives

This chapter covers the following performance criteria:

10.1.1 The general purpose of financial statements used in various organisations is identified.

10.2.6 Confidentiality procedures are followed at all times.

10.2.7 The organisation's policies, regulations, procedures and timescales relating to financial statements are observed at all times.

10.2.8 Discrepancies, unusual features or queries are identified and either resolved or referred to the appropriate person.

At the end of this chapter, you should be able to:

♦ understand the legal and professional framework which governs the drafting of financial statements; and

♦ understand the other professional considerations which govern the work of an accountant.

Introduction

The main purpose of financial statements is to provide information to a wide range of users.

The *balance sheet* provides information on the financial position of a business (its assets and liabilities at a point in time).

The *profit and loss account* provides information on the performance of a business (the profit or loss which results from trading over a period of time).

The *cash flow statement* provides information on the financial adaptability of a business (the movement of cash into and out of the business over a period of time).

Financial statements also show the results of the *stewardship* of a business. Stewardship is the accountability of management for the resources entrusted to it by the owners. This applies to the financial statements of many limited companies.

All users of financial statements need information on financial position, performance and financial adaptability. However, many different groups of people may use financial statements and each group will need particular information. Users of financial statements may include investors, management, employees, customers, suppliers, lenders, the government and the public. Investors need to be able to assess the ability of a business to pay dividends and manage resources. Management need information with which to assess performance, take decisions, plan, and control the business. Lenders, such as banks, are interested in the ability of the business to pay interest and repay loans. The Inland Revenue uses financial statements as the basis for tax assessments.

The law requires limited companies to prepare financial statements annually. These financial statements must be filed with the Registrar of Companies and are then available to all interested parties. Most businesses, whether incorporated or not, are required to produce financial statements for submission to the Inland Revenue.

In the UK, the form and content of limited company accounts is laid down within the Companies Acts. The preparation of limited company accounts is also subject to regulations issued by the Accounting Standards Board.

The form and content of the accounts of other businesses is not prescribed by law. However, the accounts of sole traders and partnerships should be prepared in accordance with current best accounting practice.

Companies Act 1985

Introduction

The Companies Act 1985 contains the following:

- formats
- fundamental accounting principles
- valuation rules

Formats

Companies must prepare their annual accounts in accordance with certain formats. There are two formats specified for the balance sheet and four formats specified for the profit and loss account. These formats specify the items which must be disclosed in the financial statements and the order in which they must be shown, although they do provide some flexibility in relegating details to the notes to the accounts. We shall study these formats in the sessions on company accounts.

Fundamental accounting principles

The law embodies five accounting principles:

- going concern
- consistency
- prudence
- accruals
- no offset

These accounting principles are well known to accountants and the first four are listed as fundamental accounting concepts in SSAP2 *Disclosure of accounting policies*, which we shall examine later.

When the directors depart from these accounting principles, a note to the accounts must provide particulars of the departure, the reasons for it and its effect.

Valuation rules

The Companies Act 1985 embodies two sets of valuation rules: the **historical cost accounting rules** and the **alternative accounting rules**.

- *Historical cost accounting rules*

    Under these rules, assets are shown on the basis of their purchase price or production cost. Fixed assets with a finite useful economic life must be depreciated on a systematic basis over their useful economic life. Current assets (eg. stocks) must be written down if the net realisable value is lower than the cost.

- *Alternative accounting rules*

    Under these rules, fixed assets other than goodwill, stocks and short-term investments may be shown at their current cost.

Companies Act 1989

The Companies Act 1989 has to some extent increased the volume of disclosure that companies are required to make in their financial statements. These disclosures are dealt with in later sessions.

One of the most significant requirements is that accounts of public and large private companies must state whether they have been prepared in accordance with applicable accounting standards (ie. SSAPs and FRSs – see below) and give details of, and the reasons for, any material departures.

Accounting standards

Accounting standards give guidance in specific areas of accounting. There are two types of accounting standard currently in issue:

- *Statements of Standard Accounting Practice (SSAPs)*

    SSAPs were created by a body known as the Accounting Standards Committee (ASC). The ASC was abolished in July 1990.

- *Financial Reporting Standards (FRSs)*

    The Accounting Standards Board (ASB) took over the role of setting accounting standards from the ASC in August 1990. One of the ASB's first acts was to adopt all 22 existing SSAPs. The SSAPs therefore continue to be applicable to all sets of accounts until they are replaced or withdrawn.

    The accounting standards created by the ASB are known as *Financial Reporting Standards*. In preparing company accounts, both SSAPs and FRSs should be complied with. Failure to do so can lead to the company being ordered to redraft its accounts (*S12 CA 1989*).

    The board consists of approximately ten qualified accountants and is monitored and funded by a body, the Financial Reporting Council, whose members are drawn from accounts user groups (eg. Stock Exchange, CBI) as well as the accounting profession.

Financial Reporting Review Panel (FRRP)

The Financial Reporting Review Panel is also guided and monitored by the FRC. It enquires into material departures from the requirements of the Companies Act or of accounting standards in the annual accounts of public and large private companies. The Review Panel can require companies to amend their accounts and has the power to prosecute them under the Companies Act if they refuse to do so voluntarily. Although a number of public companies have agreed to amend their accounts since the Review Panel was set up in 1990, no case has yet reached the courts.

Urgent Issues Task Force (UITF)

This is a committee of the ASB. It deals with urgent and emerging issues, particularly where the normal standard setting process would be too slow to implement changes. It issues consensus pronouncements which are known as *UITF Abstracts*.

The Public Sector and Not for Profit Committee

This is another sub-committee of the ASB. It maintains contact between the ASB and public sector accounting by advising the ASB on ways of minimising differences between public sector and private sector accounting practices. It also comments on FRSs before they are issued from the point of view of public sector and 'not for profit' organisations.

Aims of accounting standards

The aim of the ASB is to establish and improve standards of financial accounting and reporting for the benefit of users, preparers and auditors of financial information.

Accounting standards:

- are authoritative statements of how particular types of transaction and other events should be reflected in financial statements
- are applicable to all financial statements that are intended to give *a true and fair view*
- need not be applied to immaterial items.

Compliance with accounting standards will normally be necessary for financial statements to give a true and fair view. Only in exceptional circumstances will departure from the requirements of an accounting standard be necessary in order for financial statements to give a true and fair view.

Members of professional bodies are expected to observe accounting standards, whether they are acting as directors or officers of a company or as auditors or reporting accountants. They should use their best endeavours to ensure that accounting standards are observed by others and that significant departures found to be necessary are adequately disclosed and explained in the financial statements.

The standard setting process

There are several stages in the development of a new FRS:

1. A topic is identified and a member of the ASB's staff carries out research.
2. The ASB issues a Discussion Paper, which sets out the issues and discusses the possible alternative approaches. This is circulated to interested parties, who comment.
3. A Financial Reporting Exposure Draft (FRED) is published. This is a draft version of the new FRS. Again, this is circulated to interested parties. The proposals may be amended as a result of their comments.
4. The FRS is published.

The ASB issues standards on its own authority. Although it does take comments into account, the ultimate content of an FRS depends on its own judgement based on research, public consultation and careful deliberation about the benefits and costs of providing the resulting information in the financial statements.

Main types of standard

There are four main types of standard, although several contain features of more than one type:

(a) *Informational:* These require explanation of what has been done. The best example is SSAP2 *Disclosure of accounting policies*, discussed below.

(b) *Additional disclosure:* Some standards call for the disclosure of information not required by law. Thus FRS1 *Cash flow statements* requires all but small companies to include a cash flow statement in their financial statements.

(c) *Presentation:* These require a standard presentation of information. An example is FRS3 *Reporting financial performance*, which requires, for example, analysis of results between continuing operations and discontinued operations. In many British standards, guidance on presentation is relegated to non-mandatory appendices.

(d) *Valuation (or measurement):* These standards contain rules on how items in a balance sheet and profit and loss account should be valued (or measured). An example is SSAP9 *Stocks and long-term contracts*.

While there has been relatively little opposition to standards of the first type, many have spoken out against standards of the other three types, particularly those which specify valuation or measurement rules. It has been argued that these restrict the exercise of professional judgement by the accountant.

Management accounts

As well as producing financial statements for external users, businesses may also produce financial statements for internal use. These are often known as *management accounts*.

These accounts provide the information which management needs in order to control the business, to take decisions and to plan for the future. Therefore they are likely to be very much more detailed than the financial statements produced for external users. Whereas published financial statements are based on historical information, management accounts may include forecast information, such as cash flow statements.

Financial statements intended for third parties are normally produced annually. Management accounts may be produced quarterly or monthly.

Management accounts do not have to comply with the requirements of the Companies Acts. They may be drafted in whatever form management wish.

Management accounting as such (for example, recording cost information) is outside the scope of this unit. The emphasis of this unit falls upon financial accounting, that is, drafting financial statements primarily intended for external users.

Other professional requirements

Confidentiality

In the course of preparing accounts, you are likely to acquire confidential information. This applies whether you are working in practice and preparing accounts for a client or whether you are preparing accounts for your own employer.

Confidential information should not be disclosed, either to anyone within the organisation or to a third party unless permission has been obtained from the client, employer or other proper source. Under very exceptional circumstances, an accountant may have a legal duty to disclose information to a third party (for example, if a client has committed an illegal act).

An accountant should not make use of confidential information for personal gain, for example, by dealing in the shares of a client company.

Some businesses treat the financial statements themselves as strictly confidential, at least until they are published. This is particularly likely in the case of a public company or a large partnership, but may apply to any business.

There are obvious examples of the type of information which is likely to be confidential (for example, directors' salaries). Other information may be less obviously sensitive but still regarded as confidential in some organisations. In practice, confidentiality procedures vary from organisation to organisation, but they must always be followed strictly.

Policies and procedures

Most organisations are likely to have their own policies, regulations and procedures for preparing financial statements. These govern the method of preparing the financial statements, the accounting policies and systems used, and the way in which financial information is presented. Accounting procedures will vary according to the size and structure of the organisation and the nature of the business.

Timescales are likely to be important in most organisations. Limited company final accounts must be filed with the Registrar of Companies within ten months of the end of the financial year (or seven months if the company is a public company). Deadlines are likely to be particularly tight if the company has to report its results to the public and the financial press, or where it is owned by another company, particularly if that company is overseas.

Many businesses are required to produce accounts within a timescale in order to raise finance or as a condition of continued support from banks.

The professional accountant must observe the policies, regulations, procedures and timescales of the organisation for which financial statements are prepared.

Dealing with discrepancies and unusual items

In drawing up financial statements you are likely to have to resolve matters such as discrepancies and the treatment of unusual items.

Earlier in your studies you will have learned the importance of procedures such as reconciling control accounts and ensuring that the trial balance balances. Extending the trial balance may give rise to differences, especially where the nominal ledger contains a large number of individual accounts. When producing the first draft of a set of accounts, it is not uncommon to find that the balance sheet does not balance or that the figure for retained profit in the profit and loss account does not agree to the figure in the balance sheet! A methodical approach is necessary in order to resolve all discrepancies (unless they are immaterial enough to be safely ignored).

Drafting final accounts, particularly statutory accounts for limited companies, can be a complex operation. Accurate information about items contained in the accounts is essential so that the correct accounting treatment can be determined and the correct disclosures made. You may not necessarily have access to all the information which you need. For example, if a business acquires a type of fixed asset which it has not previously held, it will be necessary to determine its useful economic life in order to decide how it should be depreciated. If you cannot resolve items yourself, you should refer them to the appropriate person.

There is another reason why it is important to identify discrepancies and unusual items. An accounting system which is not properly controlled increases the scope for errors in the financial statements and may be an invitation to fraud.

Summary

The legal and professional framework for preparing financial statements consists of:

- the Companies Acts (which apply to limited company financial statements)

- Accounting Standards (which apply to all financial statements giving a true and fair view)

The professional accountant must observe the requirements of the Companies Acts and Accounting Standards and must also:

- follow confidentiality procedures;

- observe the policies, regulations, procedures and timescales of the organisation for which financial statements are prepared.

CHAPTER 2

The Conceptual Framework

Objectives

This chapter covers the following performance criteria:

10.1.1 The general purpose of financial statements used in various organisations is identified.

10.1.2 Elements of financial statements used in various organisations are identified.

10.1.3 The relationship of elements within financial statements is identified.

At the end of this chapter, you should be able to:

- understand the fundamental accounting concepts contained in the Companies Act 1985 and in SSAP 2

- understand the main points in the ASB's draft Statement of Principles, including:

    - the objectives of financial statements

    - the users of financial statements

    - the characteristics that make financial information useful

    - the elements of financial statements

Accounting concepts

Introduction

- The Companies Act 1985 and SSAP2 *Disclosure of accounting policies* outline the four most fundamental accounting concepts recognised by the accountancy profession.

- The Companies Act 1985 outlines a further principle of non-aggregation (no offset).

- Current accounting practice recognises other important concepts of materiality and commercial substance over legal form.

- The Companies Act 1985 identifies the *true and fair* principle.

SSAP2: Disclosure of accounting policies

Introduction

SSAP2 states that 'it is fundamental to the understanding and interpretation of financial accounts that those who use them should be aware of the main assumptions on which they are based'.

To achieve this, the statement defines accounting concepts and bases (on which accounting policies depend) and recommends disclosure in accounts of significant accounting policies.

Definition of concepts, bases and policies

- **Fundamental accounting concepts**

    - These are the *broad basic assumptions* which underlie the periodic financial accounts of business enterprises.

    - SSAP2 recognises four fundamental concepts.

    - The relative importance of each will vary according to the circumstances of the particular case.

The going concern concept

It is assumed that the enterprise will continue in operational existence for the foreseeable future.

The accruals concept

Revenues and costs are 'matched' with one another in the period to which they relate. If this conflicts with prudence, prudence must prevail.

The consistency concept

Like items are treated in a similar manner within each accounting period and from one period to the next.

The prudence concept

Revenues and profits are not included in the accounts until they are realised but provision is made for losses and liabilities immediately, even if the loss will not occur until the future.

- **Accounting bases**

    - These are the *methods* developed for applying fundamental accounting concepts to financial transactions and items, for the purpose of financial accounts.

    - In order to decide in which periods revenue and expenditure will be brought into the profit and loss account and the amounts at which material items should be shown in the balance sheet, business enterprises will select specific accounting bases most appropriate to their circumstances and adopt them.

◆ **Accounting policies**

These are the specific accounting bases judged by the business enterprises to be most appropriate to their circumstances and adopted by them for the purpose of preparing their financial accounts.

Illustration

Consider fixed assets and depreciation.

The company's accounting *policy* would be to depreciate plant and machinery.

The accounting *base* would be to depreciate plant and machinery over an expected useful life of ten years. Thus a change in the average expected useful life would be a change in accounting base but *not* a change in accounting policy.

Since depreciation should be allocated so as to charge a fair proportion of the cost or valuation of the asset to each accounting period expected to benefit from its use, it is invoking the *accruals concept*.

SSAP2 – Text

The text of the standard is as follows:

◆ *Disclosure of adoption of concepts which differ from those generally accepted*

If accounts are prepared on the basis of assumptions which differ in material respects from any of the generally accepted fundamental concepts, the facts should be explained.

In the absence of a clear statement to the contrary, there is a presumption that the four fundamental concepts have been observed.

◆ *Disclosure of accounting policies*

The accounting policies followed for dealing with items which are judged material or critical in determining profit and loss for the year and in stating the financial position should be disclosed by way of notes to the accounts. The explanation should be clear, fair and as brief as possible.

Non-aggregation principle (CA 1985)

In determining items in the accounts, assets and liabilities should not be offset against one another.

Illustrations

◆ Compensating inaccuracies in individual accounts should not be lost in one large total.

◆ If a company borrows money to buy a building, the building should be shown in fixed assets and the loan in creditors.

The concept of 'true and fair'

The Companies Act 1985 section 226 requires the directors of a company to prepare for each financial year of the company a balance sheet as at the last day of the year and a profit and loss account.

It continues, insisting that the balance sheet shall give a *true and fair* view of the state of the affairs of the company as at the end of the financial year and the profit and loss account shall give a *true and fair* view of the profit or loss of the company for the financial year.

So, where accounts are drawn up to comply with the Companies Acts, the concept of *true and fair* is a legal one.

Truth implies that the figures are mathematically accurate and factually correct.

Fairness implies that the information is presented in a manner which is free from bias.

The question as to whether or not a particular company's financial statements are true and fair can ultimately be decided by the courts.

The concept of true and fair may also apply to the financial statements of sole traders and partnerships.

Other important accounting concepts

- *Substance over form*

    Under this concept, transactions and other events are accounted for and presented in financial statements in accordance with their economic substance and financial reality and not merely with their legal form.

    For example, leasehold buildings are owned by the landlord rather than the occupier, but the occupier is using them for his business in the same way as if they were freehold. Thus it is appropriate to treat them as a fixed asset, provided that it is made clear that the premises are leasehold.

- *Materiality*

    - The omission or mis-statement of an item in a financial statement is material if, in the light of surrounding circumstances, the magnitude of the item is such that it is probable that the judgement of a reasonable person relying upon the report would have been changed or influenced by the inclusion or correction of the item.

    (Statement of Financial Accounting Concept No 2 issued by FASB)

    - There is no rigid or officially recognised definition. It is a practical rule.

    - It allows other rules to be ignored if the consequences of doing so are considered insignificant and cut off all proportion to the time and cost involved in rigidly following those other rules.

    - Accounting standards do not apply to immaterial items.

- *Realisation*

    Transactions are normally recorded when there is a legal requirement to accept liability for them; that is, when the legal title is transferred.

    This means that a transaction may be included in an earlier accounting period than the one in which cash is eventually exchanged.

- *Historical cost*

    Quantitative information recorded in monetary values is normally retained at its historical cost.

    In the case of goods purchased, this will be at the price originally paid for them and, in the case of sales, at the agreed price for which the goods were eventually sold.

- *Relevance*

    The overall message that the accounts are trying to relay may be obscured if too much information is presented.

    Accounting statements should contain only information that complies strictly with the specific requirements of the user.

- *Objectivity*

    The preparation of accounting statements involves a considerable amount of individual discretion.

    They should be prepared with the minimum amount of personal bias and the maximum amount of overall objectivity.

The Statement of Principles

Introduction

One of the first priorities of the ASB has been to develop a Statement of Principles. At present it exists as an Exposure Draft.

The aim of the Statement of Principles is to develop a conceptual framework for the preparation of financial statements. A conceptual framework is a basic set of rules or principles. From these basic rules, more detailed rules for specific issues can logically be developed.

A conceptual framework provides a clear and authoritative statement and includes the following:

- the primary statements to be presented
- the qualities they should possess
- the meaning of key accounting terms
- the criteria which must be met before items are recognised in the financial statements
- the amounts at which recognised items should be measured

UK accounting practice has been consistently criticised for its lack of coherent and consistent underlying principles. Unlike some other standard setting bodies, such as the International Accounting Standards Committee and the Financial Accounting Standards Board in the United States, the ASC did not develop any kind of conceptual framework.

The Statement of Principles will not become an accounting standard. It will influence the content of future accounting standards, but it will not be the only influence on standard setting. The ASB will also take legal requirements, cost-benefit considerations and other issues into account in developing new standards.

The remainder of this section summarises key points from the Draft Statement of Principles.

The objective of financial statements

The objective of financial statements is to provide information about the reporting entity's financial performance and financial position that is useful to a wide range of users for assessing the stewardship of management and for making economic decisions.

Users and their information needs

User group	Needs information to decide/assess:
Investors	♦ stewardship of management ♦ risk inherent in, and return provided by, their investments ♦ the entity's financial performance, financial position, cash generation abilities and financial adaptability
Lenders/potential lenders	♦ whether their loans will be repaid ♦ whether the interest will be paid when due ♦ whether to lend to the entity and on what terms
Suppliers and other creditors	♦ whether to sell to the entity ♦ the likelihood that amounts owing to them will be paid when due
Employees	♦ stability and profitability of employers ♦ the ability of their employer to provide remuneration, employment opportunities and retirement benefits
Customers	♦ the entity's continued existence (especially when they are dependent on it eg, for specialised replacement parts)
Governments and their agencies	♦ the allocation of resources ♦ the activities of entities ♦ how to regulate the activities of entities and assess taxation These users also need information as a basis for national statistics.
Public	♦ trends and recent developments in the entity's prosperity and the range of its activities
All users	♦ financial performance ♦ financial position

Financial statements cannot meet the information needs of all users. Because investors focus on financial performance and financial position it can be assumed that financial information that meets the needs of investors will meet many of the needs of other user groups.

Information required by investors

- The **financial performance** of an entity includes:
    - the return it obtains on the resources it controls;
    - the components of that return;
    - the characteristics of those components.

- The **financial position** of any entity includes:
    - the economic resources it controls;
    - its financial structure;
    - its liquidity and solvency;
    - its capacity to adapt to changes in the environment in which it operates.

- An entity's **financial adaptability** is its ability to take effective action to alter the amount and timing of its cash flows so that it can respond to unexpected needs or opportunities.

The reporting entity

An entity should prepare and publish financial statements if:

- it is a cohesive economic unit; and
- there is a legitimate demand for the information that its financial statements would provide.

Financial statements report on all the activities and resources under the control of the entity that has prepared them.

Single entity financial statements report on the activities and resources under the entity's direct control. Consolidated financial statements report on the activities and resources under the entity's direct and indirect control (that is, the activities carried out by itself and its subsidiaries and the assets and liabilities owned by itself and by its subsidiaries).

To have control, an entity must:

- be able to deploy the economic resources involved; and
- be able to benefit or suffer from their deployment.

The qualitative characteristics of financial information

Information provided by financial statements needs to be:

- relevant
- reliable
- comparable
- understandable.

Information is *relevant* if it has the ability to influence the economic decisions of users.

Information is *reliable* if:

- it can be depended upon to represent faithfully what it appears to represent (eg it represents the substance of transactions); and
- it is free from deliberate or systematic bias (is neutral), material error and is complete; and
- a degree of caution (prudence) has been applied in exercising the judgements necessary under conditions of uncertainty.

Information is *comparable* if it enables users to compare the nature and effects of transactions and other events:

- over time; and
- across different entities.

Information is *understandable* if its significance can be perceived by users that have a reasonable knowledge of business and economic activities and accounting and are willing to study the information with reasonable diligence.

Conflicts between the characteristics

The most relevant information may not be the most reliable or vice versa. For example:

- the relevance of the financial statements is reduced if they are not published until several months after the year-end, but the delay may be necessary in order to ensure that the information in them is reliable;
- information based on current values is normally more relevant to users than information based on historic cost, but information based on historic cost is normally more reliable than information based on current values.

Neutrality implies freedom from bias, while prudence is a potentially biased concept. It seeks to ensure that, under conditions of uncertainty, gains and assets are not overstated and losses and liabilities are not understated.

Where there is a conflict, a balance between the two characteristics must be found that still enables the objective of financial statements to be met. It is usually appropriate to use the information that is most relevant of whichever information is reliable.

Information that is relevant and reliable should not be excluded from the financial statements simply because it is too difficult for some users to understand.

Materiality

Information is *material* if its misstatement or omission might reasonably be expected to influence the economic decisions of users.

Materiality is a threshold quality. Information that is not material is not useful and should not be included in the financial statements.

The elements of financial statements

Assets

Assets are rights or other access to future economic benefits controlled by an entity as a result of past transactions or events.

- An asset is not the item of property itself, but the rights to future economic benefits. This does not necessarily involve legal ownership (eg under certain types of lease contract an entity has the right to use an asset to generate income although it does not legally own it).

- Future economic benefits eventually result in receipt of cash. For example, if an entity has a factory it uses it to produce goods which may be sold for cash. The future economic benefit need not be certain. For example, there is always a risk that the factory may be destroyed in a fire.

- Control is the ability to obtain the economic benefits and to restrict the access of others to those benefits.

Liabilities

Liabilities are obligations of an entity to transfer economic benefits as a result of past transactions or events.

- An obligation means that the entity is not free to avoid the outflow of resources. Future costs are not liabilities if the entity can choose to avoid the expenditure.

- The transfer of economic benefits usually involves an outflow of cash, but could also be a transfer of another asset away from the entity, or the provision of a service (for example, for payments received in advance).

Ownership interest

Ownership interest is the residual amount found by deducting all the entity's liabilities from all of the entity's assets.

The exact composition of ownership interest depends on the type of entity:

- Sole trader
- Capital introduced + accumulated net profits – drawings

- Partnership
- Partners' capital accounts + partners' current accounts (appropriations of profit – drawings)

- Limited company
- Share capital + reserves (accumulated net profits – dividends)

- Not-for-profit organisation (eg, public sector, charity, club, society)
- Accumulated funds (accumulated income – expenditure)

Gains

Gains are increases in ownership interest not resulting from contributions from owners.

Losses

Losses are decreases in ownership interest not resulting from distributions to owners.

Contributions from owners

Contributions from owners are increases in ownership interest resulting from transfers from owners in their capacity as owners.

Distributions to owners

Distributions to owners are decreases in ownership interest resulting from transfers to owners in their capacity as owners.

Relationship of elements

Earlier in your studies, you learned the accounting equation:

> Assets – Liabilities = Capital + Profits – Drawings

The Statement of Principles restates this as:

> Assets – Liabilities = Ownership interest; or
>
> Assets – Liabilities = Contributions from owners + Gains – Losses – Distributions to owners

Recognition in financial statements

A new asset or liability, or an addition to an existing asset or liability, is recognised if:

- sufficient evidence exists that the new asset or liability has been created or that there has been an addition to an existing asset or liability; and

- the new asset or liability or the addition can be measured at a monetary amount with sufficient reliability.

An asset or liability is wholly or partly derecognised if:

- sufficient evidence exists that a transaction or other past event has eliminated a previously recognised asset or liability; or

- although an item continues to be an asset or liability, the criteria for recognition are no longer met.

Assuming that no contribution from owners or transfer to owners is involved:

- if net assets increase, gain is recognised; and

- if net assets are reduced or eliminated, a loss is recognised.

Again, this can be stated in terms of the accounting equation:

> Closing net assets – Opening net assets = Profit/loss or surplus/deficit for the period

Presentation of financial information

Financial statements consist of primary financial statements and supporting notes. The primary financial statements are:

- the statement(s) of financial performance (profit and loss account and statement of total recognised gains and losses)

- the statement of financial position (balance sheet)

- the cash flow statement.

The presentation of information on *financial performance* focuses on the components of financial performance and their characteristics.

The presentation of information on *financial position* focuses on the types and functions of assets and liabilities held and on the relationships between them.

The presentation of *cash flow information* shows the extent to which the entity's various activities generate and use cash.

The notes and primary financial statements form an integrated whole. The notes amplify and explain the financial statements by providing:

- more detailed information on items recognised in the primary financial statements

- an alternative view of items recognised in the primary financial statements (for example, by disclosing a range of possible outcomes for a liability that is in dispute, or by disclosing segmental information)

- relevant information that it is not practicable to incorporate in the primary financial statements (for example, because of uncertainty).

Disclosure of information in the notes to the financial statements is not a substitute for recognition. It does not correct or justify any misrepresentation or omission in the primary financial statements.

Financial statements are often accompanied by other information, for example:

- historical summaries, trend information, directors' reports, chairman's statement, non-accounting and non-financial information; and

- highlights and summary indicators.

Question

Briefly define the four fundamental accounting concepts referred to in SSAP2.

Summary

SSAP2 sets out the four fundamental accounting principles:

- going concern
- accruals
- consistency
- prudence

The Companies Act 1985 sets out the same fundamental principles with one further addition:

- non-aggregation (no offset)

The objective of financial statements is to provide information about the reporting entity's financial performance and financial position that is useful to a wide range of users for assessing the stewardship of management and for making economic decisions.

The qualitative characteristics of financial information are:

- relevance;
- reliability;
- comparability; and
- understandability

The elements of financial statements are:

- assets;
- liabilities;
- ownership interest;
- gains;
- losses;
- contributions from owners; and
- distributions from owners.

CHAPTER 3

Introduction to Final Accounts

> ## Objectives
>
> This chapter covers the following performance criteria:
>
> **10.1.1** The general purpose of financial statements used in various organisations is identified.
>
> **10.2.1** Financial statements are accurately drafted from appropriate information.
>
> **10.2.2** Subsequent adjustments are correctly implemented.
>
> **10.2.5** Year-end financial statements are presented for approval to the appropriate person in a clear form.
>
> At the end of this chapter, you should be able to:
>
> - discuss the advantages and disadvantages of various types of business organisation
> - understand the main characteristics of non-profit making entities
> - draft final accounts for a sole trader from an extended trial balance

Types of business organisation

There are three main types of profit making business organisation:

- sole trader (sole proprietor)
- partnership
- limited company

Sole trader

As the name suggests, this is an organisation owned by one person.

Accounting conventions recognise the business as a *separate entity* from its owner. However, legally, the business and personal affairs of a sole trader are not distinguished in any way. The most important consequence of this is that a sole trader has complete personal unlimited liability. Business debts which cannot be paid from business assets must be met from the sale of personal assets, such as a house or car.

Sole trading organisations are normally small because they have to rely on the financial resources of their owner.

The advantages of operating as a sole trader include flexibility and autonomy. A sole trader can manage the business as he or she likes and can introduce or withdraw capital at any time.

Partnership

A partnership is two or more persons associated for the purpose of a business or a profession. Like a sole trader, a partnership is not legally distinguished from its members. Personal assets of the partners may have to be used to pay the debts of the partnership business.

The advantages of trading as a partnership stem mainly from there being many owners rather than one. This means that:

- more resources may be available, including capital, specialist knowledge, skills and ideas;

- administrative expenses may be lower for a partnership than for the equivalent number of sole traders, due to economies of scale; and

- partners can substitute for each other.

Partners can introduce or withdraw capital at any time, provided that all the **partners agree**.

Limited company

A limited company is a distinct, artificial 'person' created in order to separate legal responsibility for the affairs of a business (or any other activity) from the personal affairs of the individuals who own and/or operate the business.

The owners are known as *shareholders* (or members) and the people who run the business are known as *directors*. In a small corporation, owners and directors are often the same person.

Sometimes the owner of a company is another company; at some stage in the chain, however, there will be human owners! If one company owns another company, the owner is known as the parent company and the other company is known as the subsidiary company; collectively, the two companies are known as a *group*.

The consequences of separate legal personality

Limited liability

The company's debts and liabilities are those of the company and not those of the members.

Each member of a limited company is liable to contribute if called on to do so only the amount he has agreed to pay on his shares.

Perpetual succession

Unless the company is wound up, it continues in existence regardless of the death, bankruptcy, mental disorder or retirement of any of its members (this is in contrast with the position of a partnership which automatically dissolves where one of the partners dies or retires).

Property holding

The property of a registered company belongs to the company. A change in the ownership of shares in the company will have no effect on the ownership of the company's property. (Compare this with partnerships where the firm's property belongs directly to the partners who can take it with them if they leave the partnership.)

Transferable shares

Shares in a registered company can often be transferred without the consent of the other shareholders. (In the absence of agreement to the contrary, a new partner cannot be introduced into a firm without the consent of all existing partners.)

Contracts with members

A registered company can contract with its members and can sue and be sued on such contracts. (A partner cannot enter into contracts with his own firm.)

Suing and being sued

As a separate legal person, a company can sue and be sued in its own name. Judgements relating to companies do not affect the members personally.

Number of members

There is no upper limit on the number of members in a company.

In a partnership, except in certain restricted categories, such as accountants and stockbrokers, the maximum number of partners is 20. This limitation on numbers makes it difficult for a partnership to raise large amounts of capital.

Security for loans

A company has greater scope for raising loans by, for example, borrowing on debentures (long-term borrowings) and may secure them with floating charges.

(A floating charge is a mortgage over the constantly fluctuating assets of a company providing security for the lender of money to a company. It does not prevent the company dealing with the assets in the ordinary course of business. Such a charge is useful when a company has no fixed assets such as land, but does have a large and valuable stock in trade.)

The law does not permit partnerships or individuals to secure loans with a floating charge.

Taxation

Because a company is legally separate from its members, it is taxed separately from its members. Tax payable by companies is known as *corporation tax*. Partners and sole traders are personally liable for tax on the profits made by their businesses.

The rate of corporation tax (currently 30%) is lower than the top rate of income tax (currently 40%).

Disadvantages of incorporation

The disadvantages arise principally from the restrictions imposed by the *Companies Act 1985*.

Formalities, publicity and expenses

When they are being formed, companies have to register and to file a Memorandum and Articles of Association (formal constitution documents) with the Registrar. Registration fees and legal costs have to be paid.

Most limited companies' accounts are subject to an annual audit inspection (although this requirement has been lifted for small companies). The costs associated with this can be high. Partnerships and sole traders are not subject to this requirement unless as members of professional bodies whose own rules apply.

A registered company's accounts and certain other documents are open to public inspection. The accounts of sole traders and partnerships are not open to public inspection.

Capital maintenance

Limited companies are subject to strict rules in connection with the introduction and withdrawal of capital and profits.

Management powers

Members of a company may not take part in its management unless they are directors, whereas all partners are entitled to share in management, unless the partnership agreement provides otherwise.

Non-profit making entities

Although you will not be expected to draft accounts for non-profit making entities, you may be required to interpret them. Therefore you must have an understanding of the ways in which their accounts differ from those of profit making entities.

The main types of non-profit making entity are:

- clubs and societies
- charities
- public sector organisations (including central government, local government and National Health Service bodies).

Profit making and 'not for profit' entities compared

Objectives

The main objective of sole traders, partnerships and limited companies is to make a profit.

The main objective of charities, clubs and societies is to carry out the activities for which they were created. In order to do this, they need to attract or generate sufficient income to cover their expenditure, including administration costs. A large surplus of income over expenditure in the accounts of a charity is normally regarded as a bad sign, as it suggests that donors' money is not being used for the purpose for which it was intended.

The main objective of public sector organisations is to provide services to the general public. Like charities, their long term aim is normally to break even, rather than to generate a surplus.

Other differences

These are summarised in the table below:

	Profit making	**Clubs, societies, charities**	**Public sector**
Managed by:	Sole traders, partners, directors (who may also be shareholders)	Depends on constitution/other internal regulations	Elected officials, eg MPs councillors
Main sources of finance	Equity, debt	Donations, membership fees	Taxation
Stewardship responsibilities to: (likely to be main users of financial statements)	Shareholders	Members, donors, beneficiaries	The general public
Financial statements used to assess:	Financial performance, whether to hold or sell investment	Whether resources have been used efficiently to achieve objectives	Level of spending in relation to services provided, whether services provide value for money, whether services have been provided economically efficiently, effectively.

Accounts of non profit making entities

Most non–profit making entities prepare a statement of financial performance (the equivalent of a profit and loss account for a profit making entity) and a balance sheet. Many entities also prepare a cash flow statement. Increasingly, non–profit making entities are adopting commercial style accounting practices, so that the basic principles used to prepare accounts are very similar to those used by a profit making entity. This is particularly true of the public sector. Many charities are companies and must therefore comply with the accounting requirements of the Companies Act.

Statement of financial performance

The statement of financial performance for a non profit making entity is either:

♦ a receipts and payments account (on a cash basis); or

♦ an income and expenditure account (on an accruals basis).

Most entities prepare an income and expenditure account, which may be called a *revenue statement* or an *operating cost statement*. Until recently, the most important exception to this was central government, which now prepares financial statements on an accruals basis (known as 'resource accounting'). The terms *surplus* and *deficit* are used instead of profit and loss. Accounts may also refer to an *excess of income over expenditure* and vice versa.

Funds

The balance sheet of a non-profit making entity lists its assets and liabilities in the same way as that of a profit making entity. Ownership interest is represented by *funds* rather than by capital. Funds are accumulated income less accumulated expenditure.

Many not for profit entities have a single fund, known as the *accumulated fund*. Others may have several funds. Special funds are normally represented by particular assets and liabilities which may only be used for the purpose for which they have been designated. For example:

- an educational charity receives a legacy with the condition that it is used to provide a scholarship;

- a local authority receives money from central government. The money may only be used to build a new hospital.

Illustration: Accounts of a non-profit making entity

Summarised income and expenditure account for the year ended 31 December 19X8

	£	£
General Fund		
Income		
Subscriptions	189,000	
Donations	33,000	
Investment income	8,000	
		230,000
Expenditure		
Education and training	86,000	
Member services	104,000	
Administrative experience	30,000	
		(220,000)
Surplus of income over expenditure		10,000
Library Fund		
Income: Investment income		25,000
Expenditure: Library services		(27,000)
Deficit of expenditure over income		(2,000)

Summarised balance sheet at 31 December 19X8

	£	£	£
Fixed assets			
Tangible assets		590,000	
Investments: General Fund	248,000		
Library Fund	45,000		
		293,000	
			883,000
Current assets			
Debtors		35,000	
Cash at bank and in hand			
General Fund	9,000		
Library Fund	1,600		
		10,600	
		45,600	
Creditors: Amounts falling due within one year		(63,400)	
Net current liabilities			(17,800)
			865,200

	£	£
General Fund		
Balance at 1 January 19X8	808,600	
Transferred from income and expenditure account	10,000	
		818,600
Library fund		
Balance at 1 January 19X8	48,600	
Transferred from income and expenditure account	(2,000)	
		46,600
Total accumulated funds		865,200

Preparing final accounts

Final accounts are the end result of a process of summarising, classifying and structuring large quantities of data. The objective of preparing final accounts is to turn individual transactions into useful information.

Whether the accounts are being prepared for a sole trader, a partnership or a limited company, the steps in the process are basically the same.

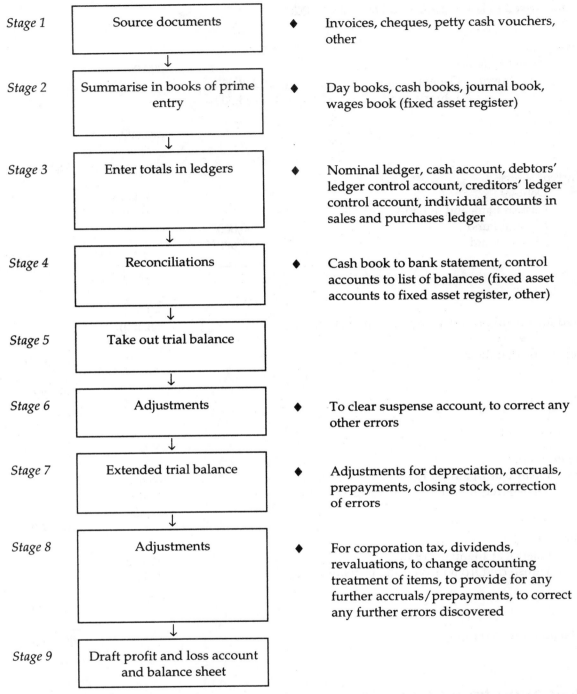

The first few stages should be familiar to you as you have covered them in your earlier studies. Your studies for Unit 10 will focus on the later stages:

♦   making final adjustments
♦   drafting the final accounts

In practice, there is normally a further set of adjustments, particularly where the accounts to be drafted are those of a limited company. These adjustments arise from the review of the draft accounts by management and from the audit.

The accounts of a sole trader

The profit and loss account

The *profit and loss account* is a summary of a business' transactions for a given period. In practice, as you will see from the following pro forma, it is commonly split into two parts and referred to as a *trading and profit and loss account*.

Pro forma trading and profit and loss account for the year ended ...

		£	£
Sales			X
Less: **Cost of sales**			
① Stock, at cost on 1 January (opening stock)	X	
Add: Purchases of goods	X	
		X	
Less: Stock, at cost on 31 December (closing stock)	(X)	
			(X)
Gross profit			X
Sundry income:			
Discounts received	X	
Commission received	X	
Rent received	X	
		X
			X
Less: Other expenses:			
② Rent	X	
Rates	X	
Lighting and heating	X	
Telephone	X	
Postage	X	
Insurance	X	
Stationery	X	
Office salaries	X	
Depreciation	X	
Accountancy and audit fees	X	
Bank charges and interest	X	
Bad and doubtful debts	X	
Delivery costs	X	
Van running expenses	X	
Advertising	X	
Discounts allowed	X	
			(X)
Net profit			X

① – **Trading account**
② – **Profit and loss account**

Explanations

- The *trading account* discloses the *gross profit* generated by the business by comparing sales with the cost of those sales. A shopkeeper, for example, will purchase for resale items from various suppliers (wholesalers); by adding a profit margin to this cost, the selling price of the goods will be computed and this margin is the *gross profit*.

- *Cost of sales* is calculated by taking the cost of the goods available for sale during the year of period (ie. opening stock plus purchases) and deducting the cost of the goods which were unsold (ie. closing stock). Sales and cost of goods sold relate to the *same* number of units.

- The *profit and loss account* shows other items of income and expenditure earned or incurred by the business, in order to arrive at *net profit*.

- In a manufacturing industry, further analysis is needed of the figure for cost of sales. This is dealt with in Chapter 6. Similarly, service industries may have different ways of defining goods and net profit.

The balance sheet

The *balance sheet* is a statement of the financial position of a business at a given date, usually the end of the period covered by the *profit and loss account*. It is a snapshot at one given moment.

Pro forma balance sheet at ......

	Cost £	Depreciation £	£
Fixed assets			
Freehold factory	X	X	X
Machinery	X	X	X
Motor vehicles	X	X	X
	X	X	X
Current assets			
Stocks		X	
Debtors	X		
Less: Provision for doubtful debts	(X)	X	
Prepayments		X	
Cash at bank		X	
Cash in hand		X	
		X	
Current liabilities			
Trade creditors	X		
Accrued charges	X		
		(X)	
Net current assets			X
Long-term liabilities			X
12% loan			(X)
Net assets			X

	£
Representing:	
Capital at 1 January	X
Profit for the year	X
	X
Less: Drawings	(X)
Proprietor's funds	X

Explanations

- *Fixed assets:* Assets acquired for use within the business with a view to earning profits, but not for resale. They are normally valued at cost less accumulated depreciation.

- *Current assets:* Assets acquired for conversion into cash in the ordinary course of business; they should not be valued at a figure greater than their realisable value.

- *Current liabilities:* Amounts owed by the business, payable within one year.

- *Net current assets:* Funds of the business available for day-to-day transactions. This can also be called *working capital*.

- *Long-term liabilities:* Funds provided for the business on a medium to long-term basis by an individual or organisation other than the proprietor. Long-term liabilities are repayable in more than one year.

Within these main headings, the following items should be noted:

- *Fixed assets*

    Depreciation is an amount charged in the accounts to write off the cost of an asset over its useful life.

- *Current assets*

    Debtors are people who owe amounts to the business.

    Provision for doubtful debts refers to those amounts owed which the proprietor is unsure of collecting.

    Prepayments are items paid by the company before the balance sheet date but relating to a subsequent period.

- *Current liabilities*

    Trade creditors are those suppliers to whom the business owes money.

    Accrued charges are amounts owed by the business, but not yet paid, for other expenses at the date of the balance sheet.

    Current liabilities are repayable within one year.

Making adjustments

Adjustments to the initial trial balance, the extended trial balance and the draft accounts are made by drawing up and posting a *journal entry*.

In practice, journals may be used in several ways:

- to record major or unusual transactions;
- to record period-end adjustments (eg. depreciation, stock, doubtful debts); and
- to facilitate the correction of errors, and to explain the nature of the errors.

Journals are recorded in the journal book. This is a book of prime entry and is not part of the double entry. From the journal book, the journals are posted to the relevant accounts in the nominal ledger.

Example I

On 31 March 19X5 we purchased a new motor vehicle for £20,000 in cash. If we were going to record this in the books we would:

Debit:	Motor vehicles	£20,000
Credit:	Cash	£20,000

This statement of the double-entry is sometimes known as a *journal*.

In the journal book itself, the transaction would be recorded as follows:

Date	Narrative	Account No	Dr £	Cr £
31.3.X5	Dr Motor Vehicles	M1	20,000	
	Cr Cash	C41		20,000
	Purchase of new motor vehicle (registration P666 BLR)			

When period-end adjustments are made, the journal is drawn up and the trial balance or draft accounts are adjusted. (These journals are not normally posted to the nominal ledger until the accounts have been finalised. The nominal ledger accounts are then balanced off and the new balances brought down for the start of the next accounting period.)

Example 2

Flagg extracted the following trial balance from his ledgers at 31 March 19X4:

	£	£
Petty cash	48	
Capital		3,830
Drawings	3,360	
Sales		49,457
Purchases	37,166	
Purchases returns		504
Stock (1 April 19X3)	5,057	
Fixtures and fittings	1,704	
Debtors	4,366	
Sundry creditors		4,987
Carriage on purchase	262	
Carriage on sales	442	
Rent and rates	1,104	
Light and heat	180	
Postage and telephone	204	
Sundry expenses	456	
Cash at bank	4,328	
	58,677	58,778

The trial balance did not agree. On investigation, Flagg discovered the following errors:

(1) In extracting the schedule of debtors, the credit side of a debtor's account had been overcast by £24.

(2) An amount of £10 for carriage on sales had been posted in error to the carriage on purchases account.

(3) A credit note for £41 received from a creditor had been entered in the purchase returns book but no entry had been made in the creditor's account.

(4) £84 charged for repairs to Flagg's private residence had been charged, in error, to the sundry expenses account.

(5) A payment of a telephone bill of £51 had been entered correctly in the cash book but had been posted, in error, to the postage and telephone account as £15.

Solution

The adjustments are as follows:

			Dr £	Cr £
1	Debit	Debtors	24	
	Credit	Suspense account		24
	Being correction of undercast in debtor's account			
2	Debit	Carriage on sales	10	
	Credit	Carriage on purchases		10
	Being correction of wrong posting			
3	Debit	Creditors	41	
	Credit	Suspense account		41
	Being correction of omitted entry			
4	Debit	Drawings	84	
	Credit	Sundry expenses		84
	Being payment for private expenses			
5	Debit	Postage and telephone	36	
	Credit	Suspense account		36
	Being correction of transposition error			

Journals 1, 3 and 5 clear the suspense account:

Suspense account

	£		£
Difference per trial balance	101	Debtors	24
		Creditors	41
		Postage	36
	101		101

The trial balance is then corrected:

	Opening £	Adjustments £	Dr £	Cr £
Petty cash	48		48	
Capital	(3,830)			3,830
Drawings	3,360	84	3,444	
Sales	(49,457)			49,457
Purchases	37,166		37,166	
Purchases returns	(504)			504
Stock at 1 April 19X3	5,057		5,057	
Fixtures and fittings	1,704		1,704	
Debtors	4,366	24	4,390	
Creditors	(4,987)	41		4,946
Carriage on purchases	262	(10)	252	
Carriage on sales	442	10	452	
Rent and rates	1,104		1,104	
Light and heat	180		180	
Postage and telephone	204	36	240	
Sundry expenses	456	(84)	372	
Cash at bank	4,328		4,328	
	(101)	101	58,737	58,737

The extended trial balance

A trial balance is simply a list of all the balances on the ledger accounts *before* year-end adjustments are made. These adjustments need to be made before the preparation of the profit and loss account and balance sheet and they normally include the following:

- correction of errors
- recognition of accruals and prepayments
- provision of the year's depreciation charge
- review of the charge for bad and doubtful debts
- inclusion of closing stock

The extended trial balance is a worksheet which takes us from the trial balance to the profit and loss account and balance sheet.

Layout of a typical extended trial balance

Account	Trial balance		Adjustments		Profit and loss account		Balance sheet	
	Dr	Cr	Dr	Cr	Dr	Cr	Dr	Cr
	£	£	£	£	£	£	£	£

The names of the ledger accounts and the corresponding amounts per the trial balance are entered into the first three columns.

The adjustments columns are used for all of the year-end adjustments mentioned above.

Example 3

Trial balance at 31 December 19X6

	Dr £	Cr £
Shop fittings at cost	2,000	
Depreciation provision at 1 January 19X6		100
Leasehold premises at cost	12,500	
Depreciation provision at 1 January 19X6		625
Stock in trade at 1 January 19X6	26,000	
Debtors at 31 December 19X6	53,000	
Provision for doubtful debts at 1 January 19X6		960
Cash in hand	50	
Cash at bank	2,250	
Creditors for supplies		65,000
Proprietor's capital at 1 January 19X6		28,115
Drawings to 31 December 19X6	2,000	
Purchases	102,000	
Sales		129,000
Wages	18,200	
Advertising	2,300	
Rates for 15 months to 31 March 19X7	1,500	
Light and heat	1,800	
Bank charges	200	
	223,800	223,800

The following adjustments are to be made:

(1) Depreciation of shop fittings   £100
       Depreciation of leasehold premises   £625

(2) A debt of £500 is irrecoverable and is to be written off; the doubtful debts provision is to be increased to 2% of the debtors.

(3) Advertising fees of £200 have been treated incorrectly as wages.

(4) The proprietor has withdrawn goods costing £1,000 for his personal use; these have not been recorded as drawings.

(5) The stock in trade at 31 December 19X6 is valued at £30,000.

(6) The electricity charge for the last three months of 19X6 is outstanding and is estimated to be £400.

Solution: Preparation of the extended trial balance

Stage 1: The balances per the trial balance are recorded in the correct columns and the total of the debit balances is agreed to the total of the credit balances.

Stage 2: We shall now deal with the adjustments (apart from accruals and prepayments).

- **Correction of errors**

    Two errors need to be corrected. One of the errors concerns the drawings of the proprietor, ie. the fact that some of the purchases were bought for his own use. To correct this, we should decrease the purchases and increase the drawings, ie:

Debit	Drawings	1,000	
Credit	Purchases		1,000

    The other error concerns the mis-classification of advertising fees as wages. To correct this, the following adjustment is necessary:

Debit	Advertising	200	
Credit	Wages		200

- **Provision of the year's depreciation charge**

    The charge for the year is £725 and we need to charge this to the *depreciation expense* account and also to increase the *provision for depreciation*, ie. the accumulated depreciation carried forward. The double-entry is:

Debit	Depreciation expense account	725	
Credit	Provision for depreciation: shop fittings		100
Credit	Provision for depreciation: leasehold premises		625

    We will need to set up the depreciation expense account as none exists.

- **Provision for doubtful debts**

    The debtors amount to £52,500 after the write-off of the bad debt of £500. A provision of £1,050 (£52,500 × 2%) is therefore required at 31.12.X6. The provision brought forward at the beginning of the year was £960; therefore it should be increased by £90 (1,050 − 960). The total charge to the profit and loss account is £590 (the debt written off plus the increase in the provision). The double-entry is:

Debit	Bad and doubtful debts expense	590	
Credit	Provision for doubtful debts		90
Credit	Debtors		500

    The bad debt expense account will need to be created.

- **Inclusion of closing stock**

    Closing stock appears in both the profit and loss account and the balance sheet.

    - In the profit and loss, it is a reduction of cost of goods sold and hence is a *credit*.
    - In the balance sheet, it is an asset and hence is a *debit*.

    Accordingly we set up two stock accounts: one for the balance sheet and one for the profit and loss account. The adjustment is:

Debit	Stock (balance sheet)	30,000	
Credit	Stock (profit and loss account)		30,000

    If you turn to the extended trial balance on page 38, you will see that each of these pairs of double-entry has been recorded in the adjustment columns. As the debit entries should always equal the credit entries, it is a useful check to cast the debit and credit adjustment columns to see that the totals are equal.

Stage 3: We now have to deal with the last adjustments, ie. the accruals and prepayments.

- **Electricity**

    The profit and loss account charge for the year needs to be increased by £400 and a creditor for £400 must be established. The double-entry is:

Debit	Light and heat	400	
Credit	Accruals		400

    The accruals account will need to be set up.

- **Rates**

    The profit and loss account charge for the year should be £1,200 (12/15 × £1,500), and there should be a prepayment of £300. The double-entry is:

Debit	Prepayments	300	
Credit	Light and heat		300

Stage 4: We have now recorded all of the adjustments and we need to prepare the trading and profit and loss account and balance sheet. This is achieved by the following:

- Cross-cast each account and enter the total in the appropriate column of the profit and loss account or balance sheet. Some examples are as follows:

    - Fittings (2,000 + 0 = £2,000) are recorded in the *debit* column of the *balance sheet*.

    - Provision for depreciation on fittings (100 + 100 = £200) is recorded in the *credit* column of the *balance sheet*.

    - Purchases (102,000 – 1,000 = £101,000) is recorded in the *debit* column of the *profit and loss account*.

    Note: Accruals are added to the original trial balance amount whereas prepayments are subtracted.

- Add the debit and credit sides of the profit and loss account. The differences between these two columns is a profit (if the credits exceed the debits) or a loss (if the debits exceed the credits). The difference is recorded in the correct column of the profit and loss account (so that the two sides now balance) and the double-entry is with the balance sheet.

- Add the debit and credit columns of the balance sheet. These should agree unless you have made any errors.

Stage 5: The trading and profit and loss account and balance sheet are then prepared from the relevant columns.

The completed extended trial balance is shown overleaf:

Chapter 3 Introduction to Final Accounts

Extended trial balance at 31 December 19X6

Account	Trial balance Dr £	Trial balance Cr £	Adjustments Dr £	Adjustments Cr £	Profit and loss account Dr £	Profit and loss account Cr £	Balance sheet Dr £	Balance sheet Cr £
Shop fittings	2,000						2,000	
Provision for depreciation 1.1.X6		100		100				200
Leasehold premises	12,500						12,500	
Provision for depreciation 1.1. X6		625		625				1,250
Stock 1.1.X6	26,000		30,000	30,000	26,000	30,000	30,000	
Debtors	53,000			500			52,500	
Provision for doubtful debts 1.1.X6		960		90				1,050
Cash in hand	50						50	
Cash at bank	2,250						2,250	
Creditors		65,000						65,000
Capital		28,115						28,115
Drawings	2,000						3,000	
Purchases	102,000		1,000	1,000	101,000			
Sales		129,000				129,000		
Wages	18,200			200	18,000			
Advertising	2,300		200		2,500			
Rates	1,500			300	1,200			
Light and heat	1,800		400		2,200			
Bank charges	200				200			
Depreciation – shop fittings			100		100			
Depreciation – leasehold premises			625		625			
Bad debts expense			590		590			
Prepayments			300				300	
Accruals				400				400
	223,800	223,800	33,215	33,215	152,415	159,000	102,600	
Net profit					6,585			6,585
					159,000	159,000	102,600	102,600

39

The trading and profit and loss account and balance sheet are now drafted from the extended trial balance. (For the purpose of this example, we are assuming that there are no further adjustments to the extended trial balance; in practice, this might not be the case. Any further adjustments would be made by drawing up and posting journal entries, exactly as before.)

Trading and profit and loss account for the year ended 31 December 19X6

		£	£
Sales			129,000
Less:	Cost of sales		
	Opening stock	26,000	
	Purchases	101,000	
		127,000	
	Closing stock	(30,000)	
			(97,000)
Gross profit			32,000
Less:	Expenses		
	Wages	18,000	
	Advertising	2,500	
	Rates	1,200	
	Light and heat	2,200	
	Charges	200	
	Depreciation (100 + 625)	725	
	Bad debts	590	
			(25,415)
Net profit			6,585

Balance sheet at 31 December 19X6

	Cost £	Accumulated depreciation £	Net book value £
Fixed assets			
Shop fittings	2,000	200	1,800
Leasehold premises	12,500	1,250	11,250
	14,500	1,450	13,050
Current assets			
Stocks		30,000	
Debtors (52,500 – 1,050)		51,450	
Prepayments		300	
Cash at bank		2,250	
Cash in hand		50	
		84,050	
Current liabilities			
Creditors	65,000		
Accruals	400		
		(65,400)	
Net current assets			18,650
Total assets less current liabilities			31,700

	£
Represented by:	
Capital	28,115
Add: Net profit for the year	6,585
	34,700
Less: Drawings	(3,000)
	31,700

Further points

Users of the accounts and their needs

The form and content of sole trader accounts are not prescribed by law. Therefore the accounts of sole traders may be drawn up in any format that the owner wishes. This is determined by the needs of the users of the accounts.

For a sole trader, the most probable users are:

- the owner of the business (who is almost certainly also the manager of the business)
- the Inland Revenue
- any third parties which may have provided finance (normally the bank)

The owners of a business are interested in its profitability and in the components of that profit. They need detailed information about the cost of sales and expenses. They probably need to compare the performance of the business in the current period with its performance in previous periods. The owners of a business should also be interested in its solvency. Even if the business is making profits, it cannot survive without cash, or the ability to generate cash.

The Inland Revenue uses the accounts to determine the amount of tax payable. This is based on adjusted net profit. Certain expenses are not allowable for tax purposes. Depreciation and losses on sales of fixed assets are not allowable as deductions from profit. However, capital allowances, calculated in a form prescribed by the Inland Revenue, are allowable. For these reasons, accounts should include details of expenses and of additions and disposals of fixed assets.

Loan creditors are primarily interested in the ability of the business to pay interest and to repay loans. They are likely to focus on the balance sheet as well as on the profit and loss account.

The form of accounts

General principles which should be observed in preparing accounts include the following:

- *Aggregation:* information must be detailed enough to be useful but not so detailed as to obscure the general picture. For example, descriptions of each transaction or event taking place during the period would be of little use.

- *Classification:* items should be grouped according to their nature or function and items which have similar characteristics should be grouped together. For example, all fixed assets appear under the same heading and cost of sales is differentiated from other expenses.

- *Structure:* the prominence given to disclosure should be appropriate to the overall significance of the item within the accounts as a whole. For example, if a business were required to supply a breakdown of individual items within a particular account heading, this information would normally be disclosed in a note, rather than on the face of the profit and loss account.

- *Consistency:* because businesses need to compare their current performance and position with those of previous periods, accounts should normally be presented in the same format each year.

Current best practice

Sole traders are not obliged to follow accounting standards when drawing up accounts. However, accounts should normally be drawn up in accordance with current best practice (which may mean compliance with accounting standards). It should be noted that accounts cannot show a true and fair view unless they comply with accounting standards.

In practice, many accounting standards are unlikely to be relevant to the accounts of sole traders. Those which are most likely to apply include the accounting standards which you have already met earlier in your studies:

- SSAP2 *Disclosure of accounting policies*
- SSAP5 *Accounting for value added tax*
- SSAP9 *Stocks and long-term contracts*

Other accounting standards likely to be relevant to sole traders include the following:

- SSAP17 *Accounting for post balance sheet events*
- FRS5 *Reporting the substance of transactions*
- FRS10 *Goodwill and intangible assets*
- FRS12 *Provisions, contingent liabilities and contingent assets*
- FRS15 *Tangible fixed assets*

These accounting standards are covered later in this Study Pack.

Questions

1 VB Ltd

VB Ltd, a chemical company, extracted a trial balance from its ledgers on 30 April 19Y0 and found that the sum of the debit balances did not equal the sum of the credit balances. A suspense account was opened and used to record the difference. VB Ltd does not use control accounts for its customer and supplier accounts.

The company carried out an investigation into the cause of the difference and found the following:

(1) Cash sales of £246 had been debited to the sales returns account and the cash book.

(2) An invoice to a customer for £1,249 had been posted to the customer's account as £1,294.

(3) Bank charges of £37 had not been entered in the cash book.

(4) Value added tax of £45 had been included in the sum posted to the purchases account from a supplier's invoice.

(5) A contra entry of £129 had been debited to the customer account and credited to the supplier account.

(6) An invoice for rates for the six-month period ending 30 September 19Y0 amounting to £13,500 had not been entered in the ledgers and remained unpaid on 30 April 19Y0.

(7) A carriage invoice of £52 had been debited to carriage outwards but it related to the purchase of goods from a supplier of the company.

(8) A bad debt of £40 which should have been written off had been forgotten and remained as a balance on the customer's account.

Required

Show the journal entries necessary to correct *each* of the above (including a narrative) and state the effect of each correction on the profit of the company for the year ended 30 April 19Y0.

Summary

The journal is used to record period-end adjustments. It must be accompanied by narrative stating the nature of the transaction.

The extended trial balance is simply a worksheet showing the adjustments made to the figures in the trial balance to lead to the profit and loss account and balance sheet.

Procedure:

- Set out initial trial balance.

- Deal with adjustments.

- Deal with accruals and prepayments.

- Add the columns across into P + L and B/S columns.

- Add the columns down.

- Prepare profit and loss account and balance sheet from the relevant columns.

Sole traders are not required to prepare their accounts in a standard format or to observe accounting standards. In practice, applicable accounting standards should normally be followed.

CHAPTER 4

The Accounts of Partnerships

Objectives

This chapter covers the following performance criteria:

10.2.1 Financial statements are accurately drafted from appropriate information.

10.2.2 Subsequent adjustments are correctly implemented.

10.2.3 Draft accounts comply with domestic standards and legislation and, where relevant, partnership agreement.

10.2.5 Year–end financial statements are presented for approval to the appropriate person in a clear form.

At the end of this chapter, you should be able to:

♦ draft final accounts for a partnership.

Introduction

What is a partnership?

The Partnership Act 1890 defines a partnership as 'the relation which subsists between persons carrying on a business in common with a view of profit'.

The existence of a partnership is usually a matter of fact constituted by agreement (either orally or in writing) between those who wish to carry on business together. The essence of a partnership is that each partner is an agent of all the others for the purposes of the business. Each partner is bound by the acts of all the other partners and each partner can be sued in his own name for the whole of any partnership debts.

Basic rules

Let us look first at the basic rules you must know before starting partnership accounts.

♦ To record a partner's interests in the business, we will need:

(i) a *capital* account, which shows his share of fixed capital of the firm, and

(ii) a *current* account recording his share of profits/losses and his drawings.

There will be one account for *each* partner and these accounts should always be shown in *columnar* form.

Capital and current accounts normally appear as *credit* balances. The partnership (ie. the business) has a liability to the partners as individuals. A debit balance on a current account means that the partner is a *debtor* of the business. This occurs if a partner draws more money out of the business than his profit share entitles him to draw.

- Whether you need both capital and current accounts depends on the instructions of the particular question you are dealing with. If the option is left open to you, use one account only and call it the *capital account*.

- If you do need both, there is a general rule as to the distinction between the two accounts and the types of item which should be passed through them. It is best to use the capital account to record adjustments to the amount of fixed capital of any partner and the effect of any alteration in the value of goodwill, ie. items of a permanent nature.

Partnership agreement

The basis of a partnership is agreement and trust. It is much better to have a written agreement to which reference may be made by all partners. An agreement may however be created in any of the following ways:

- deed
- writing
- word of mouth
- course of dealing

The agreement will cover rights and duties of partners and is likely to include a number of items of accounting importance including:

- partners' capital and current accounts
- profit and loss sharing ratio
- partners' drawing rights
- interest on capital, current and drawings accounts
- partners' salaries
- valuation of goodwill
- provision relating to death or retirement of partners

Rights of partners

The division of profits and losses between partners depends upon the arrangements laid down in the partnership agreement.

The following provisions of the Partnership Act 1890 (S24) give the rights of partners to the following *in the absence of agreement to the contrary*:

- All partners are entitled to share equally in capital and profits and must contribute equally to losses.

- Partners are not entitled to interest on capital.

- Partners are not entitled to salaries.

- A partner is entitled to interest at 5% per annum on advances beyond the amount of his agreed capital (ie. on loans).

Questions normally give all relevant details of the partnership agreement. In the absence of this information you should apply the provisions above.

Appropriation of profit

The profit and loss account of a partnership is the same as that of any other trading entity but, once the net trading profit has been found, a further account is necessary to show the implementation of the partnership agreement and the resulting division of profits between the partners. This is called an *appropriation account*. Thus the appropriation account does not contain items that are charges against profit; it simply shows how the final profit is divided. Where changes have occurred to the partnership during the accounting period, it may be necessary to allocate or apportion profit between the periods and to construct a separate appropriation account for each period.

Profit and loss appropriation account

This account starts with the net profit divisible between the partners and shows the division between them. It may reflect any or all of the following:

- interest on current accounts;
- interest on capital accounts;
- salaries;
- division of remaining profit in agreed ratio;
- any adjustment to reach guaranteed minimum share for one of the partners.

Interest on capital and current accounts is normally calculated on the balance at the period-end. A partnership agreement may provide for interest on debit balances as well as on credit balances. Interest on debit balances is a deduction from profit share.

It is important to remember that any interest on loans from partners, in excess of agreed capital, is a charge against profit (ie. an expense), and does not appear in the appropriation account.

Example

A, B and C are in partnership. Their first year's trading produces a profit of £27,000 before taking account of the items covered below. The partnership agreement specifies:

Interest on capital at 10% per annum; no interest on drawings.

A is to receive a salary of £6,000 per annum.

Profits are to be shared 1:2:3 between A, B and C respectively.

Partners' capitals are:

A	£6,000
B	£4,000
C	£8,000

In addition to the above capital, C has advanced a further £15,000 and interest on this amount has been agreed at 12% per annum.

Drawings during the year were as follows:

A	£8,000
B	£5,000
C	£10,000

Solution

The first step is to find the net profit divisible between the partners as follows:

	£
Profit in question	27,000
Deduct: Interest on loan – £15,000 × 12%	1,800
Divisible profit	25,200

Next we construct a profit and loss appropriation account giving effect to the agreement between the partners.

Profit and loss appropriation account

		£	£
Net profit (as above)			25,200
Interest on capital			
A	10% × 6,000	600	
B	10% × 4,000	400	
C	10% × 8,000	800	
			(1,800)
			23,400
Salary A			(6,000)
			17,400
Profit in agreed ratios			
A	1/6 × 17,400	2,900	
B	2/6 × 17,400	5,800	
C	3/6 × 17,400	8,700	
			17,400

Finally, we must construct the partners' current accounts to reflect the other side of these entries.

Partners' current accounts

	A £	B £	C £		A £	B £	C £
Cash book – drawings	8,000	5,000	10,000	Interest on loan			1,800
				Interest on capital	600	400	800
				Salary	6,000		
Balances c/f	1,500	1,200	1,300	Profit share	2,900	5,800	8,700
	9,500	6,200	11,300		9,500	6,200	11,300

Although interest on the loan is charged to profit and loss account, it is still credited to the current account of C. Drawings are debited directly to the current accounts and must *never* appear in the profit and loss account or appropriation account.

Changes during a year

Where a change takes place in a partnership during an accounting period, it will be necessary to produce two appropriation accounts dealing with each period separately. In order to do this the profit must be divided between the periods before and after the change. This may involve the following:

(a) a simple time-apportionment of profit on a month-by-month basis.

(b) a time-apportionment of gross profit on a month by month basis and a division of other expenses on either a time basis or according to factual information;

(c) an apportionment of gross profits according to the level of sales in each period and a breakdown of expenses using the following methods:

    (i)   *pro rata* to sales;
    (ii) apportioned on a time basis;
    (iii) according to the facts given.

The last of these three methods, (c), is the most complicated so we will examine this method using a simple illustration. Remember, methods (a) and (b) use part of the methods we will adopt here, but both are simplifications of this approach.

Example

A and B are in partnership sharing profits and losses equally. The profit and loss account for the year to 31 December 19X1 was as follows.

	£	£
Sales		60,000
Cost of sales		30,000
Gross profit		30,000
Packing and distribution	9,000	
Rent, rates etc.	6,000	
Depreciation – car	800	
		15,800
Net profit		14,200

Owing to the workload taken on by B following A's illness in June, it was agreed that B should receive a salary of £6,000 pa and the remaining profits should be shared A $2/3$ and B $1/3$. This new agreement was to operate as from 1 July 19X1.

Sales in the period January to June were £20,000.

B was also to have personal use of the firm's motor car which was purchased on 1 July.

Solution

The first step is to work out the net profit for each period. Expenses will be apportioned as follows:

Cost of sales   )
Packing and distribution)   in proportion to sales
Rent and rates etc.   -   time basis
Depreciation – car   -   last period only

Profit and loss appropriation account

	1 January to 30 June £	1 January to 30 June £	1 July to 31 Dec £	1 July to 31 Dec £
Sales		20,000		40,000
Cost of sales		(10,000)		(20,000)
		10,000		20,000
Packing and distribution	3,000		6,000	
Rent, rates etc.	3,000		3,000	
Depreciation	-		800	
		(6,000)		(9,800)
Net profit		4,000		10,200
Appropriations				
Salary – B	-		3,000	(3,000)
		4,000		7,200
Share of profit A	2,000		4,800	
B	2,000		2,400	
		4,000		7,200

Goodwill

Definition

There are many ways in which goodwill can be defined – the most generally accepted definition is:

> 'Goodwill is the difference between the value of a business as a whole and the fair value of its identifiable net assets'.

So a business may have net assets that have a current market value of, say, £50,000 yet someone may be prepared to pay £80,000 for the business as a whole. Why? What does the extra £30,000 goodwill represent?

Chapter 4 The Accounts of Partnerships

Sources of goodwill

Goodwill may arise from a large number of sources, some of which are:

- reputation of owners;
- quality of goods;
- site monopoly or advantage;
- advantageous patents or trade marks;
- growth element.

Unrecorded goodwill

It is normal for a business to show no value for goodwill on its balance sheet because of its volatile nature and the uncertainty as to its true value (you will recall a company can only include purchased goodwill in its balance sheet).

Whenever a change occurs in a partnership, it is necessary to record the goodwill prior to making the change and normally it is then written off once the change has occurred.

This adjustment in respect of unrecorded goodwill is required whenever any of the following takes place:

(a) admission of a new partner;
(b) retirement of a partner;
(c) death of a partner;
(d) change in profit-sharing ratio;
(e) any combination of (a) to (d) above.

The adjustment to be made in respect of unrecorded goodwill is always the same:

Credit Old partners' capital accounts with unrecorded goodwill in the old profit-sharing ratio
Debit Goodwill account

This records the goodwill and the change may now be made.

Credit Goodwill account
Debit New partners' capital accounts in the new profit-sharing ratio

This now eliminates goodwill from the balance sheet of the firm.

Often, no goodwill account is opened. This does not mean that goodwill can be ignored but that a shortcut is taken. The entries are commonly shortened to:

Credit Old partners in old profit-sharing ratio
Debit New partners in new profit-sharing ratio

Example

A and B are in partnership sharing profits equally. No goodwill exists in the books of the partnership and the partners wish to continue this policy. They agree that in the future A should receive 60% of the profits and B only 40%.

Goodwill is valued at £60,000.

Solution

		£	£
Credit	A Capital account		30,000
	B Capital account		30,000
Debit	Goodwill	60,000	
Credit	Goodwill		60,000
Debit	A Capital account	36,000	
	B Capital account	24,000	

This would appear in the ledger accounts as follows:

Goodwill

	£		£
Capital	60,000	Capital	60,000

Capital

		A £	B £			A £	B £
G'w'l		36,000	24,000	G'w'l		30,000	30,000
c/f			6,000	c/f		6,000	
		36,000	30,000			36,000	30,000
b/f			6,000	b/f		6,000	

The entries in the goodwill account may be omitted because the £60,000 is simply entered and then written out.

Why do this? To ensure that B gets full credit for his 50% share of goodwill generated to the date of change of profit share ratio.

Suppose that, one year later, the goodwill had risen to £80,000 and that the partnership was sold, realising this in the form of a profit. Ignoring the other assets of the business, the effects on the partners would be:

Goodwill

	£		£
Capital	80,000		

Capital

		A £	B £			A £	B £
b/f		6,000		b/f			6,000
c/f		42,000	38,000	G'w'l		48,000	32,000
		48,000	38,000			48,000	38,000
				b/f		42,000	38,000

The capital accounts therefore reflect the proper claims the partners have on the realised goodwill:

	A	B
50% share of original goodwill	30,000	30,000
60%/40% share of goodwill generated in last year (£20,000)	12,000	8,000
	42,000	38,000

Other assets

Before any change can occur in a partnership, all assets and liabilities must be recorded at their correct value just like the goodwill we saw above. Unlike the goodwill, these assets are normally left at their new values in the partnership books.

The entries required when an asset is to be increased in value are therefore:

Debit Asset account with the amount of the revaluation
Credit Old partners in old profit-sharing ratio

(The reverse entry is made to reduce an asset in value.)

Where a number of assets are to be revalued, it is normal to open a revaluation account into which all the increases and decreases may be collected, with the net difference being transferred to the partners' capital accounts in their profit-sharing ratio.

Example

A and B are in partnership, sharing capital and profits in the ratio 1:1. They decide to change the profit ratio to 2:1. The book value of the assets and their true value at the date of change are as follows:

	Book value £	Revalued value £
Freehold land and buildings	100,000	200,000
Motor vehicles	25,000	35,000
Debtors	30,000	20,000
Creditors	10,000	10,000
Total net assets	165,000	265,000

Ignore goodwill.

Required

Write up the ledger accounts to record the revaluation.

Solution

Steps

(1) The partners' capital accounts must show a total of £165,000 (the total net assets) divided in the ratio 1:1 (£82,500 : £82,500). They will appear as follows:

Capital account

	A £	B £		A £	B £
			b/f	82,500	82,500

(2) The asset accounts will be debited or credited with the increase or decrease in value, and the appropriate amount entered in the revaluation account. These later entries are shown below (the entries in the asset accounts are not shown).

Revaluation account

	£	£		£	£
Debtors	10,000		Freehold		100,000
			Vehicles		10,000

(3) The balance on the revaluation account is written off to the capital account in the ratio 1:1 – the old profit-sharing ratio.

Capital account

	A £	B £		A £	B £
			b/f	82,500	82,500
			Revaluation	50,000	50,000

Revaluation account

	£	£		£	£
Debtors		10,000	Freeholds		100,000
Capital accounts		100,000	Vehicles		10,000
		110,000			110,000

Note: The fact that the profit-sharing ratio has changed does not alter the partners' ownership of the assets that exist at the date of change, in exactly the same way that their share of goodwill existing at the date of change did not change.

Admission of new partners

Cash paid by incoming partners

All cash paid by an incoming partner, however described, must be credited to his account in the partnership.

Transactions of this type are often described in somewhat confusing and misleading terms. The most common descriptions are outlined below.

(a) C is admitted as a partner and introduces cash of £12,000.

Entries		£	£
Debit	Cash	12,000	
Credit	C's capital account		12,000

(b) C is admitted as a partner and pays A and B £6,000 each.

		£	£
Debit	A's capital account	6,000	
	B's capital account	6,000	
Credit	C's capital account		12,000

(c) C is admitted as a partner and pays A and B £6,000 each, purchasing one sixth share of goodwill from each.

The entries are the same as in (b) above but this also tells us C's share of profit:

$1/3$ $(1/6 + 1/6)$

and the valuation of goodwill: $1/6$ = £6,000 ∴ Goodwill = £36,000

Chapter 4 The Accounts of Partnerships

Example

A and B are in partnership, sharing profits 1:1. The total net assets (excluding goodwill) amount to £200,000. No goodwill account is maintained in the books. They agree to admit C into partnership on 1 January 19X5, when the new profit-sharing ratio will be 1:1:1. C agrees to pay £20,000 for his share of the goodwill.

Required

Show how the above transaction will be recorded in the books of the partnership.

Solution

Steps

(1) Calculate the goodwill.

C's share of goodwill is $1/3$ = £20,000
Therefore the goodwill = £60,000

(2) Write the goodwill into the books in the old profit ratio (A:B; 1:1).

(3) Write the goodwill out of the books in the new profit ratio (A:B:C; 1:1:1).

(4) Record the payment of £20,000 by C.

The partners' capital account will appear as follows (S = Step):

Capital account

	A £	B £	C £		A £	B £	C £
C/f	130,000	130,000		B/f	100,000	100,000	
				Goodwill (S1, 2)	30,000	30,000	
	130,000	130,000			130,000	130,000	
				B/f	130,000	130,000	
Goodwill (S3)	20,000	20,000	20,000	Cash book (S4)			
C/f	110,000	110,000	-				20,000
	130,000	130,000	20,000		130,000	130,000	20,000
				B/f	110,000	110,000	-

Comment on solution

If the goodwill were written back again in the new profit ratio 1:1:1, each partner would be credited with £20,000, giving A and B £130,000 (ie. their original share of the net assets and goodwill) and C £20,000 (the value of the cash paid in).

Example

Merriman, Jolly and Jape were in partnership, sharing profits one-half, one-third, one-sixth respectively.

On 1 January 19X1 they admitted Giggle into partnership on the following terms.

Giggle to have one-sixth share which he purchased entirely from Merriman, paying him £4,000 for that share of goodwill. Of this amount, Merriman retained £3,000 and put the balance into the firm as additional capital. Giggle also brought £2,500 capital into the firm.

It was agreed that the investments should be reduced to their market value of £1,800 and that the plant should be reduced to £2,900 as on 31 December 19X0.

The balance sheet of the old firm at 31 December 19X0 was as follows.

	£	£
Fixed assets		
Plant	3,500	
Furniture	1,000	
Investments	3,000	
		7,500
Current assets		
Stock	5,000	
Debtors	6,000	
Cash at bank	4,000	
	15,000	
Current liabilities		
Creditors	10,500	
		4,500
		12,000
Capital accounts		
Merriman		6,000
Jolly		4,000
Jape		2,000
		12,000

Required

(a) Prepare the opening balance sheet of the new firm as at 1 January 19X1.

(b) Prepare the capital accounts of the partners for the year to 31 December 19X1.

Solution

The steps involved in solving this problem are as follows:

Steps

(1) Prepare the revaluation account, identify the profit or loss and transfer it to the old partners in their profit-sharing ratio.

(2) Work out the total value of goodwill.

$1/6$ = £4,000, total goodwill = £4,000 × 6 = £24,000

Credit the old partners in the old ratio and debit the new partners in the new ratio.

(3) Calculate the new ratio.

Merriman's share $= 1/2 - 1/6 = 1/3$

Therefore, new ratio is $1/3 : 1/3 : 1/6 : 1/6 = 2:2:1:1$

(4) Record the private settlement between Merriman and Giggle.

(5) Record the cash introduced by Merriman and Giggle.

(6) Balance the partners' capital accounts and draft the new balance sheet.

The answer would appear as follows.

(a) **Balance sheet at 1 January 19X1 (Step 6)**

	£	£
Fixed assets		
Plant	2,900	
Furniture	1,000	
Investments	1,800	
		5,700
Current assets		
Stock	5,000	
Debtors	6,000	
Cash at bank	7,500	
	18,500	
Current liabilities		
Creditors	10,500	
		8,000
		13,700

	£
Capital accounts	
Merriman	6,100
Jolly	3,400
Jape	1,700
Giggle	2,500
	13,700

(b)

Partners' capital accounts

	M £	Jo £	Ja £	G £		M £	Jo £	Ja £	G £
Revaluation	900	600	300	–	Bal b/f	6,000	4,000	2,000	–
Bal c/f	6,100	3,400	1,700	2,500	Cash	1,000	–	–	2,500
	7,000	4,000	2,000	2,500		7,000	4,000	2,000	2,500
					Bal b/f	6,100	3,400	1,700	2,500

Note: There is no entry in the partners' capital accounts for goodwill as the settlement between Merriman and Giggle took place outside the partnership, ie. Giggle gave Merriman a cheque for £4,000. Alternatively, the transaction could have gone through the books and appeared as follows:

Partners' capital accounts

	M £	Jo £	Ja £	G £		M £	Jo £	Ja £	G £
Revaluation	900	600	300	–	Bal b/f	6,000	4,000	2,000	–
Goodwill	8,000	8,000	4,000	4,000	Goodwill	12,000	8,000	4,000	–
Cash	3,000	–	–	–	Cash	–	–	–	6,500
Bal c/f	6,100	3,400	1,700	2,500					
	18,000	12,000	6,000	6,500		18,000	12,000	6,000	6,500
					Bal b/f	6,100	3,400	1,700	2,500

Workings

Revaluation account (Step 1)

	£		£
Investments	1,200	Partners' capital accounts	
Plant	600	Merriman	900
		Jolly	600
		Jape	300
	1,800		1,800

Cash at bank

	£		£
Balance b/f	4,000		
Merriman (Step 5)	1,000		
Giggle (Step 5)	2,500	Balance c/f	7,500
	7,500		7,500
Balance b/f	7,500		

Retirement of partners

Introduction

If a partner retires, he will be sacrificing his share of future profits and will, therefore, want compensation for this.

He will also want his share of existing assets of the business.

Partnership Act 1890

Section 42 gives the following rights to an outgoing partner:

(a) Where a partner dies or ceases to be a partner and the surviving partner continues in business without a settlement of accounts, the outgoing partner is entitled (in the absence of any agreement to the contrary) to (i) or (ii) below:

 (i) such post-dissolution profits as the court may find attributable to the use of his share;

 (ii) interest at 5% per annum on the amount of his share.

(b) Where, by agreement, an option is given to surviving partners to purchase the interest of an outgoing or deceased partner and that option is exercised, the outgoing partner (or his estate) is not entitled to any further share in profits.

 If this option is *not* exercised (a) applies.

Section 43 provides that, subject to agreement to the contrary, the amount due to an outgoing partner (or his estate) is a debt accruing from the date of dissolution or death.

Goodwill

On retirement, a partner will want his share of the goodwill that he has helped the business acquire over the years.

Double-entry

Dr Goodwill account
 Cr Partners' capital account in the old profit-sharing ratio

To bring goodwill temporarily into the books.

Dr Partners' capital account in new profit-sharing ratio
 Cr Goodwill

To remove goodwill from the books.

These are exactly the same entries as on admission.

Revaluation account

The retiring partner will also want his share of the existing assets. Since balance-sheet values are unlikely to reflect the true asset values (especially property), some assets will have to be revalued.

Double-entry

(a) To revalue an asset upwards:

  Dr Asset account
    Cr Revaluation account

  with increase in value.

(b) To revalue an asset downwards:

  Dr Revaluation account
    Cr Asset account

  with decrease in value.

(c) The revaluation account is cleared to the existing partners' capital accounts.

(d) If the revaluation account is not to remain in the books, then the procedure is reversed and the revaluation account is cleared to the new partners' capital accounts in the new profit-sharing ratio.

Example

M, N and P are in partnership sharing profits and losses equally. P wishes to retire.

The partnership balance sheet shows:

	£
Property (market value £80,000)	60,000
Debtors (recoverable value £9,500)	10,000
Bank	50,000
	120,000

	£
Capital accounts	
M	40,000
N	40,000
P	40,000
	120,000

Required

(a) Prepare the revaluation account.

(b) Prepare the partners' capital accounts.

(c) Prepare the revised balance sheet – the partners do not wish the revaluations to remain in the books.

Solution

(a) **Revaluation account**

Revaluation account

		£		£
Debtors	(2)	500	Property account (1)	20,000
M	(3)	6,500		
N	(3)	6,500		
P	(3)	6,500		
		20,000		20,000

Narrative

				£	£
(1)	Dr	Property account		20,000	
		Cr Revaluation account			20,000

With increase in value of property.

				£	£
(2)	Dr	Revaluation account		500	
		Cr Debtors account			500

With decrease in recoverable value of debtors.

(3)

			£	£
Dr	Revaluation account		19,500	
Cr	Partner's capital account			
		M		6,500
		N		6,500
		P		6,500

To clear balance to the partners in the old profit–sharing ratio.

The balance sheet would now incorporate revaluations showing:

	£
Property	80,000
Debtors	9,500
Bank	50,000
	139,500

	£
Capital accounts	
M	46,500
N	46,500
P	46,500
	139,500

Capital account

	M £	N £	P £		M £	N £	P £
				Bal b/f	40,000	40,000	40,000
Bal c/f	46,500	46,500	46,500	Revaluation a/c	6,500	6,500	6,500
	46,500	46,500	46,500		46,500	46,500	46,500

(b) P retires and the business must pay him the amount he is owed, ie. the balance on his capital account.

Dr   P Capital account   £46,500
     Cr   Bank account   £46,500

The balance sheet now shows the following.

	£
Property	80,000
Debtors	9,500
Bank	3,500
	93,000

	£
Capital accounts	
M	46,500
N	46,500
	93,000

Capital account

	M £	N £	P £		M £	N £	P £
Bank			46,500	Bal b/f (a)	46,500	46,500	46,500
Bal c/f	46,500	46,500	–				
	46,500	46,500	46,500		46,500	46,500	46,500

(c) The revaluation account is not to remain in the books. It must be reversed.

                                                                   £   £

(1)   Dr   Revaluation account   20,000
           Cr   Property account   20,000
      with increase in value of property.

(2)   Dr   Debtors' account   500
           Cr   Revaluation account   500
      with reversal of revaluation entries.

(3)   Dr   Partners' capital account   M   9,750
                                    N   9,750
           Cr   Revaluation account   19,500

clear revaluation account to partners' capital account in the new profit-sharing ratio.

Showing the accounts in full now:

Revaluation account

	£		£
Debtors	500	Property	20,000
Capital accounts			
M	6,500		
N	6,500		
P	6,500		
	20,000		20,000
Property (1)	20,000	Debtors (2)	500
		Capital accounts	
		M (3)	9,750
		N (3)	9,750
	20,000		20,000

Capital accounts

	M £	N £	P £		M £	N £	P £
Bank a/c			46,500	Bal b/f	40,000	40,000	40,000
Revaluation (c) (3)	9,750	9,750		Revaluation (a)	6,500	6,500	6,500
Balance c/f	36,750	36,750	–				
	46,500	46,500	46,500		46,500	46,500	46,500

Revised balance sheet for MN at 31 December 19XX

	£
Property	60,000
Debtors	10,000
Bank	3,500
	73,500

	£
Capital accounts	
M	36,750
N	36,750
	73,500

Dissolution

A partnership may be ended for various reasons – the partners' wish to retire, or to pursue other interests, or to take advantages of the status of a limited company.

The approach is similar to the changes in partnership, with the use of a realisation account instead of revaluation account.

On dissolution, the assets of the partnership will have to be sold and the liabilities met. It may happen that the proceeds are not equal to the net book value of the net assets of the partnership and this will give rise to a profit or loss on realisation. This must be credited or debited to the partners in their profit-sharing ratio.

Example

Ted, Tony, Jim and Willie run a business in partnership. At 31 December 19X4 the partners decide to sell their business to one of their competitors. The balance sheet showed the following position, the partners sharing profits equally:

Balance sheet at 31 December 19X4

	Cost £	Dep'n £	£
Fixed assets			
Lease	10,000	3,000	7,000
Fixtures and fittings	1,500	900	600
Motor van	800	250	550
	12,300	4,150	8,150
Current assets			
Stock		8,500	
Debtors		7,600	
Bank		3,200	
		19,300	
Current liabilities			
Creditors		3,900	
			15,400
			23,550
Capital accounts			
Ted			6,000
Tony			4,000
Jim			3,000
Willie			2,000
			15,000
Current accounts			
Ted		2,080	
Tony		2,460	
Jim		2,120	
Willie		1,890	
			8,550
			23,550

Chapter 4 The Accounts of Partnerships

The following assets were sold for cash:

	£
Lease	9,000
Fixtures and fittings	400
Stock	8,200
Debtors	7,500
Goodwill	12,000
Total proceeds	37,100

The motor van was taken over by Jim at a valuation of £630. The creditors were paid in full and the bank account was closed.

Required

Close off the books of the following partnership as at 31 December 19X4.

Solution

Step 1: Prepare a realisation account.

As the partnership is terminating, all the ledger accounts in the partnership's books have to be closed. The most practical way of doing this is to transfer all the assets that are being sold or taken over to a **realisation account**, the journal entry being:

Dr: Realisation account
Cr: Asset accounts

with the book value of the assets being sold or taken over.

In the case of this business all the assets, except the bank account, are being disposed of, so the realisation account after the above journal entry should look like this:

Realisation account

	£
Lease	7,000
Fixtures and fittings	600
Motor van	550
Stock	8,500
Debtors	7,600
	24,250

Step 2: Deal with the sale proceeds of the assets.

The realisation account must be credited with the sale proceeds of the assets (including goodwill) sold for cash as well as the value at which Jim (who becomes a debtor) is going to take over the motor van, the journal entries being:

Dr: Bank account
Cr: Realisation account

with the assets being sold for cash (see ledger account in step 3 below).

Dr: Partner's current account
Cr: Realisation account

with the asset being taken over by one of the partners at the agreed value (see ledger account in step 3 below).

65

AAT Unit 10 Study Pack

Step 3: Close off the realisation account.

The realisation account, which is similar to a disposal of fixed assets account, now shows a profit which is divided between the partners in their profit-sharing ratio and transferred to their respective current accounts as shown.

Realisation account

	£	£		£
Sundry assets		24,250	Bank (assets sold for cash)	37,100
			Jim's current account	630
Profit of £13,480				
Ted (¼)	3,370			
Tony (¼)	3,370			
Jim (¼)	3,370			
Willie (¼)	3,370			
		13,480		
		37,730		37,730

Step 4: Close off the remaining accounts.

The only accounts left in the books now are the partners' capital and current accounts, the creditors' accounts, and the cash book. After paying off the creditors there should be just enough money in the bank to pay the amounts due to the partners. The partners' current and capital accounts can be combined at this stage.

Cash book

	£		£	£
Balance per balance sheet	3,200	Creditors		3,900
Realisation account	37,100	Partners' capital accounts		
		Ted	11,450	
		Tony	9,830	
		Jim	7,860	
		Willie	7,260	
				36,400
	40,300			40,300

Partners' capital accounts

	Ted £	Tony £	Jim £	Willie £		Ted £	Tony £	Jim £	Willie £
Realisation account					Balance per balance sheet	6,000	4,000	3,000	2,000
Motor van			630		Current a/c balances	2,080	2,460	2,120	1,890
Cash book	11,450	9,830	7,860	7,260	Realisation a/c Profit	3,370	3,370	3,370	3,370
	11,450	9,830	8,490	7,260		11,450	9,830	8,490	7,260

As you can now see there was exactly enough money in the bank to pay off the partners so the books have now been closed.

Drafting partnership accounts

Partnerships are not required to draw up accounts in a prescribed format.

The comments made in Chapter 3 regarding the users of sole trader accounts, general principles of drafting accounts and applicable accounting standards also apply to partnerships.

Questions

1 Brick and Stone

The following list of balances as at 30 September 19Y0 has been extracted from the books of Brick and Stone trading in partnership, sharing the balance of profits and loss in the proportions 3 : 2 respectively.

	£
Printing, stationery and postage	3,500
Sales	322,100
Stock in hand at 1 October 19X9	23,000
Purchases	208,200
Rent and rates	10,300
Heat and light	8,700
Staff salaries	36,100
Telephone charges	2,900
Motor vehicle running costs	5,620
Discounts allowable	950
Discounts receivable	370
Sales returns	2,100
Purchases returns	6,100
Carriage inwards	1,700
Carriage outwards	2,400
Fixtures and fittings	
At cost	26,000
Provision for depreciation	11,200
Motor vehicles	
At cost	46,000
Provision for depreciation	25,000
Drawings	
Brick	24,000
Stone	11,000
Current account balances at 1 October 19X9	
Brick	3,600 credit
Stone	2,400 credit
Capital account balances at 1 October 19X9	
Brick	33,000
Stone	17,000
Debtors	9,000
Creditors	8,400
Balance at bank	7,700 debit

Additional information

(1) £10,000 is to be transferred from Brick's capital account to a newly opened Brick loan account with effect from 1 July 19Y0.

The terms of the loan applied a rate of 10% per annum.

(2) Stone is to be credited with a salary at the rate of £12,000 per annum from 1 April 19Y0.

(3) Stock in hand at 30 September 19Y0 has been valued at cost at £32,000.

(4) Telephone charges accrued due at 30 September 19Y0 amounted to £400 and rent of £600 was prepaid at that date.

(5) During the year ended 30 September 19Y0, Stone has taken goods costing £1,000 for his own use.

(6) Depreciation is to be provided at the following annual rates on the straight-line basis:

Fixtures and fittings	10%
Motor vehicles	20%

Required

(a) Prepare a trading and profit and loss account for the year ended 30 September 19Y0.

(b) Prepare a statement showing the appropriation of profit for the year ended 30 September 19Y0.

(c) Prepare a balance sheet as at 30 September 19Y0 which should include summaries of the partners' capital and current accounts for the year ended on that date.

Summary

- The amount owed by the business to each partner is reflected in the total of each partner's capital and current account.

- Typically, the capital account is used for recording fixed capital.

- The current account is used for all other items, the most important of which are profit share and drawings.

- Profit is shared by the partners in accordance with their agreement.

- If there is no agreement, the Partnership Act 1890 states how profit is to be shared.

- Double-entry:

Drawings	Dr	Partners' current account
	Cr	Bank account
Interest on loan to partnership	Dr	Profit and loss loan interest account
	Cr	Partners' current account
Interest on capital, salaries, and profit share	Dr	Appropriation account
	Cr	Partners' current account

- On the admission or retirement of a partner, the assets and future profits (goodwill) must be valued.

- Goodwill adjustments

  Dr   Goodwill account
        Cr   Partners' capital account in the old profit-sharing ratio (PSR)

  with goodwill temporarily created in the books.

  Dr   Partners' capital account in the new PSR
        Cr   Goodwill account

  with goodwill removed from the books.

CHAPTER 5

Introduction to Limited Company Accounts

Objectives

This chapter covers the following performance criteria:

10.2.1 Financial statements are accurately drafted from appropriate information.

10.2.2 Subsequent adjustments are correctly implemented.

10.2.3 Draft accounts comply with domestic standards and legislation and, where relevant, partnership agreement.

10.2.5 Year–end financial statements are presented for approval to the appropriate person in a clear form.

At the end of this chapter, you should be able to:

- understand the ways in which the accounts of a limited company differ from those of a sole trader or a partnership

- draft a profit and loss account and a balance sheet for a limited company

- account for share issues

Introduction

We have already seen that a limited company is regarded as separate from its owners, the shareholders. The 'limited' part of a company's name refers to the fact that the shareholders are limited in their liability for the company's debts – the most they can lose is the total amount paid/payable on the shares held by them.

This means that companies will often be owned by shareholders who are independent of the management. They may also have other major loan investors. The financial statements therefore are of great importance in communicating between the company and its investors.

The main differences between the accounts of a company and those of a sole trader are:

- the format of the company accounts, which is governed by Schedule 4 of the Companies Act 1985, as modified by the Companies Act 1989;

- the treatment of profit in the profit and loss account;

- the composition of capital in the balance sheet.

Pro forma company profit and loss account

	£
Turnover	X
Cost of sales	(X)
Gross profit	X
Distribution costs	(X)
Administrative expenses	(X)
Other operating income	X
	X
Interest payable and similar charges	(X)
Profit on ordinary activities before taxation	X
Corporation tax	(X)
Profit on ordinary activities after taxation	X
Dividends paid and proposed	(X)
Profit for the financial year	X
Retained profit brought forward	X
Retained profit carried forward	X

Analysis of expenses

Unlike the profit and loss account of a sole trader, the profit and loss account of a limited company does not show the different types of expenses separately. Instead, expenses are grouped under the headings 'distribution costs' and 'administrative expenses'.

The best approach is:

- cross-reference workings for the main headings (distribution costs and administrative expenses);

- as you come across each expense, put it under the appropriate working heading;

- transfer the total at the end into the profit and loss account.

Do not spend hours deciding which heading for each expense – it won't really matter, as long as you've dealt correctly with the obvious ones and have shown clearly what you've included.

As a rule of thumb, you could use the following guide:

Distribution costs

- Salesmen's salaries and commissions
- Depreciation of showroom, delivery vehicles and salesmen's cars
- Advertising
- Delivery costs

Administrative expenses

Other expenses that are not shown under distribution costs, interest payable, tax or dividends!

This will include rent, light and heat, directors' remuneration, auditors' remuneration, depreciation on offices and staff cars, and other overheads.

Other operating income

The main example you might come across under this heading is rent receivable.

Corporation tax

The company is a separate legal entity and is subject to tax. Tax payable by companies is known as *corporation tax*. This is an appropriation of the company's profits and therefore appears in the profit and loss account.

Generally, tax will be paid nine months after the year end so the accounting entries are:

Debit Profit and loss account
Credit Corporation tax creditor (shown as a current liability in the balance sheet)

In the next year, when the tax is likely to be paid, the entry will be:

Debit Corporation tax creditor
Credit Cash

Dividends

The actual amount of dividend to be paid by a company will be determined by many factors, the main one being the need to retain sufficient profits to provide for the future working capital and fixed asset requirements of the company.

Some companies pay an amount on account of the total dividend before the end of the year. This is known as an *interim dividend* – the bookkeeping entry is:

Debit Dividend account
Credit Cash

(The dividend account is closed off to the profit and loss account at the year-end.)

It will only be at the end of the year, when the company's results for the whole accounting period are known, that the directors can declare a final dividend.

As the payment of the final dividend takes place after the year-end, the figure in the accounts will again represent a provision. The entries are therefore:

Debit Profit and loss account
Credit Dividends proposed account (shown as current liability)

Hence we will have two debits for dividends in the profit and loss account – one paid and one proposed.

Pro forma company balance sheet

	Cost £	Dep'n £	£
Fixed assets			
Land and buildings	X	X	X
Plant and machinery	X	X	X
Fixtures, fittings, tools and equipment	X	X	X
Current assets			
Stocks		X	
Debtors		X	
Cash at bank and in hand		X	
		X	
Creditors: amounts falling due within one year			
Trade creditors		X	
Accruals and deferred income		X	
		X	
Net current assets			X
Total assets less current liabilities			X
Creditors: amounts falling due after more than one year			
Debenture loans			(X)
			X
Capital and reserves			
Share capital			X
Share premium account			X
Other reserves			X
Profit and loss account			X
Shareholders' funds			X

Share capital

When a company is formed, it usually raises its initial capital by issuing a number of shares.

The people who buy the shares and are the owners of the company are known as its *members* or *shareholders*.

Shareholders

The proportion of the company which each member owns can thus be calculated by reference to the number of shares he holds. For example, if a member holds 750 shares in a company which has 1,000 shares in issue, he has a 75% stake in the company.

The advantage of the share system is that members can easily transfer their interest in the company by selling their shares and the company can raise new capital by issuing more shares.

Shares have a face value which is also called the *nominal value* or *par value*. This is distinct from their *market value*.

Suppose a company issues 100 shares with a nominal value of £1 for £100 in total.

Mrs X   25 shares
Mrs Y   75 shares

The double entry is:

Debit   Cash   100
Credit Share capital   100

If Mrs Y sells her shares to Mrs Z, this has no effect on the amount of share capital received by the company, so no entry is made in the share capital account.

If the stock market decides that the shares are worth only 80p each, no entry is made in the share capital account because, again, this has no effect on the capital received by the company.

Types of share capital

A company may issue different types (classes) of shares, by far the most important of which are:

- *Ordinary shares*

    The majority of companies will only have this type of share, whose holders usually have a right to vote at meetings and are therefore effectively the owners of the company.

- *Preference shares*

    'Preference' in this context means that the owners of these shares will have priority over the ordinary shareholders in the payment of their dividend, which is usually of a fixed amount.

    In addition, if the company winds up (ceases to exist) the preference shareholders will normally be repaid their capital before the ordinary shareholders.

The difference between these two classes of shares is in essence the difference between the risk-takers (the ordinary shareholders), whose reward will be geared to how well the company performs, and the non-risk-takers (the preference shareholders) whose entitlement is fixed.

Other terms

Authorised share capital

A company's Memorandum of Association states the amount of shares which it is allowed to issue to its shareholders. This is the *authorised share capital* of the company. A company does not necessarily issue all of the shares which it is authorised to issue.

Issued share capital

The number of shares actually issued is known as the *issued share capital*.

Called up share capital and paid up share capital

Once the company has asked its shareholders to pay for the shares it has issued to them, the shares are said to be *called up*. Once those shareholders have paid the company for the shares they are said to be *paid up*.

Reserves

Reserves are the cumulative total of the company's retained profits.

A company may if it wishes, set aside some of its profits for a specific purpose. For example:

	£
Called-up share capital	1,000
Profit and loss account	1,000
	2,000

The company wishes to set aside £500 for replacement of fixed assets.

	£
Called-up share capital	1,000
Fixed asset replacement reserve	500
Profit and loss account	500
	2,000

This does not affect its total reserves, which remain at £1,000.

Share premium account

This arises when a company issues shares for more than their nominal value. The *premium* over this amount must be credited to a *share premium* account.

Example

Enterprise Ltd makes an issue of 10,000 £1 ordinary shares for £1.60 each. The entries are:

Debit	Cash account	£16,000	
Credit	Share capital account		£10,000
	Share premium account		£6,000

Note that a share premium account does *not* arise if the market value subsequently increases to more than the nominal value.

The share premium account cannot be distributed to shareholders.

It may only be used for:

- making bonus share issues;
- writing off preliminary expenses (expenses incurred before a company is incorporated);
- writing off expenses of, or the commission paid or discount allowed on, any issue of shares or debentures;
- providing for the premium payable on redemption of debentures.

Bonus issues

Introduction

Sometimes, extra shares may be issued to existing shareholders without any more money having to be paid for them. Such an issue of share is known as a *bonus* issue or a *scrip* or *capitalisation* issue. The extra shares are issued to existing shareholders in proportion to their present shareholdings. Since no cash changes hands, the exercise is merely a bookkeeping one.

The accounting entries are as follows:

    Debit   Reserves
    Credit   Ordinary share capital.

With the nominal value of the bonus shares issued.

Example

A public limited company has an authorised share capital of 2,000,000 ordinary shares of £1 each, and an issued and fully paid share capital of 600,000 ordinary £1 shares. At 30 June 19X1 its reserves amounted to £900,000. The company proposes to make a bonus issue of one share for every share held (a one for one bonus issue).

Required

Prepare an extract of A plc's balance sheet (a) immediately before; and (b) immediately after the issue of the bonus shares.

Solution

A plc
Balance sheet at 30 June 19X1

		(a)	Before £'000	(b)	After £'000
Net assets			1,500		1,500
Share capital					
Authorised:	ordinary shares £1 each		2,000		2,000
Issued and fully paid:	ordinary shares £1 each		600		1,200
Reserves			900		300
Shareholders' funds			1,500		1,500

Commentary

It can be seen from the above illustration that shareholders' funds are not changed by the bonus issue. However, the number of shares in issue and their total nominal value has increased by £600,000 (from £600,000 to £1,200,000), but the reserves have decreased by an equivalent amount (from £900,000 to £300,000). No change has taken place in the total value of the net assets.

Rights issues

A rights issue differs from a bonus issue in that the company actually raises cash through an additional issue of shares at a favourable price to the existing shareholders. Existing shareholders are given the exclusive right to take up a new issue of shares at a specific price. The number of shares that they are entitled to take up is in proportion to their existing holdings; for example, with a one for five rights issue, a shareholder with 100 shares has the right to subscribe for twenty shares. The issue price is normally below the market price.

Example

XYZ plc has 2,000,000 25p ordinary shares in issue and its summarised balance sheet is given below:

	£'000
Net assets	2,300
Share capital	500
Reserves	1,800
	2,300

The company decides to make a rights issue of one for every five held at £1 each.

Show the balance sheet after the rights issue is complete.

Solution

The rights issue is 400,000 shares @ £1 each and will raise cash of £400,000 which can be split between nominal value and premium as follows:

Nominal value 400,000 × 25p	100,000
Share premium (75p each)	300,000
Cash	400,000

The balance sheet is as follows:

	£'000
Net assets (2,300 + 400)	2,700
Share capital	600
Share premium	300
Reserves	1,800
	2,700

Shareholders' options

A shareholder who receives a rights offer has three options open to him. These are as follows:

(a) Take up rights and pay the required amount to the company, increasing his shareholding.
(b) Sell his rights to a third party who may then buy the shares from the company.
(c) Do nothing and let his rights lapse.

Option (a) above may be considered the normal course for a shareholder to follow, but some shareholders may not wish to take up the offer, or may not be in a position to do so. In this case they would adopt (b) or (c) as their course of action.

Debentures

Debentures are a long-term loan. They are named after the legal agreement detailing the loan.

It is likely that there will be a number of debenture-holders in the same way that there are a number of shareholders. In other words, the company may well be borrowing from a number of people or organisations rather than just one.

Capital instruments

FRS4 *Capital instruments* defines capital instruments as 'all instruments issued as a means of raising finance'.

Limited companies have more scope for raising finance than other forms of business organisation. We have seen that finance can be raised in two main ways:

- share capital (ordinary shares are sometimes referred to as 'equity')
- debentures (sometimes referred to as 'loan capital' or 'debt').

Until quite recently, and in the majority of cases, finance was capable of being fairly easily classified as share capital or loan capital. However, during the 1980s, some companies began to raise capital using more complex capital instruments, which grant rights other than simple interest or dividend participation. Many of these capital instruments have the characteristics of both debt and equity and it is often difficult to decide how to classify them and how to treat them in the accounts.

FRS4 states that capital instruments should be presented in financial statements in a way that reflects the *obligations of the issuer*:

- capital instruments should be classified as liabilities if they contain an obligation to transfer economic benefits

- capital instruments should be classified as shareholders' funds if they do not contain an obligation to transfer economic benefits.

If a company issues a debenture, it must pay interest to the debenture holders; therefore a debenture is a liability. If a company issues ordinary shares, members pay cash to the company for the right to be a member. The company may pay dividends to shareholders, but it is not obliged to do so. Therefore ordinary shares are classed as shareholders' funds. (Preference shares are classed as shareholders' funds because preference dividends may only be paid if there are distributable profits available whereas debt interest must be paid in all circumstances.)

Detailed accounting for, and disclosure of, complex capital instruments is beyond the scope of this Unit. You are merely required to have an appreciation of the definition of a capital instrument.

Types of company

There are two types of limited company, public and private. A public company must include in its name the letters 'plc' standing for public limited company. Private companies must include 'Limited' ('Ltd') in their name.

The main difference is that a private company may not offer its shares or debentures to the public and so all companies listed on the Stock Exchange are public companies.

The duties of companies regarding accounting records

By S221 CA 1985, every company must keep accounting records which are sufficient to show and explain the company's transactions to disclose, with reasonable accuracy, the financial position of the company at any time.

Any officer who knowingly or wilfully authorises or permits his company to keep inadequate accounting records commits an offence.

Private company accounting records must be preserved by the company for three years from the date on which they were made; those of public companies must be preserved for six years.

The accounting records of a company must contain:

- a day book or journal;
- a record of assets and liabilities of the company;
- if the company's business involves dealing with goods:
  - statements of stock held by the company at the end of each financial year;
  - the stocktaking records from which those statements are derived; and
  - statements of all goods sold other than by ordinary retail trade and of all goods purchased, in sufficient detail to enable the goods, the buyers and the sellers to be identified.

Annual accounts

Contents of annual accounts

Profit and loss account and balance sheet

The directors of every company must prepare:

- a profit and loss account for each financial year; and
- a balance sheet as at the end of that financial year.

Directors' report

The balance sheet must be accompanied by a directors' report which details certain matters in relation to the company.

Auditors' report

The company's auditors must report to the members on the accounts examined by them and the report must state whether the accounts give a true and fair view of the state of the company's affairs and of its results for the period ending on the accounting date. The auditors' report must be signed by them and must state their names.

Normally, each year, the directors must lay copies of the balance sheet, profit and loss account, directors' report and auditors' report before the annual general meeting of the company. However, a private company may pass an elective resolution to dispense with the requirement to lay accounts and reports before general meetings.

A copy of these accounts must usually be sent to every member of the company not less than 21 days before the general meeting at which they will be considered.

However, listed companies can now send their shareholders summary financial statements instead of the full audited accounts. Shareholders have a right to ask for a full set of accounts.

Accounting reference periods

The key factor in arriving at the time limits for the preparation of annual accounts is the accounting reference period – the company's financial year.

The day on which the accounting reference period ends is known as the *accounting reference date*. A company has nine months from the date of incorporation to notify the Registrar of its accounting reference date. The first accounting reference date cannot be more than eighteen months after incorporation.

If a company does nothing to establish its own accounting reference date, this date will be the end of the month in which the anniversary of incorporation falls.

In the case of a private company, its annual accounts must be laid before a general meeting and filed with the Registrar within ten months after the end of the accounting reference period. In the case of a public company, the time limit is seven months.

Questions

1 Billesley Ltd

Billesley Ltd has authorised share capital of 500,000 50 pence ordinary shares and 300,000 6% £1 preference shares.

The trial balance of Billesley Ltd at 30 June 19X2 was as follows:

	£	£
Land and buildings (cost and depreciation)	500,000	80,000
Plant (cost and depreciation)	180,000	105,000
Vehicles (cost and depreciation)	150,000	90,000
Issued share capital		
Ordinary shares		200,000
Preference shares		200,000
Share premium account		25,000
General reserve		10,000
Capital redemption reserve		20,000
Sales		500,000
Administrative expenses	110,000	
Selling expenses	65,000	
Provision for doubtful debts		12,000
12% Debentures		150,000
Creditors and accruals		74,000
Debtors and prepayments	116,000	
Purchases	280,000	
Stock	46,000	
Investment	75,000	
Profit and loss account		135,000
Interim dividends paid		
– ordinary	10,000	
– preference	6,000	
Cash at bank	63,000	
	1,601,000	1,601,000

The stock at 30 June amounted to £52,000 and the investment, which was a short-term use of surplus cash, had a market value of £79,000 at that date.

The directors wish to provide for a final ordinary dividend of 4% and the final preference dividend together with a transfer to the general reserve of £5,000.

Corporation tax of £12,000 is to be provided for.

The debenture loans were issued on 30 June 19X2.

Required

(a) Prepare the profit and loss account for Billesley Ltd for the year ended 30 June 19X2 together with a balance sheet at that date, in a format suitable for publication.

(b) One of your clients is a small shareholder in Billesley Ltd and has the following concerns about items in the accounts that he has received. Write a short response to each of his questions.

1 How many ordinary shares does Billesley actually have in issue at 30 June 19X2?

2 How and why was the share premium account created?

3 What are the company's management accounts and will they be the same as the accounts produced here?

Summary

- Differences between sole traders' and companies' accounts:
    - treatment of profit;
    - composition of capital in the balance sheet; and
    - requirements of the Companies Acts 1985 and 1989 (note a company is a separate legal entity).

- Corporation tax:
    - a tax based on profits for a year; and
    - amount due shown as a current liability.

- Dividends:
    - amounts paid by the company to its shareholders, corresponding to drawings by a sole trader.

- Shares:
    - Ordinary
        - give control of the company; and
        - dividend dependent upon profitability.
    - Preference
        - do not give control; and
        - priority over ordinary shares in payment of dividend and (normally) on winding up.

- Reserves:
    - cumulative total of a company's retained profits – there may be several different reserves intended for specific purposes.

- Share premium account:
    - amount paid for shares over and above their nominal value.

- Debenture:
    - an acknowledgement by a company of a long-term loan made to it.

- Public company:
    - name has suffix 'plc'; and
    - may issue shares to the public.

- Private company
    - name has suffix 'Ltd'; and
    - may not issue shares to the public.

- The directors of every company must prepare:
    - a profit and loss account for each financial year; and
    - a balance sheet at the end of that financial year.

CHAPTER 6

Manufacturing Accounts

Objectives

This chapter covers the following performance criteria:

10.2.1 Financial statements are accurately drafted from appropriate information.

10.2.2 Subsequent adjustments are correctly implemented.

10.2.5 Year–end financial statements are presented for approval to the appropriate person in a clear form.

At the end of this chapter, you should be able to:

♦   prepare a manufacturing account.

Introduction

So far we have worked with trading accounts of the form:

	£	£
Sales		X
Opening stock	X	
Purchases	X	
	X	
Closing stock	(X)	
Cost of sales		(X)
Gross profit		X

This is perfectly satisfactory for a retail organisation that purchases and resells goods. A manufacturing company will need further details of the cost of manufacturing its products and these details can be set out in the form of a manufacturing account.

Definitions

♦   *Direct costs* are those which can be attributed to a particular unit of production and will normally include raw materials, productive wages and other expenses capable of direct identification with production. These three are often called *direct materials, direct wages* and *direct expenses*.

♦   *Indirect expenses* are production expenses which cannot be attributed to a particular unit of production. They are often called *manufacturing* or *works overheads* and will include such items as factory power, plant repairs etc.

♦   *Prime cost* is the total of the direct expenses.

♦   *Factory cost or works cost* is prime cost plus a share of the factory indirect expenses.

Stocks

A trading firm has stocks in only one form (ie. goods held for resale), but a manufacturing firm will have three forms of stocks:

- *direct materials* – items of raw materials which have not yet been issued to production;
- *work in progress* – items of partly completed goods;
- *finished goods* – items which are completed but unsold.

The pro forma manufacturing account

Basic format

The manufacturing account summarises the costs of production in the factory:

	£
Direct materials	X
Direct labour	X
Direct expenses	X
Prime cost	X
Manufacturing overheads	X
Factory cost	X

Detailed layout of manufacturing account

Pro forma manufacturing account

	£	£
Materials consumed		
Opening stock of raw materials	X	
Purchases of raw materials	X	
	X	
Less: Closing stock of raw materials	(X)	
		X
Direct wages		X
Direct expenses		X
		X
Prime cost		
Works indirect expenses		
Factory power	X	
Factory rent/rates	X	
Factory insurance	X	
Factory light and heat	X	
Plant repairs	X	
Plant depreciation	X	
		X
		X
Add: Opening work in progress		X
Less: Closing work in progress		(X)
Factory cost of goods produced – transfers to warehouse		X

Trading and profit and loss account

The trading and profit and loss account, which takes account of selling and distribution costs and administration expenses, will be in a reasonably familiar format:

Trading and profit and loss account

	£	£
Sales		X
Less: Cost of goods sold		
Opening stock of finished goods	X	
Transfers from factory	X	
	X	
Less: Closing stock of finished goods	(X)	
		(X)
Gross profit		X
Less: Distribution costs	X	
Administrative expenses	X	
		(X)
Net profit		X

Preparation of the manufacturing account

Illustration

The following represent details of the factory costs of J White for the year ended 31 December 19X7.

	£
Opening stock of raw materials	1,000
Raw materials purchased	12,000
Direct (manufacturing) wages	24,000
Factory rent	800
Depreciation of plant in factory	850
General indirect expenses	550
Closing stock of raw materials	1,200
Work in progress	
1 January 19X6	4,000
31 December 19X6	6,000

Given that we have a basic format, we can now use the above information to demonstrate a developed layout.

J White
Manufacturing account for the year ended 31 December 19X7

	£	£
Direct materials		
Opening stock	1,000	
Purchases	12,000	
Carriage inwards	–	
Less: Returns	–	
	13,000	
Less: Closing stock	(1,200)	
		11,800
Direct wages		24,000
Direct expenses		–
Prime cost		35,800
Factory overhead		
Rent	800	
Plant depreciation	850	
General expenses	550	
		2,200
		38,000
Add: Opening work in progress		4,000
		42,000
Less: Closing work in progress		(6,000)
Manufacturing cost of goods completed		36,000

Note that opening and closing stocks of raw materials and work in progress are included in the manufacturing account. Stocks of finished goods are dealt with in the trading account, as is normal.

Certain overhead costs may require apportionment amongst these functional headings. For example, rent of premises may be £1,000 per annum. How should this be split between manufacturing, administration and selling? In such a case, the likely answer is on the basis of floorspace used. Thus the apportionment might be:

	Area (m²)	Apportionment £	
Factory	6,000	500	Manufacturing account
Administration offices	3,600	300)	Profit and loss account
Sales offices	2,400	200)	
	12,000	1,000	

If you are required to apportion expenses, you will be told which basis to use.

The double-entry

In the trading account the manufacturing cost of goods completed will appear in the place of purchases as shown below. Thus a credit has been made to manufacturing account and a debit to trading account.

J White
Trading account for the year ended 31 December 19X7

	£	£
Sales (say)		60,000
Less: Cost of sales		
Opening stock (say)	6,000	
Cost of manufacture	36,000	
	42,000	
Less: Closing stock (say)	(5,000)	
		(37,000)
Gross profit		23,000

Questions

1   Punch

Punch is a sole trader engaged in the manufacture of toys. The following trial balance was extracted from the books at 31 March 19X1.

	Debit	Credit
	£	£
Capital		39,390
Freehold land and buildings at cost	45,000	
Plant and machinery at cost	36,500	
Motor vans at cost	19,800	
Provision for depreciation – Land and buildings		2,700
– Plant and machinery		4,500
– Motor vans		3,700
Stocks at 1.4.X0 – Raw materials	12,725	
– WIP	18,000	
– Finished goods	20,500	
Purchases	82,550	
Sales		362,720
Wages – Factory	64,750	
– Administration	24,360	
– Sales	26,920	
Rent (nine months to 31.12.X0)	22,000	
Repairs to buildings	5,500	
Sales expenses	22,000	
Electricity and power	17,600	
Administration expenses	5,900	
Provision for doubtful debts		1,560
Debtors	38,970	
Creditors		42,230
Bank		6,320
Cash in hand	45	
	463,120	463,120

You are given the following information.

(1) Provision is to be made for commission due to the sales manager. The commission is 20% of his own department's net profit after charging such commission.

(2) Closing stocks on 31 March 19X1:

	£
Raw materials	9,650
WIP	21,000
Finished goods	24,500

(3) Annual depreciation is to be provided at the following rates on the straight-line basis:

Land and buildings	2%
Plant and machinery	10%
Motor vans	25%

(4) Debtors include an amount of £700 due from Sonic Ltd. Punch does not expect to be paid and has decided to write it off.

A general provision of 5% is to be maintained on remaining debts.

(5) Factory rent for the 12 months to 31.12.X1 is £26,500.

(6) Expenses are to be allocated as follows:

	Factory	Administration
Rent	7/10	3/10
Repairs	4/5	1/5
Electricity and power	2/3	1/3
Buildings depreciation	8/10	2/10

(7) The following amounts were outstanding at the year-end:

	£
Electricity	960
Telephone (60% Sales, 40% Admin.)	240
Accountancy fees (Admin.)	850

Required

Prepare the manufacturing, trading and profit and loss accounts for the year ended 31 March 19X1 and the balance sheet at that date.

Summary

Manufacturing accounts provide a detailed analysis of the *cost of goods produced*.

For a manufacturing business, cost of goods sold includes:

- raw materials;

- production labour; and

- production overheads (direct and indirect).

Production overheads need to be distinguished from selling and administrative expenses.

CHAPTER 7

Limited Company Accounts: the Balance Sheet

Objectives

This chapter covers the following performance criteria:

10.2.1 Financial statements are accurately drafted from appropriate information.

10.2.3 Draft accounts comply with domestic standards and legislation and, where relevant, partnership agreement.

10.2.5 Year–end financial statements are presented for approval to the appropriate person in a clear form.

At the end of this chapter, you should be able to:

- prepare the balance sheet of a limited company in the format required by the Companies Act 1985

- prepare notes to the balance sheet that disclose the additional information required by the Companies Act

Introduction

The financial statements of a company comprise:

- balance sheet and notes;

- profit and loss account and notes;

- statement of total recognised gains and losses;

- cash flow statement and notes;

- accounting policies note; and

- comparative figures.

In this session and the following session we will study the form and content of the balance sheet and profit and loss account which are required by the Companies Acts. In later sessions we will look at the detailed accounting and disclosure requirements of the various accounting standards.

Form of accounts

The Companies Act 1985 requires that published accounts follow certain prescribed formats.

A number of different layouts are given in the Act for both the balance sheet and the profit and loss account, but once a company has adopted one of these formats it cannot be changed in future years unless the directors consider there are special reasons for doing so.

The formats given are only those which are most commonly used.

In reading the formats, you should be aware of the following points:

- Although only one year's figures are indicated on the pro forma, corresponding amounts for the previous year must be shown (these are not normally required by assessment questions).

- Headings are prefixed by a letter A, B, C or a number, I, II, III (Roman numerals), 1, 2, 3, 4 (Arabic numerals). These letters and numbers are not required in published statements or in assessment answers.

- Items prefixed by letters A, B, C etc. and by Roman numerals I, III, III, IV etc. may be omitted but not changed.

- Items prefixed by Arabic numerals 1, 2, 3, 4 etc. may be omitted, combined or described differently if necessary. If Arabic items are combined on the face of the balance sheet or profit and loss account, an analysis should be given in the notes to the accounts.

- Any item for which there is no amount to be shown for both the current and preceding years may be omitted.

Balance sheet – formats

Two formats exist for the balance sheet. Format 1, often referred to as the *vertical format*, is the most common and is normally used in practice. Format 2 is often referred to as the *horizontal format* and is not very common in practice.

Balance sheet – Format 1

				£	£	£
A	Called-up share capital not paid*					X
B	Fixed assets					
	I	Intangible assets				
		1	Development costs	X		
		2	Concessions, patents, licences, trade marks and similar rights and assets	X		
		3	Goodwill	X		
		4	Payments on account	X		
					X	
	II	Tangible assets				
		1	Land and buildings	X		
		2	Plant and machinery	X		
		3	Fixtures, fittings, tools and equipment	X		
		4	Payments on account and assets in course of construction	X		
					X	

				£	£	£
	III	Investments				
		1	Shares in group undertakings	X		
		2	Loans to group undertakings	X		
		3	Participating interests	X		
		4	Loans to undertakings in which the company has a participating interest	X		
		5	Other investments other than loans	X		
		6	Other loans	X		
		7	Own shares	X		
					X	
		(Total of B)				X
C	**Current assets**					
	I	Stocks				
		1	Raw materials and consumables	X		
		2	Work in progress	X		
		3	Finished goods and goods for resale	X		
		4	Payments on account	X		
				X		
	II	Debtors				
		1	Trade debtors	X		
		2	Amounts owed by group undertakings	X		
		3	Amounts owed by undertakings in which the group has a participating interest	X		
		4	Other debtors	X		
		5	Called-up share capital not paid*	X		
		6	Prepayments and accrued income*	X		
				X		
	III	Investments				
		1	Shares in group undertakings	X		
		2	Own shares	X		
		3	Other investments	X		
				X		
	IV	Cash at bank and in hand		X		
		(Total of C)			X	
D	**Prepayments and accrued income***				X	
		(Total of C + D)				X

				£	£	£
E	Creditors: Amounts falling due within one year					
	1	Debenture loans		X		
	2	Bank loans and overdrafts		X		
	3	Payments received on account		X		
	4	Trade creditors		X		
	5	Bills of exchange payable		X		
	6	Amounts owed to group undertakings		X		
	7	Amounts owed to undertakings in which the group has a participating interest		X		
	8	Other creditors including taxation and social security		X		
	9	Accruals and deferred income*		X		
				───		
					(X)	
F	Net current assets (liabilities) (C + D – E)					X
G	Total assets less current liabilities (A + B + F)					X
H	Creditors: Amounts falling due after more than one year					
	1	Debenture loans		X		
	2	Bank loans and overdrafts		X		
	3	Payments received on account		X		
	4	Trade creditors		X		
	5	Bills of exchange payable		X		
	6	Amounts owed to group undertakings		X		
	7	Amounts owed to undertakings in which the group has a participating interest		X		
	8	Other creditors including taxation and social security		X		
	9	Accruals and deferred income*		X		
				───		
					(X)	
I	Provisions for liabilities and charges					
	1	Pensions and similar obligations		X		
	2	Taxation, including deferred taxation		X		
	3	Other provisions		X		
				───		
					(X)	
J	Accruals and deferred income*					(X)
						───
						X
K	Capital and reserves					
	I	Called-up share capital				X
	II	Share premium account				X
	III	Revaluation reserve				X
	IV	Other reserves				
		1	Capital redemption reserve		X	
		2	Reserve for own shares		X	
		3	Reserves provided for by the articles of association		X	
					───	
						X
	V	Profit and loss account				X
						───
						X

* alternative positions for the items marked

Balance sheet – disclosures

Fixed assets

Note that tangible assets are just one of the three categories of fixed assets. Remember that assets are classified as fixed assets 'if they are intended for use on a continuing basis in the company's activities'.

The disclosures required in respect of fixed assets may be broken down into:

(a) *General movements*

For each item under fixed assets, state the following (comparatives not required):

(i) The aggregate purchase price or production cost, or valuation as at the beginning and end of the financial year.

(ii) The effect on any amount shown in the balance sheet in respect of each fixed asset item as a result of any:

- revaluation made during the year;
- acquisitions during the year;
- disposals during the year;
- transfers (between category of fixed asset) during the year.

(iii) In respect of provisions for depreciation or diminution in value:

- the cumulative amount of such provisions as at the beginning and end of the year;
- the amount provided during the year;
- the amount of any adjustments made during the year in consequence of the disposal of any asset.

Example

The following extracts from the trial balance of Alpine Athletic Training plc relate to tangible fixed assets.

Trial balance at 31 December 19X7

	£	£
Premises at cost	600,000	
Plant and machinery at cost	135,000	
Provision for depreciation on plant and machinery at 1.1.X7		60,000
Motor vehicles at cost	54,000	
Provision for depreciation on motor vehicles at 1.1.X7		24,000

The following information is relevant to the year ended 31 December 19X7.

Depreciation is to be provided for the year as follows:

Buildings	2% on cost
Plant and machinery	10% on cost
Motor vehicles	25% on written down value

The only changes in fixed assets during the year were an addition to plant and machinery in early January 19X7 costing £30,000 and the purchase of premises for £600,000 comprising £150,000 for buildings and £450,000 for land.

Required

Produce in a form suitable for publication, the required information for fixed assets.

Solution

The first step is to work out the depreciation charge for the current year as follows:

Freehold premises

$$2\% \times 150,000 = £3,000$$

Plant and machinery

$$10\% \times 135,000 = £13,500$$

Motor vehicles

$$25\% \times (54,000 - 24,000) = £7,500$$

We can now construct a suitable note for inclusion in the notes to the accounts which would appear as follows.

Notes to the accounts (extract)

Note 1

Tangible fixed assets

	Freehold land and buildings £	Plant and machinery £	Motor vehicles £	Total £
Cost 1.1.X7	–	105,000	54,000	159,000
Addition during year	600,000	30,000	–	630,000
Cost 31.12.X7	600,000	135,000	54,000	789,000
Accumulated depreciation at 1.1.X7	–	60,000	24,000	84,000
Charge for year	3,000	13,500	7,500	24,000
Accumulated depreciation at 31.12.X7	3,000	73,500	31,500	108,000
Net book value at 31 12.X7	597,000	61,500	22,500	681,000
Net book value at 1.1.X7	–	45,000	30,000	75,000

The straight-line method of depreciation is applied to buildings and plant and machinery using 2% and 10% respectively. Vehicles are depreciated according to the reducing balance method at 25%.

Balance sheet (extract)

	19X7 £	19X6 £
Fixed assets		
Tangible assets (Note 1)	681,000	75,000

(b) *When fixed assets are stated at a valuation*

State

   (i)   the dates and amounts of the last revaluation;

   (ii)   the corresponding historical cost amounts;

   (iii) where the revaluation has been made during the year, the names or qualifications of the valuers and the basis of valuation used.

(c) *Analysis of land and buildings*

Analyse net book amount of land and buildings under:

   (i)   freehold;

   (ii)   long leasehold (ie. not less than 50 years remaining unexpired at the end of the financial year); and

   (iii) short leasehold.

Illustration

The analysis of land and buildings is achieved by creating separate headings in our fixed asset note for each group that exists. Our example of a fixed asset note above contained £600,000 in respect of freehold premises. Had this amount in fact been split between freehold and leasehold, our note might have appeared as follows.

Tangible fixed assets

	Freehold premises £	Long leasehold £	Plant & machinery £	Motor vehicles £	Total £
Cost 1.1.X7	–	–	105,000	54,000	159,000
Addition during year	400,000	200,000	30,000	–	630,000
Cost 31.12.X7	400,000	200,000	135,000	54,000	789,000
Accumulated depreciation 1.1.X7	–	–	60,000	24,000	84,000
Charge for year	1,000	2,000	13,500	7,500	24,000
Accumulated depreciation 31.12.X7	1,000	2,000	73,500	31,500	108,000
Net book value 31.12.X7	399,000	198,000	61,500	22,500	681,000
Net book value at 1.1.X7	–	–	45,000	30,000	75,000

Where such an analysis is too cumbersome, a note as follows will suffice.

The net book value of land and buildings is made up as follows:

	£
Freehold premises	399,000
Long leasehold	198,000
Total per original analysis	597,000

(d) *Investments (both fixed asset and current asset)*

    (1) Aggregate amount of listed investments.

    (2) For each item which includes listed investments disclose:

        – the aggregate market value of the listed investments where it differs from their balance sheet amount;

        – both the market value and stock exchange value where the market value is taken as being higher than the stock exchange value.

Illustration

Such information will be given in a note to the accounts which may appear as follows:

Note: Investments

The total of investments of £400,000 given on the balance sheet comprises:

	£
Listed investments	250,000
Other investments	150,000
	400,000

The market value of the listed investments at 31.12.X7 was £284,000.

    (3) Details of each investment where the investing company holds 20% or more of the nominal value of any class of share or where the investment represents 20% of the book value of investing company's assets:

        – name;
        – country of incorporation (if outside Great Britain) ;
        – description and proportion of each class of shares held.

Current assets

The additional requirements in respect of current assets are considerably simpler than those for fixed assets.

Note that current assets are those not intended for use on a continuing basis in the company's activities, ie. all assets are either fixed or current.

(a) *Stocks*

  (i) Sub-classify the main categories of stock and work in progress in a manner appropriate to the business. This would normally comprise the following:

  - finished goods and goods for resale;
  - raw materials and consumables;
  - work in progress.

  (ii) Where the purchase price or production cost of any item of stock is materially different from the replacement cost of that item, state the amount of the difference by way of a note.

(b) *Debtors*

  For each item under debtors, show separately the amount falling due after more than one year.

  Debtors falling due after more than one year should be disclosed on the face of the balance sheet, rather than in the notes to the accounts if they are so material that readers might otherwise misinterpret the accounts.

Liabilities and provisions

(a) *Creditors – general*

  For each balance sheet item shown under creditors, disclose by way of a note the following:

  (i) amounts falling due within one year or after more than one year:

  - the aggregate amount of secured liabilities;
  - an indication of the nature of the security given;

  (ii) amounts falling due after more than one year:

  - amount due for repayment after more than five years from the balance sheet date;
  - terms of repayment and rate of interest for any such amounts.

(b) *Debentures*

  (i) Where the company has issued any debentures during the financial year, disclose by way of a note:

  - the classes of debenture issued;
  - in respect of each class, the amount issued and the consideration received.

  (ii) Show separately the amount of any convertible loans.

(c) *Taxation*

  Identify separately amounts payable in respect of mainstream corporation tax and other tax and social security.

Illustration

This merely requires a note giving an analysis of the items included under the heading 'Other creditors including taxation and social security'. Typically this analysis for creditors falling due within one year would be:

	£
Corporation tax (mainstream)	64,000
Social security	4,300
Other creditors	23,000
	91,300

(d) *Dividends*

    (i) Amount of proposed dividends, which should be included as a current liability.

    (ii) Amount of any arrears of fixed cumulative dividends and the period for which each class is in arrears. Note that these are not provided for in the accounts and are only a contingent liability.

(e) *Provisions – general*

    (i) Disclose by way of a note particulars of each material provision included under 'other provisions' in the balance sheet (comparatives not required).

    (ii) Where there is any movement on provisions, disclose (comparatives not required):

- the amount of the provision as at the beginning and end of the financial year,
- the amount transferred to or from the provisions during the year.

(f) *Contingent liabilities*

For possible material contingent liabilities not provided against and which are not remote, disclose:

- the nature of the contingency,
- the uncertainties relating to the amount of timing of any outflow,
- an estimate of its financial effect,
- details of any security provided.

(g) *Commitments*

    (i) Disclose by way of a note aggregate or estimated amounts of capital commitments not provided for.

    (ii) Particulars of any other financial commitments which:

- have not been provided for,
- are relevant to assessing the company's state of affairs.

Chapter 7 Limited Company Accounts: the Balance Sheet

(iii) Distinguish separately any commitments made on behalf of:

- any parent company or fellow subsidiary of the company,
- any subsidiary of the company.

Capital and reserves

The disclosures in respect of capital and reserves are straightforward and should present few problems.

(a) *Share capital*

    (i) Authorised share capital.

    (ii) Amount of allotted share capital and amount of called-up share capital which has been paid up.

    (iii) Number and aggregate nominal value of allotted shares of each class where more than one class of shares have been allotted.

    (iv) Where the company has allotted any shares during the financial year:

- the classes of shares allotted, and
- for each class of shares, the number allotted, their aggregate nominal value and the consideration received by the company.

    (v) Particulars of debentures which may be converted to shares:

- the number, description and amount of the shares in question,
- the period during which the right is exercisable, and
- the price to be paid for the shares allotted.

    (vi) Number, description and amount of shares in the company held by its subsidiaries or their nominees.

(b) *Redeemable shares*

    (i) Earliest and latest dates of redemption by company.
    (ii) Whether redemption at company's option or in any event.
    (iii) Whether any (and if so what) premium is payable on redemption.

(c) *Reserves*

Where there is any movement on reserves, disclose (comparatives not required):

    (i) the amount of the reserves as at the beginning and end of the financial year,
    (ii) any amount transferred to or from the reserves during the year.

(d) *Revaluation reserve*

If assets are revalued, the revaluation surplus must be credited to a revaluation reserve (shown separately as item K III in balance sheet: format 1).

An amount may only be transferred from the revaluation reserve:

(i) if the revalued asset is disposed of, when the revaluation credit may be transferred to the profit and loss account;

(ii) on capitalisation.

Illustration

A typical note showing movements on reserves might appear as follows:

	Share premium £	Revaluation reserve £	Profit and loss account £
Balance at 1 January 19X7	160,000	122,000	614,000
Share issue during year	84,000	–	–
Capitalised on bonus issue	(125,000)	–	–
Revaluation during year	–	60,000	–
Retained profit	–	–	47,000
Balance at 31 December 19X7	119,000	182,000	661,000

Questions

1 Radical Ltd

After closing off the profit and loss account for the year ended 30 September 19X2, the following trial balance was extracted from the nominal ledger of Radical Ltd:

	£	£
Stocks on hand, at cost	192,734	
Debtors	172,062	
Cash in hand	2,431	
Balance at bank	42,735	
Freehold property, at cost	131,000	
Motor vehicles, at cost	406,795	
Ordinary shares in Midland Bank plc, at cost	22,632	
Prepayments	2,596	
Ordinary share capital		250,000
Preference share capital		100,000
9½% Loan stock		150,000
Creditors		64,700
Aggregate depreciation		
Freehold property		5,000
Motor vehicles		196,530
Provision for bad debts		13,420
Profit and loss account		89,185
Share premium account		52,400
Corporation tax at 30%		26,750
Proposed ordinary dividend		25,000
	972,985	972,985

You also obtain the following information:

(1) The company has an authorised and issued share capital of £350,000 divided into 200,000 8% cumulative preference shares of 50p each and 1,000,000 ordinary shares of 25p each.

(2) The 9½% loan stock is unsecured and repayable on 1 October 19Y9.

(3) The balance on corporation tax account was due for payment nine months after the year-end.

(4) Additional motor vehicles were purchased during the year at a cost of £40,450 and additions to freehold property were £26,000.

(5) Depreciation has been charged during the year as follows:

Freehold buildings £2,500
Motor vehicles   £84,000

Required

Prepare the company's balance sheet as at 30 September 19X2, in a form suitable for presentation to members. Ignore the requirement to produce a statement of accounting policies.

Corresponding figures are not required and the information given may be taken as if it included all that is necessary to satisfy the requirements of the Companies Act 1985.

Summary

In this chapter we have covered:

♦ the format of the balance sheet;

♦ the additional disclosures required by the Companies Acts.

You will need to use this chapter and the next as reference material when you begin to practise drafting detailed company accounts.

CHAPTER 8

Limited Company Accounts: the Profit and Loss Account

Objectives

This chapter covers the following performance criteria:

10.2.1 Financial statements are accurately drafted from appropriate information.

10.2.3 Draft accounts comply with domestic standards and legislation and, where relevant, partnership agreement.

10.2.5 Year–end financial statements are presented for approval to the appropriate person in a clear form.

At the end of this chapter, you should be able to:

- prepare the profit and loss account of a limited company in the format required by the Companies Act 1985

- prepare notes to the profit and loss account that disclose the additional information required by the Act

- calculate earnings per share

Profit and loss account – formats

The Act permits a choice of four profit and loss account formats. Format 1 is the most commonly used in practice.

The vertical profit and loss account – Format 1

		£	£
1	Turnover		X
2	Cost of sales		(X)
3	Gross profit or loss		X
4	Distribution costs		(X)
5	Administrative expenses		(X)
6	Other operating income		X
7	Income from shares in group undertakings		X
8	Income from participating interests		X
9	Income from other fixed asset investments		X
10	Other interest receivable and similar income		X
11	Amounts written off investments		(X)
12	Interest payable and similar charges		(X)
13	Tax on profit or loss on ordinary activities		(X)
14	Profit (or loss) on ordinary activities after taxation		X
15	Extraordinary income	X	
16	Extraordinary charges	(X)	
17	Extraordinary profit or loss		X
18	Tax on extraordinary profit or loss		(X)
19	Other taxes not shown under the above items		(X)
20	Profit (or loss) for the financial year		X

Note: All the lines in the profit and loss account are given Arabic numerals; this means that technically all of this information could be included in the notes to the accounts rather than on the face of the profit and loss account! The following items *must* be shown on the face of the profit and loss account:

(a) profit (or loss) on ordinary activities before taxation – a subtotal between lines 12 and 13;
(b) dividends paid and proposed; and
(c) transfers to or from reserves.

Profit and loss account – disclosures

Analyses of turnover and profit before tax

Disclose by way of a note, an analysis of turnover by:

(i) class of business,
(ii) geographical market,

where, in the opinion of the directors, there is more than one class and/or market.

Illustration

A typical note covering these requirements may be as follows.

Analysis of turnover

An analysis of the group's activities shows:

	Turnover £
Wholesaling	694,000
Retailing	276,000
	970,000

Turnover was distributed as follows:

	£
United Kingdom	846,000
Europe	115,000
Other	9,000
	970,000

Note: Further analysis of this nature may be required under SSAP25 if the company is large enough (see Chapter 17).

Particulars of staff

Disclose by way of a note:

(a) average number of persons employed by the company and (in the group accounts) by its subsidiaries during the financial year, analysed by category;

(b) (i) wages and salaries paid/payable in respect of those persons,
    (ii) social security costs thereon,
    (iii) other pension costs thereon.

Directors' emoluments

Disclose by way of a note:

(a) Aggregate amount of:

- emoluments (including salary, fees, bonuses, benefits in kind, 'golden hellos')

- gains on the exercise of share options (listed companies only)

- money and value of assets (excluding share options) receivable by directors under long term incentive schemes in respect of qualifying services

- company contributions paid to a pension scheme in respect of directors' qualifying services

- compensation for loss of office

- amounts paid to third parties to secure the services of a director.

(b) The number of directors who are accruing benefits under:

- money purchase pension schemes
- defined benefit pension schemes.

(c) Where the combined total of directors emoluments, (including gains on the exercise of share options and amounts receivable under long term incentive schemes) is £200,000 or more the following additional information must be given in respect of the **highest paid director**:

Aggregate amounts of:

- emoluments;
- company contributions paid to a pension scheme; and
- accrued retirement benefits (if the highest paid director is a member of a defined benefit pension scheme).

Illustration

A typical note covering the above can be constructed from the following information.

Waugh plc has three directors whose emoluments are as follows:

Name	Fees as directors	Salaries as executives	Cash received under incentive scheme	Pension contributions
	£	£	£	£
X	4,000	94,000	2,000	14,000
Y	4,000	136,000		21,000
Z	2,000	44,000		3,500

All pension contributions relate to a money purchase pension scheme.

Note to accounts

Directors' remuneration

The amounts paid to directors were:

	£
Emoluments	284,000
Cash received under long term incentive scheme	2,000
Pension contributions	38,500

During the year, three directors accrued benefits under money purchase pension schemes.

Amounts paid to the highest paid director were:

	£
Emoluments	140,000
Pension contributions	21,000

Sundry charges

Disclose by way of a note:

(a) Amounts of provisions made for depreciation or diminution in value of tangible and intangible fixed assets.

(b) Effect on depreciation charge of any change from one method of depreciation to another, in year of change, if material.

(c) Effect on depreciation charge of any revaluation of assets, in year of revaluation, if material.

(d) Hire of plant and machinery.

(e) Auditors' remuneration, including audit expenses.

(f) Exceptional items.

Income from listed investments

Should be disclosed by way of a note.

Interest payable

Disclose by way of a note:

The amount of the interest on:

(a) bank loans and overdrafts, and loans made by the company (other than bank loans and overdrafts) which fall due for repayment within five years; and

(b) all other loans.

Taxation

Disclose by way of a note:

(a) Tax charge divided between:

    (i) UK corporation tax,
    (ii) deferred taxation.

(b) Where applicable, distinguish the amounts attributable to taxation on ordinary and extraordinary activities.

(c) If corporation tax rate not known for any part of period, use and disclose latest known rate.

See the session on taxation in company accounts for examples of this disclosure.

Extraordinary and exceptional items

(a) Particulars of extraordinary income and charges, including separate disclosure of any related taxation.

(b) Amount of profit or loss after extraordinary items.

    Note: Following the publication of FRS3, extraordinary items are now very rare.

(c) Exceptional items are disclosed within the sundry items note (other than those shown on the face of the profit and loss account per FRS3 – see Chapter 9).

Dividends

(a) Aggregate dividends paid ⎫ In respect
(b) Aggregate dividends proposed ⎬ of each class of share
(c) (Disclosure of the dividend per share is **desirable**.)

Sundry matters

- **Disclosure of accounting policies**

    The accounting policies used by the company must be disclosed by note.

- **Compliance with accounting standards**

    It must be stated whether the accounts have been prepared in accordance with accounting standards. If not, details of material departures from the standards must be given, with reasons.

The directors' report

Introduction

In addition to a balance sheet and profit and loss account, shareholders must also receive a report prepared on behalf of the directors. The report must be signed by a director or the company secretary. Although the Companies Act specifies the contents of this report no formal layout is included in the Act.

Contents

The directors' report must contain:

- a fair review of the development of the business of the company during the year;
- its position at the end of the year;
- principal activities during the year and significant changes in activities;
- difference between book value and market value of land and buildings, if significant;
- proposed dividends;
- names of directors who served at any time during the year;
- directors' interests (including nil holdings) in the shares or debentures of the company or any other company in the group
    - there must be shown for each director:
    - the number held in each body corporate at the beginning of the year, or, if he became a director during the year, at that date; and
    - the number held at the year–end;
- particulars of important events affecting the company or its subsidiary undertakings which have occurred since the end of the year;
- an indication of likely future developments in the business;
- an indication of the activities in the field of research and development;

- the separate totals of political and charitable contributions, if, taken together, these exceed £200;

- the amount and name of recipients of individual political contributions exceeding £200;

- a statement of the company's policy on the employment, training and career development of disabled people where the average number of employees exceeds 250;

- a statement describing the action that has been taken during the financial year to introduce, maintain or develop arrangements aimed at employee communication, consultation, involvement and awareness, where the average number of employees exceeds 250;

- a statement on the company's policy on payment of its suppliers, for the financial year immediately following that covered by the directors' report, (where the company is public or a large private company which is a subsidiary of a public company):

    - companies which follow any code or standard must state which code or standard is followed;

    - companies which do not follow such a code or standard must give a fuller statement of their payment practices.

FRS 14: Earnings per share

The price earnings ratio is an indicator used by investment analysts. It is therefore important that the figure for earnings per share, which is used for calculating that ratio, should be calculated and disclosed on a comparable basis between one company and another.

Scope of FRS 14

FRS 14 applies to companies whose ordinary shares are publicly traded. Any company which voluntarily discloses earnings per share must also comply with the requirements of FRS 14.

Requirements of FRS 14

Earnings per share must be disclosed on the face of the profit and loss account. This applies even if the amount disclosed is negative (a loss per share). Comparative figures are required.

Calculation of earnings per share (EPS)

The basic calculation is:

$$\frac{\text{Net profit or loss for the period attributable to ordinary shareholders}}{\text{Weighted average number of ordinary shares outstanding during the period}}$$

The net profit or loss for the period is after deducting tax, exceptional items and extraordinary items.

The net profit or loss for the period attributable to ordinary shareholders is the net profit or loss after deducting preference dividends.

Example

Given below is the summarised profit and loss account of ABC plc, a listed company.

	19X5 £	19X4 £
Operating profit	6,420,000	5,680,000
Interest payable	(780,000)	(780,000)
Profit before taxation	5,640,000	4,900,000
Taxation	(2,440,000)	(1,980,000)
Profit after taxation	3,200,000	2,920,000
Dividends		
Preference dividend – paid	52,500	52,500
– proposed	52,500	52,500
Ordinary dividend – paid	160,000	130,000
– proposed	920,000	720,000
Retained profit for the year	2,015,000	1,965,000

The company's capital is as follows:

	£
Authorised share capital	
40,000,000 Ordinary shares 25p each	10,000,000
10,000,000 7% Preference shares 25p each	2,500,000
	12,500,000
Issued and fully paid	£
20,000,000 Ordinary shares 25p each	5,000,000
6,000,000 7% Preference shares 25p each	1,500,000
	6,500,000

Required

Calculate, for disclosure, the earnings per share for 19X5 on the face of the company's profit and loss account.

Solution

Earnings	19X5 £	19X4 £
Profit after tax	3,200,000	2,920,000
Deduct: Preference dividend	105,000	105,000
Earnings	3,095,000	2,815,000
Number of equity (ordinary) shares in issue	20,000,000	20,000,000

$$\text{EPS 19X5} = \frac{3,095,000 \times 100}{20,000,000} = 15.475\text{p}$$

Comparative figure (also required):

$$\text{EPS 19X4} = \frac{2,815,000 \times 100}{20,000,000} = 14.075\text{p}$$

Disclosure

Disclose the following:

♦ the amount used as the numerator and a reconciliation of that amount to the net profit or loss for the period; and

♦ the number of shares used as the denominator.

Accounts for small and medium-sized companies

Introduction

Certain small and medium-sized companies can take advantage of accounting exemptions in section 247 of Companies Act 1985 permitting them to prepare two sets of accounts, normal full accounts for their shareholders and abbreviated accounts which are filed at Companies House.

These exemptions are optional.

Small and medium sized companies are exempt from the requirement to state whether their accounts have been prepared in accordance with applicable accounting policies, regardless of whether they choose to file abbreviated accounts.

Conditions for exemption

♦ A company 'qualifies' as small or medium-sized if it meets two out of the following three size criteria in a particular year:

	Small	Medium–sized
Turnover not more than	£2,800,000	£11,200,000
Fixed and current assets not more than	£1,400,000	£5,600,000
Average number of employees not more than	50	250

Note that this does not on its own entitle a company to file abbreviated accounts (see below).

♦ A company is entitled to file abbreviated accounts for a particular year if it satisfies two of the following three criteria:

- 'qualifies' this year;
- 'qualified' last year;
- was entitled to file abbreviated accounts last year.

Thus, we need to look at two years together to see if the conditions are met.

♦ If the qualifying conditions are met in the company's first financial year, it can file abbreviated accounts in that year.

- Whatever their size, there are some companies which can never file abbreviated accounts. These are as follows:

    - public companies;
    - banking and insurance companies;
    - companies authorised to carry out investment business;
    - companies in a group which contains a public company, a banking or insurance company, or a company authorised to carry out investment business.

Exemptions permitted for medium-sized companies

- In the profit and loss account, turnover, cost of sales, gross profit and other operating income are combined as one figure.

- No analysis of turnover by class of business or geographical destination.

Exemptions permitted for small-sized companies

- **Profit and loss account**

    Not required.

- **Balance sheet**

    Only items which bear a letter or Roman numeral (ie. the main headings).

- **Notes to the accounts**

    Only the following notes are required:

    (i) accounting policies;
    (ii) share capital;
    (iii) debtors recoverable after more than one year;
    (iv) creditors due after more than five years;
    (v) secured creditors;
    (vi) the movements (in total) on intangible fixed assets, tangible fixed assets and fixed asset investments.

Advantages and disadvantages of filing abbreviated accounts

Abbreviated accounts enable a company to maintain a certain degree of confidentiality. Information which might be of interest to competitors is not made public. This is particularly true of abbreviated accounts for small companies, which do not contain a profit and loss account. Accounts for medium sized companies do not disclose turnover or profit margins.

The main disadvantage of filing abbreviated accounts is the additional cost and work required since the company still has to prepare full audited accounts for the members.

Other exemptions for small companies

Regardless of whether a small company (as previously defined) has chosen to *file* abbreviated accounts, it may take advantage of certain additional exemptions when *preparing* full accounts for distribution to shareholders.

These exemptions result in a simplified balance sheet format, with some of the items bearing an Arabic numeral being combined. For example:

- Tangible assets have only two categories: 'land and buildings' and 'plant and machinery, etc.'.

- All categories of stock are combined, with the exception of payments on account.

- The nine separate headings under creditors in the full format are reduced to four.

The profit and loss account remains the same.

There is also a considerable reduction in the number of notes required; for example, security of creditors, particulars of staff, emoluments of directors, taxation notes are all not required.

Financial reporting standard for smaller entities (FRSSE)

The Financial Reporting Standard for Smaller Entities (FRSSE) is a special financial reporting standard designed for small entities. 'Small' companies as defined by the Companies Act and other entities that would be 'small' if they were companies may choose to prepare financial statements in accordance with the requirements of the FRSSE. This exempts them from complying with existing accounting standards.

The FRSSE contains the requirements of existing accounting standards that are most relevant to smaller entities. Many of the more complex disclosure requirements in existing standards have been omitted and some of the other requirements have been simplified.

Summary financial statements

The Companies Act 1989 introduced summary financial statements. These may be produced by public limited companies which have a full Stock Exchange Listing (not USM companies) as an alternative to producing full accounts.

This recognises that the vast amount of detail as required by full Companies Act formats and disclosures may not be of relevance or interest to all shareholders.

Requirements

Companies must always file a full set of accounts with the Registrar of Companies.

The company must ascertain whether its shareholders wish to receive full or summary financial statements. This will usually be achieved by writing to each shareholder. Once a shareholder's preference has been ascertained, it will be up to the shareholders to notify the company of any change in future years. The shareholders will always have the right to demand a full set of accounts.

The contents of the summary financial statements must be derived from the full accounts. No additional information can be included which is not in the full accounts.

The summary financial statements will carry a 'health warning' to advise shareholders not to take investment decisions based on the contents of these statements.

Contents

Profit and loss account

	£
Turnover	X
Aggregate of income from shares in investments held	X
Net aggregate of interest receivable and payable	X
Profit or loss on ordinary activities before tax	X
Tax on profit on ordinary activities	(X)
Net aggregate of extraordinary income and charges after tax	X
Profit or loss for the financial year	X
Aggregate dividends paid and proposed	(X)
	───
Aggregate directors' emoluments	X
	───

Balance sheet

	£	£
Fixed assets		X
Current assets	X	
Prepayments and accrued income	X	
Creditors: Amounts falling due within one year	(X)	
	───	
Net current assets (liabilities)		X
Total assets less current liabilities		X
Creditors: Amounts falling due after more than one year		(X)
Provisions for liabilities and charges		(X)
Accruals and deferred income		(X)
		───
		X
		───
Capital and reserves		X
		───

Questions

1 Church's Ltd

Church's Ltd, a company which manufactures footwear, makes up its accounts to 31 December in each year. The company has an authorised share capital of £300,000, divided into 150,000 6½% preference shares of £1 each and 300,000 ordinary shares of 50p each. It is not a member of a group.

The following balances have been extracted from the ledger for the year ended 31 December 19X0.

Debit	£	**Credit**	£
Cost of sales	349,996	Sales	595,932
Motor expenses	79,842	Discounts received	420
Depreciation of motor vehicles	5,290	Investment income received:	
Other distribution costs	39,420	Unlisted	546
Wages and salaries	62,917	Listed	780
Other administrative costs	5,746		
Audit fee	700		
Depreciation of fixtures and fittings	520		
Depreciation of buildings	1,000		
Pension to former director's widow	750		
Superannuation scheme	4,250		
Corporation tax	12,410		
Debenture interest	800		
Preference dividend paid on 30 September 19X0	6,500		

You are given the following additional information:

(1) Wages, salaries, pension and superannuation are to be broken down as follows:

	Distribution £	Administration £
Wages and salaries	34,715	28,202
Pension to former director's widow	–	750
Superannuation scheme	2,250	2,000

The charge for wages and salaries includes the salaries of the managing director £13,500 and sales director £13,000. Superannuation scheme also includes £858 on their behalf. Provision is to be made for directors' fees of £7,500, being £2,500 for each director, including the chairman, who does not receive a salary. The company has employed an average of 10 people in the year.

(2) The charge for corporation tax in the profit and loss account is the amount estimated to be payable on the profits for the year at 30%.

(3) The directors recommend payment of an ordinary dividend of 5.2p per share. The ordinary share capital in the balance sheet is £100,000.

(4) The debentures are repayable in 19Z9.

Required

Prepare the company's profit and loss account and associated notes for the year ended 31 December 19X0 in accordance with generally accepted accounting principles and in a form suitable for presentation to members. (An accounting policies note is not required.)

Summary

In this chapter we have covered:

- the format of the profit and loss account;

- the additional disclosures required by the Companies Acts.

In order to become proficient at drafting limited company financial statements, you must practise whenever possible.

You should also try to look at as many sets of published accounts as you can.

CHAPTER 9

Reporting Financial Performance

> ### Objectives
>
> This chapter covers the following performance criteria:
>
> **10.2.1 Financial statements are accurately drafted from appropriate information.**
>
> **10.2.3 Draft accounts comply with domestic standards and legislation and, where relevant, partnership agreement.**
>
> At the end of this chapter, you should be able to:
>
> - prepare a profit and loss account in accordance with the requirements of FRS 3
>
> - prepare a statement of total recognised gains and losses
>
> - prepare a note of historical cost profits and losses and a reconciliation of movements in shareholders' funds

Introduction

FRS3 *Reporting Financial Performance* is intended to provide users of financial statements with information about important components of financial performance. It achieves this in two ways:

- by requiring companies to make detailed disclosures of a range of items included in the profit and loss account; and

- by setting out the permitted accounting treatment for these items so that all companies are required to account for them in the same way.

The term *reporting entity* is used throughout the FRS. A reporting entity is any business which prepares financial statements which are intended to show a true and fair view. A reporting entity need not be a limited company. However, the requirements of FRS3 are most likely to apply to limited companies.

Continuing operations, acquisitions and discontinued operations

FRS3 requires businesses to analyse their results between continuing operations, acquisitions (as a component of continuing operations) and discontinued operations.

An operation may be represented by a separate class of business within a single company or, if group accounts are prepared, a company or companies within a group. The requirements of the FRS apply to both these situations.

An *acquisition* is an operation that is acquired in the period.

A *discontinued operation* is an operation that is sold or terminated.

Disclosures

FRS3 requires all the standard profit and loss account headings to be analysed between continuing operations, acquisitions (as a component of continuing operations) and discontinued operations, down to the level of operating profit.

Operating profit is not a term used in the Companies Act formats and the FRS does not formally define it. However, operating profit is normally profit before income from shares in group undertakings, ie. gross profit and other operating income less distribution costs and administrative expenses.

Turnover and operating profit must be analysed on the face of the profit and loss account. The analysis of the other headings may be shown either on the face of the profit and loss account or in the notes.

Obviously, where a company has no acquisitions and no discontinued operations there is no need for the additional analysis.

Illustration

PROFIT AND LOSS ACCOUNT

	£'000	£'000
Turnover		
Continuing operations		550
Acquisitions		50
		600
Discontinued operations		175
		775
Cost of sales		(620)
Gross profit		155
Distribution costs		(44)
Administrative expenses		(80)
Other operating income		10
Operating profit		
Continuing operations	20	
Acquisitions	6	
	26	
Discontinued operations	15	
		41
Profit on sale of fixed assets in continuing operations		22
Profit on ordinary activities before interest		63
Other interest receivable and similar income		2
Interest payable		(20)
Profit on ordinary activities before taxation		45
Tax on profit on ordinary activities		(14)
		31
[Extraordinary items] (included only to show positioning)		–
Profit for the financial year		31
Dividends		(8)
Retained profit for the financial year		23

Notes to the financial statements

	Continuing £'000	Discontinued £'000	Total £'000
Cost of sales	485	135	620
Distribution costs	31	13	44
Administrative expenses	68	12	80
Other operating income	10	–	10

The total figures for continuing operations include the following amounts relating to acquisitions: cost of sales £40,000, distribution costs £3,000, administrative expenses £3,000 and other operating income £2,000.

Exceptional items

Definition

Exceptional items are defined as those which:

(a) are material;

(b) derive from events or transactions that fall within the ordinary activities of the business;

(c) need to be disclosed separately by virtue of their size or incidence if the financial statements are to give a true and fair view.

All three criteria must be present for an item to be classed as exceptional.

Examples

FRS3 does not give examples of exceptional items other than to specify three types of exceptional item which should be separately disclosed on the face of the profit and loss account (see below).

Exceptional items might include:

- redundancy costs;
- amounts transferred to employee share schemes;
- profits or losses on the disposal of fixed assets;
- abnormal charges for bad debts and write-offs of stock and work in progress;
- abnormal provisions for losses on long-term contracts; and
- surpluses arising on the settlement of insurance claims.

Accounting entries

Exceptional items are accounted for in the normal way. For example, an exceptionally large bad debt is debited to profit and loss account, with the corresponding credit entry being made in the provision for bad debts account or the individual debtors account as appropriate.

Disclosure

In published accounts, exceptional items are normally included under the statutory headings of 'cost of sales' 'administrative expenses' or 'distribution costs' in line with a company's policy, but because they are material items further information must be given.

Normally, exceptional items will be disclosed as separate items in the note to the published accounts which discloses the other items required to be shown by the Companies Act. For example:

Operating profit has been arrived at after charging:

	£
Depreciation	3,714,000
Audit fee	162,000
Directors' remuneration	732,000
Exceptional item – bad debt arising on liquidation of major customer	1,680,000

FRS3 specifies that there are three types of exceptional item which must always be disclosed on the face of the profit and loss account. These are:

- Profits or losses on the sale or termination of an operation.

- Costs of a fundamental reorganisation or restructuring, having a material effect on the nature and focus of the reporting entity's operations.

- Profits or losses on the disposal of fixed assets.

Other types of exceptional item should be shown on the face of the profit and loss account if they are so material that it is thought necessary for the accounts to show a true and fair view.

If exceptional items are shown on the face of the profit and loss account, they are disclosed separately after operating profit and before interest. Look at the formats shown earlier in the session.

Exceptional items must be included under the appropriate heading of continuing or discontinued operations.

Illustration

Consider an investment that is held by a company that occasionally deals in investments (although this is not its main area of operation). Assume that it purchases the investment for £600,000 and sells it for £1,400,000, making a profit of £800,000 which is considered to be exceptional.

The profit and loss account extract would be as follows.

	£
Operating profit (say)	4,000,000
Profit on sale of investments (1,400,000 – 600,000)	800,000
Profit on ordinary activities before interest	4,800,000

The vital point to understand is that the exceptional item is charged against profit before taxation. This differentiates the treatment of exceptional and extraordinary items.

Extraordinary items

Definition

Extraordinary items are defined as those which:

- are material;
- possess a high degree of abnormality;
- arise from events or transactions that fall outside the ordinary activities of the business;
- are not expected to recur.

Again, all four criteria must be present for an item to be classed as extraordinary.

FRS3 also defines ordinary activities. Ordinary activities are any activities which are undertaken by a reporting entity (for example, a company) as part of its business. They include:

- Such related activities in which the reporting entity engages in furtherance of, incidental to, or arising from its main activities.

- The effects on the reporting entity of any event in the various environments in which it operates, including the political, regulatory, economic and geographical environments, irrespective of the frequency or unusual nature of the events. (Examples of these would include changes in the law, which might mean that a particular item could no longer be produced, or an economic recession resulting in closures and redundancies.)

This definition of 'ordinary activities' is extremely wide. Virtually all activities are ordinary activities.

This in turn means that in practice extraordinary items are extremely rare. The FRS does not give any examples of extraordinary items.

Prior-period adjustments

Definition

Prior-period adjustments are those material adjustments applicable to prior periods arising from

(a) changes in accounting policies; or
(b) the correction of fundamental errors.

A fundamental error is one of such significance as to destroy the true and fair view and hence the validity of a set of accounts, and which would have led to their withdrawal had the error been recognised at the time.

Normal recurring corrections and adjustments of accounting estimates made in prior years do not constitute prior-year adjustments.

Examples

Examples of changes in accounting policies which are likely to give rise to prior-year adjustments are:

(a) method of valuing stock;
(b) method of accounting for development costs.

Fundamental errors are particularly unique events but size is of considerable importance and the amount involved should be judged not only by reference to its impact on the assets of the enterprise but also by its effect upon profits.

Accounting entries

When a change in basis of accounting occurs, it is important that the accounts are prepared on a consistent basis. It therefore follows that the new accounting policy must be applied to those assets or liabilities standing in the books at the commencement of the current year, thereby adjusting the opening figures to the new basis.

Illustration

A company decides that, given the current situation in the business and the likely future trend, a new basis of accounting is more appropriate to the valuation of their stock than the method previously adopted. It changes from the average method of valuation to a first in, first out basis.

The profits retained at the last balance sheet date amount to £16,483,000 and the stock at that time and the current stock at the end of our financial year have been valued on both the old and new basis as follows:

	Old basis £	New basis £
Opening stock brought forward from last year	946,000	998,000
Closing stock at the end of the current year	1,117,000	1,206,000

Before the accounts relating to the current year are prepared, the stock account will contain only the amount brought forward from the previous year.

Stock account

	£		
Balance b/f			
- Opening stock at old value	946,000		

This stock should now be adjusted to the new method of valuation by a prior-period adjustment of £52,000 (£998,000 – £946,000)

Stock account

	£		
Balance b/f	946,000		
Period-period adjustment	52,000		
	998,000		

The retained profits brought forward will reflect this adjustment.

	£
Profits retained in previous years	16,483,000
Prior-period adjustment on change in basis of accounting	52,000
New retained profit brought forward	16,535,000

The accounts for the current year can now be prepared, using the new method of valuation consistently.

Stock account

	£		£
Balance b/f	946,000	Trading account (current year)	
Prior-year adjustment		- Opening stock at new value	998,000
- Retained profit	52,000	Balance c/f	1,206,000
Trading account (current year)			
- Closing stock at new value	1,206,000		
	2,204,000		2,204,000

Disclosure

Prior-period adjustments should be accounted for by restating the prior period profit, with the result that the opening balance of retained profits is altered (as shown above). The effect of the change should be disclosed, where practicable, by showing separately, the restatement of the previous period profit and the amount involved.

This restatement must immediately follow the profit and loss account, or alternatively be shown by way of note with a reference to its location on the face of the profit and loss account.

An illustration of this restatement, with the figures from the previous section, is as follows:

Statement of retained profits

	£'000
Retained profits brought forward	
– as previously reported	16,483
– prior-period adjustment	52
– as restated	16,535
Retained profits for the financial year	X
Retained profits carried forward	X

Statement of total recognised gains and losses

Introduction

FRS3 requires all reporting entities to prepare a statement of total recognised gains and losses. This must be presented with the same prominence as the other primary statements.

Recognised gains and losses include the following:

- the profit or loss for the period;
- surpluses or deficits on revaluation of properties;
- changes in the value of an investment property;
- prior-period adjustments.

Some of these items may be taken directly to reserves, rather than pass through the profit and loss account. The purpose of the statement of total recognised gains and losses is to show all the gains and losses which have been recognised in a period and which are available to shareholders.

If there are no recognised gains and losses other than the profit or loss for the period, there should be a statement to that effect immediately below the profit and loss account.

Realised and unrealised gains – an example

A common example of a recognised gain which does not pass through the profit and loss account is an unrealised surplus on revaluation of fixed assets.

The double entry for revaluing a fixed asset upward is

		£	£
Dr	Fixed asset (at cost)	X	
Dr	Accumulated depreciation	X	
	Cr Revaluation reserve		X

It is not prudent to recognise the increase in value in the profit and loss account since it is unrealised. However, when the fixed asset is sold and the gain becomes realised it cannot then be reversed out of the statement of recognised gains and losses and included in the profit and loss account. The profit or loss on disposal must be calculated on the revalued amount.

Illustration

Bell Ltd revalued land costing £20,000 to £30,000. Three years later, it sold the land for £25,000.

The initial double-entry is:

Dr	Land at cost	£10,000	
	Cr Revaluation reserve		£10,000

at the time the revaluation takes place.

The unrealised gain of £10,000 is included in the statement of recognised gains and losses in the period in which the revaluation takes place.

The subsequent double-entry is :

Dr	Cash	£25,000	
Dr	Loss on disposal	£5,000	
	Cr Fixed assets		£30,000

at the time the disposal takes place. The £5,000 loss is recognised in the profit and loss account for the period in which the disposal takes place (as an exceptional item, if material).

The previous revaluation surplus of £10,000 will be transferred from the revaluation reserve to the profit and loss *reserve* as it is now realised. This will have no net effect on the statement of recognised gains and losses.

Without FRS3 it would be possible to account for the disposal as follows:

Dr	Cash		£25,000	
Dr	Revaluation reserve		£10,000	
	Cr	Fixed assets		£30,000
	Cr	Disposals		£5,000

which would give rise to a realised profit of £5,000 which would be included in the profit and loss account (this will, in fact, be disclosed in the note of historical cost profits).

Under FRS3 a net 'recognised gain' of £5,000 has been included in the statement of recognised gains and losses instead:

	£
Unrealised gain (when revalued)	10,000
Loss on disposal (through profit and loss)	(5,000)
	5,000

Disclosure

Pro forma statement of total recognised gains and losses

	19X3 £	19X2 (as restated) £
Profit for the financial year	X	X
Unrealised surplus on revaluation of properties	X	
Unrealised (loss)/gain on trade investment	(X)	X
Total recognised gains and losses relating to the year	X	X
Prior-period adjustment (as explained in note X)	(X)	
Total gains and losses recognised since last annual report	X	

There are two things to note:

- profit for the financial year is before dividends; and
- the disclosure of the prior-period adjustment.

Note of historical cost profits and losses

FRS3 requires this note to be prepared where there is a material difference between an entity's result as disclosed in the profit and loss account and its result on the historical cost basis.

In practice, the note will normally be required where the accounts contain properties included at a valuation rather than at cost.

The note should include a reconciliation of the reported profit on ordinary activities before taxation to the historical cost profit on ordinary activities before taxation. The note should also show the retained profit for the financial year reported on the historical cost basis.

The note should be presented immediately following the profit and loss account or the statement of total recognised gains and losses.

Pro forma note of historical cost profits and losses

	£
Reported profit on ordinary activities before taxation	X
Realisation of property revaluation gains of previous years	X
Difference between a historical cost depreciation charge and the actual depreciation charge for the year calculated on the revalued amount	X
Historical cost profit on ordinary activities before taxation	X
Historical cost profit for the year retained after taxation, minority interests, extraordinary items and dividends	X

Reconciliation of movements in shareholders' funds and statement of reserves

FRS3 requires a reconciliation of the opening and closing totals of shareholders' funds of the period.

Shareholders' funds include share capital and share premium as well as all reserves.

The purpose of this statement is to summarise all changes in net assets between the opening and closing balance sheets, including items which are not recognised gains and losses (eg. issues of shares).

The Companies Act requires a statement of reserves showing all movements on reserves in the year.

Reconciliation of movements in shareholders' funds

	£
Profit for the financial year	X
Dividends	(X)
	X
Other recognised gains and losses relating to the year (net) #	X
New share capital subscribed	X
Net addition to shareholders' funds	X
Opening shareholders' funds (£Y before prior year adjustment of £Z)	X
Closing shareholders' funds	X

From the statement of total recognised gains and losses.

Statement of reserves (required by the Companies Act)

	Share premium account £	Revaluation reserve £	Profit and loss account £	Total* £
At beginning of year:				
As previously stated	X	X	X	X
Prior year adjustment			(X)	(X)
As restated	X	X	X	X
Premium on issue of shares (nominal value £X)	X			X
Transfer from profit and loss account for the year			X	X
Decrease in value of trade investment		(X)		(X)
Surplus on property revluations		X		X
Transfer of realised profits		(X)	X	
At end of year	X	X	X	X

* This is not strictly necessary under the Companies Act. Also, the Act does not require comparatives for the statement of reserves. FRS3 does however require a comparative for the reconciliation of movements in shareholders' funds.

Comprehensive example

Extracts from the accounts of Lincoln Ltd for the year ended 31 December 19X7 are as follows:

Profit and loss account

	£'000
Profit on ordinary activities before taxation	50
Taxation	(10)
Profit on ordinary activities after taxation	40
Dividends	(10)
Retained profit for the year	30

The profit and loss account reserve has been reduced by a prior year adjustment of £30,000.

Balance sheet

		19X7 £'000	19X6 £'000
Share capital		100	100
Revaluation reserve		335	235
Profit and loss account	(19X6 figure is after dealing with prior year adjustment)	170	70
		605	405

Fixed assets – land and buildings

	Valuation £'000	Historical cost £'000
Cost/valuation		
At 1 January 19X7	500	250
Additions	75	75
Disposals	(130)	(55)
Revaluations	120	–
At 31 December 19X7	565	270
Depreciation		
At 1 January 19X7	45	40
Charge	15	5
Disposals	(10)	(5)
Revaluations	(50)	–
At 31 December 19X7	–	40
Net book value at 31 December 19X7	565	230

Disposal proceeds amounted to £135,000.

Required

Prepare a statement of total recognised gains and losses, a note of historical cost profits and losses, a reconciliation of movements in shareholders' funds and a statement of reserves for the year ended 31 December 19X7.

Solution

Statement of total recognised gains and losses for the year ended 31 December 19X7

	£'000
Profit for the financial year	40
Unrealised surplus on revaluation of properties (120 + 50)	170
Total recognised gains and losses relating to the year	210
Prior year adjustment	(30)
Total gains and loss recognised since last annual report	180

Note of historical cost profits and losses

	19X7 £'000
Reported profit on ordinary activities before taxation	50
Realisation of property revaluation gains of previous years (W)	70
Difference between historical cost depreciation charge and the actual depreciation charge for the year calculated on the revalued amount (15 – 5)	10
Historical cost profit on ordinary activities before taxation	130
Historical cost profit for the year retained after taxation, minority interests and dividends	110

Reconciliation of movements in shareholders' funds

	19X7 £'000
Profit for the financial year	40
Dividends	(10)
	30
Other recognised gains and losses relating to the year	170
Net addition to shareholders' funds	200
Shareholders' funds at 1 January 19X7 (originally £435,000 before deducting prior year adjustment of £30,000)	405
Shareholders' funds at 31 December 19X7	605

Statement of reserves

	Revaluation reserve £000	Profit and loss account £000	Total £000
At 1 January 19X7			
As previously stated	235	100	335
Prior year adjustment	-	(30)	(30)
	235	70	305
Transfer from profit and loss account for the year	-	30	30
Surplus on property revaluations	170	-	170
Transfer of realised profits	(70)	70	-
At 31 December 19X7	335	170	505

Working

Realisation of property revaluation gains

	£'000
Valuation NBV (130 – 10)	120
Historic cost NBV (55 – 5)	50
	70

Questions

1 Claret

Claret Ltd has an issued share capital of 2,000,000 50p ordinary shares all of which were issued at par on incorporation.

The balance on the profit and loss account at 1 January 19X8 was £20,658,000 and the draft retained profit for the year was £1,825,000. The directors had decided to propose a dividend of £250,000 for the year.

At 1 January 19X8 the balance on the revaluation reserve was £83,000. On 31 December 19X8 a property was revalued to £430,000. It was purchased on 1 January 19X1 for £650,000 and is being depreciated over 20 years.

During the year the company issued 160,000 50p ordinary shares at a market price of 210p per share.

After the preparation of the draft accounts had been completed, it was discovered that the method of valuing closing stock had been incorrectly applied for the last three years resulting in the following overvaluations of stock.

	£'000
At 31 December 19X6	40
At 31 December 19X7	55
At 31 December 19X8	62

Required

Prepare the following extracts from the financial statements of Claret Ltd as at 31 December 19X8:

(a) statement of total recognised gains and losses;

(b) note on reconciliation of shareholders' funds.

Ignore the requirement to produce comparative figures.

Summary

The key points to learn are:

- Exceptional items arise from the ordinary activities of the business, whereas extraordinary items do not. Extraordinary items are extremely rare.

- Prior period adjustments are necessary in only two situations:
    - changes in accounting policies; and
    - correction of fundamental errors.

- Items must be material.

You must be able to prepare the following:

- Statement of total recognised gains and losses (a primary statement)

- Note of historical cost profits and losses

- Reconciliation of movements in shareholders' funds

136

CHAPTER 10

Fixed Assets: Tangible Assets

Objectives

This chapter covers the following performance criteria:

10.2.1 Financial statements are accurately drafted from appropriate information.

10.2.2 Subsequent adjustments are correctly implemented.

10.2.3 Draft accounts comply with domestic standards and legislation and, where relevant, partnership agreement.

At the end of this chapter, you should be able to:

- understand how tangible fixed assets should be treated in the profit and loss account and balance sheet

- apply the main principles of FRS 15, SSAP 19 and SSAP 4

- disclose information about tangible fixed assets in the financial statements

FRS 15: Tangible fixed assets

Introduction

FRS 15 defines tangible fixed assets as assets that have physical substance and are held for use in the production or supply of goods or services, for rental to others, or for administrative purposes on a continuing basis in the reporting entity's activities.

In other words, fixed assets are not intended for resale, but for the entity to use in the long term.

FRS 15 applies to all tangible fixed assets except investment properties, which are dealt with in SSAP 19.

Cost

FRS 15 states that a tangible fixed asset should initially be measured at its *cost*. An asset's cost is:

> its purchase price, **less** any trade discounts or rebates, **plus** any further costs directly attributable to bringing it into working condition for its intended use.

In many cases, the cost of a fixed asset simply consists of its purchase price. Occasionally, an entity may incur other expenditure in acquiring a fixed asset, especially if it purchases a building or constructs an asset itself. FRS 15 gives some examples:

- acquisition costs (eg stamp duty, import duties, non-refundable purchase taxes)
- the cost of site preparation and clearance
- delivery and handling costs
- installation costs
- professional fees (eg legal, architects and engineers fees).

If an entity constructs an asset, it will incur the cost of materials, labour and overheads, such as heat, light and power.

Only costs that are *directly attributable to bringing the asset into working condition for its intended use* should be included.

Illustration

An entity builds a factory for its own use. It incurs the following costs:

	£
Land at purchase price	175,000
Legal fees	20,000
Stamp duty	10,000
Architect's fees	25,000
Materials and labour	300,000
Administrative overheads	50,000
	580,000

Material and labour costs include an amount of £30,000 that was incurred as the result of faulty design work.

The cost of the factory is:

	£
Total cost as above	580,000
Less: abnormal costs (design fault)	(30,000)
Administrative overheads	(50,000)
	500,000

FRS 15 states that abnormal costs and administrative and general overheads are not directly attributable costs and must be excluded. Other abnormal costs might relate to industrial disputes, idle capacity, wasted materials and production delays.

Finance costs

Entities may have to take out loans in order to finance the purchase or construction of a tangible fixed asset. It can be argued that interest on these borrowings is part of the cost of a fixed asset and should therefore be included in the amount that is capitalised.

Capitalisation of finance costs is optional. However, FRS 15 sets out the following rules:

- If an entity adopts a policy of capitalising finance costs, then this must be *applied consistently*. In other words, an entity cannot decide to capitalise finance costs relating to some tangible fixed assets but not others.

- Only finance costs that are directly attributable to the construction of a tangible fixed asset should be capitalised as part of the cost of that asset.

- Finance costs should only be capitalised while:

    (i) finance costs are being incurred; and
    (ii) expenditures for the asset are being incurred; and
    (iii) activities that are necessary to get the asset ready for use are in progress.

Subsequent expenditure

An entity may need to incur costs in relation to a tangible fixed asset during its useful economic life. This may be:

- to maintain or service the asset; or
- to improve or upgrade the asset.

Expenditure to maintain or service an asset is revenue expenditure. It simply maintains the performance of the asset and should be treated as an expense of the period in the profit and loss account.

Expenditure to improve or upgrade an asset may be effectively an addition to fixed assets. It should be capitalised where it provides an enhancement of the economic benefits of the tangible fixed asset in excess of its previously assessed standard of performance.

FRS 15 gives examples of subsequent expenditure that should be capitalised:

- modification of an item of plant to extend its useful economic life or increase its capacity
- upgrading machine parts to achieve a substantial improvement in the quality of output.

Depreciation

Most fixed assets wear out or become obsolete. The purpose of depreciation is to reflect this wearing out by making a charge against income for a business, thereby matching the cost of the asset with the income it generates. This is an example of the accruals concept, which is one of the four fundamental accounting concepts contained in SSAP 2.

FRS 15 defines depreciation as:

> 'the measure of the cost or revalued amount of the economic benefits of the tangible fixed asset that have been consumed during the period'

Consumption includes the wearing out, using up or other reduction in the useful economic life of a tangible fixed asset whether arising from use, effluxion of time or obsolescence through either changes in technology or demand for the goods and services produced by the asset.

Other key definitions

The *depreciable amount* is the cost of a tangible fixed asset (or, where an asset is revalued, the revalued amount) less its residual value.

Residual value is the net realisable value of an asset at the end of its useful economic life.

The *useful economic life* of a tangible fixed asset is the period over which the entity expects to derive economic benefit from that asset.

Allocation

FRS 15 states that:

- The depreciable amount of a tangible fixed asset should be allocated on a systematic basis over its useful economic life.

- The depreciation method used should reflect as fairly as possible the pattern in which the asset's economic benefits are consumed by the entity.

- The depreciation charge for each period should be recognised as an expense in the profit and loss account.

To determine the useful economic life and residual value of an asset and the depreciation method to be used, it is necessary to consider:

- The expected usage of the asset by the entity. This may depend on the asset's expected capacity or physical output.

- The expected physical deterioration of the asset through use or effluxion of time. This may depend on repairs and maintenance.

- Economic or technological obsolescence, for example arising from changes or improvements in production, or a change in the market demand for the product.

- Legal or similar limits on the use of the asset, such as expiry dates or related leases.

FRS 15 does not prescribe a method of depreciation, but states that the method chosen should result in a depreciation charge throughout the asset's economic life and not just towards the end of its economic life or when the asset is falling in value. It does briefly discuss the two methods most commonly used in practice:

- straight line, which should be used when the pattern of consumption of an asset's economic benefits is uncertain; and

- reducing balance, which is suitable for assets which provide fewer economic benefits as they become older (eg as a result of wear or technical obsolescence).

Change in method of depreciation

A change from one method of providing depreciation to another (for example, from machine hour rate to straight line) is only allowed if the 'new method will give a fairer presentation of the results and of the financial position'.

However, this is treated as a change in accounting policy, meaning that there is no prior year adjustment. Instead, the carrying amount of the tangible fixed asset is depreciated using the new method over the asset's remaining useful economic life, beginning in the period in which the change is made.

Illustration

Ford plc makes up its accounts to 31 December each year. On 1 January 19X0, it bought a machine for £100,000, and started depreciating it at 15% per annum, on the reducing-balance basis. On 31 December 19X3 the machine would be included in Ford plc's accounts at:

	£
Cost	100,000
Accumulated depreciation	47,800
Net book value	52,200

During 19X4, the company decided to change the basis of depreciation to straight-line, over 10 years.

In accordance with FRS 15 the unamortised cost at 1 January 19X4 of £52,200 must be written off over the six years remaining of the ten-year life.

The new annual charge will be:

$$\frac{£52,200}{6 \text{ years}} = £8,700 \text{ per annum}$$

- Balance sheet presentation would be:

	19X4 £	19X3 (not restated) £
Cost	100,000	100,000
Accumulated depreciation	56,500	47,800
Net book value	43,500	52,200

- Profit and loss account would show:

    (i) Charge for the year £8,700

    (ii) Note: As a result of the change in depreciation policy from 15% reducing balance to 10% straight-line, the charge for depreciation is £870 (£8,700 − 15% × £52,200) higher than it would otherwise have been.

Useful economic lives and residual values

The length of a fixed asset's life is clearly a very important number in a depreciation calculation. However, it is an estimate, as it is necessary to make predictions about the future.

Both the useful economic life and the residual value (if material) of a tangible fixed asset should be reviewed at the end of each reporting period. They should be revised 'if expectations are significantly different from previous estimates'. Reasonably expected technological changes based on prices prevailing at the date of acquisition (or revaluation) should be taken into account.

If either a useful economic life or a residual value is revised, the accounting treatment is to depreciate the new net book amount over the revised remaining useful economic life.

Illustration

A moulding machine cost £50,000 on 1 January 19X1 and at the date of purchase had an estimated useful economic life of ten years. Its estimated residual value is £Nil.

Initially the annual depreciation charge is:

$$\frac{£50,000}{10 \text{ years}} = £5,000 \text{ pa}$$

At 31 December 19X4 the machine would be stated in the accounts at:

	£
Cost	50,000
Less: Accumulated depreciation (four years @ £5,000)	(20,000)
Net book value	30,000

It has a remaining useful economic life of six years.

In 19X5 the management decided that the machine was wearing out more rapidly than expected and revised its remaining useful life down to three years.

Therefore, the new annual depreciation charge is:

$$\frac{£30,000}{3 \text{ years}} = £10,000 \text{ pa}$$

At 31 December 19X5 the machine would be included in the accounts at:

	£
Cost	50,000
Less: Accumulated depreciation (£20,000 + £10,000)	(30,000)
Net book value	20,000

Revaluations

It is common practice for companies to include fixed assets in their historical cost accounts at their current values, rather than original cost. (The Companies Act allows tangible fixed assets to be carried either at historic cost or at a valuation).

Depreciation of such assets must be based on the revalued amounts and the remaining useful economic lives.

Illustration

Ferrari plc bought an office building with a 50-year lease, on 1 January 19X1, for £3 million. The company's accounting policy is that depreciation is provided for on the straight-line method over the useful lives of the assets.

Five years later, on 1 January 19X6, the office block has a market value of £4.5 million. Ferrari plc decides to incorporate this into its financial statements. At 31 December 19X5 the office building would be stated in the accounts at historical cost less related depreciation.

	£
Cost	3,000,000
Accumulated depreciation (3,000,000 ÷ 50 for 5 years)	300,000
Net book value	2,700,000

If the revaluation takes place on 1 January 19X6, to incorporate the valuation in the company's books it is necessary to increase the cost of the building to valuation and write back any accumulated depreciation. The corresponding credit entries are to a revaluation reserve. The double-entry is:

		£	£
Dr	Fixed assets – cost	1,500,000	
Dr	Fixed assets – accumulated depreciation	300,000	
Cr	Revaluation reserve		1,800,000

If accounts are prepared on 1 January 19X6, the building will be included at £4,500,000.

The depreciation charge for 19X6 will be based on this value and the remaining useful life of the building, ie:

$$\frac{£4,500,000}{45 \text{ years}} = £100,000$$

As we saw in Chapter 9, revaluation gains are not taken to the profit and loss account, because they are not realised. Instead they are disclosed in the statement of total recognised gains and losses.

Disposal of revalued assets

Profits and losses on disposal of fixed assets are recognised in the profit and loss account of the period in which the disposal occurs. FRS 3 and FRS 15 both require that the profit or loss on the disposal of a revalued fixed asset is the difference between the net sale proceeds and the carrying amount.

Frequency and basis of valuation

Revaluation of fixed assets is *optional*.

Revaluation increases the relevance of the information in the financial statements to users. However, information about asset values may be useless if it is not kept up to date.

Therefore FRS 15 states that the carrying amount of a revalued fixed asset should be its *current value* at the balance sheet date. This is defined as follows:

- The *current value* of a tangible fixed asset to the business is the lower of replacement cost and recoverable amount. *Recoverable amount* is the higher of net realisable value and value in use.

This does not necessarily mean that once fixed assets have been revalued, the valuation exercise must be carried out every year:

- Where a reliable market value exists for an asset, this should be updated each year. (Reliable market value exist for many fixed asset investments and for some other assets, such as motor vehicles.)

- Otherwise, a full valuation should be carried out at least every five years, with an interim (less thorough) valuation in Year 3 or where it is likely that there has been a material change in value. A full valuation must be carried out by a qualified valuer. If the valuation is carried out by an internal valuer (a director, officer or employee of the entity), the valuation should be reviewed by a qualified external valuer (defined as a person who is not an internal valuer and does not have a significant financial interest in the entity).

FRS 15 states that the following valuation bases should be used:

Type of asset	Basis of valuation
♦ non specialised properties	existing use value (open market value to be disclosed if materially different)
♦ specialised properties	depreciated replacement cost
♦ properties surplus to an entity's requirements	open market value less expected direct selling costs if material
♦ other tangible fixed assets	market value, or where this is not obtainable, depreciated replacement cost

Before FRS 15 was issued, some entities revalued assets very selectively. For example, where there were several freehold properties, only those whose current value was above historic cost would be included in the balance sheet at a valuation. Any properties whose current value was below historic cost would not be revalued. Not only did this practice reduce the usefulness of the financial statements, but it also contravened the fundamental concept of consistency.

It is still possible for an entity to revalue some tangible fixed assets and not others. However if an entity chooses to revalue some of its assets it must apply the policy consistently to all tangible fixed assets in the same class, that is, all assets that have 'a similar nature, function or use in the business of the entity'. A class can be quite narrow, for example, an entity can decide to revalue only specialised properties. It cannot revalue some specialised properties and not others.

Depreciating revalued assets

FRS 15 requires that all tangible fixed assets are depreciated over their useful economic lives and that the depreciation charge is based on the revalued amount. The only exception to this is freehold land, which has an indefinite useful economic life (unless it is used for mining or landfill).

Some entities have not charged depreciation on revalued buildings on the grounds that they are maintained to such a standard that their useful economic lives are very long. In this situation, the depreciation charge is immaterial.

The ASB has accepted that in rare cases, assets such as heritage properties may have their useful economic lives extended by maintenance and repair. However, FRS 15 states that 'expenditure on a tangible fixed asset that maintains or enhances the previously assessed standard of performance of the asset does not negate the need to charge depreciation'.

FRS 15 does not actually prohibit non-depreciation on the grounds that the charge is immaterial. It discourages it by requiring that the asset must be reviewed for impairment at the end of each reporting period. This also applies where the estimated remaining useful economic life of the tangible fixed asset exceeds 50 years. If an asset is impaired in value, it must be written down to its recoverable amount. (Impairment reviews are covered in Chapter 11).

Disclosure requirements of FRS 15

- An accounting policy note giving details of the depreciation methods used and useful economic lives or depreciation rates, for each major class of fixed asset.

  A typical depreciation note:

  Depreciation on property and equipment, excluding freehold land, is provided for on the straight-line method based upon the estimated useful lives of the various assets as follows:

	Estimated useful life
Freehold buildings	60 years
Short leasehold property	life of lease
Plant and machinery	5 to 10 years
Fixtures and fittings	5 to 10 years
Motor vehicles	5 years

- Total depreciation charged for the year. This information is normally shown in the note:

  Operating profit is stated after charging:

	£
Depreciation on tangible fixed assets	X

- For each class of tangible fixed assets: the cost or revalued amount, cumulative provisions for depreciation and the net carrying amount at the beginning and end of the period. Also provide a reconciliation of the movements. This information is included in the standard fixed asset note to the balance sheet which is required by the Companies Act 1985.

- A note explaining the reason and effect of a change in the method of depreciation.

- A note explaining the effect of a change in useful economic lives or residual value (if this is material).

Where fixed assets have been revalued, the financial statements are prepared under the **alternative accounting rules** rather than the historical cost accounting rules. Under these rules CA 1985 and FRS 15 requires the following extra disclosures in the notes to the balance sheet:

- the corresponding historical cost amount and, if relevant, accumulated depreciation, or the difference between the historical cost amount and the amount included in the balance sheet;

- the years in which the assets were valued and the various values;

- in the case of assets valued during the year, the names of the valuers or particulars of their qualifications and the bases of valuation used

- whether the valuers are internal or external to the business

- if the valuation has not been updated because the directors are not aware of any material change, a statement to that effect.

If finance costs have been capitalised, the following disclosures are required:

- an accounting policy note stating that this is the case;
- the total amount of finance costs included in the cost of tangible fixed assets;
- the amount of finance costs capitalised during the period; and
- the interest rate used to determine the amount of finance costs capitalised during the period.

SSAP19: Accounting for investment properties

It has been seen that property held for its investment potential is outside the scope of FRS 15. SSAP19 was developed to cover the specific problem of investment properties.

Definition

An investment property is an interest in land and/or buildings:

- in respect of which construction work and development have been *completed*; and
- which is held for its *investment potential*, any rental income being negotiated at arm's length.

The following are exceptions from the definition:

- a property which is owned and occupied by a company for its own purposes is not an investment property;
- a property let to and occupied by another group company is not an investment property for the purposes of its own accounts or the group accounts.

Principles

In broad terms, the standard requires investment properties to be included in the balance sheet at their open market value and any surplus or deficit on revaluation to be reported as a movement on an 'investment revaluation reserve'. In practice this means that investment properties are revalued annually.

Treatment of revaluation surpluses and deficits

The period's net revaluation surplus (deficit) should be credited (debited) to an investment revaluation reserve. It should not be dealt with in the profit and loss account. Changes in market value are shown in the statement of total recognised gains and losses. The exception to this is where a revaluation deficit on an individual property is expected to be permanent. In this case, the full amount of the deficit should be charged in the profit and loss account for the period. This would be disclosed as an exceptional item in accordance with FRS3, if material.

Depreciation

SSAP 19 requires that investment properties should not be depreciated. The exception is that properties held on lease with an unexpired period not exceeding 20 years should be amortised over the remaining useful life. This is because shorter leases lose value through the effluxion of time and therefore should be depreciated through the profit and loss account in accordance with FRS 15. This would additionally mean that the rents receivable from the property are matched with the associated cost (loss in value of the property) in the profit and loss account in accordance with SSAP2.

Example

Centreblock plc has three freehold investment properties, each of which originally cost £1m. At 31 December 19X1, the open market value of the properties was as follows:

	£'000
Property 1	1,250
Property 2	1,100
Property 3	750
	3,100

Before accounting for these valuations, the carrying value of the properties was £3,150,000 and the credit balance on the investment revaluation reserve was £150,000. The fall in value of property 3 has arisen because of technical obsolescence and is expected to be permanent. Prior to this valuation, property 3 had been included in the balance sheet at £1,050,000.

Required

Show the journal to incorporate the valuations into the accounts for the year ending 31 December 19X1.

Solution

			£'000	£'000
Dr		Profit and loss account for year (750 – 1,050) (permanent diminution for property 3)	300	
	Cr	Investment revaluation reserve (2,350 – 2,100) (gain on properties 1 and 2)		250*
	Cr	Fixed assets: Investment properties (3,100 – 3,150)		50

* = included in statement of total recognised gains and losses

Previous surplus on property 3 can be transferred to the profit and loss reserve as a reserve movement (not affecting earnings):

			£'000	£'000
Dr		Investment revaluation reserve	50	
	Cr	Profit and loss reserve		50

Key disclosures

- Names or qualifications of valuers and basis of valuation used.

- If the valuer is an employee or officer of the company or group, the notes must state this.

- Display prominently in the accounts:
    - the carrying value of investment properties; and
    - the investment revaluation reserve.

Investment properties are usually shown as a separate category of tangible fixed asset.

Companies Act 1985 and SSAP19

The Companies Act 1985 requires that all fixed assets with a limited useful economic life should be systematically depreciated over that life. The application of SSAP19 obviously is a departure from this requirement in order to give a true and fair view, which is permissible under the Act. However, particulars of the departure, the reasons for it and its effect should be given in a note to the accounts.

Additionally, since investment properties are not carried at a figure based on cost, the Act requires that the following be disclosed by way of note:

- the corresponding historical cost amount and, if relevant, accumulated depreciation; or

- the difference between the historical cost amount and the amount included in the balance sheet.

SSAP4: Accounting for government grants

Introduction

Government grants are available in various forms. The two most common are:

- grants to cover all or part of the cost of specific capital expenditure, for example, on particular fixed assets (capital-based grants);

- grants to cover all or part of specific expenses, for example, on a particular project (revenue-based grants)

Government grants include grants from local government agencies and EC bodies.

Accounting for grants (particularly capital-based grants) may present two problems:

- the grant must be matched with the expenditure towards which it is intended to contribute (applying the accruals concept);

- the grant should not be recognised until the business has complied with any conditions for its receipt (applying the prudence concept).

Capital-based grants

Grants must be matched with the expenditure to which they are intended to contribute. Expenditure on fixed assets appears in the profit and loss account as depreciation. This means that a grant received to finance the purchase of a fixed asset must be matched with the depreciation charged in respect of that asset.

Illustration

Nissan plc purchases a fixed asset for £6,000 in 19X5 and receives a 20% government grant. The asset has an expected life of three years at the end of which it is expected to have nil scrap value.

Solution

Treat the amount of the grant as a deferred credit, a portion of which is transferred to revenue annually. The deferred credit is shown under accruals and deferred income in the balance sheet.

Profit and loss account	19X5 £	19X6 £	19X7 £
Depreciation charge	2,000	2,000	2,000
Related government grant credit	(400)	(400)	(400)

Balance sheet at end of year	19X5 £	19X6 £	19X7 £
Fixed assets: Cost	6,000	6,000	6,000
Less: Accumulated depreciation	2,000	4,000	6,000
Net book value	4,000	2,000	–
Accruals and deferred income			
Government grants	(800)	(400)	–

Revenue-based grants

The general principle is that the grant must be matched, as far as possible, with the expenditure to which it relates.

Grants made:

- to give immediate financial support or assistance to an enterprise; or

- to reimburse costs previously incurred

should be recognised in the profit and loss account of the period in which they become *receivable*.

Grants made:

- to finance the general activities of an enterprise over a specific period; or

- to compensate for a loss of current or future income

should be recognised in the profit and loss account of the period in respect of which they are *paid*.

In practice, this may mean that a debtor or creditor must be set up if the grant is actually received in a different period from the one in which the expenditure is incurred.

Prudence

A grant should not be recognised in the profit and loss account until all conditions for its receipt have been complied with and there is reasonable assurance that the grant will be received.

Occasionally, there may still be a potential liability to repay a grant in the future. For example, if a grant is received in respect of building work, one of the conditions might be that the building should not be sold within a certain period of time. A provision should be made where repayment is probable. This should be set off against any unamortised deferred credit and any excess charged in the profit and loss account immediately.

Disclosure

Disclosure of the following matters is required by SSAP4 (revised):

- the accounting policy adopted for government grants;

- the effects of government grants on the results for the period and the financial position of the enterprise;

- where material assistance has been received by forms of government assistance other than grants, details of that assistance;

- potential liabilities to repay grants, in accordance with FRS 12.

Questions

1   Ford plc

The following fixed asset balances have been extracted from the books of Ford plc as at 31 December 19X7.

	£'000	£'000
Freehold factory cost at 1 January 19X7	1,440	
Freehold factory revaluation	760	
Freehold factory additions	500	
Freehold factory depreciation at 1 January 19X7		144
Freehold factory revaluation adjustment	144	
Freehold factory depreciation charge		60
Plant and machinery cost at 1 January 19X7	1,968	
Plant and machinery additions	75	
Plant and machinery depreciation at 1 January 19X7		257
Plant and machinery depreciation charge		233
Motor vehicles cost at 1 January 19X7	449	
Motor vehicles additions	35	
Motor vehicles depreciation at 1 January 19X7		194
Motor vehicles depreciation charge		87
Office equipment and fixtures cost at 1 January 19X7	888	
Office equipment and fixtures additions	22	
Office equipment and fixtures depreciation at 1 January 19X7		583
Office equipment and fixtures depreciation charge		182

You are given the following information for the year ended 31 December 19X7:

(1) The factory was acquired in March 19X2 and is being depreciated over 50 years.

(2) At 1 January 19X7, depreciation was provided on cost on a straight-line basis. The rates used were 20% for office equipment and fixtures, 25% for motor vehicles and 10% for plant and machinery.

(3) Early in the year the factory was revalued to an open market value of £2.2 million and an extension was built costing £500,000.

(4) During the year the directors decided to change the method of depreciating motor vehicles to 30% reducing balance to give a fairer presentation of the results and of the financial position. The effect of this change was to reduce the depreciation charge for the year by £34,000.

(5) It is the company's policy to charge a full year's depreciation in the year of acquisition.

Required

Prepare the disclosure notes for fixed assets for the year ended 31 December 19X7 required by FRS 15 and CA 1985 in so far as the information permits.

Summary

FRS 15

- Tangible fixed assets should initially be measured at cost.

- Subsequent expenditure on an asset should only be capitalised where it enhances the asset's performance, otherwise it must be treated as an expense.

- The depreciable amount of a tangible fixed asset should be allocated on a systematic basis over its useful economic life.

- Revaluation of fixed assets is optional. If an entity has a policy of revaluing assets, this must be applied consistently to all assets in the same class. Revaluations must be kept up to date.

SSAP19

- Investment properties should be revalued each year to their open market value.

- Any surplus or deficit on revaluation is to be reported as a movement on an 'investment revaluation reserve'.

SSAP4

- Grants should be recognised in the profit and loss account in order to match them with the expenditure towards which they are intended to contribute.

- A capital-based grant should be credited to revenue over the useful life of the asset concerned, usually by setting up a deferred credit, which is transferred to revenue over the same length of time as the asset is depreciated.

CHAPTER 11

Fixed Assets: Intangible Assets

Objectives

This chapter covers the following performance criteria:

10.2.1 Financial statements are accurately drafted from appropriate information.

10.2.2 Subsequent adjustments are correctly implemented.

10.2.3 Draft accounts comply with domestic standards and legislation and, where relevant, partnership agreement.

At the end of this chapter, you should be able to:

- understand how intangible fixed assets should be treated in the profit and loss account and balance sheet

- understand the nature and the problems of accounting for goodwill

- apply the main principles of SSAP 13, FRS 10 and FRS 11

- disclose information about intangible fixed assets in the financial statements

SSAP13: Accounting for research and development

Introduction

It has proved extremely difficult to standardise the accounting treatment of research and development (R & D) expenditure, because this is an area where two fundamental accounting concepts, accruals and prudence, come into head-on conflict.

From one point of view, R & D expenditure is incurred for the future development of business, with a view to decreasing future costs or increasing future revenue. The accruals concept would therefore have R & D expenditure which leads to reduced costs or increased sales carried forward and written off over all the accounting periods which benefit from that expenditure.

On the other hand, it can be argued that it is impossible to be certain of the future benefits of R & D expenditure, since some projects may be abortive and others may result in lower than anticipated benefits. Therefore, in accordance with the prudence concept, all such expenditure should be written off in the year in which it is incurred.

SSAP13 gives guidance regarding the appropriate accounting treatment for R & D expenditure and sets out disclosure requirements.

Definitions

The SSAP classifies R & D expenditure in the following broad categories:

- *Pure (or basic) research* – experimental or theoretical work undertaken primarily to acquire new scientific or technical knowledge for its own sake rather than directed towards any specific aim or application.

- *Applied research* – original or critical investigation undertaken in order to gain new scientific or technical knowledge and directed towards a specific practical aim or objective.

- *Development* – use of scientific or technical knowledge in order to produce new or substantially improved materials, devices, products or services, to install new processes or systems prior to the commencement of commercial applications, or to improve substantially those already produced or installed.

Exceptions

Research and development expenditure as defined by SSAP13 does *not* include:

- Expenditure incurred in locating and exploiting oil, gas and mineral deposits in the extractive industries.

- Situations where companies enter into a firm contract:
    - to carry out development work on behalf of third parties on such terms that the related expenditure is to be fully reimbursed; or
    - to develop and manufacture at an agreed price calculated to reimburse expenditure on development as well as on manufacture.

Accounting treatment

- *Fixed assets* – The cost of fixed assets acquired or constructed in order to provide facilities for research and development activities over a number of accounting periods should be capitalised and written off through the profit and loss account over their useful economic lives. Depreciation is calculated in accordance with FRS 15 and such depreciation may itself form part of development expenditure (covered below) which could be carried forward to later periods.

- *Other expenditure* – Expenditure on pure and applied research (other than on fixed assets) should be written off through the profit and loss account in the year of expenditure.

In general, the standard requires that development expenditure should also be written off in the year of expenditure. However, development expenditure can be deferred to future periods if *all* the following criteria are met:

- There is a clearly defined project.

- The related expenditure is separately identifiable.

- The outcome of such a project has been assessed with reasonable certainty as to:

  - its technical feasibility;

  - its ultimate commercial viability considered in the light of factors such as likely market conditions (including competing products), public opinion, consumer and environmental legislation.

- The aggregate of the deferred development costs, any further development costs and related production, selling and administration costs is reasonably expected to be exceeded by related future sales or other revenues.

- Adequate resources exist, or are reasonably expected to be available, to enable the project to be completed and to provide any consequential increases in working capital.

Development expenditure which has been deferred is included in the balance sheet as an intangible fixed asset and amortised.

Amortisation

SSAP13 states that, if development costs are deferred to future periods, they should be amortised. The amortisation should start with the commercial production or application of the product, service, process or system and should be allocated on a systematic basis to each accounting period, by reference to either (i) the sale or use of the product, service, process or system, or (ii) the period over which these are expected to be sold or used.

Illustration

A company has incurred development expenditure of £250,000 in relation to product X. This development expenditure meets all the criteria for deferral laid down in SSAP13.

Production of product X has now commenced and sales are expected to take place as follows:

	Number of units
19X1	75,000
19X2	150,000
19X3	75,000

After 19X3 sales are expected to decline dramatically.

The deferred development expenditure will be amortised as follows:

	Charge £
19X1 (75/300 × £250,000)	62,500
19X2 (150/300 × £250,000)	125,000
19X3 (75/300 × £250,000)	62,500

The note to the balance sheet will appear as follows:

Intangible fixed assets – development costs

	19X1 £	19X2 £	19X3 £
Cost at beginning and end of year	250,000	250,000	250,000
Amortisation			
At beginning of year	–	62,500	187,500
Charge for year	62,500	125,000	62,500
At end of year	62,500	187,500	250,000
Net book value at end of year	187,500	62,500	–
Net book value at beginning of year	250,000	187,500	62,500

Deferred development expenditure for each project should be reviewed at the end of each accounting period and, where the circumstances which have justified the deferral of the expenditure no longer apply or are considered doubtful, the expenditure should be written off immediately, project by project, to the extent to which it is considered to be irrecoverable.

Disclosure

- The accounting policy on R & D expenditure should be stated and explained.

- The total amount of R & D expenditure charged in the profit and loss account should be disclosed, analysed between the current year's expenditure and amounts amortised from deferred expenditure.

- Movements on deferred development expenditure and the amount carried forward at the beginning and the end of the period should be disclosed.

- Deferred development expenditure should be disclosed under intangible fixed assets in the balance sheet.

Scope

The disclosure requirement outlined above applies only to the following:

- public limited companies; special category companies (ie. banking, insurance, shipping companies); holding companies with a plc or special category company as a subsidiary;

- companies that exceed the criteria, multiplied by 10, for defining a medium-sized company (S248 CA 1985).

All the other requirements of SSAP13 apply to all financial statements intended to give a true and fair view.

FRS 10: Goodwill and Intangible Assets

Nature and meaning of goodwill

The value of a business as a whole will often be different from the total value of its individual net assets. The difference, which may be positive or negative, is described as *goodwill*.

Goodwill is therefore, by definition, incapable of realisation separately from the business as a whole; that is, you cannot sell off pieces of goodwill in a business. This characteristic of goodwill distinguishes it from all other items in the accounts.

Definitions

Purchased goodwill is the difference between the cost of an acquired entity and the aggregate of the fair values of that entity's identifiable assets and liabilities.

Identifiable assets and liabilities are the assets and liabilities of an entity that are capable of being disposed of or settled separately, without disposing of a business of the entity.

Identifiable net assets are not purely tangible assets; they can include intangible assets such as concessions, patents, licences and trade marks.

There are two types of goodwill:

- *purchased goodwill* is goodwill which is established as a result of the purchase of a business;
- *non-purchased goodwill* is any goodwill other than purchased goodwill.

Other phrases which you need to understand are:

Fair value – the amount for which an asset (or liability) could be exchanged in an arm's length transaction.

Useful economic life of purchased goodwill – the best estimate of the life of such goodwill at the date of purchase.

Other points to consider are that:

- the value of goodwill has no reliable or predictable relationship to any costs which may have been incurred;

- individual intangible factors which may contribute to goodwill cannot be valued;

- the value of goodwill may fluctuate widely according to internal and external circumstances over relatively short periods of time; and

- the assessment of the value of goodwill is highly subjective.

Therefore, any amount attributed to goodwill is unique to the valuer and to the specific point in time at which it is measured, and is only valid at that time and in the circumstances then prevailing.

There is no difference in character between purchased goodwill and non-purchased goodwill. However, the value of purchased goodwill, although arising from a subjective valuation of the business, is established as a fact at a particular point in time by a market transaction; this is not true of non-purchased goodwill which, while it may be presumed to exist, has not been evidenced in a purchase transaction.

Factors which may contribute to goodwill

There are many practical reasons why positive goodwill arises such as:

- market dominance arising from the purchase;
- superior management;
- strategic location;
- excellent reputation of products or service.

Accounting treatment of goodwill

- *Non-purchased goodwill*: No amount should be attributed to non-purchased goodwill in the balance sheets of companies or groups. This has always been the case. FRS 10 was issued to standardise the treatment of purchased goodwill.

- *Purchased goodwill*: Two alternative treatments are possible here. We can examine these by means of an illustration.

Illustration

Suppose that Harvey acquires the business of Wallbanger for £250,000 in cash. Immediately prior to the purchase, the balance sheets of the two businesses can be summarised as follows:

	Harvey £	Wallbanger £
Tangible fixed assets	750,000	130,000
Net current assets	350,000	70,000
Capital and reserves	1,100,000	200,000

We can also assume that the book values of Wallbanger's assets are equal to their current market value (or fair value).

Therefore Harvey has paid £250,000 for a business whose separable net assets reach a total of just £200,000. It is clear that the difference paid represents goodwill of £50,000.

If Harvey now pools the Wallbanger assets in its balance sheet, it should appear as follows:

	£
Purchased goodwill	50,000
Tangible fixed assets £(750,000 + 130,000)	880,000
Net current assets £(350,000 + 70,000 − 250,000)	170,000
Capital and reserves	1,100,000

Clearly Harvey has acquired purchased goodwill from Wallbanger. It is also probable that Harvey's business contains some goodwill, but this cannot be disclosed in the balance sheet, since it represents non-purchased goodwill.

How should this purchased goodwill which Harvey has bought be dealt with in its accounts?

Option 1

One method is to adopt the approach used in the above example. The purchased goodwill bought by Harvey is carried in the balance sheet, just like any other capital asset. It is argued that Harvey has paid cash in exchange for an asset and, as such, the goodwill represents a real asset. However, should the goodwill not be depreciated in Harvey's balance sheet just like other fixed assets?

Option 2

Another method is to eliminate goodwill from the accounts by immediately writing it off, which is consistent with the accepted practice of excluding non-purchased goodwill from the accounts. The immediate write-off of purchased goodwill should be made against reserves, *not* as a charge to the profit and loss account. This follows the concept of prudence, particularly given the characteristics of goodwill, as an asset which is often difficult to measure.

FRS 10 states that positive purchased goodwill should be capitalised and classified as an asset on the balance sheet (Option 1). It has prohibited immediate elimination against reserves (Option 2).

In almost all cases, goodwill has a limited useful economic life and therefore, like any other fixed asset, it should be amortised (depreciated) on a systematic basis over that life. There is a rebuttable presumption that the useful economic life of purchased goodwill is 20 years or less.

In our illustration, suppose that the goodwill arising on the acquisition of Wallbanger has a useful economic life of five years. This means that at the end of the first year after the acquisition, goodwill will appear in the balance sheet as follows:

	£
Fixed assets:	
Intangible assets: Goodwill	40,000

There will be a charge of £10,000 to the profit and loss account for each of the five years.

FRS 10 states that:

- no residual value may be assigned to goodwill;

- the straight line method of amortisation should normally be used;

- the useful economic life of goodwill should be reviewed at the end of each reporting period and revised if necessary; and

- goodwill should be reviewed for impairment:

    - at the end of the first full financial year following the acquisition; and

    - in other periods if events or changes in circumstances indicate that the carrying value may not be recoverable.

Negative purchased goodwill

Negative goodwill arises where an entity is purchased for less than the total fair values of its identifiable net assets, for example when:

- a business is sold at a bargain price because the vendor needs to achieve a quick sale; or
- the purchase price is reduced to take account of probable future losses.

Negative goodwill is rare. It should be recognised and separately disclosed on the face of the balance sheet, immediately below the goodwill heading, followed by a subtotal showing the net amount of the positive and negative goodwill. It should then be recognised (as a credit) in the profit and loss account in the periods expected to benefit.

Other intangible assets

Intangible assets are non-financial fixed assets that do not have physical substance but are identifiable and are controlled by the entity through custody or legal rights.

They may include:

- brand names
- publishing titles
- patents
- franchises
- licences
- trade marks.

They are distinguished from goodwill because they are identifiable, that is, they could be disposed of without disrupting the business of the entity. Skilled staff or a portfolio of clients are not treated as intangible assets because they are not usually controlled by the entity (they can change jobs or suppliers).

FRS 10 applies to all intangible assets other than research and development expenditure (covered by SSAP 13) and any other intangible asset covered by another accounting standard.

The way in which an intangible asset is treated depends on its type.

- An intangible asset purchased separately from a business should be capitalised at its cost. Examples: copyrights, patents, licences.

- An intangible asset acquired as part of the acquisition of a business should be capitalised separately from goodwill if its value can be measured reliably on initial recognition. It should initially be recorded at its *fair value*.

- If its value cannot be measured reliably, an intangible asset purchased as part of the acquisition of a business should be subsumed within the amount of the purchase price attributable to goodwill. (Most purchased brand names fall into this category).

- An internally developed intangible asset may be capitalised only if it has a readily ascertainable market value. (This is consistent with the treatment of internally generated goodwill.)

- If an intangible asset is recognised, it is then amortised over its useful economic life in exactly the same way as purchased goodwill.

Where useful economic life is longer than 20 years

A useful economic life may be regarded as longer than 20 years or indefinite if:

- the durability of the acquired business or intangible asset can be demonstrated and justifies estimating the useful economic life to exceed 20 years;

- the goodwill or intangible asset is capable of continued measurement (so that it can be reviewed for impairment); and

- an impairment review is carried out at the end of each reporting period.

Where there has been an impairment in value, the goodwill or intangible asset is written down to its recoverable amount.

If goodwill and intangible assets are regarded as having indefinite useful economic lives, they are carried indefinitely in the balance sheet, subject to the results of impairment reviews. The Companies Acts require that all fixed assets are amortised over their useful economic lives. Therefore the 'true and fair view override' is invoked.

Disclosure

The accounting policy followed in respect of goodwill and intangible fixed assets should be explained in the notes to the accounts.

Goodwill and intangible assets are shown as separate items under intangible fixed assets in the balance sheet until they are fully amortised. Negative goodwill is separately disclosed.

The following should also be disclosed:

- The method used to value intangible assets.

- The following information separately for positive goodwill, negative goodwill and each class of intangible asset included on the balance sheet:

    - cost or valuation at the beginning and end of the year;

    - the cumulative amount of provisions for amortisation and impairment at the beginning and end of the year;

    - a reconciliation of the movements; and

    - the net carrying amount at the balance sheet date.

- Methods and periods of amortisation of goodwill and intangible assets and the reasons for choosing those periods.

- Changes in amortisation period or method.

- Grounds for amortising goodwill or intangible assets over a period that exceeds 20 years (if applicable).

- The periods in which negative goodwill is being written back in the profit and loss account.

- Separate disclosure of the fair value of the consideration and the amount of purchased goodwill arising on each acquisition during the period, including the method of dealing with goodwill.

- Provision of a table showing the book value of each major category of assets and liabilities as in the records of the acquired company. Any differences between these book values and the fair values should be explained and analysed between:
    - revaluations;
    - provisions for future trading losses;
    - other provisions;
    - adjustments to bring accounting policies into line with those of the acquiring group;
    - any other major item.

- When a business that has been acquired is sold, disclose:
    - the profit or loss on disposal;
    - the amount of purchased goodwill attributable to the business sold and how it has been treated in calculating the profit or loss on the disposal.

FRS 11: Impairment of fixed assets and goodwill

Introduction

Impairment is a reduction in the recoverable amount of a fixed asset or goodwill below its carrying amount. It is measured by comparing the carrying value of the asset with its recoverable amount. If the carrying amount exceeds the recoverable amount, the asset is impaired and should be written down.

Definitions

Recoverable amount is the higher of the amounts that can be obtained from selling the asset (net realisable value) or using the asset (value in use).

Net realisable value is the amount at which an asset could be disposed of, less any direct selling costs.

Value in use is the present value of the future cash flows obtainable as a result of an asset's continued use, including those resulting from its ultimate disposal.

When an asset is stated at the higher of net realisable value or value in use it is recorded at its greatest value to the entity. This is because, when a fixed asset becomes impaired, the decision must be made whether to continue to use it or to sell it. The entity will not continue to use the asset if it can realise more cash by selling it and vice versa.

Illustration

Montgomery Ltd has three assets:

	Net book value £	Net realisable value £	Value in use £
Asset 1	80,000	120,000	100,000
Asset 2	90,000	70,000	80,000
Asset 3	100,000	70,000	130,000

The recoverable amounts of the three assets are:

	£
Asset 1	120,000
Asset 2	80,000
Asset 3	130,000

Asset 2 is impaired and must be written down by £10,000 to its recoverable amount of £80,000.

Scope of FRS 11

FRS 11 applies to purchased goodwill that is recognised in the balance sheet and all fixed assets except investment properties as defined by SSAP 19.

Signs that an asset may be impaired

FRS 11 gives the following examples:

- a current operating loss, combined with past or expected future losses;

- a current net cash outflow from the operating activities of the business, combined with past or expected future net cash outflows;

- a significant decline in a fixed asset's market value during the period;

- evidence of obsolescence or physical damage to the fixed asset; or

- a significant adverse change in the business or the market in which the fixed asset or goodwill is involved (eg the entrance of a major competitor).

A fixed asset must be reviewed for impairment if one of these events or any similar event occurs. Impairment reviews are also required when:

- an asset is not depreciated on the grounds that the charge would be immaterial (FRS 15); or

- the estimated remaining useful economic life of an asset (other than non–depreciable land) is more than 50 years (FRS 15); or

- goodwill and intangible assets have a useful life exceeding twenty years (FRS 10).

Accounting for impairment losses

The asset's value is written down to its recoverable amount. This is normally done by making an additional charge for depreciation.

Illustration

On 1 January 19X4, a company invested £20,000 in plant for a new project, which was expected to last for 5 years.

After 2 years a competitor entered the market. An impairment review was carried out, and the recoverable amount of the plant was estimated at £9,000. At this point in time the net book value of the plant is:

	£
Cost	20,000
Less: Accumulated depreciation (2 years)	(8,000)
	12,000

The plant is written down to £9,000:

		£	£
Dr	Profit and loss account	3,000	
	Cr Accumulated depreciation		3,000

FRS 11 states that the remaining useful economic life and residual value of the asset should be reviewed and revised if necessary. The revised carrying amount should be depreciated over the revised estimate of the remaining useful economic life.

In this case, the remaining useful economic life is still three years and so the annual depreciation charge is:

$$\frac{9,000}{3 \text{ years}} = £3,000$$

In 19X6 the total charge to the profit and loss account is £6,000, being the impairment and the annual charge.

The impairment loss may need to be disclosed as an exceptional item, if material.

Chapter 11 Fixed Assets: Intangible Assets

Questions

1 Newprods Ltd

During the course of a year, Newprods Ltd incurred expenditure on many research and development activities. Details of three of them are given below.

Project 3   To develop a new compound in view of the anticipated shortage of a raw material currently being used in one of the company's processes. Sufficient progress has been made to suggest that the new compound can be produced at a cost comparable to that of the existing raw material.

Project 4   To improve the yield of an important manufacturing operation of the company. At present, material input with a cost of £100,000 pa becomes contaminated in the operation and half is wasted. Sufficient progress has been made for the scientists to predict an improvement so that only 20% will be wasted.

Project 5   To carry out work, as specified by a creditworthy client, to attempt to bring a proposed aerospace product of that client into line with safety regulations.

Costs during the year

	Project 3 £	Project 4 £	Project 5 £
Staff salaries	5,000	10,000	20,000
Overheads	6,000	12,000	24,000
Plant at cost (life of ten years)	10,000	20,000	5,000

Required

(a) Define the following:

    (i)   pure research expenditure;

    (ii)   applied research expenditure;

    (iii)   development expenditure.

(b) State the circumstances in which it may be appropriate to carry forward research and development expenditure to future periods.

(c) Show how the expenditure on projects 3, 4 and 5 would be dealt with in the balance sheet and profit and loss account in accordance with SSAP13.

Summary

SSAP13

- Research and development expenditure falls into three categories:
    - pure research
    - applied research
    - development expenditure

- Development expenditure (only) can be deferred to future periods if it meets the criteria laid down in the SSAP.

- If development expenditure is deferred, it should be amortised.

FRS 10

- Non-purchased goodwill should never appear in the balance sheet.

- Positive purchased goodwill should be capitalised.

- An intangible asset should be capitalised if:
    - it has been purchased separately from a business (capitalise at cost); or
    - its value can be measured reliably (capitalise at fair value).

    Otherwise it should be treated as part of goodwill.

- An internally developed intangible asset should only be capitalised if it has a readily ascertainable market value.

- Goodwill and intangible assets that have been capitalised should be amortised over their useful economic lives (presumed to be 20 years or less).

FRS 11

- If the recoverable amount of a fixed asset is less than its carrying amount (net book value), it is impaired and must be written down.

- Recoverable amount is higher of net realisable value and value in use.

- An impairment loss is normally treated as additional depreciation.

CHAPTER 12

Stocks and Long–Term Contracts

Objectives

This chapter covers the following performance criteria:

10.2.1 Financial statements are accurately drafted from appropriate information.

10.2.2 Subsequent adjustments are correctly implemented.

10.2.3 Draft accounts comply with domestic standards and legislation and, where relevant, partnership agreement.

At the end of this chapter, you should be able to:

- understand how stocks should be treated in the profit and loss account and balance sheet
- apply the main principles of SSAP 9
- disclose information about stocks and long term contracts in the financial statements

Stock

Accounting treatment

Stocks should be stated at the lower of *cost* and *net realisable value*.

Cost

SSAP9 defines cost as: 'that expenditure which has been incurred in the *normal course of business* in bringing the product or service to its *present location and condition*'.

This means that two identical items may have different costs if they are in different locations. For example, the cost of an item which has been shipped to a distribution centre in France will include the normal transport costs to France and hence will have a higher cost than a similar item held in the factory in England.

Note that only costs incurred in the *normal* course of business should be included. If the lorry taking items to France broke down, the costs of the breakdown would not be included as part of the transport costs since they are considered abnormal.

Cost includes the following.

- *Cost of purchase* which comprises:
    - purchase price – including import duties, transport, handling costs and any other directly attributable costs; less
    - trade discounts, rebates and subsidies.

- *Cost of conversion* which comprises:
    - costs which are specifically attributable to units of production – direct labour, direct expenses and subcontracted work;
    - production overheads;
    - other overheads, if any, attributable in the particular circumstances of the business to bringing the product or service to its present location and condition.

Illustration

The Standard Company plc has stock at 31 December 19X7 and has gathered the following information together in order to determine its cost.

	£
Cost of original materials	16,000
Cost of work on material	
Labour 1,000 hours @ £2.50	2,500
Variable overhead	700
Fixed production overhead during the period 1 October to 31 December 19X7	40,000
Number of hours worked in the period 1 October to 31 December 19X7	18,000 hours

You also discovered that 2,000 hours of work were lost during December due to an industrial dispute over the holiday work programme.

Selling and distribution costs during the quarter were £10,000.

The value of the stock held at 31 December 19X7 is:

	£
Material cost	16,000
Labour cost	2,500
Variable overhead	700
Fixed overhead $\dfrac{£40,000}{20,000 \text{ hrs}} \times 1,000 \text{ hrs}$	2,000
	21,200

Fixed overheads are absorbed on a basis of the labour hours worked, 1,000 hours, as a proportion of normal working hours for the period, 20,000 hours.

The industrial dispute will not increase the value of the stock even though it reduced the number of hours actually worked in the quarter.

Selling and distribution overheads have been ignored as the goods in stock have not been sold or distributed.

Net realisable value

Net realisable value is defined as the actual or estimated selling price (net of trade but before settlement discounts) less:

- all further costs to completion;
- all costs to be incurred in marketing, selling and distributing the product.

Settlement discounts are those discounts which are offered as an inducement for early payment of an invoice; as such, they are more akin to an interest or finance expense than to a true discount and hence are not deducted in determining net realisable value.

Illustration

The Standard Mix Company plc has the following items in stock at its year-end:

	Cost £	Selling price £
Item A	7,000	10,000
Item B	8,400	10,200
Item C	9,200	10,400

Item A is ready for immediate sale.

Item B is also ready for sale but, due to falling demand, a 25% special discount will be needed to encourage a buyer to come forward.

Item C requires packaging before it can be sold and this cost is estimated at £1,800.

The net realisable values of these items are:

			£	£
Item A	NRV			10,000
Item B	Selling price		10,200	
	Discount 25%		(2,550)	
	NRV			7,650
Item C	Selling price		10,400	
	Packaging		(1,800)	
	NRV			8,600

For stock purposes, these items will be valued as follows:

Item	Cost £	NRV £	Stock value £
A	7,000	10,000	7,000
B	8,400	7,650	7,650
C	9,200	8,600	8,600
Stock at lower of cost and net realisable value			23,250

The comparison of cost and net realisable value needs to be made in respect of each item of stock *separately*. If this is difficult in practice, similar groups or categories of stock should be taken together.

By comparing the total realisable value of stocks with the total cost, you could net off foreseeable losses against unrealised profits. This is not acceptable under SSAP9 and the Companies Act.

Methods of costing

In practice, it is often difficult to relate expenditure to specific units of stocks. This is because a number of identical items may have been purchased or made at different times.

SSAP9 permits the use of any of the following methods, consistently applied:

- *Unit cost* – The actual cost of purchasing or manufacturing identifiable units of stock.

- *Weighted average cost* – The calculation of the cost of stocks and work in progress on the basis of the application to the unit of stocks on hand of an average price computed by dividing the total cost of units by the total number of such units (this average price may be arrived at by means of a continuous calculation, a periodic calculation or a moving periodic calculation).

- *FIFO (first in, first out)* – The calculation of the cost of stocks and work in progress on the basis that the quantities in hand represent the latest purchases or production.

- *Standard cost* – The calculation of the cost of stocks and work in progress on the basis of periodically predetermined costs calculated from management's estimates of expected levels of costs, operations, operational efficiency and the related expenditure.

  There is a proviso. Standards must be reviewed frequently to ensure that they bear a reasonable relationship to the actual costs of the period.

- *Selling price less an estimated profit margin* – This is acceptable only if it can be clearly shown that it gives a reasonable approximation of the actual cost.

The following methods should *not* normally be used:

- *LIFO (last in, first out)* – The calculation of stocks and work in progress on the basis that the quantities in hand represent the earliest purchases or production.

- *Base stock* – The calculation of the cost of stocks and work in progress on the basis that a fixed unit value is ascribed to a predetermined number of units of stock, any excess over this number being valued on the basis of some other method. If the number of units in stock is less than the predetermined minimum, the fixed unit value is applied to the number in stock.

- *Replacement cost* – The cost at which an identical asset could be purchased or manufactured at the balance sheet date.

The Companies Act 1985 states that the following methods are acceptable:

- first in, first out (FIFO);
- last in, first out (LIFO);
- a weighted average price;
- any other method similar to the methods mentioned above.

The method of valuation used should provide the fairest practicable approximation to actual cost.

You should be familiar with most of these methods of valuation from your earlier studies.

Long-term contract work in progress

Introduction

Long-term contracts (for example, building a dam or constructing a road) generally extend over a number of years. The length of time taken to complete such projects presents a special problem in accounting terms. If we wait for completion of the contract before taking any of the profit it earns, we will find that the first years of a contract show no return on the investment made in it. A very large profit will arise, however, when the project is completed. In order to overcome this problem, part of the contract's turnover and profit is recognised each year as it proceeds.

Definitions

- *Long-term contracts* are contracts entered into for the design, manufacture or construction of a single substantial asset or the provision of a service where the time taken substantially to complete the contract is such that the contract activity falls into different accounting periods.

  A contract that is required to be accounted for as long-term by this Accounting Standard will usually extend for a period exceeding one year. However, a duration exceeding one year is not an essential feature of a long-term contract. Some contracts with a shorter duration than one year should be accounted for as long-term contracts if they are sufficiently material to the activity of the period that not to record turnover and attributable profit would lead to a distortion of the period's turnover and results such that the financial statements would not give a true and fair view, provided that the policy is applied consistently within the reporting entity and from year to year.

- *Attributable profit* is that part of the total profit currently estimated to arise over the duration of the contract, after allowing for estimated remedial and maintenance costs and increases in costs so far as not recoverable under the terms of the contract, that fairly reflects the profit attributable to that part of the work performed at the accounting date.

- *Foreseeable losses* are those which are currently estimated to arise over the duration of the contract (after allowing for estimated remedial and maintenance costs and increases in costs so far as not recoverable under the terms of the contract). This estimate is required irrespective of:

  - whether or not work has yet commenced on such contracts;
  - the proportion of work carried out at the accounting date;
  - the amount of profits expected to arise on other contracts.

- *Payments on account* are all amounts received and receivable at the accounting date in respect of contracts in progress.

Accounting treatment

Attributable profit is that part of the total contract profit which has been earned to date. By including such profit in its accounts, a company could be anticipating unrealised profits. This treatment is not prudent unless the company is reasonably certain in advance about the contract's outcome.

Where the outcome of a contract can be foreseen with reasonable certainty, SSAP9 states that attributable profit should be calculated on a prudent basis and included in the accounts. The amount of profit taken up should reflect the proportion of work carried out at the accounting date.

Where the outcome of a contract cannot be assessed with reasonable certainty, no profit should be reflected in the profit and loss account in respect of that contract.

If an ultimate loss on the contract is expected, all the loss should be recognised as soon as it is foreseen.

Illustration

You will not be assessed on detailed accounting for long term contracts. However, it is useful to have an appreciation of the technique in order to understand the issues involved.

Spade Ltd has one long-term contract in progress in the year ending 30 June 19X4, the details of which are as follows:

	£'000
Contract price	2,000
Costs incurred to date	1,200
Estimated further costs to complete	600
Value of work done (work certified)	1,400
Amounts invoiced	1,250

The contract commenced in the current year.

We begin by identifying whether the contract is expected to make a profit or loss overall, as this is crucial to the rest of the workings. We calculate the total estimated profit or loss as follows:

	£'000	£'000
Contract price		2,000
Less: Costs incurred to date	1,200	
All further costs to completion	600	
		(1,800)
Total estimated profit		200

At the year-end, we calculate turnover and attributable profit, or foreseeable loss, for each contract, giving cost of sales as the balancing figure.

Turnover

As this is the first year of the contract, turnover for the year is the value of work certified, £1,400. (If this were the second or subsequent year of the contract, turnover for the year would be the cumulative value of work certified less turnover previously recognised in the profit and loss account.)

Gross profit

The contract is expected to make a profit overall. We calculate the *attributable profit* from the start of the contract to the balance sheet date and deduct any amounts included in the profit and loss account in earlier years to obtain the current year's gross profit figure. However, if the contract is not far enough advanced to assess the outcome with reasonable certainty, we cannot recognise any profit.

Methods of calculating attributable profit

SSAP9 does not specify how to calculate attributable profit but does state that it should reflect the proportion of work carried out at the balance sheet date and take account of any known inequalities of profitability in the various stages of the contract. There are three possible methods:

(i) Using: $\dfrac{\text{Work certified}}{\text{Contract price}} \times \text{Total estimated profit}$

Attributable profit = $\dfrac{1,400}{2,000} \times 200 = £140,000$

(ii) Using: $\dfrac{\text{Cost to date}}{\text{Total estimated cost}} \times \text{Total estimated profit}$

Attributable profit = $\dfrac{1{,}200}{1{,}800} \times 200 = £133{,}333$

(iii) Using: Turnover to date – Cost to date

Attributable profit = 1,400,000 – 1,200,000 = £200,000

In this case, method (iii) is not likely to be appropriate as it is unlikely to be prudent to recognise the whole profit before the contract is finished.

Note: If the contract is expected to make a loss overall, we must recognise the full loss in the profit and loss account immediately, less any amounts already recognised in earlier years. This applies even if we have not yet started work and even if other contracts are profitable. We include in cost of sales whatever figure is needed to make gross profit for the contract equal the foreseeable loss, whether or not the relevant costs have been incurred yet (if they have not, we will set up a provision).

Cost of sales

The easiest way to deal with this figure is to treat it as the balancing figure in the profit and loss account workings. For the purpose of this example, we will assume that attributable profit is to be calculated using work certified as a proportion of total contract price [Method (i)].

This gives us the profit and loss account figures:

	£'000
Turnover (work certified)	1,400
Cost of sales (β)	(1,260)
Gross profit	140

The balance sheet

The figures which appear in the balance sheet arise from the matching process that we have just carried out in order to determine turnover and attributable profit.

We have earned more revenue than we have billed, and we include the balance in:

	£
Debtors: Amounts recoverable on contracts	**150**

The balance is calculated as follows:

	£
Cumulative turnover from start of contract to balance sheet date (Dr)	1,400
Less: Amounts invoiced (SSAP9 calls this *payments on account*)(Cr)	(1,250)
	150

We have charged more costs to the profit and loss account than we have so far incurred. Hence, we make an accrual or provision (the distinction is not significant):

	£
Provisions for liabilities and charges	**60**
OR	
Accruals and deferred income	**60**

The balance is calculated as follows:

	£
Costs incurred from start of contract to balance sheet date (Dr)	1,200
Less: Cumulative cost of sales to date (Cr)	(1,260)
	(60)

Disclosure requirements

Accounting policies

Accounting policies adopted in calculating the following must be disclosed:

- cost;
- net realisable value;
- turnover;
- attributable profit;
- foreseeable losses.

Stocks and work in progress

Total stocks and work in progress should be subclassified in a manner appropriate to the business so as to indicate the amount held in each of the main categories. This is usually achieved by giving the analysis required in the balance sheet formats by CA 1985.

	£
Raw materials and consumables	X
Work in progress	X
Finished goods and goods for resale	X
Payments on account	X
	X

Question

1 S Ltd

S Ltd is a manufacturing company. It held its annual stock count on 31 March 19X2, the company's year-end. The accounts department is currently working its way through the stock sheets placing a value on the physical stocks. The company has had a difficult year and profits are likely to be lower than in the previous year.

Raw materials

Stocks of raw materials are valued at cost. The finance director has suggested that the cost has been understated in previous years because the company has not taken the costs of delivery or insurance into account. These can be substantial in the case of imported goods. It has been proposed that these costs be taken into account in the valuation of closing stocks of raw materials.

Work in progress

The cost of work in progress includes an element of overheads. The following table of figures has been prepared in order to assist in the calculation of the overhead absorption.

	£
Fixed costs	
Factory rent, rates and insurance	150,000
Administration expenses	240,000
Factory security	110,000
Variable costs	
Factory heat, light and power	300,000
Sales commissions and selling costs	120,000
Depreciation of machinery	200,000
Depreciation of delivery vehicles	70,000

Overheads are usually absorbed on the basis of labour hours. The stock sheets suggest that 500 labour hours have been included in work in progress. A total of 70,000 hours have been worked by production staff during the year. The figure is, however, much lower than the normal figure of 95,000 hours.

Finished goods

Finished goods have already been valued at £400,000. This figure includes some obsolete stocks which cost £70,000 to produce, but which are likely to be sold at a scrap value of £500. There are also several batches of a new product which will be launched early in the new financial year. These cost £90,000 to manufacture. Independent market research suggests that it is very likely that the new product will be sold for considerably more than this. If, however, the launch is unsuccessful, the new product will have to be sold as scrap for £1,000. The finance director has said that the aggregate net realisable value of all closing stocks of finished goods is at least £500,000 and so there is no need to worry about the obsolete and new stock products.

Required

(a) (i) Explain whether the costs of delivery and insurance should be included in the valuation of raw materials.

(ii) Assuming that the change is made, state how the change should be accounted for.

(b) (i) Explain how SSAP 9 requires overheads to be treated in the valuation of closing stocks.

(ii) Calculate the value of overheads to be absorbed into S Ltd's closing stock of work in progress.

(c) (i) Explain whether the valuation of closing stocks at the lower of cost and net realisable value should be done on an item–by–item basis or on the basis of the aggregate cost of all items as compared with their aggregate net realisable value.

(ii) State how you would value the obsolete items and the new product line, giving reasons for your valuation in each case.

Summary

Stocks and short-term WIP

- Remember the key phrase is lower of cost and net realisable value.

    (i) Determine costs (purchase price of goods plus attributable overheads).

    (ii) Compare costs with net realisable value (usually selling price less additional costs to complete or sell).

- Disclosure requirements:

    (i) accounting policies;
    (ii) stocks and work in progress note.

Long-term contract WIP

- Long-term contracts should be assessed on a contract by contract basis and reflected in the profit and loss account by recording turnover and related costs as contract activity progresses.

- Attributable profit should be recognised in the profit and loss account where it is considered that the outcome of the contract can be assessed with reasonable certainty.

CHAPTER 13

Accounting for Leases and Hire Purchase Contracts

Objectives

This chapter covers the following performance criteria:

10.2.1 Financial statements are accurately drafted from appropriate information.

10.2.2 Subsequent adjustments are correctly implemented.

10.2.3 Draft accounts comply with domestic standards and legislation and, where relevant, partnership agreement.

At the end of this chapter, you should be able to:

♦ understand how leases and hire purchase contracts should be treated in the profit and loss account and balance sheet.

Types of transaction

Legally, there are three main types of 'extended credit' transaction:

♦ credit sale
♦ hire purchase
♦ lease

Traditionally, they have been accounted for in accordance with their legal form as shown in the following table:

	Credit sale	Hire purchase	Lease
Title	Passes to buyer immediately	Passes to buyer at the end of the agreement	Never passes to the lessee (buyer)
Buyer/lessee	Asset capitalised Liability recognised Interest and depreciation charged to profit and loss	Asset capitalised Liability recognised Interest and depreciation charged to profit and loss	Rentals charged to profit and loss account
Sellor/lessor	Debtor recognised Finance income spread over agreement	Debtor recognised Finance income and gross profit spread over agreement	Asset capitalised Rental income credited to profit and loss account

The problem

Similar transactions may be accounted for in different ways. A leasing transaction may be very similar in substance to a hire purchase transaction.

The solution

Transactions should be accounted for in accordance with their *commercial substance* and not merely their *legal form*.

Types of lease

Finance lease

A lease that transfers substantially all the risks and rewards of ownership of an asset to the lessee.

Operating lease

A lease other than a finance lease.

Commercial substance of finance and operating leases

A *finance lease* is similar in substance to the ownership of an asset, financed by a loan repayable by instalments over the period of the lease. The lessee would normally have sole use of the asset and would be responsible for its maintenance, repair and insurance even though legal title to the asset remains with the lessor. An *operating lease*, on the other hand, is the 'short-term' hire of an asset.

Finance lease

SSAP21 requires that finance leases (or equivalent agreements) are capitalised in the lessee's balance sheet by including both the

- value of the asset in fixed assets;
- the outstanding leases commitments in creditors.

The profit and loss account is charged with depreciation on the asset and an appropriate share of the finance charge.

The problems

The two critical questions to be answered are:

(a) At what value should the asset be capitalised?
(b) What finance charge should be made in the profit and loss account?

The capitalised value in the balance sheet

At the start of the lease, the sum to be recorded both as an asset and as a liability should be *the present value of the minimum lease payments*, derived by discounting them at the interest rate implicit in the lease.

In practice, in the case of a finance lease the *fair value* of the asset will often be a sufficiently close approximation to the present value of the minimum lease payments and may in these circumstances be substituted for it.

The finance charge

The excess of the minimum lease payments over the initial capitalised value represents the finance charge. The total finance charge should be allocated to accounting periods during the lease term so as to produce a constant periodic rate of charge on the remaining balance of the obligation for each accounting period (ie. the actuarial method), or a reasonable approximation thereto.

The lessor will account for future amounts receivable under finance leases as a debtor, which are then allocated to the profit and loss over the term of the lease.

Operating lease

An operating lease is effectively a short-term rental agreement, with no option to purchase the goods. The supplier retains title throughout and usually undertakes to keep them in good working order. The domestic rental of a television or video recorder would generally constitute such an agreement.

In this case, it is the lessor that records the asset as a fixed asset and depreciates it. Rental is recognised on a straight-line basis in both the lessee's and lessor's books over the lease term.

Hire purchase

Hire purchase contracts could fall into either of these categories, depending upon the terms of the agreement, and SSAP21 requires that they be accounted for accordingly. It is usual that they are treated as a finance lease. A difference may be that the hire purchase seller takes credit not only for finance income, but also for gross profit on the actual sale of the asset.

Summary

SSAP21 is an important contribution in the development of Accounting Standards since it represents the application of commercial substance as the solution to one form of off-balance sheet finance. The important matters which you must appreciate are:

- the problem of reflecting the commercial substance of a transaction rather than strict legal form;

- the distinction between a finance lease and an operating lease.

CHAPTER 14

Taxation in Company Accounts

Objectives

This chapter covers the following performance criteria:

10.2.1 Financial statements are accurately drafted from appropriate information.

10.2.2 Subsequent adjustments are correctly implemented.

10.2.3 Draft accounts comply with domestic standards and legislation and, where relevant, partnership agreement.

At the end of this chapter, you should be able to:

♦ account for and disclose corporation tax, value added tax and deferred tax in the financial statements

♦ understand the nature of deferred taxation

Corporation tax

The basics

Companies pay corporation tax on their profits. The current rate of corporation tax is 30%.

Clearly corporation tax cannot be paid until after the annual profit figure has been found; therefore, when preparing a profit and loss account, a provision must be made for the corporation tax payable on those profits.

Illustration 1

A company makes an operating profit before taxation of £300,000 in the year ended 31 December 19X7. Corporation tax is estimated at £90,000. (Note that in practice the tax will be 30% of *taxable* profits, which will not usually equal *operating* profits.)

Profit and loss account (extract) 19X7

	£
Profit on ordinary activities before taxation	300,000
Tax on profit on ordinary activities	
Corporation tax on income @ 30%	(90,000)
Profit on ordinary activities after taxation	210,000

Corporation tax account

	£		£
Balance c/f	90,000	Profit and loss account	90,000
	90,000		90,000
		Balance b/f	90,000

The balance on the corporation tax account is carried forward and will appear on the balance sheet under the creditors heading.

The full description given in the profit and loss account above is required either on the face of the profit and loss account as shown or in the notes to the accounts.

Due dates for payment

Corporation tax is normally payable nine months after the end of the company's accounting period.

In the profit and loss account above, being to 31 December 19X7, the corporation tax we have identified will be payable on 1 October 19X8.

In the statutory accounts the amount of £90,000 will be included in:

> 'Creditors : amounts falling due within one year'

Within that heading it will be included within the description:

> 'Other creditors including taxation and social security'

Adjustments relating to prior years

When the provision for corporation tax is made in the accounts, it is only an estimate of the actual liability which will eventually be agreed with HM Inspectors of Taxes. Any difference between the original estimate and the actual figure will be adjusted in the next year's charge. If material, this figure will be disclosed separately.

Illustration 1 (continued)

In 1 October 19X8 the company pays £84,000 corporation tax on the 19X7 profit, not the £90,000 as estimated. The profit for the year 19X8 is £400,000 and corporation tax is estimated at £120,000.

Profit and loss account (extract) 19X8

	£	£
Profit on ordinary activities before taxation		400,000
Tax on profit on ordinary activities		
Corporation tax on income @ 30%	120,000	
Adjustment for overprovision in previous year	(6,000)	
		(114,000)
Profit on ordinary activities after taxation		286,000

Corporation tax account

		£			£
1.10.X8	Cash – actual charge	84,000	1.1.X8	Balance b/f – provision	90,000
1.10.X8	Profit and loss account – overprovision	6,000	31.12.X8	Profit and loss account – 19X8 expected charge	120,000
31.12.X8	Balance c/f	120,000	1.1.X9	Balance b/f	
		210,000			120,000
					120,000

Accounting for value added tax

Introduction

VAT is collected by businesses on behalf of the government. VAT is incurred by a business within the price paid for supplies purchased (an input tax) and levied by the business when it charges for goods sold to its customers (an output tax). The difference between the amount levied and the amount incurred is paid quarterly to HM Customs and Excise. The current rate is 17.5%. The eventual payer is the consumer who stands at the end of the manufacturing and distribution chain.

Illustration

Goods purchased for £117.50 – Debit purchases £100, VAT £17.50
Goods sold for £352.50 – Credit sales £300, VAT £52.50

Thus revenue and costs are not affected by VAT, but the net amount (£35) collected for value added by the business and owed to Customs and Excise is shown in the VAT account.

VAT account

	£		£
Input tax on purchases	17.50	Output tax on sales	52.50
Balance due to HM Customs and Excise c/f	35.00		
	52.50		52.50
Cash	35.00	Balance b/f	35.00

The standard

SSAP5 deals with the very straightforward problem which raises no controversy at all. The Standard consists of two short paragraphs which are reproduced below, followed by a brief explanation.

Turnover

Turnover shown in the profit and loss account should exclude VAT on taxable outputs. If it is desirable to show the gross turnover also, the VAT relevant to that turnover should be shown as a deduction in arriving at the turnover exclusive of VAT.

Irrecoverable VAT

Irrecoverable VAT allocable to fixed assets and to other items disclosed separately in published accounts should be included in their cost where practicable and material.

Explanation

Turnover

Since the trader who is registered for VAT is merely acting as a tax collector by adding VAT to his prices and then paying it over to HM Customs and Excise, it is reasonable and correct to exclude the VAT from turnover.

Irrecoverable VAT

When a trader actually bears VAT, it is again reasonable and correct that capital revenue items affected should include that VAT. A trader is unable to offset VAT suffered on his purchases when, for example, he is not registered for VAT.

Accounting for deferred tax

Introduction

There are two types of difference between profits chargeable to corporation tax and profits as stated in the financial statements: permanent differences and timing differences.

Permanent differences

These arise from items of income and expenditure which are never included in arriving at taxable profits (eg. disallowed entertaining).

Timing differences

These arise from items of income and expenditure which are included in both financial statements and tax computations but in different years (eg. capital allowances in excess of related depreciation charges). *Such differences may originate but must, by definition, reverse over a period of time.*

Because of these timing differences, the taxation charge as calculated by the tax authorities may not represent the charge on the accounting profits.

Illustration

A company buys a fixed asset for £20,000 on 1 January 19X1 and disposes of it on 31 December 19X4. Profit before taxation is £50,000 for each of the four years. Details of capital allowances and depreciation are as follows.

	19X1 £	19X2 £	19X3 £	19X4 £
Depreciation	5,000	5,000	5,000	5,000
Capital allowances	8,000	3,000	2,250	6,750

The rate of corporation tax is 30%. If the tax charge were computed on the unadjusted profit before taxation it would be £15,000 for each of the four years.

The actual tax charge for each of the four years is as follows:

	19X1 £	19X2 £	19X3 £	19X4 £
Profit before taxation	50,000	50,000	50,000	50,000
Add back depreciation	5,000	5,000	5,000	5,000
Deduct capital allowances	(8,000)	(3,000)	(2,250)	(6,750)
	47,000	52,000	52,750	48,250
Corporation tax at 30%	14,100	15,600	15,825	14,475

The total amount of tax paid over the four year period is the same amount that would have been paid if the tax charge had been based on accounting profit. However, the timing differences give rise to fluctuations in the *annual* tax charge.

SSAP2 states that a company should match the expenses incurred in a period with profits earned in that period. In order to ensure that the total tax charge relates to accounting profits earned, extra tax can be charged or released through a deferred taxation account.

Deferred tax is the tax attributable to timing differences.

The calculation of deferred tax is beyond the scope of Unit 10. You are only required to understand the concept and to be able to make the accounting entries.

The accounting entries for deferred taxation

In periods when corporation tax is reduced by timing differences, a charge to deferred taxation is made in the profit and loss account and a provision is set up in the balance sheet. The double entry is:

Dr   Deferred tax charge (profit and loss account)
    Cr   Provision for deferred tax (balance sheet)

This increases the tax charge in the profit and loss account.

To reverse the provision, the entries are:

Dr   Provision for deferred tax
    Cr   Deferred tax charge

This has the effect of reducing the tax charge.

Illustration

Profit before taxation for the year ended 31 December 19X1 is £160,000. The corporation tax charge for the year has been estimated at £40,000. The provision for deferred tax brought forward at the start of the year was £60,000. The deferred tax provision is to be increased by £8,000.

How will this information appear in the accounts for the year ended 31 December 19X1?

To increase the deferred tax provision, the following adjustment is required:

Dr   Deferred tax charge   £8,000
    Cr   Provision for deferred tax   £8,000

The information will be disclosed as follows:

Profit and loss account (extract)

	£
Profit on ordinary activities before taxation	160,000
Tax on profit on ordinary activities	(48,000)
Profit on ordinary activities after taxation	112,000

Notes to the profit and loss account

Tax on profit on ordinary activities

	£
Corporation tax on profits	40,000
Deferred taxation	8,000
	48,000

Balance sheet (extract)

Provisions for liabilities and charges

	£
Deferred taxation	68,000

Notes to the balance sheet

Deferred taxation

	£
At 1 January 19X1	60,000
Profit and loss account	8,000
At 31 December 19X1	68,000

Summary

- Disclose the following in the notes to the profit and loss account:

  – Corporation tax on profits for the year

  – Adjustment for under/(over) provision in previous year

- The corporation tax liability is included in:

  Creditors: Amounts falling due within one year:
  Other creditors including taxation and social security

- Turnover should be disclosed in the published accounts net of VAT.

- Deferred tax should be charged/(released) to/(from) the profit and loss account to match the tax charge for a period with profits earned in that period.

CHAPTER 15

Post Balance Sheet Events, Provisions and Contingencies

Objectives

This chapter covers the following performance criteria:

10.2.1 Financial statements are accurately drafted from appropriate information.

10.2.2 Subsequent adjustments are correctly implemented.

10.2.3 Draft accounts comply with domestic standards and legislation and, where relevant, partnership agreement.

At the end of this chapter, you should be able to:

- understand how post balance sheet events, provisions and contingencies should be treated in the profit and loss account and balance sheet

- apply the main principles of SSAP 17 and FRS 12

- disclose information about post balance sheet events, provisions and contingencies in the financial statements

SSAP17: Accounting for post balance sheet events

Introduction

Post balance sheet events are those events, both favourable and unfavourable, which occur between the balance sheet date and the date on which the financial statements are approved by the board of directors.

It is necessary to have a standard on the accounting treatment of post balance sheet events to provide sufficient information for the users of the financial statements.

The explanatory foreword to SSAP17 gives the following reasons for the standard:

> 'Events arising after the balance sheet date need to be reflected in financial statements if they provide additional evidence of conditions that existed at the balance sheet date and materially affect the amounts to be included.

> 'To prevent financial statements from being misleading, disclosure needs to be made by way of notes of other material events arising after the balance sheet date which provide evidence of conditions not existing at the balance sheet date. Disclosure is required where the information is necessary for a proper understanding of the financial position.'

Types of event

The standard distinguishes two types of post balance sheet event: *adjusting events* and *non-adjusting events*.

Adjusting events

These require the accounts to be adjusted to reflect their impact. They are defined as being 'post balance sheet events which provide additional evidence of conditions existing at the balance sheet date'.

Such events are relevant because they relate to items appearing in the accounts or transactions reported in them.

Examples of these, given in the appendix of SSAP17, are as follows.

- *Fixed assets* – The subsequent determination of the purchase price or of the proceeds of sale of assets purchased or sold before the year-end.

- *Property* – A valuation which provides evidence of an impairment in value.

- *Investments* – The receipt of a copy of the financial statements or other information in respect of an unlisted company which provides evidence of an impairment in the value of a long-term investment.

- *Stocks and work in progress*

    (i) The receipt of proceeds of sales after the balance sheet date or other evidence concerning the realisable value of stocks.

    (ii) The receipt of evidence that the previous estimate of accrued profit on a long-term contract was materially inaccurate.

- *Debtors* – The renegotiation of amounts owing by debtors or the insolvency of a debtor.

- *Dividends receivable* – The declaration of dividends by subsidiaries relating to periods prior to the balance sheet date of the holding company.

- *Taxation* – The receipt of information regarding rates of taxation.

- *Claims* – Amounts received or receivable in respect of insurance claims which were in the course of negotiation at the balance sheet date.

- *Discoveries* – The discovery of errors or frauds which show that the financial statements were incorrect.

Non-adjusting events

These are merely noted in the accounts *if material*. They are post balance sheet events which concern conditions which did not exist at the balance sheet date. Consequently they do not result in changes in amounts in financial statements. They may, however, be of such materiality that their disclosure is required by way of notes to ensure that the financial statements are not misleading.

Examples of these, given in the appendix to SSAP17, are as follows.

- Mergers and acquisitions

- Reconstructions and proposed reconstructions

- Issues of shares and debentures

- Purchase and sale of fixed assets and investments

- Losses of fixed assets or stocks as a result of a catastrophe such as a fire or flood

- Opening new trading activities or extending existing trading activities

- Closing a significant part of the trading activities if this was not anticipated at the year-end

- Decline in the value of property and investments held as fixed assets, if it can be demonstrated that the decline occurred after the year-end

- Government action, such as nationalisation

- Strikes and other labour disputes

Window-dressing

The balance sheet is a 'snapshot' of the affairs of the business at a particular moment. This does not necessarily mean that it shows the typical financial position throughout the year. For example, if a business makes most of its sales in the period shortly before Christmas, debtors are likely to be at their highest and stocks are likely to be at their lowest on 31 December.

A business may enter into transactions which are *primarily undertaken* to improve the appearance of the balance sheet. After the year-end, these transactions may reverse. This practice is known as *window-dressing*.

Under SSAP17, a material post balance sheet event should be disclosed where it is the reversal or maturity of a transaction which was entered into primarily to alter the appearance of the company's balance sheet.

Disclosure requirements

- Financial statements should be prepared on the basis of conditions existing at the balance sheet date and should disclose the date they were approved by the board of directors.

- A material post balance sheet event requires changes in the amounts to be included in financial statements where:

    – it is an adjusting event; or

    – it indicates that application of the going concern concept to the whole or a material part of the company is not appropriate.

This second point considers the situation where post year-end events indicate that the company is no longer a going concern. Clearly the accounts will need to be adjusted if they were originally prepared on a going concern basis.

- A material post balance sheet event should only be disclosed where:

    - it is a non-adjusting event of such materiality that its non-disclosure would affect the ability of the users of financial statements to reach a proper understanding of the financial position; or

    - it is the reversal or maturity after the year-end of a transaction entered into before the year-end, the substance of which was primarily to alter the appearance of the company's balance sheet (ie. a 'window-dressing' transaction).

In respect of each post balance sheet event which is required to be disclosed, the following information should be stated by way of notes in financial statements:

- the nature of the event; and

- an estimate of the financial effect, or a statement that it is not practicable to make such an estimate.

Companies Act 1985

The Companies Act 1985 requires disclosure of particulars of any important events affecting the company or any of its subsidiaries which have occurred since the end of that year.

This disclosure required by the Act is to be contained in the directors' report; SSAP17 on the other hand requires that these items be shown as a note to the accounts. Accordingly, there is likely to be some duplication of disclosure and it will not be sufficient for the directors' report merely to refer to the appropriate note in the accounts.

The Companies Act makes no distinction between adjusting and non-adjusting events.

FRS 12: Provisions, contingent liabilities and contingent assets

Provisions

Preparers of accounts often have to exercise judgement in conditions of uncertainty. For example, a legal claim may have been lodged against a company and the situation may not have been resolved at the time that the accounts are finalised. In a situation like this, the directors must estimate the likelihood of the claim succeeding and the amount that the company will have to pay if this happens. The prudence concept requires that all known liabilities are provided for whether or not the amount is known with certainty. Therefore if the directors believe that they will have to pay material damages a provision will be made in the financial statements.

Provisions may have to be made where:

- a company has guaranteed the completion of a contract or the borrowings of another entity;

- products have been sold with warranties to make good any defects;

- a business has to clean up environmental damage that it has caused.

You will be familiar with 'provisions' for depreciation and for doubtful debts. These are not true provisions, but normal accounting estimates.

FRS 12 covers all provisions which are not covered by another accounting standard. For example, provisions for future losses on long term contracts are required by SSAP 9.

Definitions

FRS 12 defines a *provision* as a liability of uncertain timing or amount. A *liability* is an obligation to transfer economic benefits as a result of past transactions or events. Uncertainty is what distinguishes a provision from another type of liability (such as a trade creditor or an accrued expense). The important word here is *obligation*.

An obligation can be:

- legal (deriving from a contract, legislation or other operation of law); or
- constructive.

A *constructive obligation* occurs where:

- an entity indicates that it will accept certain responsibilities (for example, by past practice, published policies or statements); and

- as a result, the entity has created a valid expectation on the part of those other parties that it will discharge those responsibilities.

For example, a store has a policy of refunding purchases by dissatisfied customers, even though it is not legally obliged to do so and this policy is generally known. The store has a constructive obligation to make refunds.

Recognition

Three conditions must be met before a provision can be recognised.

- An entity has a present obligation as a result of a past event. (This is the case if it is *more likely than not* that a present obligation exists at the balance sheet date).

- It is probable that a transfer of economic benefits will be required to settle the obligation. (Again, probable means *more likely than not*.)

- A reliable estimate can be made of the amount of the obligation. (Only in extremely rare cases will this not be possible.)

The amount recognised should be the best estimate of the expenditure required to settle the present obligation at the balance sheet date.

A provision should only be used for expenditures for which it was originally recognised.

Provisions should not be recognised for future operating losses. These do not meet the definition of a liability.

Contingent liabilities

A *contingent liability* is:

- a possible obligation that arises from past events and whose existence will be confirmed only by the occurrence of one or more uncertain future events not wholly within the entity's control; or

- a present obligation that arises from past events but is not recognised because;

    - it is not probable that a transfer of economic benefits will be required to settle the obligation; or

    - the amount of the obligation cannot be measured with sufficient reliability.

Because it is only possible, not probable, that the expenditure will actually be incurred, contingent liabilities are not recognised. In other words, no provision is made for them. However, users of the financial statements need to be aware of their existence, so that they can make informed judgements on the basis of the financial statements. Information about contingent liabilities is disclosed in the financial statements unless the possibility of a transfer of economic benefits is remote.

Contingent assets

A *contingent asset* is a possible asset that arises from past events and whose existence will be confirmed only by the occurrence of one or more uncertain future events not wholly within the entity's control.

Contingent assets should not be recognised, because it is not prudent to do so. If the possibility of an inflow of economic benefits is probable they should be disclosed.

If a gain is virtually certain it represents an actual asset, rather than a contingent asset. Therefore it should be recognised.

Disclosure

For each class of provision, disclose:

- carrying amount at the beginning and end of the period
- additional provisions made in the period
- amounts used during the period; and
- unused amounts reversed during the period.

There should also be disclosed:

- a brief description of the nature of the obligation and expected timing of any resulting transfers of economic benefit; and

- an indication of the uncertainties about the amount or timing of those transfers of economic benefit.

For each class of contingent liability and for probable contingent assets disclose:

- a brief description of the nature of the liability;
- an estimate of its financial effect; and
- an indication of the uncertainties relating to the amount or timing of any outflow.

Disclosures are not required if the possibility of a transfer of economic benefits is remote.

Companies Act 1985

The Companies Act 1985 requires information to be given with respect to the amount, or estimated amount, of any contingent liability not provided for, its legal nature and any valuable security provided.

Questions

1 Trunfair Ltd

The directors of Trunfair Ltd, a trading company, are about to approve the company's financial statements for the year ended 31 July 19X3.

Since the financial statements were originally prepared, the following material information has become available:

(1) On 15 September 19X3 torrential rain caused flooding at the company's riverside warehouse resulting in an uninsured stock loss totalling £200,000.

(2) Year-end debtors included £120,000 owed by a customer who went into liquidation on 16 September 19X3. The invoice was dated 15 July 19X3.

Required

Advise the directors on the effect the above information should have on the financial statements for the year ended 31 July 19X3, giving your reasons.

Summary

Post balance sheet events

Does the event provide additional evidence of *conditions existing at the balance sheet date*?

- If so, you must *adjust* the financial statements.
- If not, you must *disclose* the event (if it is material).

Provisions and contingent liabilities

Do *all* the following conditions exist?

- There is a present *obligation* as the result of a past event; and
- a transfer of economic benefits is *probable*; and
- a reliable estimate can be made of the amount of the obligation.

If so, recognise a provision. Otherwise, there is a contingent liability if:

- there is a present obligation, but a transfer of economic benefits is only possible; or
- there is a *possible* obligation as the result of a past event; or
- there is a present obligation and a transfer of economic benefits is probable but no reliable estimate can be made of the amount of the obligation.

Contingent liabilities are *disclosed* unless the possibility of a transfer of economic benefits is *remote*.

Contingent assets

The treatment depends on the likelihood of an inflow of economic benefits;

- Virtually certain   Recognise (because *not* contingent)
- Probable   Do not recognise, but disclose
- Possible or remote   Do nothing.

CHAPTER 16

Cash Flow Statements

Objectives

This chapter covers the following performance criteria:

10.2.1 Financial statements are accurately drafted from appropriate information.

10.2.3 Draft accounts comply with domestic standards and legislation and, where relevant, partnership agreement.

10.2.4 A cash flow statement is correctly prepared and interpreted where required

At the end of this chapter, you should be able to

- prepare a cash flow statement
- interpret a cash flow statement
- discuss the advantages of cash flow information for the user of the financial statements

The purpose of the cash flow statement

Accruals accounting deliberately removes the effect of *cashflows* from the profit and loss account. It is important, however, for users of financial statements to get information about the amount of cash available to and required by an enterprise.

Cash is of great importance to the continuing existence of an enterprise. For instance, cash is needed to pay existing liabilities (including corporation tax) and to fund future investment (including the purchase of fixed assets).

The cash flow statement looks at the cash inflows and outflows of a business in a particular accounting period.

Basic illustration

Let us consider Rathbone Ltd, a company which operates entirely on a cash basis.

The profit and loss account for the first year of trading was:

	£
Sales	500
Costs	300
	200

From this, we can assume that the cash balance of the company will have increased by £200 at the end of the year.

Let us now suppose that the sales had been made on credit and at the year-end there were debtors of £50. The cash balance would have increased by £150 [(500 – 50) – 300].

We could reconcile the profit for the year with the increase in cash.

	£
Profit for the year	200
Increase in debtors	(50)
Increase in cash (450 – 300)	150

In addition let us now suppose that the purchases had been made on credit and that £30 was outstanding at the year-end.

	£
Profit for the year	200
Increase in debtors	(50)
Increase in creditors	30
Increase in cash (450 – 270)	180

Finally let us suppose that there was stock of £20 on hand at the year-end, ie:

	£
Costs: Purchases	320
Closing stock	(20)
	300

The reconciliation would then be:

	£
Profit for the year	200
Increase in debtors	(50)
Increase in creditors	30
Increase in stock	(20)
Increase in cash (450 – 290)	160

There might, however, be other cash inflows and outflows. Suppose the company issued some share capital during the year and bought a fixed asset for cash. Our statement would then look like this:

	£
Profit for the year	200
Increase in debtors	(50)
Increase in creditors	30
Increase in stock	(20)
	160
Issue of share capital	150
Payments to purchase fixed assets	(80)
Increase in cash (450 – 290 + 150 – 80)	230

This is a basic cash flow statement.

Cash

Definition

Cash comprises cash in hand and deposits repayable on demand less overdrafts repayable on demand.

Cash inflows and outflows

Cash inflows and outflows are shown under seven headings.

Operating activities

The main source of cash inflow for most businesses is its operating activities.

Returns on investments and servicing of finance

This heading covers the payments made to providers of finance, excluding dividends paid to equity shareholders which are shown separately.

It also covers receipts from third parties for whom the business provides finance.

Taxation

This heading covers payments of tax.

Capital expenditure and financial investment

Payments for the purchase of fixed assets and receipts from the sale of fixed assets are included under this heading.

Equity dividends paid

This heading covers the payments made to ordinary shareholders by way of dividend.

Management of liquid resources

Liquid resources are current asset investments which are readily disposable without causing disruption to the business. They must also be either readily convertible into known amounts of cash at or close to the carrying amount or traded in an active market.

This heading, therefore, includes payments to or withdrawals from short term deposits and payments to acquire or receipts from selling liquid investments.

Financing

This heading deals with receipts and repayments of capital and long-term loans.

Example – inflows and outflows

Limited company	Sole trader or partnership
Operating activities	
Profit before interest and tax, adjusted to remove accruals effect	Net profit adjusted to remove accruals effect
Returns on investments and servicing of finance	
Preference dividends paid Interest paid and received Dividends received	Drawings Interest paid and received Dividends received
Taxation	
Corporation tax paid	For businesses, other than companies, tax is assessed on the individual owners, not the business itself
Capital expenditure and financial investment	
Purchase of fixed assets	Purchase of fixed assets
Sale of fixed assets	Sale of fixed assets
Purchase or sale of investments which are not liquid resources	Purchase or sale of investments which are not liquid resources
Equity dividends paid	
Dividends paid to ordinary shareholders	Not applicable as there are no shareholders
Management of liquid resources	
Payments into short term deposits Payments to acquire liquid investments	Payments into short term deposits Payments to acquire liquid investments
Withdrawals from short term deposits Receipts from selling liquid investments	Withdrawals from short term deposits Receipts from selling liquid investments
Financing	
Issue of shares Issue of debentures Raising of long-term loans	Raising of long-term loans Capital introduced by owners
Payment and redemption of share capital Redemption of debentures Repayment of long-term loans	Repayment of long-term loans Repayment of capital

Format of the cash flow statement

Financial Reporting Standard 1 (FRS1) (Revised 1996) deals with cash flow statements. It prescribes the following format:

Pro forma per FRS1 (Revised)

Pro forma cash flow statement for the year ended 31 March 19X2 for a single company with required supporting notes

Reconciliation of operating profit to net cash inflow from operating activities

	£
Operating profit	X
Depreciation charges	X
Increase in stocks	(X)
Increase in debtors	(X)
Increase in creditors	X
Net cash inflow from operating activities	A

CASH FLOW STATEMENT

	£	£
Net cash inflow from operating activities		A
Returns on investments and servicing of finance		
Interest received	X	
Interest paid	(X)	
		(X)
Taxation		(X)
Capital expenditure		
Payments to acquire intangible fixed assets	(X)	
Payments to acquire tangible fixed assets	(X)	
Receipts from sales of tangible fixed assets	X	
		(X)
Equity dividends paid		(X)
		X
Management of liquid resources		
Purchase of treasury bills	(X)	
Sale of treasury bills	X	
		(B)
Financing		
Issue of ordinary share capital	X	
Repurchase of debenture loan	(C)	
Expenses paid in connection with share issues	(X)	
		X
Increase in cash		D

Reconciliation of net cash flow to movement in net debt (note)

	£	£
Increase in cash in the period	D	
Cash to repurchase debenture	C	
Cash used to increase liquid resources	B	
Change in net debt		X
Net debt at 1 April 19X1		(X)
Net debt at 31 March 19X2		(X)

Note: Analysis of changes in net debt

	At 1 April 19X1 £	Cash flows £	Other changes £	At 31 March 19X2 £
Cash in hand, at bank	X	X		X
Overdrafts	(X)	X		–
		D		
Debt due within 1 year	(X)	C	(X)	(X)
Debt due after 1 year	(X)		X	(X)
Current asset investments	X	B		X
Total	X	X	X	X

Explanatory notes to the pro forma

♦ *Net cash inflow from operating activities*

In the pro forma, the net cashflow has been reported. However, gross cash inflows and outflows may also be shown. If this additional information is disclosed, it appears on the face of the cash flow statement.

	£	£
Operating activities		
Cash received from customers	X	
Cash payments to suppliers	(X)	
Cash paid to and on behalf of employees	(X)	
Other cash payments	(X)	
Net cash inflow from operating activities		A

This analysis appears on the face of the cash flow statement. This is sometimes known as the *direct method* of preparing a cash flow statement.

- *Reconciliation of operating profit to net cash inflow from operating activities*

    This reconciliation showing separately the movements in stocks, debtors and creditors relating to operating activities and other differences between cashflows and profits (eg. depreciation) may be given either immediately above the cash flow statement or as a note. It should always be presented separately from the cash flow statement itself and clearly labelled.

- *Reconciliation of net cash flows to movement in net debt*

    Net debt comprises borrowings less cash and liquid resources.

    If cash and liquid resources together exceed debt then it is classified as net funds.

    The reconciliation analyses changes in net debt from b/f to c/f component amounts showing separately those arising from

    - the entity's cash flows
    - other non-cash changes
    - recognition of changes in market value.

    This reconciliation may either be presented below the cash flow statement or as a note.

Exceptional and extraordinary items

Cashflows relating to exceptional items or extraordinary items should be shown under the appropriate standard headings according to their nature.

In both cases, the nature of the cashflows should be disclosed in a note so as to explain the effect of the underlying transactions on the entity's cashflows.

Where cash flows are exceptional because of their size or incidence but are not related to items treated as exceptional or extraordinary in the profit and loss account, sufficient disclosure should be given to explain their cause and nature.

Major non-cash transactions

If a company has undertaken a material transaction which has not resulted in movements of cash – for example, the inception of a finance lease or an exchange of assets – this should not appear in the cash flow statement. However, sufficient disclosure should be given so that the underlying transaction may be understood.

Preparation of the cash flow statement

The practical preparation of a cash flow statement using the FRS1 pro forma is looked at below.

Example

The draft accounts of Precipitate Ltd for the year ended 30 April 19X7 are set out below:

Balance sheet at 30 April 19X7

	19X7 £'000	19X6 £'000
Fixed assets (Note)	491	643
Current assets		
Stocks	893	688
Trade debtors	793	608
Cash at bank and in hand	7	10
	1,693	1,306
Creditors due within one year		
Trade creditors	583	563
Dividends proposed	62	28
Taxation	44	12
	(689)	(603)
Creditors due after more than one year		
Loans and debentures	(416)	(555)
	1,079	791
Share capital	820	720
Profit and loss account	259	71
	1,079	791

Note

Fixed assets

	£'000
(1) Freehold property	
At cost 30 April 19X6	455
At cost 30 April 19X7	340

Properties which originally cost £235,000 were sold during the year for £425,000.

(2) Plant and equipment

	Cost £'000	Depreciation £'000
On 30 April 19X6	282	94
Additions at cost	53	
Disposals	(109)	(25)
Provision for the year		6
On 30 April 19X7	226	75

Profit and loss account for the year ended 30 April 19X7

	19X7 £'000	19X7 £'000	19X6 £'000	19X6 £'000
Turnover		2,930		1,563
Less: Directors' emoluments	70		70	
Auditors' remuneration	6		5	
Interest on loans and debentures	39		46	
Depreciation	6		5	
Other operating expenses	2,724		1,431	
		(2,845)		(1,557)
Net trading profit		85		6
Profit on sale of fixed assets		205		–
		290		6
Taxation		(40)		(2)
		250		4
Proposed dividend		(62)		(28)
Retained profit for year		188		(24)
Balance brought forward		71		95
Balance carried forward		259		71

Step 1

To prepare the cash flow statement, we should start with the reconciliation of operating profit to net cash inflow from operating activities.

We are here trying to find by how much the cash balance has increased due to our operating activities.

To do this, we start with operating profit and firstly take out all items which will have no impact on cash (eg. depreciation and the increase in stocks during the year) and secondly, remove any increase in debtors and creditors during the year.

The reconciliation will appear as follows:

Reconciliation of operating profit to net cash inflow from operating activities

	£'000
Operating profit (85 + 39)	124
Depreciation charge	6
Increase in stocks	(205)
Increase in debtors	(185)
Increase in creditors	20
	(240)

We now have the first figure to go on the face of our cash flow statement.

Step 2

Next we need to calculate the dividend paid, interest paid and tax paid. The best approach is to use a T-account to work out cash paid in the year:

Dividends

	£'000		£'000
Cash paid in year (balancing figure)	28	b/f (per balance sheet)	28
c/f (per balance sheet)	62	Proposed in year (per profit and loss account)	62

Taxation

	£'000		£'000
Tax paid	8	b/f (per balance sheet)	12
c/f (per balance sheet)	44	Charge (per profit and loss account)	40

The interest paid is £39,000 per the profit and loss account as there is no creditor at the start or end of the year.

Step 3

The fixed asset note needs to be looked at next. During the year, freehold property and plant have been disposed of. In our cash flow statement we need to determine the *cash proceeds of sale*.

	£'000
Proceeds of sale of freehold (per question)	425
Profit on sale of freehold (425 – 235)	190
∴ Profit on sale of plant (205 – 190)	15

	£'000
Proceeds of sale of plant	
NBV (109 – 25)	84
Add: Profit on sale	15
	99

Therefore total proceeds on sale of fixed assets (99 + 425) = 524

The *payments to acquire fixed assets* can be found as follows:

	£'000
Freehold property	
Cost at 30.4.X6	455
Disposal	(235)
Purchases (balancing figure)	120
Cost at 30.4.X7	340
Plant and equipment (per question)	53

Step 4

Finally, the financing section needs completion. It can be seen from the question that loans of £139,000 [£555,000 – £416,000] have been repaid and that cash of £100,000 has been received from the issue of shares (£820,000 – £720,000).

We can now put the statement together and complete the notes as follows:

Precipitate Ltd
Cash flow statement for the year ended 30 April 19X7

Reconciliation of operating profit to net cash outflow from operating activities

	£'000
Operating profit	124
Depreciation charge	6
Increase in stocks	(205)
Increase in debtors	(185)
Increase in creditors	20
Net cash outflow from operating activities	(240)

CASH FLOW STATEMENT

	£'000	£'000
Net cash outflow from operating activities (Note 1)		(240)
Returns on investments and servicing of finance		
Interest paid		(39)
Taxation		(8)
Capital expenditure		
Payments to acquire tangible fixed assets (120 + 53)	(173)	
Receipts from sales of tangible fixed assets (425 + 99)	524	
		351
Equity dividends paid		(28)
		36
Financing		
Issue of ordinary share capital	100	
Repayment of loan and debentures	(139)	
		(39)
Decrease in cash		(3)

Reconciliation of net cash flow to movement in net debt (note)

	£'000	£'000
Decrease in cash in the period	(3)	
Repayment of loans and debentures	139	
Change in net debt		136
Net debt at 1 May 19X6		(545)
Net debt at 30 April 19X7		(409)

Note:

Analysis of changes in net debt

	At 1 May 19X6 £'000	Cash flows £'000	At 30 April 19X7 £'000
Cash at bank and in hand	10	(3)	7
Debt due after 1 year	(555)	139	(416)
Balance at 30 April 19X7	(545)	136	(409)

Interpreting a cash flow statement

Interpreting a cash flow statement is usually reasonably straightforward. As we have seen, the headings in the cash flow statement show the different categories of cash flows and therefore enable the user to understand the reasons for a net inflow or outflow of cash.

Look at the cash flow statement of Precipitate Ltd. We will use this as an illustration.

Net cash inflow/outflow

An increase or decrease of cash should be interpreted in the context of the entity's cash and bank balances. These are given in the note analysing changes in net debt. For example:

- Does the entity have positive or negative cash balances?
- How material is the increase/decrease in relation to total cash balances?

A decrease in cash is not necessarily a bad sign. For example, there may have been an unusually high cash balance at the beginning of the period.

Precipitate Ltd has a net cash outflow of £3,000 for the year ended 30 April 19X7. Cash at bank and in hand has fallen from £10,000 to £7,000. There is not bank overdraft. On the basis of this information alone, the company does not appear to be experiencing cash flow problems.

Operating activities

The note reconciling operating profit to net cash flow from operating activities enables us to compare these two figures and gives us information about the possible reasons for the difference. If an entity is going to survive it must be both profitable and generate cash in the long term.

Signs that an entity may have serious cash flow problems are:

- high profits with material cash outflows
- material increases in stocks, debtors and creditors.

Precipitate Ltd appears to be in exactly this situation. Although operating profits are £142,000, the cash outflow is £240,000, almost twice that amount. The reason for this is that debtors and stocks have increased dramatically in the year. Creditors have only increased by £20,000. Either the company's operations are expanding rapidly, (which often gives rise to cash flow problems in the short term) or stock levels and credit control are badly managed. The fact that there is a net cash outflow from operations and that it is significant in the context of the other figures suggests that the company may experience serious cash flow problems in the near future.

Return on investments and servicing of finance and taxation

If an entity has financed its operations by issuing debentures or by borrowing, cash must be available to pay the interest, otherwise its creditors have the power to recall the loans. This will probably result in its liquidation. An entity cannot avoid paying corporation tax on its profits. Operating activities should normally generate enough cash for both these payments.

Precipitate Ltd has paid loan and debenture interest of £39,000 and taxation of £8,000. These were not covered by cash from operating activities. As it still has long term loans, it will have to continue to pay interest in future periods. Because profits for the current year are high, the taxation charge will be significantly greater next year.

Capital expenditure and financial investment

In order to generate profit and cash, entities need to invest in assets. Therefore a cash outflow on capital expenditure is usually a healthy sign. It means that there will probably be increased profits and cash inflows from operations in the long term. It is important to notice how the entity has financed the investment. The main possibilities are:

- operating activities
- a share issue
- borrowing (long term loans or debentures)
- increasing short term finance (eg overdraft).

Typically finance comes from more than one source. Investment financed from operating activities and/or a share issue probably indicates financial health. Investment from borrowing is normally acceptable as long as the entity can meet the interest payments. Capital investment should not normally be financed by increasing the overdraft.

Although Precipitate Ltd has purchased tangible fixed assets costing £173,000, it has generated a cash inflow of £524,000 by selling assets. As there have been material cash outflows during the year, it is possible that this may have been done as an emergency measure to raise cash. If this is the case, it is a bad sign. Firstly, the company has reduced its fixed assets at a time when it appears to be expanding rapidly. It is unlikely that profits can be maintained (and cash generated) unless there is more capital expenditure in the near future. Secondly, the fact that the company has had to take this action suggests that it has not been possible to raise finance from other sources.

Equity dividends paid

Equity dividends, unlike interest, do not have to be paid. An entity can take the availability of cash, as well as the level of profit, into account when proposing dividends.

Precipitate Ltd's cash outflow from equity dividends is £28,000, which is covered by the cash inflow from capital expenditure. However, the dividend for the current year is significantly larger (because profits have risen) and will have to be paid in the near future.

Management of liquid resources and financing

This section shows whether and how the entity has raised finance from external sources and how it has managed its current asset investments. This information should be interpreted in the context of the needs of the entity and the overall level of net funds or net debt. The reconciliation of net debt and the analysis of movements in net debt (if they are available) give useful additional information. The important questions to ask are:

- Does the entity need additional finance?
- If so, how could it be obtained?
- Can the entity service/repay its finance?
- Is net debt/net funds increasing or decreasing?

Because Precipitate Ltd has raised cash by selling fixed assets, it actually has a net cash inflow of £64,000 before financing, but it has a net cash outflow of £39,000 from financing. This has arisen because it has repaid long term loans of £139,000. Given the company's current situation, the reason for this is not clear. The analysis note shows that all debt is due after one year.

Precipitate Ltd has also issued ordinary shares, giving rise to a cash inflow of £100,000. As it is a private company, it is unlikely that it can raise any more finance in this way. At 30 April 19X7, the company still has net debt of £409,000. There are no liquid resources.

Conclusion

Although Precipitate Ltd has a positive cash balance at 30 April 19X7 and there has been only a small decrease in cash during the year, it appears to be suffering severe cash flow problems, possibly as a result of over expansion. Although the company is profitable, it has a net cash outflow of £240,000 from operating activities and has had to significantly reduce its fixed asset base in order to generate cash. Its prospects for raising further finance from equity or from debt appear to be poor.

For the purpose of this illustration, we have assumed that the only information available is the cash flow statements and notes. In practice, a cash flow statement should always be analysed in conjunction with the balance sheets and profit and loss account if these are provided. All the primary financial statements articulate to give a complete picture of the financial performance, position and financial adaptability of an entity.

Further points

The purpose of this section is to explain how certain specific situations are treated in the cash flow statement.

Provision for doubtful debts

This is not an unusual item but its treatment in the cash flow statement warrants consideration.

You will recall that the profit and loss account charge for depreciation, loss on disposal of fixed assets etc. is added back to the profit before tax to calculate cashflow from operating activities.

The charge for increasing the provision for doubtful debts is not added back in this way. This is because the provision will reduce debtors and hence any adjustment will be effected through the movement in debtors.

Fixed asset revaluations

These need to be considered in calculating how much *cash* was spent on acquiring fixed assets.

It is permissible to revalue fixed assets. The double entry (ignoring depreciation) is:

Dr	Fixed asset		X	
	Cr	Revaluation reserve		X

The revaluation reserve does not pass through the profit and loss account but goes directly to the balance sheet.

Example

Extracts from the balance sheet of Don Ltd show:

	19X1 £	19X0 £
Fixed assets at cost/valuation	150	100
Revaluation reserve	20	–

There were no disposals of fixed assets.

How much was spent on fixed assets?

A T-account approach is the most effective.

Fixed assets

	£		£
Balance b/f	100		
Revaluation	20		
Cash	30	Balance c/f	150
	150		150

- ♦ Fixed assets have increased by £50.

- ♦ £20 of the increase is the result of a revaluation.

- ♦ Therefore £30 cash must have been spent on fixed assets. This is the figure that will appear in the cash flow statement.

Advantages of producing a cash flow statement

- The cash flow statement focuses attention on *cash*. A business has to generate cash in order to remain viable.

- The cash flow statement gives indications of *liquidity* and *viability*. (It is possible for companies to fail due to lack of cash while apparently generating profits.)

- It gives indications of *financial adaptability* (eg. ability to generate cash by selling assets or raising additional capital).

- The profit and loss account and the balance sheet are prepared on *accruals basis* and are therefore to some extent *subjective*. They may be affected by an entity's choice of accounting policies. Cash flows are a matter of *fact* and difficult to manipulate.

- The note reconciling operating profit to net cash flow from operating activities highlights techniques which enhance profit performance with no cash flow advantage (eg. pre-acquisition write-downs). The cash flow statement shows how much cash has actually been generated from operating activities and therefore an entity's *ability to turn profit into cash*.

- Cash flow information has *predictive value* (cash flow is likely to have many common components from year to year).

Criticisms of the cash flow statement

- The additional disclosure of gross cash flows (the direct method) is *optional*. Most businesses *will not report them*, therefore depriving users of accounts (and themselves) of vital information.

- Current cash flows *may not be a reliable indicator of future cash flows* (eg. material items accrued/prepaid may result in cash flows and will not appear in the statement).

Questions

1 Lucy Ltd   (AAT Pilot CA D94)

Data

You are employed in the business services department of a firm of chartered accountants. The directors of Lucy Ltd have approached your firm for assistance with the preparation of a cash flow statement.

A trainee in the firm has produced a cash flow statement for the year ended 31 March 1994 for Lucy Ltd.

Cash flow statement of Lucy Ltd for year ended 31 March 1994

	£	£
Net cash inflow from operating activities		75,000
Returns on investments and servicing of finance		
Dividends paid		(7,500)
Taxation		(35,000)
Investing activities		
Interest paid	4,500	
Payments to acquire fixed assets	9,500	
		(14,000)
Financing		
Loan repayment		5,000
Increase in cash		23,500

Further information

(1) A fixed asset which originally cost £10,000 and was 40% depreciated was sold for £15,000 during the year. This amount has yet to be included.

(2) An issue of shares was made on the last day of the period. The shares are £1 nominal value ordinary shares. They were issued at a 50p premium; 50% of the issue price was paid on application. The total number of shares issued (application monies received in full) was 100,000.

Assessment tasks

Task 1

Make any adjustments to the cash flow statement prepared by the trainee that you consider necessary, taking into account the further information provided.

Task 2

List FOUR advantages of cash flow accounting.

Task 3

From what would the differences between operating profit and net cash flow from operating activities normally arise?

Summary

A cash flow statement shows the *cash inflows* and *cash outflows* in a business during an accounting period.

It also shows the increase or decrease in *cash*.

Cash flows are divided into seven categories:

- operating activities
- returns on investments and servicing of finance
- taxation
- capital expenditure and financial investment
- equity dividends paid
- management of liquid resources
- financing

CHAPTER 17

Interpretation of Accounts

Objectives

This chapter covers the following performance criteria:

10.1.4 The relationship between elements of limited company financial statements is interpreted.

10.1.5 Unusual features or significant issues are identified within financial statements.

10.1.6 Valid conclusions are drawn from the information contained within financial statements.

10.1.7 Conclusions and interpretations are clearly presented.

At the end of this chapter, you should be able to:

- calculate profitability, liquidity and gearing ratios
- interpret the results of these calculations
- understand the need to disclose segmental information

Introduction

Financial statements are prepared primarily for the members of the business, but they will inevitably be used by other interested parties.

Present and potential investors (and their advisers) will want to know whether the business is a good investment.

Lenders and suppliers will want to know if the business is a good credit risk.

The government will want to make sure that the correct amount of tax is being paid.

As part of their analysis, they will almost certainly calculate ratios, ie. they will relate one figure in the accounts to another.

Note: A ratio in itself is meaningless – we need a benchmark to judge it against. Typical benchmarks include the performances of comparable enterprises, previous period's performance and the budget.

Calculations

To help you understand and then remember the various calculations, a set of figures is presented below. As you meet each ratio, work it out on the basis of these figures and then check your answer with ours. Don't at this stage attempt to draw any conclusions; these figures are only to give you practice in calculation.

JG Ltd
Summarised balance sheet at 31 December 19X1

	£'000	£'000
Fixed assets, at cost, less depreciation		2,600
Current assets		
Stocks	600	
Debtors	900	
Balance at bank	100	
	1,600	
Creditors: Amounts falling due within one year	800	
		800
		3,400
Creditors: Amounts falling due after more than one year		
Debenture stock		(1,400)
		2,000
Capital and reserves		
Ordinary share capital (£1 shares)		1,000
Preference share capital		200
Profit and loss account		800
		2,000

Summarised profit and loss account for the year ended 31 December 19X1

	£'000
Turnover	6,000
Cost of sales	(4,000)
Gross profit	2,000
Operating expenses	(1,660)
Net trading profit	340
Debenture interest	(74)
Profit before tax	266
Taxation	(106)
	160
Preference dividend	(10)
Profit available for ordinary shareholders	150

Profitability

- **Return on capital employed (return on assets)**

    Capital employed is normally measured as capital and reserves plus long-term liabilities; it represents the long-term investment in the business.

    Return on capital employed is frequently regarded as the best measure of profitability, indicating how successful a business is in utilising its assets. This ratio is only meaningful when the true values of assets are known and used in the formula.

    Return on capital employed

    $$= \frac{\text{Profit before interest and taxation}}{\text{Capital employed}} \times 100$$

    $$= \frac{£}{£} \times 100 \qquad \text{(fill in the figures yourself)}$$

    A low return on capital employed is caused by either a low profit margin or a low asset turnover or both. These two factors are measured as follows:

- **Net profit margin (on sales)**

    $$\text{Margin} = \frac{\text{Net profit before interest and taxation}}{\text{Turnover}} \times 100$$

    $$= \frac{£}{£} \times 100$$

    A low margin indicates low selling prices or high costs or both. Comparative analysis will reveal the level of prices and costs in relation to competitors'.

- **Asset turnover**

    This will show how fully a company is utilising its assets.

    $$\text{Asset turnover} = \frac{\text{Turnover}}{\text{Capital employed}}$$

    $$= \frac{£}{£} \times 100$$

    A low turnover shows that a company is not generating a sufficient volume of business for the size of the asset investment. This may be remedied by increasing sales or by disposing of some of the assets or both.

- **Gross profit margin**

    This ratio isolates the pure 'nuts and bolts' of a business, ie. ignoring indirect expenses and sundry income.

    $$\text{Margin} = \frac{\text{Gross profit}}{\text{Sales}} \times 100$$

    $$= \frac{£}{£} \times 100$$

    A low margin indicates a similar position to a low net profit margin, but the causes can be traced more readily to trends in sales and cost of sales.

- **Stock turnover**

    This ratio indicates whether a business's stocks are justified in relation to its sales. If stock turnover falls, this may indicate excess stocks or sluggish sales.

    $$\text{Stock turnover} = \frac{\text{Cost of sales}}{\text{Stocks}}$$

    $$= \frac{£}{£}$$

Liquidity

- **Current ratio**

    This is a common method of analysing working capital (net current assets) and is generally accepted as the measure of short-term solvency. It indicates the extent to which the claims of short-term creditors are covered by assets that are expected to be converted to cash in a period roughly corresponding to the maturity of the claims.

    $$\text{Current ratio} = \frac{\text{Current assets}}{\text{Current liabilities}} = \frac{£}{£} =$$

- **Acid test ratio (quick ratio)**

    This is calculated in the same way as for the current ratio but stocks are excluded from current assets.

    $$\text{Acid test ratio} = \frac{\text{Current assets - stock}}{\text{Current liabilities}} = \frac{£}{£} =$$

    This ratio is a much better test of the immediate solvency of a business because of the length of time necessary to convert stocks into cash (via sales and debtors).

    Although increased liquid resources more usually indicate favourable trading, it could be that funds are not being used to their best advantage, (eg. a large unused cash balance).

- **Debtor days (debtors' ratio)**

    Average collection period = $\dfrac{\text{Debtors}}{\text{Sales}} \times 365$

Gearing

- *Capital*

    This measures the proportion of capital employed raised by debt (eg. debentures), as opposed to shareholders.

- Borrowing ratio = $\dfrac{\text{Loan capital}}{\text{Capital employed}} \times 100$

    = $\dfrac{\text{Loans}}{\text{Share capital + reserves + preference shares + loans}}$

    = $\dfrac{£}{£}$

Answers

Before you look any further, make sure you have written down an answer for every ratio.

Return on capital employed

$$\dfrac{340}{2{,}000 + 1{,}400} = 10\%$$

Net profit margin

$$\dfrac{340}{6{,}000} = 5\tfrac{2}{3}\%$$

Asset turnover

$$\dfrac{6{,}000}{3{,}400} = 1.76 \text{ times}$$

Gross profit margin

$$\dfrac{2{,}000}{6{,}000} = 33\tfrac{1}{3}\%$$

Stock turnover

$$\dfrac{4{,}000}{600} = 6\tfrac{2}{3} \text{ times}$$

Current ratio

$$\frac{1{,}600}{800} = 2$$

Acid test

$$\frac{1{,}600 - 600}{800} = 1.25$$

Debtors' days

$$\frac{900}{6{,}000} \times 365 \cong 55 \text{ days}$$

Gearing ratio

$$\frac{1{,}400}{2{,}000 + 1{,}400} \cong 41\%$$

These are only some of the accounting ratios in current use but they cover the significant aspects of most businesses.

Now go back over them, making sure that you understand what each sets out to achieve.

Interpretation

Introduction

- In your assessment, you may be required to comment on a set of accounts or on specific figures within a set of accounts.

- Before you start calculating ratios, read the accounts to identify any obvious points. You do not need a ratio to tell you that surplus cash should be invested, for example.

- Most of the marks will be awarded for interpretation of the ratios rather than for their calculation.

- Try to look at ratios in groups rather than in isolation; a group of ratios may provide a clearer indication of where the cause lies.

- Ratios are a key tool of analysis but other sources of information are also available:

    - Absolute comparisons can provide information without computing ratios; for example, comparing the balance sheet between the current year and the previous year may show that new shares have been issued to repay borrowings or finance new investment, which may in turn impact on gearing and ROCE.

    - Background information supplied about the nature of the business may help to explain changes or trends; for example, we may be told that the business has acquired another business or made substantial fixed asset purchases.

Return on capital employed (ROCE)

$$\frac{\text{Profit before interest and tax}}{\text{Capital employed}}$$

The aim is to see how effectively the business is using the money invested in it.

- It may be invalid to compare this ratio with, say, the interest rate offered by a building society.

Example

Z Ltd has ROCE of $\frac{5,000}{50,000} = 10\%$

The Scunthorpe Building Society offers 12%.

It would appear that the building society is a better investment.

However, if Z Ltd's assets were worth only £30,000, the £30,000 would be better left in Z Ltd where it is earning £5,000 or 12½%.

- It may be invalid to compare this ratio with that of our rivals.

Example

Z Ltd's main rival is A Ltd, a long-established company. The two companies are identical except that when A Ltd started business the capital requirement was only £25,000.

A Ltd's ROCE is therefore $\frac{5,000}{25,000} = 20\%$

Clearly, the two different figures for ROCE do not imply that A Ltd is a better company than Z Ltd.

Do be aware of the age structure of companies' capital before comparing them – assets bought at earlier, lower prices can appear to be more profitable.

- Often new investment does not bring immediate profits. This may be for a number of reasons. It may take time for the company's employees to learn to use the new equipment. Alternatively it may take the company time to obtain enough orders to use the new facilities to the full. (This may result in a temporary reduction in the ROCE.)

Gross and net profit margins

$$\text{GPM} = \frac{\text{Gross profit}}{\text{Sales}} \qquad \text{NPM} = \frac{\text{Net profit}}{\text{Sales}}$$

By looking at these two ratios together, we can determine whether a fall in the gross profit margin can be explained by a misclassification of cost rather than by deteriorating trade success.

Example

	19X1	19X0
	£	£
Sales	100	100
Cost of sales	(85)	(80)
Gross profit	15	20
Overheads	(5)	(10)
Net profit	10	10
GPM	15%	20%
NPM	10%	10%

The fact that the net profit margin has remained constant while the gross profit margin has fallen would lead us to check that our costs had been properly classified.

This is an illustration of using more than one ratio to guide our thoughts.

Stock turnover

$$\frac{\text{Cost of sales}}{\text{Stock}}$$

This ratio provides an excellent example of the need to investigate the circumstances behind the figures.

Example

	19X1	19X0
Z Ltd's stock turnover	5	10

Interpretation one: A poor performance by Z Ltd. It is holding too much stock and some of it may be obsolete or unsaleable.

Interpretation two: Z Ltd's management has shown commendable foresight in building up its stocks to meet the extra demand that will arise from 19X2's new advertising campaign.

We cannot determine which interpretation, if either, is correct without further information. The contrasting nature of the two explanations simply illustrates the fact that the ratio provides no answers; it simply raises questions.

♦ Other points to consider with the stock turnover ratio are:

- goods received on sale or return have no effect because they are never included in stock; and

- stock turnover may be affected by the early manufacture of spare parts that will not be needed until the future. (Remember: a current asset does not have to be realisable within one year.)

Chapter 17 Interpretation of Accounts

Current ratio

$$\frac{\text{Current assets}}{\text{Current liabilities}}$$

The aim is to ensure that current liabilities can be met as they fall due. Sometimes textbooks suggest that if a business' current ratio is below a certain level (which is usually given as between 1.5 and 2) the business should become seriously concerned. This should not be taken to be a strict rule, because:

- current liabilities include the bank overdraft which in practice is not repayable within one year (technically, of course, repayable on demand);

- it ignores the timing of the realisation or settlement of the items,

$$\text{eg. } \frac{\text{Debtors}}{\text{Creditors}} = \frac{50{,}000}{10{,}000} = 5$$

This might appear to be an excellent situation. If the creditors are due within a month and the debtors do not pay for two months, then the situation is in fact the opposite.

Debtor days

$$\frac{\text{Debtors}}{\text{Credit sales}} \times 365$$

- Accounts do not show the split between cash and credit sales. This means that assumptions have to be made (eg. all sales on credit) that may distort the result.

- Seasonality may also distort the result. Consider the following:

    Z Ltd has a year-end of 31 December; all sales are made, on credit, in December; all customers pay at the end of February (ie. take 60 days' credit).

    Debtor days

    $$\frac{\text{Debtors}}{\text{Credit sales}} \times 365 = \frac{50{,}000}{50{,}000} \times 365 = 365 \text{ days}$$

    The ratio figure is far from reality.

Gearing ratio

$$\frac{\text{Long - term loans}}{\text{Capital employed}}$$

The greater the extent to which a business is financed by debt, the greater is the risk of investing in it.

From a lender's point of view, the more debt there is, the less likely it is that money will be recovered if the company goes into liquidation.

From a shareholder's point of view, the more debt there is the greater the variability of return.

Example

Walthamstow Ltd and Hackney Ltd are identical companies except that Hackney Ltd has £50,000 of debtor finance with interest at 10% per annum.

In 19X0 trading profits are £100,000.

In 19X1 they fall by 50% to £50,000.

In the case of Walthamstow Ltd this means that the profits available to the shareholders fall by 50% from £100,000 to £50,000.

In the case of Hackney the fall is from £95,000* to £45,000*, a fall of 53%.

The more debt there is, the riskier the investment.

* Profit available to shareholders = Trading profit minus Interest

Exactly what constitutes a long-term loan is open to discussion. Many writers argue that bank overdrafts and preference shares should be included as both have characteristics similar to long-term loans. You should either exclude these items or give a brief explanation as to why you are treating them as long-term loans.

Further points

Use of ratios

Ratios are a tool to assist analysis. They focus attention on trends and weaknesses and facilitate comparison over time and between companies.

Ratios are of no use in isolation. To be useful, we need a basis for comparison, such as:

- previous years
- other companies
- industry averages
- budgeted *v* actual (for management use)

Influences on ratios

Business factors

Ratios may change over time or differ between companies because of the nature of the business or management actions in running the business.

Examples of business factors influencing ratios:

- *Type of business (eg. retailer v manufacturer)*

    This affects the nature of the assets employed and the returns earned; for example, a retailer may have higher asset turnover but lower margins than a manufacturer.

- *Quality of management*

    Better managed businesses are likely to be more profitable and have better working capital management than businesses in which management is weak.

- *State of economy and market conditions*

    If the market or the economy in general is depressed, this is likely to have an adverse affect on companies and make most or all of their ratios appear worse.

- *Management actions*

    These will be reflected in changes in ratios; for example, price discounting to increase market share is likely to reduce margins but increase asset turnover; withdrawing from unprofitable market sectors is likely to reduce turnover but increase profit margins.

- *Changes in the business*

    If the business diversifies into wholly new areas, this is likely to change the resource structure and thus impact on key ratios. A new acquisition near the year-end will mean that capital employed will include all the assets acquired but profits of the new acquisition will only be included in the profit and loss account for a small part of the year, thus tending to depress ROCE.

Accounting policies

The accounting policies adopted by a business can significantly affect the view presented by the accounts and the ratios computed, without affecting the business's core ability to generate profits and cash.

Examples of accounting policies

- *Revaluations v Historic cost*

    If a business revalues its assets rather than carries them at historic cost, this will usually increase capital employed and reduce profit before tax (due to higher depreciation). Thus, ROCE, profit margins and gearing are all likely to be lower if a business revalues its assets.

- *Immediate write-off of development costs v Capitalisation and amortisation*

    Immediate write-off has no impact on the profit and loss account for the year (contrast with amortisation) but will reduce capital employed. ROCE, profit margin and gearing are all likely to be lower if a policy of capitalisation and amortisation is adopted.

Limitations of ratios

- Ratios use historic data which may not be predictive as this ignores future actions by management and changes in the business environment.

- Ratios may be distorted by differences in accounting policies.

- Comparisons between different types of business are difficult because of differing resource structures and market characteristics.

SSAP25: Segmental reporting

Meaning and use of segmental reporting

Segmental reporting means analysing the reported results of an enterprise which has two or more classes of business or which operates in two or more different geographical areas.

The analysis is useful to users of financial statements because different segments may:

- earn a return on investment which is out of line with the remainder of the business; or

- be subject to different degrees of risk; or

- have experienced different rates of growth; or

- have different potentials for a future development.

Disclosure requirements of SSAP25

SSAP25 requires companies within its scope to disclose for each segment the following:

- *turnover*, distinguishing between turnover derived from external customers and turnover derived from other segments – in the geographical analysis, turnover should be shown segmentally according to *destination* of sales and *origin* of sales;

- *profit or loss*, before accounting for taxation, minority interests and extraordinary items, and normally before taking account of interest (unless all or part of the business of the entity is to earn or incur interest);

- *net assets* (defined as non-interest-bearing operating assets less non-interest-bearing operating liabilities).

The total of the amounts disclosed by segment should agree with the related total in the financial statements (with a reconciliation if necessary).

Comparative segmental figures for the preceding year should be shown.

Companies within the scope of SSAP25

SSAP25 applies to:

- all public companies or companies with a public company as subsidiary;

- banking and insurance companies;

- any entity which exceeds *ten times* the medium-sized company criteria in S248 Companies Act 1985 – that is to say, any two of the following three limits:

    - turnover > £112,000,000
    - balance sheet totals > £56,000,000
    - number of employees > 2,500

Defining segments

SSAP25 requires segmental analysis from companies within its scope which carry on two or more distinguishable classes of business or which operate in two or more different geographical areas.

It is for the directors to decide whether segmental information is necessary and SSAP25 indicates the following factors which should be taken into account in reaching a decision:

- Whether several classes of business are being carried on:

    - the nature of the products or services;
    - the nature of the production processes;
    - the markets in which the products or services are sold;
    - the distribution channels for the products;
    - the manner in which the entity's activities are organised;
    - any separate legislative framework relating to part of the business (for example, a bank or an insurance company).

- Whether a geographical analysis is required:

    Geographical variations as to:

    - expansionist or restrictive economic climates;
    - stable or unstable political regimes;
    - exchange control regulations;
    - exchange rate fluctuations.

    A class of business or geographical segment should normally be regarded as significant if:

    - its third party turnover is 10% or more of the total third party turnover of the entity; or

        its segment result, whether profit or loss, is 10% or more of the combined result of all segments in profit or of all segments in loss, whichever combined result is the greater; or

    - its net assets are 10% or more of the total net assets of the entity.

Questions

1 Falcon Ltd

The draft accounts of Falcon Ltd for the years ended 30 June 19X3 and 30 June 19X2 are as follows:

Balance sheets

	19X3 £	19X3 £	19X2 £	19X2 £
Fixed assets				
Premises		125,000		75,000
Plant		130,000		70,000
		255,000		145,000
Current assets				
Stock	120,000		100,000	
Debtors	80,000		60,000	
	200,000		160,000	
Creditors: Amounts falling due within one year				
Creditors	45,000		30,000	
Overdraft	15,000		5,000	
Taxation	20,000		15,000	
	80,000		50,000	
		120,000		110,000
		375,000		255,000
Creditors: Amounts falling due after more than one year				
7% Debentures		(50,000)		(50,000)
		325,000		205,000
Capital and reserves				
£1 ordinary shares		100,000		50,000
Share premium account		90,000		35,000
Profit and loss account		135,000		120,000
		325,000		205,000

Profit and loss accounts

	19X3 £	19X2 £
Turnover	525,000	425,000
Operating profit (trading profit less depreciation)	53,500	41,000
Debenture interest	(3,500)	(3,500)
Profit before tax	50,000	37,500
Tax	(20,000)	(15,000)
Profit after tax	30,000	22,500
Dividends	(15,000)	(10,000)
Retained profit	15,000	12,500

Required

(a) Calculate the following ratios:

  (i) return on capital employed;
  (ii) profit margin;
  (iii) asset turnover;
  (iv) current ratio;
  (v) acid test ratio;
  (vi) debtor days;
  (vii) gearing ratio.

(b) Write short paragraphs commenting on the profitability, liquidity and finance of Falcon Ltd as reflected in the above ratios.

Summary

Various interested parties may need to look at a business' accounts, from various standpoints. The common approach will involve comparison of figures with those of previous periods or with other companies.

Ratio analysis is one means of making such a comparison. The three main areas of comparison are:

- profitability
- liquidity
- gearing

Profitability:

- return on capital employed
- net profit margin
- asset turnover
- gross profit margin
- stock turnover

Liquidity:

- current ratio
- acid test (or quick) ratio
- debtor days

Gearing:

- capital gearing ratio

CHAPTER 18

Sundry Accounting Problems

Objectives

This chapter covers the following performance criteria:

10.2.1 Financial statements are accurately drafted from the appropriate information.

10.2.3 Draft accounts comply with domestic standards and legislation, and, where relevant, partnership agreement.

At the end of this chapter, you should be able to:

- understand the need to translate amounts denominated in foreign currencies

- understand the need to account for pension costs

- understand the need to report the substance of transactions

- understand the need to disclose related party transactions

Foreign currency translation

A company may enter into foreign currency operations in two main ways:

- It may enter directly into business transactions which are denominated in foreign currencies.

- It may conduct operations through a foreign enterprise which maintains its accounting records in its own local foreign currency.

Transactions

Although a company enters into transactions which are denominated in foreign currency it must present its own accounts, including the effects of these transactions, in sterling.

SSAP 20 *Foreign currency translation* states that:

- Each item arising from a transaction denominated in a foreign currency should be translated into local currency at the exchange rate in operation on the date on which the transaction occurred (the historic rate). In practice, the average rate for the period is often used as an approximation.

- Non–monetary items (eg tangible fixed assets, investments, stocks) are not normally retranslated at the year end. The amounts included in the balance sheet are the amounts translated at the historic rate.

- At each balance sheet date, monetary assets and liabilities denominated in a foreign currency (eg debtors, creditors, cash) should be retranslated using the rate of exchange at that date (the closing rate).

- All exchange gains and losses on settled transactions and unsettled monetary items should be taken to the profit and loss account for the year.

Illustration

On 27 April 19X4 Spall plc buys goods from a French supplier for FF 585,000 when the rate of exchange is FF10 = £1.

The supplier is not paid until after the year end of 30 June 19X4, when the rate of exchange is FF9 = £1.

Accounting entries

On 27 April 19X4 (FF585,000 ÷ 10 = 58,500)

Dr	Purchases		£58,500	
	Cr	Creditors		£58,500

On 30 June 19X4 (FF585,000 ÷ 9 = 65,000)

Dr	Exchange differences (65,000 – 58,500)		£6,500	
	Cr	Creditors		£6,500

Because the exchange rate has changed between the date on which the goods were bought and the year end, the amount that Spall plc owes the French supplier increases by £6,500. There is an exchange loss, which must be treated as an expense in the profit and loss account.

Foreign enterprises

Where a company has a foreign subsidiary, it prepares group accounts. (The methods used to prepare group accounts are covered in Chapters 19–22.) Before it can do this, it needs to translate the accounts of the subsidiary into sterling.

Translation of the accounts of foreign subsidiaries is beyond the scope of Unit 10.

However, you should be aware that there are two methods of translation. The method used depends on the nature of the relationship between the parent and the subsidiary.

- Where the subsidiary is effectively held for its investment potential and is at least semi-autonomous, the closing rate method is used. This involves translating the amounts in the subsidiary's accounts at the rate of exchange ruling at the balance sheet date. Exchange differences are taken to reserves.

- Where the subsidiary is used as an extension of the parent's own operations, the temporal method is used. This involves translating the amounts in the subsidiary's accounts as if all the transactions had been entered into by the investing company itself in its own currency.

Accounting for pension costs

Introduction

Accounting for pension costs is an extremely complex subject in practice.

The aim of this section therefore is not to give you a detailed knowledge of the ins and outs of accounting for pension costs, but to give you an appreciation of the problems involved together with the requirements of SSAP24 *Accounting for pension costs*.

Pension arrangements

There are a large number of ways in which a company may provide pensions for its employees. The most common arrangement is that in which a separate pension fund is set up under a trust deed, into which the company and possibly the employee will pay contributions and which will pay the pensions and other benefits as and when they fall due. This is illustrated in Figure 18.1.

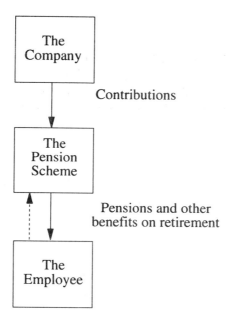

Figure 18.1 Typical structure for providing pensions to employee

Whilst the employee works for the company, the company and possibly the employee pay contributions over to the pension scheme. When the employee retires, the pension scheme will pay him a pension.

It is the job of the actuary to tell the company what contributions should be paid over to the pension fund each year in order to build up enough assets to pay the employee's pension when he retires.

Most schemes are funded, ie. the future liabilities for benefits are provided for by the accumulation of assets held externally to the employing company's business.

Types of scheme

There are two main types of pension scheme: defined benefit and defined contribution.

- A *defined contribution scheme* (sometimes called a *money purchase scheme*) is a pension scheme in which the benefits are directly determined by the value of contributions paid in respect of each member. Normally the rate of contribution is specified in the rules of the scheme.

- A *defined benefit scheme* (sometimes called a *final salary scheme*) is a pension scheme in which the rules specify the benefits to be paid and the scheme is financed accordingly. The company cannot be certain in advance that contributions plus returns on investments will equal benefits to be paid. The actuary advises the company on the level of contributions necessary to produce the defined benefits. Formal actuarial valuations of a pension scheme take place at regular intervals, normally every three years. Contributions may be varied as a result. If there is a surplus, the actuary may recommend a contribution holiday (a period during which no contributions are made). If there is a deficit, the actuary may recommend that contributions are increased for one or more years.

The accounting problem

From the point of view of the employee, a pension may be regarded as deferred remuneration. From the point of view of the employer, it is part of the cost incurred in obtaining the employee's services. Under the accruals concept, the employer should recognise the cost of providing pensions on a systematic and rational basis over the period during which he benefits from the employee's services.

Defined contribution schemes

Defined contribution schemes present no accounting problems. Because the rate of contribution is fixed, the actual contributions payable to the pension scheme (funding) represent the cost to the company of providing pensions (accounting).

Defined benefit schemes

The amount of contributions paid to the scheme by the employer may vary from year to year in order to eliminate a surplus or a deficit. The true cost to a company of providing pensions for employees only emerges over the long term.

This means that the actual contributions payable to the pension scheme for a period may *not* represent the *actual cost* to the company of providing pensions.

SSAP24 requires that the employer should recognise the expected cost of providing pensions on a systematic and rational basis over the period during which benefit is derived from the employee's services.

The expected cost of providing pensions (given by the forecast of contributions) is spread over the average remaining service lives of the employees in the scheme. This has the effect of 'smoothing' the charge to the profit and loss account.

Reporting the substance of transactions

Most transactions are reasonably straightforward and their commercial effect is the same as their strict legal form. However, in some instances this is not the case.

Example

A Ltd sells goods to B Ltd. A Ltd undertakes to repurchase the goods from B Ltd in 12 months' time.

The strict legal form of the transaction is that A has sold goods to B.

The commercial effect of the transaction is that B has made a secured loan to A.

Solution

In theory, A could record the transaction as a sale. To do so would be likely to enhance the appearance of A's financial statements. In particular, the company would appear to be less highly geared and therefore a safer investment than if A had recorded the transaction as a loan. This would, however, be very misleading.

In recent years, some companies have devised increasingly sophisticated schemes whereby it is possible for them to hold assets and liabilities which do not actually appear on the balance sheet. This practice is sometimes referred to as *off balance sheet financing*.

FRS5 *Reporting the substance of transactions* has been issued as a response to this problem. FRS5 states the following:

- An entity's financial statements should report the substance of the transactions into which it has entered.

- In order to determine the substance of a transaction, it is necessary to establish whether or not it has given rise to new assets or liabilities for the entity and whether or not it has increased or decreased the entity's existing assets and liabilities.

- Disclosure of a transaction should be sufficiently detailed to enable the user of the financial statements to understand its commercial effect.

Obviously the definition of assets and liabilities is critical. FRS5 uses the same definitions of assets and liabilities as those included in the Statement of Principles:

- *Assets* are rights or other access to future economic benefits controlled by an entity as a result of past transactions or events.

- *Liabilities* are obligations to transfer economic benefits as a result of past transactions or events.

- *Risk* is uncertainty as to amount of future benefits (gains or losses).

In addition the FRS states that:

- there is evidence that an entity has rights or other access to benefits (an asset) if it bears the *risks* inherent in the benefits.

Example

A Ltd sells goods to B Ltd under a sale and repurchase agreement (as before).

In order to determine the substance of the transaction, it is necessary to establish whether A still has rights or other access to future economic benefits associated with the goods (an asset).

Does A still have the benefits attaching to the asset?

A has a firm agreement to repurchase the goods, so it is unlikely that B has the right to sell or use them. Therefore A will eventually have the right to sell or use the goods.

Does A still bear the risks attaching to the asset?

Solution

A will eventually have the right to sell the goods. In addition, A almost certainly bears the risk that the goods will have become obsolete or otherwise fallen in value by the time that they are repurchased.

Therefore it appears that A has an asset. A also has an obligation to transfer an economic benefit (the repurchase price of the goods) to B in the future. Therefore A has a liability.

In practice, the process of determining the substance of a transaction might be very much more complicated than this. However, you are only expected to be aware of the broad principles of FRS5.

Another example of the principle of recognising the commercial substance of a transaction rather than its strict legal form is the accounting treatment of finance leases required by SSAP21.

Related party transactions

The reader of the financial statements normally assumes that transactions reflected in the financial statements are made with independent parties unless told otherwise.

Readers will also normally assume that a company is owned by a number of shareholders and is not subject to control or significant influence by any one person or company unless told otherwise, eg. through the disclosure of the identity of the parent company.

Where a company does business with "related parties" these assumptions may not be valid.

Two or more parties are related parties when at any time during the financial period:

- one party has direct or indirect control of the other party; or

- the parties are subject to common control from the same source; or

- one party has influence over the financial and operating policies of the other party to an extent that that other party might be inhibited from pursuing at all times its own separate interests; or

- the parties, in entering a transaction, are subject to influence from the same source to such an extent that one of the parties to the transaction has subordinated its own separate interests.

This definition is very wide ranging. It includes, or may include:

- other companies in the same group;
- associates and joint ventures;
- directors of the reporting entity and of other companies in the same group;
- pension funds for the benefit of employees of the reporting entity;
- key management of the reporting entity and of other companies in the same group;
- major shareholders;
- members of the close family of any individual falling under parties mentioned above; and
- partnerships, companies, trusts or other entities in which any individual or member of the close family above has a controlling interest.

FRS 8 requires the disclosure of:

- all related party transactions; and
- where the reporting entity is controlled by another party, the related party relationship and the name of that party, irrespective of whether or not any transactions have taken place between the controlling party and the reporting entity.

Summary

SSAP 20

- Items arising from a transaction denominated in a foreign currency should be translated into local currency at the exchange rate in operation on the date on which the transaction occurred. At each balance sheet date, monetary assets and liabilities denominated in a foreign currency should be retranslated at the closing rate. Exchange gains and losses are taken to the profit and loss account.

SSAP24

- The employer should recognise the expected cost of providing pensions on a systematic and rational basis over the period during which he derives benefit from the employees' services.

FRS5

- An entity's financial statements must report the substance of the transactions into which it has entered.

FRS8

- An entity's financial statements must disclose the existence of any related party transactions.

236

CHAPTER 19

Group Accounts – Basic Principles

> ## Objectives
>
> This chapter covers the following performance criteria:
>
> **10.2.1 Financial statements are accurately drafted from the appropriate information.**
>
> **10.2.2 Subsequent adjustments are correctly implemented.**
>
> **10.2.3 Draft accounts comply with domestic standards and legislation, and, where relevant, partnership agreement.**
>
> At the end of this chapter, you should be able to:
>
> ♦ understand the basic principles of consolidation.

Introduction

Until now, we have only dealt with the accounts of a single company. In this and the following chapters, we cover the major topic of group accounts.

In this chapter, we meet the basic principles of group accounts, which provide us with the foundation for studying the area in more detail in later chapters. In studying these chapters, you should always keep in mind these basic principles, as they are often of great value if you are having difficulty in trying to decide how to deal with something in a groups question.

This chapter may appear long in comparison with some others. This is because it includes several examples to illustrate the key points. If you feel that you understand the principles involved, you should treat the examples as mini-questions and work through them without looking at the solution until you have attempted the problem. As always, this is the best way to test your understanding.

Groups and group accounts

Group

A group comprises a parent company and the undertakings (usually companies) under its control, which are called *subsidiaries*. The full legal definitions of a parent and subsidiaries are dealt with in Chapter 22 and are not important at this stage. For now, we shall assume that a parent has control of another company if it holds more than 50% of that company's ordinary shares.

Gone Ltd
Summary Profit and Loss Accounts
for the year ended 31 December 19X7

	19X7	19X6
	£000	£000
Turnover	1,800	1,300
Cost of sales	1,098	715
Gross profit	702	585
Expenses	504	315
Net profit before interest and tax	198	270

Gone Ltd
Summary Balance Sheets
as at 31 December 19X7

	19X7		19X6	
	£000	£000	£000	£000
Fixed assets		3,463		1,991
Current assets	460		853	
Current liabilities	(383)		(406)	
Net current assets		77		447
Long-term loan		(1,506)		(500)
		2,034		1,938
Share capital		800		800
Revaluation reserve		164		164
Profit and loss account		1,070		974
		2,034		1,938

The industry average ratios are as follows:

	19X7	19X6
Return on capital employed	13.4%	13.0%
Gross profit percentage	44.5%	43.2%
Net profit percentage	23.6%	23.2%
Current ratio	2.0:1	1.9:1
Gearing	36%	34%

Task 1.3

In the Answer Book, prepare a report for the directors recommending whether or not to use Gone Ltd as a supplier for Bins Ltd given the information contained in the financial statements and the industry averages supplied. Your answer should comment on the profitability, liquidity and the level of gearing in the company, and how they have changed over the two years, and compare it with the industry as a whole.

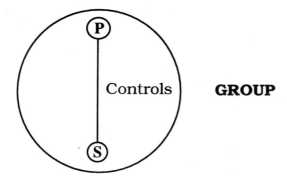

Figure 19.1 Single entity concept

The group is viewed as a single entity.

To present the group as a single entity, the net assets and results of subsidiaries are added to those of the parent line by line to show the group's financial position and performance.

So that the group accounts do not show transactions and balances between group members, these are cancelled out on consolidation. If this were not done, the group accounts would show the effects of the group investing in and transacting with itself. In this chapter, we see how the parent's investment in the subsidiary is cancelled out on consolidation. We shall cover elimination of other transactions and balances between group members in later chapters. When dealing with these adjustments, you should always keep the single entity concept firmly in mind.

Basic principles: consolidated balance sheet

On the net assets side, we add together the net assets of the group members to show the resources under the parent's control. The parent's investment in the subsidiary is cancelled out and replaced by the underlying net assets of the subsidiary. We shall look at this aspect in more detail first.

Cancellation of cost of investment against net assets acquired

On consolidation we need to cancel out:

♦ the cost of the investment recorded in the parent company's books; against

♦ the net assets that the parent company has acquired as recorded in the subsidiary company's books. (This will be represented by the share capital and reserve balances on the date of the acquisition.)

Example 1

Russell Ltd has been trading for many years preparing accounts to 31 December each year. The directors of Russell Ltd decided to form a company, Bromley Ltd, which was to deal with the marketing side of their operations and in which Russell Ltd was to own the entire share capital.

Bromley Ltd was incorporated on 31 December 19X7 with an authorised share capital of 10,000 ordinary shares of £1 each, all of which were issued at par (ie. at their nominal value) to Russell Ltd in exchange for cash.

Deskcover Ltd
Extended Trial Balance 31 September 19X7

DESCRIPTION	Trial balance Debit £000	Trial balance Credit £000	Adjustments Debit £000	Adjustments Credit £000	Profit and Loss Debit £000	Profit and Loss Credit £000	Balance sheet Debit £000	Balance sheet Credit £000
Cash at bank	316						316	
8% debentures		3,400						3,400
Trade debtors	3,386						3,386	
Provision for doubtful debts		125		44				169
Sales		20,469				20,469		
Purchases	12,025				12,025			
Land – cost	1,602						1,602	
Buildings – cost	2,137						2,137	
Fixtures and fittings – cost	1,399						1,399	
Motor vehicles – cost	1,786						1,786	
Office equipment – cost	402						402	
Return inwards	152				152			
Stock	4,502		5,244	5,244	4,502	5,244	5,244	
Accruals				118				118
Prepayments			56				56	
Returns outwards		109				109		
Buildings – accumulated depreciation		413		214				627
Fixtures & Fittings – accumulated depreciation		404		350				754
Motor vehicles – accumulated depreciation		486		417				903
Office equipment – accumulated depreciation		45		68				113
Interim dividend	240				240			
Trade creditors		2,035						2,035
Interest	136				136			
Distribution costs	3,214		542		3,756			
Administration expenses	2,368		613		2,981			
Investment	4,010						4,010	
Share capital		4,000						4,000
Profit and loss account		4,389						4,389
Share premium		1,800						1,800
Profit					2,030			2,030
	37,675	37,675	6,455	6,455	25,822	25,822	20,338	20,338

Solution 1

Consolidated balance sheet at 31 December 19X7

	£	£
Fixed assets		
Tangible assets		30,000
Current assets (130,000 + 10,000)	140,000	
Creditors: Amounts falling due within one year	(60,000)	
		80,000
Total assets less current liabilities		110,000
Capital and reserves		
Called-up share capital		50,000
Profit and loss account		60,000
		110,000

This is very straightforward. However, once you understand this, much of what follows will fall into place easily.

Example 2

In this example, we will consider the purchase of the entire share capital of a company which has already been trading for a number of years.

Austin Ltd acquired the entire share capital of Reed Ltd for £15,000 cash on 31 December 19X7. The balance sheets of the two companies at that date were as follows:

	Austin Ltd		Reed Ltd	
	£	£	£	£
Fixed assets				
Tangible assets		80,000		8,000
Investments: Shares in Reed Ltd		15,000		
		95,000		
Current assets	200,000		24,000	
Creditors: Amounts falling due within one year	(165,000)		(17,000)	
Net current assets		35,000		7,000
Total assets less current liabilities		130,000		15,000
Capital and reserves				
Called-up share capital		100,000		10,000
Profit and loss account		30,000		5,000
		130,000		15,000

Required

Prepare the consolidated balance sheet of Austin Ltd as at 31 December 19X7.

AAT Unit 10 Study Pack

Key principle

Once again, we simply need to reflect the fact that Austin Ltd now effectively owns £15,000 worth of **net assets** of Reed Ltd rather than simply £15,000 worth of shares (single entity concept).

Procedure

As previously described.

(1) Consolidation of those net assets controlled by Austin Ltd.

					£
Fixed assets	80,000	+	8,000	=	88,000
Current assets	200,000	+	24,000	=	224,000
Creditors	(165,000)	+	(17,000)	=	(182,000)

(2) Cancellation of cost of investment against the net assets acquired.

	£	£
Shares in Reed Ltd		15,000
Net assets acquired represented by:		
Share capital	10,000	
Profit and loss account	5,000	
		15,000
		–

(Note that as the company has already been trading, its net assets at the date of acquisition are represented not only by share capital but also by a profit and loss account balance.)

Solution 2

The consolidated balance sheet of Austin Ltd is:

	£	£
Fixed assets		
Tangible assets (80,000 + 8,000)		88,000
Current assets (200,000 + 24,000)	224,000	
Creditors: Amounts falling due within one year		
(165,000 + 17,000)	(182,000)	
Net current assets		42,000
Total assets less current liabilities		130,000
Capital and reserves		
Called-up share capital		100,000
Profit and loss account		30,000
		130,000

Control and ownership

In the examples which we have looked at so far, the parent has owned the entire share capital of the subsidiary. However, this is not essential for the parent to have control. If the parent owns more than 50% of the subsidiary's shares, it will normally have control, assuming one vote per share. Hence the parent will be able to decide how all of the subsidiary's net assets are utilised, even though it does not own all of the subsidiary. Therefore, all of the subsidiary's net assets are added to the parent's own net assets to show the resources under the parent's control in the consolidated balance sheet.

The capital and reserves side of the consolidated balance sheet shows the ownership of the net assets controlled. The part of group net assets owned by the parent's shareholders is represented by the parent's share capital and reserves and its share of the subsidiary's reserves (covered in more detail later). The part of the subsidiary's net assets owned by the subsidiary's other shareholders (called minority interests) is shown separately under capital and reserves.

The consolidated profit and loss account, which we shall look at in detail later, is prepared using exactly the same principle. The results of the parent and subsidiary are combined in full to give the group's profit after tax, generated from the net assets controlled. This is then apportioned between the minority interests and the parent's shareholders according to ownership.

The following example illustrates how to prepare the consolidated balance sheet where there are minority interests in the subsidiary.

Example 3

Let us assume the same figures as in example 2, except that we will now assume that Austin Ltd acquired 80% of Reed Ltd's shares for £12,000 cash on 31 December 19X7 and that the current assets of Austin Ltd are £3,000 higher.

The balance sheets of the two companies at 31 December 19X7 are as follows:

	Austin Ltd		Reed Ltd	
	£	£	£	£
Fixed assets				
Tangible assets		80,000		8,000
Investments: Shares in Reed Ltd		12,000		
		92,000		
Current assets	203,000		24,000	
Creditors: Amounts falling due within one year	(165,000)		(17,000)	
Net current assets		38,000		7,000
Total assets less current liabilities		130,000		15,000
Capital and reserves				
Called-up share capital		100,000		10,000
Profit and loss account		30,000		5,000
		130,000		15,000

Required

Prepare the consolidated balance sheet of Austin Ltd at 31 December 19X7.

Key principle

The distinction between control and ownership now becomes significant. As Austin Ltd has control, we need to add together the net assets of the two companies as previously, but we now need to show in the consolidated balance sheet that Austin Ltd's shareholders do not own all of those net assets. Instead, 20% of Reed Ltd's net assets are owned by the minority interests in Reed Ltd.

Procedure

We now need to add to our previous procedure. To help us identify the status of companies (eg. whether they are subsidiaries) and to enable us to deal with the various calculations, we need to identify the group structure before proceeding further.

(1) Identify the group structure.

The remaining 20% of Reed Ltd is held by minority interests.

(2) Cancellation of cost of investment against net assets acquired.

Although Austin Ltd controls all of Reed Ltd's net assets, it does not own all of them. Austin Ltd has only invested in 80% of Reed Ltd's net assets, and on consolidation, Austin Ltd's investment is cancelled against its share of Reed Ltd's net assets:

	£	£
Shares in Reed Ltd		12,000
Share of net assets acquired, represented by:		
Share capital	10,000	
Profit and loss account	5,000	
	15,000	
Austin Ltd's share: 80% × 15,000		(12,000)
		–

(3) Calculation of minority interests in Reed Ltd.

This is a new step. In the capital and reserves side of the consolidated balance sheet, we include a figure for minority interests which represents their share of Reed Ltd's net assets included in the consolidated balance sheet:

	£
Minority interests	
20% (from group structure) × £15,000 (Reed Ltd's net assets)	3,000

Solution 3

The consolidated balance sheet of Austin Ltd is as follows:

	£	£
Fixed assets		
Tangible assets (80,000 + 8,000)		88,000
Current assets (203,000 + 24,000)	227,000	
Creditors: Amounts falling due within one year		
(165,000 + 17,000)	(182,000)	
Net current assets		45,000
Total assets less current liabilities		133,000
Capital and reserves		
Called-up share capital		100,000
Profit and loss account		30,000
		130,000
Minority interests		3,000
		133,000

Goodwill

In the above example, Austin Ltd paid £12,000 for an equal value of net assets. This situation is unlikely in practice because Reed Ltd has proved that it is already a profitable company by the existence of accumulated profits. Hence, Austin Ltd may need to pay more for Reed Ltd than simply the value of its net assets.

Example 4

Let us assume the same figures as in Example 3, except that the shares in Reed Ltd were bought by Austin Ltd for £14,000, and that the current assets of Austin Ltd are £2,000 lower.

The balance sheets of the two companies at 31 December 19X7 are as follows:

	Austin Ltd		Reed Ltd	
	£	£	£	£
Fixed assets				
Tangible assets		80,000		8,000
Investments: Shares in		14,000		
Reed Ltd (80%)				
		94,000		
Current assets	201,000		24,000	
Creditors: Amounts falling due within one year	(165,000)		(17,000)	
Net current assets		36,000		7,000
Total assets less current liabilities		130,000		15,000
Capital and reserves				
Called–up share capital		100,000		10,000
Profit and loss account		30,000		5,000
		130,000		15,000

Required

Prepare the consolidated balance sheet of Austin Ltd as at 31 December 19X7.

Key principle

Austin Ltd has paid £14,000 for £12,000 worth of net assets of Reed Ltd (80% × £15,000). Why has Austin paid £2,000 extra?

It must consider that Reed Ltd has *goodwill*. That is, the true value of Reed Ltd as a whole is more than that of its net assets as reflected in its balance sheet. Therefore Austin pays £12,000 for the assets in the balance sheet and £2,000 for the goodwill.

This goodwill is a value arising from the price paid of £14,000 but can only be identified and measured when we consolidate. It is therefore called *goodwill arising on consolidation*.

Procedure

Again we follow the basic two steps.

(1) Cancellation of investment (Goodwill calculation)

	£	£
Shares in Reed Ltd		14,000
Net assets acquired represented by:		
Share capital	10,000	
Profit and loss account	5,000	
	15,000	
Austin Ltd's share (80% × £15,000)		12,000
Goodwill arising on consolidation		2,000

(2) Consolidation of net assets controlled **together with the asset of goodwill arising on consolidation**

						£
Goodwill arising on consolidation						2,000
Tangible assets	80,000	+	8,000	=	88,000
Current assets	201,000	+	24,000	=	225,000
Creditors	(165,000)	+	(17,000)	=	(182,000)

Solution 4

The consolidated balance sheet of Austin Ltd is as follows:

	£	£
Fixed assets		
Intangible assets: Goodwill (arising on consolidation)		2,000
Tangible assets		88,000
		90,000
Current assets	225,000	
Creditors: Amounts falling due within one year	(182,000)	
Net current assets		43,000
Total assets less current liabilities		133,000
Capital and reserves		
Called-up share capital		100,000
Profit and loss account		30,000
		130,000
Minority interests (20% × £15,000)		3,000
		133,000

Note that there is no minority interest in goodwill.

The accounting treatment of goodwill on consolidation

The goodwill on consolidation arising in the previous example is one instance of purchased goodwill.

According to FRS 10, purchased goodwill is the difference between the cost of an acquired entity and the aggregate of the fair values of its identifiable assets and liabilities (covered in Chapter 11).

FRS 10 requires that goodwill is capitalised and amortised through the profit and loss account on a systematic basis over its useful economic life.

Example 4A

Continue with the same figures as in Example 4, with the additional information that goodwill arising on the acquisition is to be amortised through the profit and loss account over its useful economic life, which is estimated at five years. A full year's charge is to be made in the year of acquisition.

Consolidation schedules

(1) Goodwill

	£
Goodwill arising on consolidation as previously	2,000
Less: Amortisation ($1/5 \times 2,000$)	(400)
Intangible asset: Goodwill arising on consolidation	1,600

(2) Profit and loss account

	£
Austin Ltd per question	30,000
Less: Amortisation of goodwill arising on consolidation	(400)
	29,600

Solution 4A

Austin Ltd: Consolidated balance sheet

	£	£
Fixed assets		
Intangible assets: Goodwill arising on consolidation (2,000 – 400)		1,600
Tangible assets		88,000
		89,600
Current assets	225,000	
Creditors: Amounts falling due within one year	(182,000)	
Net current assets		43,000
Total assets less current liabilities		132,600
Capital and reserves		
Called-up share capital		100,000
Profit and loss account		29,600
		129,600
Minority interests		3,000
		132,600

Again the write-off is an adjustment on consolidation and will not affect the profit and loss account in the books of Austin Ltd. Next year the cumulative write-off will be £800 (ie. 2 × £400) and this amount will increase each year until it reaches £2,000 in year 5.

Example 5

The following balance sheets were extracted two years later from the books of Austin Ltd and Reed Ltd at 31 December 19X9:

	Austin Ltd £	Austin Ltd £	Reed Ltd £	Reed Ltd £
Fixed assets				
Tangible assets		85,000		11,000
Investments: Shares in Reed Ltd (80%)		14,000		
		99,000		
Current assets	217,000		33,000	
Creditors: Amounts falling due within one year	(176,000)		(25,000)	
Net current assets		41,000		8,000
Total assets less current liabilities		140,000		19,000
Capital and reserves				
Called–up share capital		100,000		10,000
Profit and loss account		40,000		9,000
		140,000		19,000

Required

Prepare the consolidated balance sheet of Austin Ltd as at 31 December 19X9, assuming that goodwill on consolidation is amortised through the profit and loss account over five years, with a full years' charge in the year of acquisition.

Summary of the situation

The net assets of Reed Ltd have increased since acquisition by £4,000 to £19,000. The £19,000 of net assets must be included in the consolidated balance sheet at 31 December 19X9 and can be analysed as follows:

- **Pre-acquisition** £15,000 – This amount is financed by share capital (£10,000) and pre-acquisition profits (£5,000) 80% of which are cancelled against the cost of shares in Reed Ltd (exactly as was done on consolidating the accounts at 31 December 19X7); and

- **Post-acquisition** £4,000 – This amount is financed by post-acquisition profits (£4,000) 80% of which is credited to the consolidated profit and loss account, along with the profit and loss account of Austin Ltd. This profit was earned under Austin Ltd's control and 80% is owned by Austin Ltd's shareholders.

- The remaining 20% of Reed Ltd's net assets at 31 December 19X9 is owned by the minority shareholders in Reed Ltd and is included in the consolidated balance sheet under minority interests [£3,800 (20% × £19,000)].

It is important that you understand that the amount of goodwill arising on consolidation as calculated in 19X7 will not alter; it is calculated once and for all based on the subsidiary's net assets at acquisition.

Consolidation schedules

(1) Goodwill

	£	£
Share in Reed Ltd		14,000
Net assets acquired represented by:		
Share capital	10,000	
Profit and loss account	5,000	
	15,000	
Austin Ltd's share (80% × £15,000)		12,000
		2,000
Less: Goodwill amortised (2,000 ÷ 5 × 3)		(1,200)
		800

(2) Profit and loss account

	£	£
Austin Ltd	40,000	
Less: Goodwill amortised	(1,200)	
		38,800
Reed Ltd per question	9,000	
Less: Pre-acquisition profits (Note)	(5,000)	
	4,000	
Austin Ltd's share (80% × 4,000)		3,200
		42,000

Note: Only post-acquisition profits are included in the group profit and loss account. These have been earned whilst under the parent's control. Pre-acquisition profits are cancelled out in the goodwill calculation.

Solution 5

Therefore the consolidated balance sheet of Austin Ltd at 31 December 19X9 is:

	£	£
Fixed assets		
Intangible assets: Goodwill arising on consolidation		800
Tangible assets (85,000 + 11,000)		96,000
		96,800
Current assets (217,000 + 33,000)	250,000	
Creditors: Amounts falling due within one year		
(176,000 + 25,000)	(201,000)	
Net current assets		49,000
Total assets less current liabilities		145,800

Chapter 19 Group Accounts – Basic Principles

	£
Capital and reserves	
Called-up share capital	100,000
Profit and loss account	42,000
	142,000
Minority interests (20% × £19,000)	3,800
	145,800

Make sure that you understand completely the above workings and how the figures in the consolidated balance sheet are arrived at before continuing.

The important point to grasp is that, for the first time in an example, the consolidated profit and loss account (£42,000) includes part of the accumulated profits of the subsidiary (£3,200). These are the subsidiary's profits that have accumulated post-acquisition, that is, since Reed Ltd came under the control of Austin Ltd, which are in substance owned by Austin Ltd's shareholders.

The net assets working

Our first consolidation schedule (the goodwill calculation) has so far been the cancellation of the cost of investment in the subsidiary against the net assets actually acquired for this consideration.

We have represented 'net assets' by share capital and the profit and loss account, applying the fundamental accounting equation.

From now on however the 'net assets' will be calculated in a separate working. This will ensure a methodical approach and assist us when questions become more complex.

The goodwill consolidation schedule would appear as follows:

	£
Cost of investment	14,000
Net assets acquired (80% × £15,000)	(12,000)
Goodwill	2,000
Less: amortisation	(1,200)
	800

Working

Net assets of subsidiary	Acquisition date
	£
Share capital	10,000
Profit and loss account	5,000
	15,000

Basic principles: Consolidated profit and loss account

Objective of the consolidated profit and loss account

The objective of the consolidated profit and loss account is to show the total results of the group as a single entity and then to show how much of that total is attributable to the members of the parent company.

This objective is achieved by aggregating the sales, expenses and profits of all companies in the group (after adjusting for intra-group transactions) and then deducting from the aggregate **profits after taxation** the profits attributable to minority interests. This will leave just the profits attributable to the members of the parent company.

Simple illustration

A simple illustration will demonstrate this approach. Suppose P Ltd has owned 80% of S Ltd for a number of years.

Profit and loss accounts for year ended 31 December 19X7

	P Ltd £		S Ltd £		Consolidated £
Profit before taxation	1,000	+	500	=	1,500
Tax	345	+	175	=	520
Profit after taxation	655	+	325	=	980
Minority interest (20% x £325)					65
Profit attributable to the members of parent company					915

In the consolidated profit and loss account, we have simply aggregated the profit before tax and the tax figures for P and S. However, P only owns 80% of S and is therefore only entitled to 80% of the profits generated by S. The remaining 20% is owned by the minority shareholders, this is reflected in the consolidated profit and loss account by deducting 20% of profit after tax of S Ltd as minority interest.

Remember that the minority interest is the minority share of S Ltd's profit after tax.

We return to the consolidated profit and loss account in more detail in Chapter 21.

Questions

1 Prince plc

On 1.1.19X4 Prince plc acquired 100% of the share capital of Madonna Ltd and Jackson Ltd, paying £60,000 and £40,000 respectively.

The balance sheets of the three companies are as follows at 31.12.X4:

	Prince £	Madonna £	Jackson £
Fixed assets: Tangible	60,000	40,000	32,000
Investments	100,000	–	–
	160,000	40,000	32,000
Current assets	90,000	86,000	52,000
Creditors: Amounts falling due within one year	(50,000)	(41,000)	(40,000)
Net current assets	40,000	45,000	12,000
Total assets less current liabilities	200,000	85,000	44,000
Creditors: Amounts falling due after more than one year	(18,000)	(30,000)	(10,000)
	182,000	55,000	34,000
Share capital	60,000	50,000	30,000
Profit and loss account	122,000	5,000	4,000
	182,000	55,000	34,000

Profit for the year:

	£
Jackson Ltd	3,000
Madonna Ltd	1,000

Goodwill arising on acquisition is amortised through the profit and loss account over three years from the date of acquisition.

Required

Show how the consolidated balance sheet would look at 31 December 19X4.

Summary

In this chapter, we have met the basic principles of group accounts. Our main focus has been on the consolidated balance sheet, as this enables us to see how to apply these principles. Once you have grasped this, you should find it relatively straightforward to apply the same principles to the consolidated profit and loss account.

In the following chapters, we shall see how to deal with the consolidated balance sheet and profit and loss account in more detail. Before proceeding further, you must make sure that you understand the concept of the group as a single entity and the distinction between control and ownership. This last point is summarised in the following table:

Consolidated balance sheet	£	Consolidated profit and loss account	£
Net assets P + S (100%)	X	Turnover P + S (100%)	X
CONTROL	X	Profit after tax (CONTROL)	X
OWNERSHIP: Capital and reserves:		OWNERSHIP: Minority interests (MI% x S's profit after tax)	(X)
Share capital (P only)	X		
Reserves (P + P% x S post acq)	X	Profit attributable to P's shareholders	X
Owned by P's shareholders	X	Dividends (P only)	(X)
Minority interests	X	Retained profit for the financial year	X
(MI% x S's net assets consolidated)	X		

Key

P = parent
S = subsidiary
P% = parent share of subsidiary
MI% = Minority interest share of subsidiary

CHAPTER 20

Group Accounts – Consolidated Balance Sheet

> ## Objectives
>
> This chapter covers the following performance criteria:
>
> 10.2.1 Financial statements are accurately drafted from the appropriate information.
>
> 10.2.2 Subsequent adjustments are correctly implemented.
>
> 10.2.3 Draft accounts comply with domestic standards and legislation, and, where relevant, partnership agreement.
>
> At the end of this chapter, you should be able to:
>
> ♦ prepare a consolidated balance sheet.

Summary of basic technique

The basic steps for the consolidated balance sheet, which we met in the previous chapter, may be summarised as follows:

For the net assets side of the balance sheet, add together the net assets of the parent and subsidiary line-by-line.

For the capital and reserves side, it is best to use a series of workings:

(1) Identify the group structure.

(2) Identify the net assets of the subsidiary at acquisition for the goodwill computation and at the balance sheet date for minority interests. Identify the net assets by reference to the capital and reserves side of the balance sheet (ie. apply the fundamental accounting equation).

This is best done in a separate net assets working using two columns (one for the date of acquisition and one for the balance sheet date). This makes it easier to identify the subsidiary's post-acquisition profits for calculation of the consolidated profit and loss account reserve.

(3) Cancel the cost of investment in the subsidiary, included in the parent's own balance sheet, against the share of the subsidiary's net assets acquired to give goodwill.

(4) Calculate the minority interest share of the subsidiary's net assets (at the balance sheet date) included in the consolidated balance sheet and include this in minority interests.

(5) Add the parent's share of the subsidiary's post-acquisition profits to the parent's own reserves and adjust for goodwill amortised to calculate the group profit and loss reserve.

The workings for goodwill, minority interests and the profit and loss reserve are often called the *consolidation schedules*. These are often set out before the group structure and net assets workings.

We can now see the techniques in action in Example 1.

Example 1

The following balance sheets have been prepared at 31 December 19X8 for Dickens Ltd and its subsidiary Jones Ltd:

	Dickens Ltd		Jones Ltd	
	£	£	£	£
Fixed assets				
Tangible assets		85,000		18,000
Investment: 24,000 shares in Jones Ltd		60,000		
		145,000		
Current assets	160,000		84,000	
Creditors: Amounts falling due within one year	(135,000)		(47,000)	
Net current assets		25,000		37,000
Total assets less current liabilities		170,000		55,000
Capital and reserves				
Called–up share capital		100,000		30,000
Profit and loss account		70,000		25,000
		170,000		55,000

Dickens Ltd acquired its holding in Jones Ltd on 31 December 19X7, when Jones Ltd's profit and loss account stood at £20,000. Goodwill arising on acquisition is to be amortised over four years, with a full year's charge in the year of acquisition.

Required

Prepare the consolidated balance sheet of Dickens Ltd at 31 December 19X8.

Solution

Consolidated balance sheet at 31 December 19X8

	£	£
Fixed assets		
Intangible assets: goodwill		10,000
Tangible assets (85 + 18)		103,000
		113,000
Current assets (160 + 84)	244,000	
Creditors: Amounts falling due within one year (135 + 47)	182,000	
Net current assets		62,000
Total assets less current liabilities		175,000
Capital and reserves		
Called-up share capital		100,000
Profit and loss account (W5)		64,000
		164,000
Minority interest (W4)		11,000
		175,000

Workings

(1) Group structure

Dickens Ltd
80%
Jones Ltd

(2) Net assets of Jones Ltd:

	31 December 19X8 £	31 December 19X7 £
Share capital	30,000	30,000
Profit and loss account	25,000	20,000
	55,000	50,000

(3) Goodwill schedule

	£
Shares in Jones Ltd	60,000
Net assets acquired [80% (W1) × 50,000(W2)]	(40,000)
	20,000
Less: amortisation (20,000 ÷ 4 × 2)	(10,000)
	10,000

(4) Minority interest schedule

	£
20% × 55,000 (W2)	11,000

(5) Profit and loss account schedule

	£
Dickens Ltd	70,000
Share of Jones Ltd post-acquisition:	
[80% (W1) × (25,000 − 20,000)(W2)]	4,000
Less: Goodwill amortised (W3)	(10,000)
	64,000

Notice that the *goodwill computation* uses *reserves of Jones Ltd as at acquisition* since together with share capital, they represent the assets acquired. The amount of goodwill arising is fixed at the date of takeover.

When calculating the *minority interest* we refer to the *reserves at the current balance sheet date* since together with share capital, they represent the assets in which the minority interest has a share as at that date.

Cancellation of intra-group balances

Introduction

As we have already discussed, when consolidating we need to cancel out items which are assets in one group company and liabilities in another.

This is an application of the single entity concept, which we met in the previous chapter:

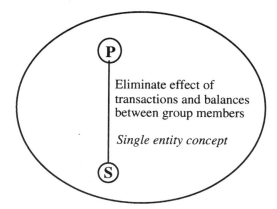

Where the group companies trade with each other, there are several ways in which balances with each other can arise. The most common of these are:

- loans and debentures
- current accounts

Loans and debentures

The cancellation process is very simple in that the credit balance of one company is offset against the debit balance of the other company, eliminating both balances from the consolidated balance sheet.

Current accounts

Current accounts are intra-group trading balances. The treatment of current accounts is the same as for loans. However, inter-company current accounts may not agree.

For example, the following balances appeared in the books of P Ltd and S Ltd in their balance sheets dated 31 December 19X0:

	Books of P Ltd £	Books of S Ltd £
S Ltd current account	10,700 Dr	
P Ltd current account		10,000 Cr

On 31 December 19X0 S Ltd had sent a cheque for £700 to P Ltd which the latter company did not record until 2 January 19X1. This is called cash-in-transit.

The necessary consolidation adjustment will be to follow the transaction to its natural conclusion by recording the receipt of the cash in P Ltd's books, thus decreasing its current account balance by £700 to £10,000, and increasing its cash balance by £700. The current account balances of £10,000 can then be cancelled out.

Example of cancellation of intra-group balances

Laura plc acquired 100% of the share capital of Ashley Ltd for £40,000 on 1 January 19X4, when the balance on the accumulated profit and loss account of Ashley Ltd stood at £8,000. The following draft balance sheets were drawn up at 31 December 19X7.

AAT Unit 10 Study Pack

	Laura plc		Ashley plc	
	£	£	£	£
Fixed assets				
Tangible assets		88,000		39,000
Investments				
Shares in Ashley ltd		40,000		–
6% debentures in Ashley Ltd		4,000		–
		132,000		39,000
Current assets				
Trade debtors	84,000		26,000	
Due from Laura plc	–		15,000	
Cash at bank and in hand	–		16,000	
	84,000		57,000	
Creditors: Amounts falling due within one year				
Trade creditors	46,000		28,000	
Due to Ashley Ltd	10,000		–	
Bank overdraft	14,000		–	
	70,000		28,000	
Net current assets		14,000		29,000
Total assets less current liabilities		146,000		68,000
Creditors: Amounts falling due after more than one year				
6% debentures		–		(12,000)
		146,000		56,000
Capital and reserves				
Called–up share capital		100,000		24,000
Profit and loss account		46,000		32,000
		146,000		56,000

You discover that Laura plc sent a cheque for £5,000 to Ashley Ltd on 30 December 19X7, which was not received until 3 January 19X8.

Goodwill arising on the acquisition is to be amortised over its useful economic life of four years.

Required

Prepare the consolidated balance sheet of Laura plc as at 31 December 19X7.

Solution

Consolidated balance sheet of Laura plc at 31 December 19X7

	£	£
Fixed assets		
Tangible assets (88 + 39)		127,000
Current assets		
Trade debtors (84 + 26)	110,000	
Cash (16 + 5)	21,000	
	131,000	
Creditors: Amounts falling due within one year		
Trade creditors (46 + 28)	74,000	
Bank overdraft	14,000	
	88,000	
Net current assets		43,000
Total assets less current liabilities		170,000
Creditors: Amounts falling due after more than one year		
6% debentures (12 – 4)		(8,000)
		162,000
Capital and reserves		
Called-up share capital		100,000
Profit and loss account		62,000
		162,000

♦ **Current accounts**

Adjust the receiving company's books, as if Ashley Ltd had received the cheque before the end of the year.

Ashley Ltd's books

		£	£
Dr	Cash	5,000	
	Cr Intra-group – due from Laura		5,000

Therefore the balance on its intra-group debtor is reduced to £10,000 and is equal to the amount shown as a creditor in Laura plc's accounts. We cancel these £10,000 balances.

♦ **6% debentures**

Laura plc owns £4,000 of the debentures issued by Ashley Ltd. This asset in Laura plc's accounts must be cancelled with the liability in Ashley Ltd's books, leaving a liability due to the other debenture holders of £8,000.

♦ Consolidation workings

(1) Group structure

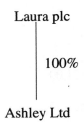

Laura plc

100%

Ashley Ltd

(2) Net assets of Ashley Ltd

	Balance sheet date £	Acquisition date £
Share capital	24,000	24,000
Profit and loss account	32,000	8,000
	56,000	32,000

(3) Goodwill schedule

	£
Shares in Ashley Ltd	40,000
Net assets acquired (W2)	(32,000)
	8,000

(4) Profit and loss account schedule

	£
Laura plc	46,000
Ashley Ltd post-acquisition [32,000 – 8,000 (W2)] (fully amortised)	24,000
Less: Goodwill (W3)	(8,000)
	62,000

Dividends

Basic approach

If a subsidiary proposes a dividend, the effects will be as follows:

- Subsidiary company books

    Dr   Profit and loss   X
        Cr   Dividend creditor   X

    with the dividend payable

- Parent company books

    Dr   Dividend debtor   X
        Cr   Profit and loss account   X

    with its share of the dividend receivable from the subsidiary company

- Consolidation adjustment

    The dividend debtor in the parent company's books is receivable from another group company, and should be cancelled out against all (if 100% owned) or part (if less than 100% owned) of the dividend creditor in the subsidiary company's books. Any balance on the dividend creditor of the subsidiary company represents the dividend owed to the minority shareholders of the company.

Example

The following are draft balance sheets as at 31 December 19X9 for Wells Ltd and its subsidiary, Christie Ltd:

	Wells Ltd £'000	Christie Ltd £'000
Fixed assets		
Tangible assets	300	100
Investment in Christie Ltd – 24,000 shares at cost	45	–
Current assets	300	168
Creditors: Amounts falling due within one year		
Trade creditors	(80)	(100)
Proposed dividends	(20)	–
Long-term loans	(175)	(60)
	370	108
Called up share capital – £1 ordinary shares	90	30
Profit and loss account	280	78
	370	108

Wells Ltd acquired its shares in Christie Ltd when the latter's reserves stood at £20,000. Christie Ltd wishes to propose a dividend of £8,000. Goodwill arising on the acquisition has been fully amortised.

Required

Prepare the consolidated balance sheet as at 31 December 19X9.

Solution

Wells Ltd consolidated balance sheet at 31 December 19X9

	£'000	£'000
Fixed assets		
Tangible assets (300 + 100)		400.0
Current assets (300 + 168 + 6.4 – 6.4)	468.0	
Creditors: Amounts falling due within one year		
Trade creditors (80 + 100)	180.0	
Proposed dividends: Parent company	20.0	
Minority interests (20% × 8,000)	1.6	
	201.6	
Net current assets		266.4
Total assets less current liabilities		666.4
Creditors: Amounts falling due after more than one year (175 + 60)		(235.0)
		431.4
Capital and reserves		
Called-up share capital		90.0
Profit and loss account		321.4
		411.4
Minority interest		20.0
		431.4

Workings

(1) Group structure

Wells Ltd
    80%
Christie Ltd

(2) Net assets of Christie:

	Balance sheet date		Acquisition date
	£'000	£'000	£'000
Share capital		30	30
Profit and loss account	78		20
Less: Proposed dividend	(8)		
		70	
		100	50

(3) Goodwill schedule

	£'000
Shares in Christie Ltd	45
Net assets acquired [80% × 50 (W2)]	(40)
Goodwill (fully amortised)	5

(4) Minority interest schedule

	£'000
20% × 100 (W2)	20

(5) Profit and loss account schedule

	£'000	£'000
Wells Ltd	280	
Add: Dividend receivable (80% × 8)	6.4	
		286.4
Share of Christie Ltd		
[80% × (70 – 20)(W2)]		40
Less: goodwill (fully amortised)		(5)
		321.4

Unrealised intra–group profit

Introduction

Where, during the period under review, goods (or assets) are transferred between group companies at prices other than cost, the transferring company can make a profit. In consolidated accounts, we want to reflect only profits made by group companies trading with third parties (single entity concept). No adjustment is necessary on consolidation if the goods (or assets) have been sold on, outside the group, within the period. However, where such goods (or assets) are still held within the group at the end of the accounting period, the consolidated accounts would not show a true and fair view of the profits of the group as a whole if the profits made on such transfers were not eliminated.

Stocks

The consolidated balance sheet should show stocks at the lower of cost and net realisable value to the group. The effects of transactions between group members should be eliminated on consolidation (single entity concept).

The adjustment for the unrealised profit on stocks is straightforward where the parent company sells goods to the subsidiary. The profit is made by the parent and recorded in its books. Hence, it is all owned by the parent.

For example, during the current accounting period P Ltd transferred goods to S Ltd for £12,000, which gave P Ltd a profit of £3,000. One third of these goods were included in the stocks of S Ltd at the balance sheet date.

The adjustment in the consolidated balance sheet would be as follows:

			£	£
Dr	Profit and loss account ($\frac{1}{3}$ x £3,000)		1,000	
	Cr	Balance sheet stocks		1,000

Sales of goods from subsidiary to parent company

On the net assets side of the balance sheet, the unrealised profit is still eliminated from stocks in full. This is because the group as a whole has bought and is holding stock, which should therefore be shown at the lower of cost and net realisable value to the group. The profit on the sale will have been recorded in the subsidiary's books. On consolidation, the adjustment to eliminate this is apportioned between the parent and minority interests according to the ownership interests in the subsidiary.

For example, during the current accounting period S Ltd sold goods to P Ltd for £18,000 which gave S Ltd a profit of £6,000. At the balance sheet date half of these goods are included in P Ltd's stock. P owns 80% of S.

The adjustment in the consolidated balance sheet would be as follows:

			£	£
Dr	Group profit and loss account (½ x 6,000 x 80%)		2,400	
Dr	Minority interest (½ x 6,000 x 20%)		600	
	Cr	Balance sheet stocks (½ x 6,000)		3,000

Fair values

Introduction

Goodwill is determined by comparing the value of the business as a whole with the aggregate of the fair values of its identifiable net assets. In our consolidation examples to date we have assumed that the fair value of the subsidiary's assets was equal to their book values. This approach is fine for questions where you are not given any information about the fair values.

If the fair value of the subsidiary's assets, at the date of acquisition, is different from their book value, the book amounts should be adjusted to fair value on consolidation.

Example

Hardy Ltd acquired 80% of the share capital of Woolf Ltd for £54,000 on 31 December 19X7. The draft balance sheets of the two companies have been drawn up on that date.

	Hardy Ltd £	Woolf Ltd £
Fixed assets		
Tangible assets	75,000	35,000
Investment in Woolf Ltd	54,000	–
Current assets	35,000	39,500
Creditors: Amounts falling due within one year	(42,000)	(16,000)
	122,000	58,500
Share capital – £1 ordinary shares	60,000	20,000
Profit and loss account	62,000	38,500
	122,000	58,500

You are given the following additional information:

The fair value of the net assets of Woolf Ltd, on 31 December 19X7, was £66,000. This increase can be attributed to freehold land.

Required

Prepare the consolidated balance sheet of Hardy Ltd as at 31 December 19X7.

Procedure

Looking at the net assets of Woolf Ltd:

	£
Fair value at 31 December 19X7	66,000
Book value at 31 December 19X7	58,500
Revaluation	7,500

We must increase the book value of Woolf Ltd's freehold land by £7,500. The necessary journal entry is:

		£	£
Dr	Fixed assets – freehold land	7,500	
	Cr Revaluation reserve		7,500

Putting through this adjustment Woolf Ltd's balance sheet becomes:

Woolf Ltd: Balance sheet at 31 December 19X7

	£
Fixed assets at valuation	42,500
Current assets	39,500
Creditors: Amounts falling due within one year	(16,000)
	66,000
Share capital – £1 ordinary shares	20,000
Revaluation reserve	7,500
Profit and loss account	38,500
	66,000

The increase in the value of Woolf Ltd's land occurred over time up to the date of takeover. The revaluation reserve is therefore a **pre–acquisition** reserve and is treated in the same way as pre–acquisition profits.

We will now prepare the consolidated balance sheet.

Solution

Hardy Ltd: Consolidated balance sheet at 31 December 19X7

	£
Fixed assets:	
Intangible assets: goodwill	1,200
Tangible assets (75 + 42.5)	117,500
Current assets (35 + 39.5)	74,500
Creditors: Amounts falling due within one year (42 + 16)	(58,000)
	135,200
Share capital – £1 ordinary shares	60,000
Profit and loss account (W5)	62,000
	122,000
Minority interest (W4)	13,200
	135,200

Consolidation workings

1 Group structure

Hardy Ltd
│ 80%
Woolf Ltd

2 Net assets of Woolf at 31 December 19X7

	£
Share capital	20,000
Profit and loss account	38,500
	58,500
Revaluation reserve	7,500
Fair value of net assets	66,000

3 Goodwill schedule

	£
Cost of shares in Woolf	54,000
Net assets acquired (80% x 66,000) (W2)	52,800
	1,200

4 Minority interest schedule

	£
20% x 66,000 (W2)	13,200

5 Profit and loss account schedule

	£
Hardy Ltd	62,000

Other considerations

Other reserves

In many cases, there is only one reserve, the profit and loss account reserve, in the subsidiary's balance sheet. The pre-acquisition profit and loss reserves are cancelled out in the goodwill computation and the parent's share of the subsidiary's post-acquisition reserves is included in the group reserves calculation.

A subsidiary may have other reserves in its balance sheet, such as a revaluation reserve. On consolidation, we treat these in exactly the same way as the profit and loss reserve. Hence, the reserves at acquisition are cancelled out in the goodwill computation and the parent's share of any post-acquisition reserves is added to the parent's own reserves. However, it is important not to mix up the different categories of reserve. Therefore, if a subsidiary has a post-acquisition revaluation reserve, for example, the parent's share goes in the consolidated balance sheet under 'revaluation reserve' not 'profit and loss account'.

Accounting policies

All balances included in consolidated accounts should be based on the same accounting policies. If a subsidiary uses different accounting policies in preparing its own accounts from those adopted by the group as a whole (eg. regarding development costs), the subsidiary's accounts should be adjusted prior to consolidation for consistency. We should make any necessary adjustment to the subsidiary's profit and loss account reserve in the net assets working prior to calculating goodwill, minority interests and group reserves.

Goodwill in a subsidiary's own books

We calculate goodwill on consolidation based on the fair value of the subsidiary's separable net assets acquired. Any goodwill recorded in the subsidiary's own balance sheet is not an asset separable from the business as a whole. Hence we need to eliminate this goodwill by adjusting the subsidiary's net assets prior to consolidating.

Note that, for uniform accounting policies, fair value adjustments and goodwill in a subsidiary's own books, we do not need to adjust in the subsidiary's own accounts as an individual company. Instead, we can make the adjustment just for the consolidated accounts.

Pro forma consolidation workings

These proformas summarise the main workings for the consolidated balance sheet. Their main purpose is to illustrate how to set out and cross-reference your workings. Clear layout is absolutely crucial as you will lose marks if the assessor cannot see how you have made your calculations. These proformas do not cover every possible situation but do illustrate the main points which we have covered so far.

Workings

(1) Group structure

(2) S Ltd: Net assets working

	Balance sheet date £'000	Balance sheet date £'000	Acquisition date £'000
Share capital		X	X
Share premium account		X	X
Revaluation reserve		X	X
Profit and loss account			
Per question	X		
Adjustments in S prior to consolidation:			
Proposed dividends (W6)	(X)		
Other (eg uniform a/c policies)	X		
Final		A	C
		B	D

Chapter 20 Group Accounts – Consolidated Balance Sheet

(3) Goodwill schedule

	Acquisition £
Cost of investment in S Ltd	X
Less: Share of net assets acquired [75% × D(W2)]	X
	X
Less: Amortisation	(X)
	X

(4) Minority interests schedule

	Balance sheet date £
Their share of S's net assets at balance sheet date [25% × B (W2)]	X

(5) Profit and loss account schedule

	Balance sheet date £
P's profit and loss account (draft per question)	X
Adjustments (in P's own books):	
P's dividends proposed (W6)	(X)
Dividend from S [75% × S's dividend proposed (W6)]	X
[P's own adjusted profit (can omit this line)	X]
P's share of S's post-acquisition retained profit	
[75% × (A − C) (W2)]	X
Goodwill amortised (W3)	(X)
	X

(6) Dividends [**Note:** Only post entries not already made in figures given in the question.]

   (a) P's dividend proposed

P's books	£	£
Dr Profit and loss account (W5)	X	
Cr Creditors (consolidated balance sheet)		X

   (b) S's dividend proposed

S's books	£	£
Dr Profit and loss account (W2 net assets)	X	
Cr Creditors (cancel 75% against P's debtor)		X
(Remaining 25% is a creditor in the		
consolidated balance sheet due to MI)		
P's books		
Dr Debtors	X	
(P's share 75% – this cancels against S's creditor)		
Cr Profit and loss account (W5)		X

AAT Unit 10 Study Pack

Questions

1   Heavy plc

As on 31 March 19X1 the draft balance sheets of Heavy plc and its subsidiary, Side Ltd showed the following positions:

	Heavy plc		Side Ltd	
	£	£	£	£
Fixed assets (tangible)		180,000		40,000
Investment in Side Ltd		49,200		–
		229,200		40,000
Current assets				
Stock	40,000		32,000	
Inter–company account	–		10,500	
Cash at bank and in hand	–		3,000	
	40,000		45,500	
Creditors: Amounts falling due within one year				
Bank overdraft	6,000		–	
Trade creditors	41,000		17,000	
Inter–company account	8,000		–	
	55,000		17,000	
Net current (liabilities)/assets		(15,000)		28,500
Total assets less current liabilities		214,200		68,500
Creditors: Amounts falling due after more than one year				
Debenture loan		(50,000)		–
		164,200		68,500
Financed by:				
Share capital – £1 ordinary shares		100,000		10,000
Share premium account		20,000		10,000
Profit and loss account		44,200		48,500
		164,200		68,500

You are given the following additional information:

(1)   Shortly before the year-end, Heavy plc paid £2,500 to Side Ltd. At 31 March 19X1, Side Ltd had not yet received this amount.

(2)   It has been decided that Heavy plc and Side Ltd should declare dividends of 10 pence per share and 20 pence per share respectively for the year ended 31 March 19X1.

(3)   Heavy plc acquired 80% of the issued share capital of Side Ltd on 1 April 19X0. Side Ltd made a profit available for distribution for the year of £10,500.

(4)   It is group accounting policy to amortise any goodwill on acquisition through the profit and loss account over five years.

Required

Prepare the consolidated balance sheet of Heavy plc as on 31 March 19X1, together with your consolidation schedules.

Summary

In this chapter we have looked in depth at how to prepare a consolidated balance sheet, including how to deal with intra-group balances, dividends and adjustments to eliminate unrealised profits.

You should now be able to:

- prepare a consolidated balance sheet together with supporting workings

- cancel out inter-company items

- adjust for dividends in the consolidated balance sheet

CHAPTER 21

Group Accounts – Consolidated Profit and Loss Account

Objectives

This chapter covers the following performance criteria:

10.2.1 Financial statements are accurately drafted from the appropriate information.

10.2.2 Subsequent adjustments are correctly implemented.

10.2.3 Draft accounts comply with domestic standards and legislation, and, where relevant, partnership agreement.

At the end of this chapter, you should be able to:

♦   prepare a consolidated profit and loss account.

Introduction

In this chapter, we switch our attention to the consolidated profit and loss account. This is prepared on the same basis as the consolidated balance sheet and thus most of the key principles will already be familiar. In particular, the single entity concept and the distinction between control and ownership are as important to the consolidated profit and loss account as they are to the consolidated balance sheet.

Basic principles

The parent's own profit and loss account as an individual company will show dividend income from the subsidiary. The consolidated profit and loss account shows the incomes generated from the group's resources. Those resources are shown by the net assets in the consolidated balance sheet.

As you will recall, when we prepared the consolidated balance sheet, we added together the net assets of the parent and subsidiary line by line to show the resources under the parent's control. We apply exactly the same principle in preparing the consolidated profit and loss account by adding together the parent's and subsidiary's income and expenses line by line. This will give us the profit after tax generated from the resources under the group's control.

In the consolidated balance sheet, we showed the ownership of the group's net assets on the capital and reserves side, where we showed the minority interests separately from the capital and reserves attributable to the parent's shareholders. In the consolidated profit and loss account, we show the ownership of the profit after tax by deducting the minority interest share of the subsidiary's profit from profit after tax, leaving us with the profit owned by the parent's shareholders.

When we looked at the consolidated balance sheet, we saw how the single entity concept was applied by cancelling out intra-group items and unrealised profits, and how we apportioned unrealised profit adjustments according to ownership. As we shall see in more detail later in the session, we apply the same principles in the consolidated profit and loss account.

We shall now see in more detail how to prepare the consolidated profit and loss account.

Detailed requirements

Pro forma

Work your way through the pro forma, referring to the tutorial notes which are referenced by letters in brackets.

Consolidated profit and loss account for the year ended....

		£
Turnover (a)		
Continuing operations		X
Acquisitions		X
		X
Discontinued operations		X
		X
Cost of sales (a)		(X)
Gross profit		X
Distribution costs		(X)
Administrative expenses		(X)
Other operating income		X
Operating profit		
Continuing operations	X	
Acquisitions	X	
	X	
Discontinued operations	(X)	
		X
Profit on the sale of fixed assets		X
Profit on ordinary activities before interest		X
Other interest receivable and similar income (b) (c)		X
Interest payable and similar charges (b)		(X)
Profit on ordinary activities before taxation (Note 1)		X
Tax on profit on ordinary activities		(X)
Profit on ordinary activities after taxation (d)		X
Minority interests (e)		(X)
Profit for the financial year attributable to parent's shareholders (Note 2)		X
Dividends (f)		(X)
Retained profit for the year		X

Statement of retained profits

Retained profits at beginning of year (g)	X
Retained profit for the financial year	X
Retained profits at end of year	X
Earnings per share	Xp

Notes to the accounts

(1) Profit on ordinary activities before taxation is stated after charging the following:

	£
Depreciation of tangible fixed assets (h)	X
Auditors' remuneration and expenses (h)	X
Directors' emoluments (i)	
As directors	X
Remuneration as executives	X

(2) The profit for the financial year of Parent Company Ltd is £X. The parent company has taken advantage of the legal exemption not to publish its own profit and loss account (j).

Tutorial notes

(a) Intra-group sales must be eliminated from both the turnover of the selling company and the cost of sales of the buying company.

(b) Any intra-group interest must be eliminated from interest receivable and interest payable respectively (single entity concept).

(c) Similarly, dividends from subsidiaries must be eliminated since the whole of the profits of those subsidiaries are being consolidated and it would be double counting to include the dividends as well.

(d) Profit on ordinary activities after taxation – Up to this point, 100% of all items for the parent company and all subsidiaries have been aggregated (subject to intra-group adjustments). It is now necessary to compute the amount of the profit after taxation that is attributable to outside (minority) shareholders.

(e) Minority interests – This is calculated by taking the minority interest's share of the subsidiary's profit after taxation.

(f) Dividends paid and proposed – These will be the dividends of the *parent company only* since a subsidiary's dividends are effectively intra-group items. No dividends to minority interests are included as their share of the subsidiary's profit after tax, whether or not paid out as a dividend, has already been taken out in the minority interest line.

(g) Retained profits at beginning of year – This figure will be the retained profits brought forward of the parent company together with the parent company's share of the post-acquisition retained profits of each subsidiary, less goodwill written off. This is the figure which would appear in the opening consolidated balance sheet.

(h) Auditors' remuneration/depreciation – This disclosure will be the simple aggregation of the amounts in the parent company and each subsidiary.

(i) **Directors' emoluments** – This disclosure is an exception to the basic rule of aggregation. The statutory requirement is to show the total of all emoluments paid by companies within the group *to directors of the parent company only*.

(j) The amount of the profit for the financial year in the accounts of the parent company will be the profit before dividends paid and proposed in its own profit and loss account. However, if the parent's own profit and loss account does not yet include dividends due from the subsidiary, these need to be added on! This note is an extra disclosure requirement when the parent does not publish its own individual profit and loss account. (Strictly speaking, this would be a note to the *individual balance sheet* of the parent company. You are unlikely to be asked to prepare this note in the assessment.)

Example

Set out below are the draft profit and loss accounts of Smiths plc and its subsidiary company Flowers Ltd for the year ended 31 December 19X7.

On 31 December 19X5 Smiths plc purchased, ex div, 75,000 ordinary shares and £10,000 10% debentures in Flowers Ltd. At that date the profit and loss account of Flowers Ltd showed a credit balance of £3,000.

The issued share capital of Flowers Ltd is 100,000 £1 ordinary shares, and it had £30,000 10% debentures outstanding on 31 December 19X7. Flowers Ltd pays its debenture interest on 31 December each year.

	Smiths plc £	Flowers Ltd £
Turnover	600,000	300,000
Cost of sales	(427,000)	(232,000)
Gross profit	173,000	68,000
Distribution costs	(41,000)	(14,000)
Administrative expenses	(52,000)	(31,000)
Income from shares in group undertakings	7,500	–
Income from other fixed asset investments (dividends from UK quoted companies)	3,000	1,000
Other interest receivable – from group companies	1,000	–
Interest payable	–	(3,000)
Profit on ordinary activities before taxation (Note)	91,500	21,000
Tax on profit on ordinary activities	(38,500)	(8,000)
Profit on ordinary activities after taxation	53,000	13,000
Dividends – proposed	(30,000)	(10,000)
Retained profit for the year	23,000	3,000
Retained profits brought forward	30,000	12,000
Retained profits carried forward	53,000	15,000

Note

Profit before taxation has been arrived at after charging:

	£	£
Depreciation	20,000	6,000
Auditors' remuneration and expenses	5,000	2,000
Directors' emoluments	10,000	4,000

The following additional information is relevant:

(1) During the year Smiths plc sold goods to Flowers Ltd for £20,000, making a profit of £5,000. These goods were all sold by Flowers Ltd before the end of the year.

(2) Included in the director's emoluments of £4,000 in Flowers Ltd's accounts is £1,000 paid to a director of Smiths plc.

Required

Prepare for presentation to members the consolidated profit and loss account for the year ended 31 December 19X7. Smiths plc does not propose to publish its own profit and loss account. Ignore goodwill.

Workings

Following through the pro forma, we will take the problems one at a time. Where you are uncertain of the treatment, refer back to the earlier tutorial notes.

Group structure

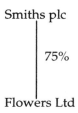

Note that there are no acquisitions or discontinued operations during the year, therefore analysis of the results between continuing operations, acquisitions and discontinued operations is not required in this example.

Turnover and cost of sales

The total turnover is £900,000 but the intra-group sale has been included as part of Smiths plc's turnover. It must be eliminated, leaving £880,000.

Similarly, total cost of sales is £659,000 but the intra-group purchase has been included in cost of sales for Flowers Ltd. Therefore eliminating it leaves £639,000.

Investment income and interest payable

- **Income from shares in group companies** represents the dividend receivable from the subsidiary (75% × £10,000). It must be excluded from the consolidated profit and loss account.

- **Interest receivable from group companies** is Smiths plc's share of the debenture interest paid by Flowers Ltd (10% × £10,000). It must be cancelled against the *interest payable* in Flowers Ltd's profit and loss account to leave the net *interest payable* to people outside the group of £2,000.

Minority interests

The minority interest is 25% of Flowers Ltd's profit after tax figure (ie. 25% × £13,000 = £3,250).

Dividends

Smiths plc's dividend only: £30,000

Retained profits brought forward

The retained profit brought forward is calculated using the profit and loss schedule which we used for the consolidated balance sheet, except that we use the figures at the *start* of the year, not the end.

Remember we only include the parent company's share of the **post-acquisition** profits of a subsidiary:

	£
Smiths plc	30,000
Flowers Ltd [75% × £(12,000 − 3,000)]	6,750
	36,750

Disclosure of directors' emoluments

Emoluments paid to directors of Smiths plc only: (£10,000 + £1,000) £11,000

Solution

Smiths plc
Consolidated profit and loss account for the year ended 31 December 19X7

	£
Turnover	880,000
Cost of sales	(639,000)
Gross profit	241,000
Distribution costs	(55,000)
Administrative expenses	(83,000)
Income from other fixed asset investments	4,000
Interest payable	(2,000)
Profit on ordinary activities before taxation (Note 1)	105,000
Tax on profit on ordinary activities	(46,500)
Profit on ordinary activities after taxation	58,500
Minority interests	(3,250)
Profit for the financial year attributable to the group (Note 2)	55,250
Dividends – proposed	(30,000)
Retained profit for the year	25,250

Statement of retained profits

	£
Retained profits brought forward	36,750
Retained profit for the year	25,250
Retained profits carried forward	62,000

Notes to the accounts

(1) Profit before taxation has been arrived at after charging:

	£
Depreciation	26,000
Auditors' remuneration and expenses	7,000
Directors' emoluments	11,000

(2) The profit for the financial year of Smiths plc is £53,000. The parent company has taken advantage of the legal exemption not to publish its own profit and loss account.

Intra-group trading and provision for unrealised profit

Introduction

We deal with intra-group trading and unrealised profit by applying the single entity concept. In the consolidated profit and loss account, we show the results of transactions which the group as a whole has made.

In the last example the two group companies traded with one another, but all of the goods had been sold on, outside the group, before the year end. The journal used was:

```
Dr   Turnover                    X
     Cr   Cost of sales                X
```

with the value of inter-company sales.

If the goods have not been sold on outside the group before the year-end, there will be two problems:

- stock in the acquiring company's balance sheet will be at cost to the acquiring company rather than to the group; and

- the profit and loss account of the selling company includes the profit on sale to the acquiring company; however this profit is not a true profit in the group accounts, since no sale has been made outside the group.

Therefore an additional correcting journal is necessary. Where the parent company has sold goods to its subsidiary, this will be as follows.

```
Dr   Cost of sales               X
     Cr   Stock (balance sheet)        X
```

with the element of inter-company profit in closing stock.

Example

Assume that in the previous example half of the goods sold by Smiths plc to Flowers Ltd were still in the stock of Flowers Ltd, and that the total profit made by Smiths plc on inter-company sales was £5,000.

Journals

			£	£
Dr	Turnover		20,000	
	Cr	Cost of sales		20,000
Dr	Cost of sales (½ x £5,000)		2,500	
	Cr	Stock		2,500

Solution

Smiths plc – Consolidated profit and loss account for the year ended 31 December 19X2 (extract)

	£
Turnover (600,000 + 300,000 – 20,000)	880,000
Cost of sales (427,000 + 232,000 – 20,000 + 2,500)	(641,500)
Gross profit	238,500

The gross profit is generated from resources controlled by the group. We next need to consider the ownership of any unrealised profits which have been eliminated.

Sales from S to P

Where the subsidiary has sold goods to the parent which remain in the parent's stocks at the year-end, we eliminate the unrealised profit in full from closing stocks in the balance sheet and profit and loss account (where opening and closing stocks are in cost of sales), as with a sale from parent to subsidiary.

However, where the subsidiary has made the intra-group sale, it will have recorded the unrealised profit. As you will recall from our study of the balance sheet, we reflected the ownership of this unrealised profit by apportioning the adjustment between the profit and loss reserve (owned by parent's shareholders) and the minority interests. In the consolidated profit and loss account, we also need to reflect the ownership of the eliminated profit. We do this by deducting the minority interest share in the minority interest computation, leaving us with the parent's share included in retained profit for the year.

The adjustment in the profit and loss account for this type of transaction will be as follows.

			£	£
Dr	Turnover		X	
	Cr	Cost of sales		X

With the value of inter–company turnover

			£	£
Dr	Cost of sales		X	
	Cr	Stock (balance sheet)		X

With the full unrealised profit on intra group sales

			£	£
Dr	Minority interest (balance sheet)		X	
	Cr	Minority interest (profit and loss account)		X

With the minority's share of the unrealised profit on sale from subsidiary to parent only.

Treatment of goodwill

Introduction

Remember that FRS 10 requires that purchased goodwill is capitalised and amortised through the profit and loss account over its useful economic life.

We will consider the effect of this using an illustration.

Illustration

A Ltd buys 90% of the shares of B Ltd on 1 January 19X9, the first day of its accounting period. Goodwill arising is £10,000, and has an estimated useful economic life of 10 years.

- Years 1–10

    The group profit and loss account each year would include a charge of £1,000. This would be included under administrative expenses.

- Year 2 onwards

    Note that the group retained profits brought forward would be net of the cumulative write-off of goodwill to date:

    Year 2   £1,000
    Year 3   £2,000
    Year 4   £3,000, etc.

Link between balance sheet and profit and loss account

In studying the consolidated profit and loss account, we have seen that the statement of reserves reconciles the opening and closing balances on the profit and loss account reserve. Where there are other reserves (eg. revaluation reserve), the statement of reserves should also include these. The main components of the statement of reserves and where we can also see the figures in the balance sheet and profit and loss account, are summarised below:

Statement of reserves (in group accounts)

	Profit and loss account £
Brought forward (per last year's consolidated balance sheet)*	X
Retained profit for the year (from the consolidated profit and loss account)	X
Goodwill amortised#	(X)
Carried forward (per this year's consolidated balance sheet)*	X

* = from profit and loss schedule at relevant date
\# = from goodwill schedule

Chapter 21 Group Accounts – Consolidated Profit and Loss Account

Questions

1 Courage Ltd

The following are the draft profit and loss accounts of Courage Ltd and Brains Ltd for the year ended 31 December 19X4:

	Courage Ltd £	Brains Ltd £
Turnover	3,000,000	900,000
Cost of sales	(1,700,000)	(600,000)
Gross profit	1,300,000	300,000
Distribution costs	(300,000)	(100,000)
Administrative expenses	(600,000)	(96,800)
Operating profit	400,000	103,200
Loss on sale of fixed asset investment	(50,000)	–
Reorganisation costs	–	(10,000)
Profit on ordinary activities before interest	350,000	93,200
Income from other fixed asset investments (dividends from UK quoted companies)	8,000	2,000
Other interest receivable – from group undertakings	1,600	–
Interest payable	–	(3,200)
Profit on ordinary activities before taxation	359,600	92,000
Tax on profit on ordinary activities	(159,600)	(40,000)
Profit on ordinary activities after taxation	200,000	52,000
Dividends: Ordinary, proposed	(20,000)	(4,000)
Retained profit for the year	180,000	48,000
Retained profits brought forward	100,000	25,000
Retained profits carried forward	280,000	73,000

You are given the following information:

(1) Issued share capital of the two companies:

    Courage Ltd   £100,000   in £1 ordinary shares
    Brains Ltd   £20,000   in £1 ordinary shares

(2) Courage Ltd bought an interest in Brains Ltd on 1 January 19X2, as follows:

    12,000 ordinary shares
    £20,000 (out of £40,000) 8% debentures

On 1 January 19X2 the balance of Brains Ltd's profit and loss account was £12,000.

(3) During the year Brains Ltd invoiced goods to Courage Ltd for £10,000. All the goods had been sold by the year–end.

(4) Brains Ltd has incurred exceptional reorganisation costs during the year. However, there are no discontinued operations.

(5) Courage Ltd does not account for dividends until they are received.

Required

Prepare the consolidated profit and loss account of Courage Ltd and its subsidiary Brains Ltd for the year ended 31 December 19X4. Ignore goodwill.

Summary

The key thing to remember is that the consolidated profit and loss account gives the results of the group trading with third parties.

Therefore the following adjustments are necessary:

- Eliminate the intra-group sales from turnover and cost of sales.

- Eliminate intra–group profit on stock held at the year–end.

- Exclude dividends received from the subsidiary.

- Include minority interest, being the minority interest's share of the subsidiary company's profit after tax.

- Only include the dividends paid and proposed by the parent company.

CHAPTER 22

Group Accounts – Legal and Professional Requirements

Objectives

This chapter covers the following performance criteria:

10.2.1 Financial statements are accurately drafted from the appropriate information.

10.2.2 Subsequent adjustments are correctly implemented.

10.2.3 Draft accounts comply with domestic standards and legislation, and, where relevant, partnership agreement.

At the end of this chapter, you should be able to:

- understand the definition of a subsidiary undertaking;

- understand the definition of an associate;

- deal with associated undertakings in the consolidated financial statements;

- understand the difference between acquisition accounting and merger accounting; and

- understand the situations in which merger accounting is appropriate.

Introduction

In this final chapter on group accounts, we shall look at the law and Standards governing this area of financial reporting. Many of the points of principle will already be familiar; the main purpose of the chapter is to draw them together.

In this chapter, we shall look at the Companies Act 1985, as amended by the 1989 Act, FRS2 *Accounting for subsidiary undertakings* and FRS 9 *Associates and joint ventures.*

Companies Act 1985 requirements

Definition of parent and subsidiary

The full definition is given in the Act and is restated in FRS2. The key points of the definition are summarised below:

An undertaking is the parent of another (a subsidiary) if *any* of the following apply:

- It holds a majority of voting rights.

- It is a member and can appoint/remove directors with a majority of votes.

- It is a member and controls a majority of votes via an agreement with other members.

- It has a participating interest and actually exercises dominant influence or the undertakings are managed on a unified basis.

FRS2 defines *dominant influence*. In essence, the term means that the parent determines the financial and operating policies of the subsidiary, which effectively means that the parent has control.

FRS2 also defines *managed on a unified basis*. This term means that the undertakings are integrated and managed as a single unit.

Requirement to prepare group accounts

A company must prepare group accounts if it is a parent company at its year-end (ie. it has one or more subsidiaries, unless it qualifies for exemption from this requirement).

Exemptions from the requirement to prepare group accounts

Inclusion in consolidated results of a larger group

A company need not prepare group accounts if:

- its immediate parent is incorporated in the European Union (EU) and prepares accounts in accordance with (EU) requirements; and

- the company seeking the exemption does not have any securities listed on a stock exchange in the EU; and

- the company is a wholly owned subsidiary of its immediate parent; or

- the parent owns over 50% and notice requiring group accounts has not been served by:
    - holders of more than half of the remaining shares *not* held by the parent; or
    - holders of 5% of total shares.

Small and medium-sized groups

- A small or medium-sized group, not containing a public company, a banking, authorised investment or insurance company, need not prepare group accounts if it:
    - meets any two of the small/medium-size limits for two consecutive years; or
    - met size criteria and was entitled to exemption last year; or
    - meets size criteria this year and was entitled to exemption last year.

Size limits:

	Before consolidation adjustments		After consolidation adjustments
Turnover not more than	£13,440,000	or	£11,200,000
Gross assets not more than	£6,720,000	or	£5,600,000
Average number of employees not more than	250		

- The totals before consolidation adjustments are obtained by adding together the amounts in the individual company accounts.

- The totals after consolidation adjustments are obtained from the group balance sheet (and profit and loss account).

Other Companies Act requirements for group accounts

- Group accounts must be consolidated.

- The parent and subsidiaries should have the same accounting period and year-end. If this is not practicable, the Act allows:

    - consolidation of a subsidiary's statutory accounts drawn up to date within three months prior to the parent's year-end; or

    - consolidation of interim accounts for the subsidiary made up to the parent's year-end; this alternative is preferred by FRS2.

- Uniform accounting policies should be used for amounts included in the group accounts. Different accounting policies may only be used in exceptional cases. The group accounts must disclose particulars of the different policies (restated in FRS2).

- Standard formats and disclosures must be used. These are set out in the chapters on company accounts.

FRS2: Accounting for subsidiary undertakings

FRS2 deals with the preparation of group accounts, including application of the Companies Act requirements.

Objective

To require parent undertakings to provide financial information about their groups in consolidated financial statements, intended to present the parent and its subsidiaries as a single economic entity.

Key definitions

- *Consolidation* is the process of adjusting and combining financial information from individual financial statements to present information for the group as a single economic entity.

- *Control* is the ability to direct the financial and operating policies of another entity.

- *Minority interests* are the interests in a subsidiary held by or on behalf of persons other than the parent and its subsidiaries.

- *Parent and subsidiary*: see section on Companies Act 1985 provisions.

Disclosures for principal subsidiary undertakings

- The proportion of voting rights held by the parent and its subsidiaries

- An indication of the nature of the subsidiary's business

Minority interests

- The consolidated balance sheet should show separately in capital and reserves the minority interest share of the subsidiary's net assets or liabilities consolidated. Note that, if the subsidiary has net liabilities, we show this as a debit balance in capital and reserves.

- The consolidated profit and loss account should show separately the minority interest share of the subsidiary's profit or loss after tax for the period.

Intra-group transactions

- Eliminate in full any profits or losses on intra-group transactions reflected in the book value of assets included in consolidation.

- Apportion the elimination of profits or losses between the parent and minority interests in proportion to their holdings in the company recording the profit or loss in its own financial statements. Hence, when the subsidiary sells goods to the parent, the subsidiary records the profit so we apportion the elimination between the parent and minority interests.

Changes in composition of a group

- Changes in membership of a group occur on the date on which control passes.

Other types of investment

We have seen that, if a company has an investment in another company, the accounting treatment of that investment depends upon whether or not that investment gives *control*. If the investment gives control, the investment is treated as a subsidiary and group accounts are prepared. If the investment does not give control, it is treated as a simple investment (see the sessions on published accounts).

In practice, there is a third possibility.

An associate is an entity (usually a company) over which the group exerts *significant influence* but *not* control. A holding of 20% to 50% usually indicates significant influence. Significant influence involves active participation in management, not simply a passive role, as would be the case with a simple trade investment.

We need to distinguish an associate from a subsidiary and from a simple trade investment because, whilst the group does not have control over the associate, it does have more than a passive interest. Hence, we need a treatment in between full consolidation and leaving the investment at cost in the group accounts.

Relationship with group

As we saw in the first session on group accounts, a group comprises a parent and its subsidiaries. As an associate is neither a parent nor a subsidiary, it is not part of the group. Instead, the group has an investment in the associate. When we identify the group structure, we include the associate, even though it is not part of the group, as this helps us to identify its status and the actual percentage interest which, as we shall see, is important. For example:

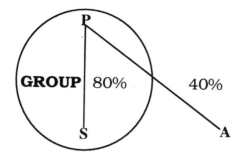

The associate is not part of the group

Treatment in investing company's own accounts

Balance sheet

We include the investment in fixed asset investments, usually at cost. In the individual company, as opposed to consolidated, balance sheet, we do not use the term *associate*. Instead, we include the investment under the sub-heading 'Participating interests'. As we shall see in more detail later, this term also includes investments other than associates. As with other investments, we may revalue this investment and must write down its value if there is a an impairment in value.

Profit and loss account

In the individual company profit and loss account (which, as you will recall, the parent does not need to publish if it publishes a consolidated profit and loss account), we include dividend income from the associate under the heading 'Income from participating interests'. Again, note that the term *associate* is not used in the individual company, as opposed to group, accounts.

Treatment in group accounts

In the group accounts, we use a technique called *equity accounting* for an associate. We also describe the associate as an *associated undertaking*. Note that we only use this technique in group accounts (ie. where the parent also has a subsidiary), which we consolidate as normal.

Instead of bringing in all of the associate's net assets and profits and then showing a minority interest to reflect the part not actually owned, we only include the *group share* of the associate's net assets and profits from the outset.

Balance sheet

In fixed asset investments, we replace the investment as shown in the investing company's own individual balance sheet with the *group share* of the associate's net assets at the balance sheet date, in one line, under 'Interests in associated undertakings'.

In group reserves, we include the parent's share of the associate's post-acquisition reserves (calculated in the same way as for a subsidiary).

We cancel the investment in the associate as shown in the investing company's own individual balance sheet against the group share of the associate's net assets at the date of acquisition (at fair value). The difference is a premium or discount on acquisition (in effect, goodwill).

Example

P Ltd owns 80% of S Ltd and 40% of A Ltd. Balance sheets of the three companies at 31 December 19X8 are:

	P Ltd £	S Ltd £	A Ltd £
Investment: Shares in S Ltd	800	–	–
Investment: Shares in A Ltd	600	–	–
Sundry net assets	3,600	3,800	4,400
	5,000	3,800	4,400
Share capital – £1 ordinary shares	1,000	400	800
Profit and loss account	4,000	3,400	3,600
	5,000	3,800	4,400

P Ltd acquired its shares in S Ltd when S Ltd's profit and loss reserves were £520 and P Ltd acquired its shares in A Ltd when A Ltd's profit and loss reserves were £400.

Assume that all goodwill arising on acquisition has been fully amortised through the profit and loss account.

Required

Prepare the consolidated balance sheet at 31 December 19X8.

Solution

P Ltd: Consolidated balance sheet as at 31 December 19X8

	£
Interest in associated undertakings (4,400 × 40%)	1,760
Sundry net assets (3,600 + 3,800)	7,400
	9,160
Share capital	1,000
Profit and loss account (W5)	7,400
	8,400
Minority interests (W4)	760
	9,160

Workings

(1) **Group structure**

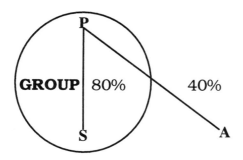

(2) **Net assets working**

S Ltd

	Balance sheet date	Acquisition
	£	£
Share capital	400	400
Profit and loss account	3,400	520
	3,800	920

A Ltd

	Balance sheet date	Acquisition
	£	£
Share capital	800	800
Profit and loss account	3,600	400
	4,400	1,200

(3) **Goodwill**

S Ltd

	£
Cost of investment	800
Net assets acquired (80% × 920 (W2))	(736)
	64

A Ltd

	£
Cost of investment	600
Net assets acquired (40% × 1,200 (W2))	(480)
	120

(4) Minority interests

	£
S Ltd only – (20% × 3,800)	760

(5) Profit and loss account

	£
P Ltd – from question	4,000
Share of S Ltd [80% × (3,400 – 520)]	2,304
Share of A Ltd [40% × (3,600 – 400)]	1,280
Less: Goodwill (64 + 120)	(184)
	7,400

Profit and loss account

The treatment of an associate in the consolidated profit and loss account is consistent with its treatment in the consolidated balance sheet.

We replace the dividend income from the investment in the associate, as shown in the investing company's own profit and loss account, with the *group share* of the associate's operating profit, in one line, as 'Income from interests in associated undertakings' or 'Share of operating profit in associates'.

If there is a charge for amortisation of goodwill, this is included in the group's share of the associate's operating profit. It should be separately disclosed.

If the associate's profit and loss account includes exceptional items, interest payable or interest receivable, the group's share of these should be included in the profit and loss account and shown separately from the amounts for the group.

We also include the group share of the associate's tax in 'Tax on profit on ordinary activities'. The group tax and the share of the associate's tax are separately disclosed in the tax note.

Do not add in the associate's turnover or expenses line by line.

Time-apportion the results of the associate if acquired mid-year.

Example

P Ltd has owned 80% of S Ltd and 40% of A Ltd for several years. Profit and loss accounts for the year ended 31 December 19X8 are:

	P Ltd £	S Ltd £	A Ltd £
Turnover	14,000	12,000	10,000
Cost of sales	(9,000)	(4,000)	(3,000)
Gross profit	5,000	8,000	7,000
Administrative expenses	(2,000)	(6,000)	(3,000)
	3,000	2,000	4,000
Income from participating interests	400	–	–
Profit on ordinary activities before taxation	3,400	2,000	4,000
Tax on profit on ordinary activities	(1,000)	(1,200)	(2,000)
Profit on ordinary activities after taxation	2,400	800	2,000
Dividends (paid)	(1,000)	–	(1,000)
Retained profit	1,400	800	1,000

Required

Prepare the consolidated profit and loss account for the year ended 31 December 19X8. Assume that all goodwill arising on acquisition has been fully amortised through the profit and loss account.

Solution

P Ltd: Consolidated profit and loss account for the year ending 31 December 19X8

	£	£
Turnover		26,000
Cost of sales		(13,000)
Gross profit		13,000
Administrative expenses		(8,000)
Operating profit		5,000
Income from interests in associated undertakings		1,600
Profit on ordinary activities before taxation		6,600
Tax on profit on ordinary activities		
Group	2,200	
Share of associated undertaking's tax	800	
		(3,000)
Profit on ordinary activities after taxation		3,600
Minority interests (W3)		(160)
Profit for the financial year attributable to the members of P Ltd		3,440
Dividends paid		(1,000)
Retained profit for the financial year		2,440

Workings

(1) Group structure

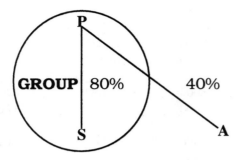

(2) Consolidation schedule

	P Ltd £	S Ltd £	A Ltd £	Consol £
Turnover	14,000	12,000		26,000
C of S	(9,000)	(4,000)		(13,000)
Admin	(2,000)	(6,000)		(8,000)
Income from assoc (40% x 4,000)			1,600	1,600
Tax – group	(1,000)	(1,200)		(2,200)
– assoc (40% x 2,000)			(800)	(800)
PAT		800		

(3) Minority interest

S Ltd (20% x 800)　　　　　　　　　　　　　　　　　　　　　　　　　£160

Associates and the Companies Act 1985

Participating interest

The term *participating interest* is defined in the Act and FRS2 restates the definition. A participating interest is one held on a long-term basis for the purpose of securing a contribution by the exercise of control or influence. This is presumed where the holding is 20% or more. Note that this does *not* automatically mean that there is significant influence as that term has a narrower meaning, given by FRS 9. We have already seen that the statutory formats distinguish a participating interest from smaller investments, which are classified as 'Other investments other than loans' in the balance sheet sub-headings.

Associated undertakings

♦ The Act defines these as undertakings, which are not subsidiaries, where the group:

– has a participating interest
– exercises significant influence

Significant influence is presumed, unless the contrary is shown, if the group's holding is 20% or more.

♦ The Act requires equity accounting for an associate in the group accounts.

FRS 9: Associates and joint ventures

Key definitions

- An *associate* is an entity (other than a subsidiary) in which another entity (the investor) has a *participating interest* and over whose operating and financial policies the investor exercises a *significant influence*.

- A *participating interest* is an interest held in the shares of another entity on a long term basis for the purpose of securing a contribution to the investor's activities by the exercise of control or influence arising from or related to that interest.

- The exercise of *significant influence* means that the investor is actively involved and is influential in the direction of its investee through its participation in policy decisions covering aspects of policy relevant to the investor, including decisions on strategic issues such as:

    (a) the expansion or contraction of the business, participation in other entities or changes in products, markets and activities of its investee; and

    (b) determining the balance between dividend and reinvestment.

Note that the FRS 9 definition of an associate is narrower than the Companies Act definition and the emphasis is different. The Companies Act definition is based on the size of the shareholding. The FRS 9 definition is based on whether significant influence is exercised in practice (on the substance of the relationship between investor and investee, rather than on its strict legal form). For example, a holding of over 20% is extremely unlikely to give rise to significant influence if the remainder of the shares are owned by another company.

Accounting treatment

- In the investing company's own accounts, the associate is included in the balance sheet as a fixed asset investment and shown either at cost (or valuation) less amounts written off.

    (The profit and loss account includes dividends received and receivable.)

- In the consolidated profit and loss account:

    Group share of associate's:

    - Operating profit
    - Exceptional items
    - Interest payable/receivable
    - Taxation

- In the consolidated balance sheet:

	£
Group share of associate's net assets	X
Goodwill arising on acquisition less amounts amortised	X
	X

Other methods of consolidation

You have learned to prepare consolidated accounts using the acquisition method of accounting. Acquisition accounting is the method used for the majority of business combinations. (*Business combination* is the generic term for transactions which result in one company becoming the subsidiary of another.)

The central idea behind acquisition accounting is that a parent *acquires* a subsidiary company. The assets and liabilities of the subsidiary company are taken over by the parent and absorbed into its operations. This scenario is typical of most business combinations.

However, some business combinations arise as the result of the uniting of interests of two companies so that neither company can be said to have acquired the other. This type of combination is popularly known as a *merger*. A different method of consolidation, known as the *merger method*, is used to prepare consolidated accounts in this situation.

The difference between an acquisition and a merger seems to be obvious. However, the essential distinction between the two depends on future intentions and the spirit in which the combination takes place. These are subjective, rather than matters of fact. Many business combinations involve complex transactions and arrangements and in practice it can be difficult to establish whether a particular combination is an acquisition or a merger.

The following definitions are contained in FRS6 *Acquisitions and mergers*.

- *Merger*

    A business combination which results in the creation of a new reporting entity formed from the combining parties, in which the shareholders of the combining entities come together in a *substantially equal partnership* for the *mutual sharing* of the risks and benefits of the combined entity, and in which *no party to the combination in substance obtains control over any other, or is otherwise seen to be dominant*, whether by virtue of the proportion of its shareholders rights in the combined entity, the influence of its directors or otherwise.

- *Acquisition*

    A business combination that is *not a merger*.

Note that, in practice, merger accounting is extremely rare.

Merger accounting method

Consolidations under acquisition accounting are based on the concept of control. This is not relevant in a merger situation where there is no control. Instead, the consolidation needs to reflect the pooling of interests of two companies.

To reflect the pooling of interests the following treatment is adopted:

(i)   The parent records the investment in the subsidiary in its own balance sheet at *nominal* value of shares issued plus fair value of any other consideration, ie. the fair value of shares issued on combination is not recorded.

(ii)   On consolidation, cancel the cost of the investment in the subsidiary against the nominal value of the subsidiary's shares obtained in exchange.

(iii) There is no need to adjust the net assets of the combining parties to fair value at combination for inclusion in the consolidated balance sheet.

(iv) Results and cash flows are consolidated as though the merger had always existed, ie. profits are included from the date of incorporation not the date of combination.

Example

Set out below are the summarised balance sheets of Coll plc and Tiree plc.

	Coll plc £'000	Tiree plc £'000
Net assets	5,000	4,000
Share capital – £1 ords	1,000	1,000
Profit and loss account	4,000	3,000
	5,000	4,000

Coll plc is to combine with Tiree plc by obtaining 100% of Tiree plc's shares. The consideration consists of 1,000,000 £1 ordinary shares valued at £6 each. The fair value of Tiree plc's assets is £4,600,000.

Required

Assuming that the combination is to be accounted for as a merger

(a) prepare the balance sheet of Coll plc reflecting the issue of shares
(b) prepare the consolidated balance sheet of the Coll group after the combination.

Solution

(a) **Balance sheet of Coll plc**

	£'000
Net assets	5,000
Investment in Tiree plc (1,000 × £1)	1,000
	6,000
Share capital (1,000 + 1,000)	2,000
Profit and loss account	4,000
	6,000

(b) **Consolidated balance sheet of Coll plc**

	£'000
Net assets (5,000 + 4,000)	9,000
Share capital	2,000
Profit and loss account (4,000 + 3,000)	7,000
	9,000

Summary

The main legal and professional requirements in respect of group accounts are set out in:

- the Companies Act 1985

- FRS2 *Accounting for subsidiary undertakings*

- FRS 9 *Associates and joint ventures*

An undertaking is the parent of another (a subsidiary) if *any* of the following apply:

- It holds a majority of voting rights.

- It is a member and can appoint/remove directors with a majority of votes.

- It is a member and controls a majority of votes via an agreement with other members.

- It has a participating interest and actually exercises dominant influence or the undertakings are managed on a unified basis.

CHAPTER 23

Answers to Chapter Questions

Chapter 2

1. *Going concern:* The business will continue to trade for the foreseeable future.

   Accruals: Revenue and expenditure are recognised in accounts as they are earned or incurred, rather than as they are received or paid.

   Consistency: There is consistency of accounting treatment of like items within each accounting period and from one period to another.

   Prudence: Revenue and profits are not anticipated, but are included only when realised. Liabilities and losses are provided for as soon as possible.

Chapter 3

1 VB Ltd

			Debit £	Credit £
(1)	Dr	Suspense	492	
	Cr	Sales returns account		246
	Cr	Sales		246

Being the correction of cash sales incorrectly debited to the sales returns account

(2)	Dr	Suspense	45	
	Cr	Customer's account		45

Being the correction of a transposition error on a posting to a customer's account

(3)	Dr	Bank charges	37	
	Cr	Cash		37

Being the posting of bank charges

(4)	Dr	VAT recoverable	45	
	Cr	Purchases		45

Being the correction of the posting of VAT on a supplier's invoice

(5)	Dr	Supplier's account	258	
	Cr	Customer's account		258

Being the correction of a contra entry wrongly posted

(6)	Dr	Rates	13,500	
	Cr	Creditors		13,500

Being the entering into the trial balance of a rates bill

(7)	Dr	Carriage inwards	52	
	Cr	Carriage outwards		52

Being the correction of a posting error

(8)	Dr	Bad debts	40	
	Cr	Customer's account		40

Being the writing-off of a bad debt

The effect on profit for the year ended 30 April 19Y0 of each of these journals is as follows:

(1) Increase profit by £492.
(2) No effect
(3) Decrease profit by £37.
(4) Increase profit by £45.
(5) No effect
(6) Decrease profit by 1/6 × £13,500 = £2,250
(7) No effect
(8) Decrease profit by £40.

Chapter 4

1 Brick and Stone

Trading and profit and loss account for the year ended 30 September 19Y0

	£	£
Sales (322,100 − 2,100)		320,000
Cost of sales		
Opening stock	23,000	
Purchases (208,200 − 1,000 − 6,100 + 1,700)	202,800	
	225,800	
Closing stock	(32,000)	
		(193,800)
Gross profit		126,200
Add: Discounts receivable		370
		126,570
Less: Printing, stationery and postage	3,500	
Rent and rates (10,300 − 600)	9,700	
Heat and light	8,700	
Salaries	36,100	
Telephone (2,900 + 400)	3,300	
Motor vehicle costs	5,620	
Discounts allowable	950	
Carriage outwards	2,400	
Depreciation		
Fixtures and fittings (26,000 × 10%)	2,600	
Motor vehicles (46,000 × 20%)	9,200	
Loan interest (W3)	250	
		(82,320)
Net profit		44,250

Appropriation statement

	Total £	Brick £	Stone £
Stone's salary (6/12 × 12,000)	6,000	–	6,000
Profit share 3:2	38,250	22,950	15,300
	44,250	22,950	21,300

Balance sheet as at 30 September 19Y0

	Cost	Provision for depreciation	NBV
	£	£	£
Fixed assets			
Fixtures and fittings	26,000	13,800	12,200
Motor vehicles	46,000	34,200	11,800
	72,000	48,000	24,000

	£	£
Current assets		
Stock		32,000
Trade debtors		9,000
Prepayments		600
Bank balance		7,700
		49,300
Creditors: Amounts falling due within one year		
Trade creditors	8,400	
Accruals (W3)	650	
		(9,050)

	40,250
	64,250
Creditors: Amounts falling due after more than one year	
Loan – Brick	(10,000)
	54,250

Represented by:

	£	£
Capital accounts (W1)		
Brick		23,000
Stone		17,000
		40,000
Current accounts (W2)		
Brick	2,550	
Stone	11,700	
		14,250
		54,250

Workings

(1) Partners' capital accounts

	Brick £	Stone £
Balance at 1 October 19X9	33,000	17,000
Less: Transfer to Brick loan Account 1 July 19Y0	(10,000)	
	23,000	17,000

(2) Partners' current accounts

	Brick	Stone
Balance at 1 October 19X9	3,600	2,400
Salary		6,000
Profit share (from appropriation statement)	22,950	15,300
	26,550	23,700
Less: Drawings		
Goods	–	(1,000)
Cash	(24,000)	(11,000)
	2,550	11,700

(3) Accruals

	£
Telephone	400
Brick's loan interest (10,000 × 10% × 3/12)	250
	650

Chapter 5

1   Billesley Ltd

(a)

Profit and loss account for the year ended 30 June 19X2

	£	£
Turnover		500,000
Cost of sales (46 + 280 – 52)		274,000
Gross profit		226,000
Distribution costs	65,000	
Administrative expenses	110,000	
		175,000
Profit on ordinary activities before taxation		51,000
Tax on profit on ordinary activities		12,000
Profit for the financial year		39,000
Dividends (10 + 6 + 8 + 6)		30,000
		9,000
Transfer to general reserve		5,000
		4,000
Profit and loss account brought forward		135,000
Profit and loss account carried forward		139,000

Balance sheet as at 30 June 19X2

	£	£	£
Fixed assets			
Land and buildings	500,000	80,000	420,000
Plant	180,000	105,000	75,000
Vehicles	150,000	90,000	60,000
	830,000	275,000	555,000
Current assets			
Stocks		52,000	
Debtors (116 – 12)		104,000	
Investment		75,000	
Cash at bank and in hand		63,000	
		294,000	
Creditors: Amounts falling due within one year			
Creditors and accruals	74,000		
Corporation tax	12,000		
Proposed dividends (8 + 6)	14,000		
		100,000	
Net current assets			194,000
Total assets less current liabilities			749,000
Creditors: Amounts falling due after more than one year			
12% debentures			150,000
			599,000
Capital and reserves			
Called-up share capital			400,000
Share premium account			25,000
Capital redemption reserve			20,000
General reserve (10 + 5)			15,000
Profit and loss account			139,000
			599,000

(b) (1) The nominal value of Billesley Ltd's ordinary share capital is £200,000. This is made up of 400,000 50 pence ordinary shares.

    (2) The share premium account is a statutory reserve that must be set up if the company issues shares at a price that is greater than their nominal value. Therefore at some time in the past Billesley Ltd must have issued some shares at a price that was £25,000 more than the nominal value of those shares.

    (3) Most companies will produce both management accounts and financial accounts. Management accounts are produced for the internal use of the management of the company. The financial accounts (as produced in part (a)) are produced for the shareholders or owners of the company. The managers and the shareholders will have different information needs and the management accounts and financial accounts will reflect these different needs.

Chapter 6

1 Punch

Manufacturing account for the year ended 31 March 19X1

	£	£
Raw materials consumed		
Opening stock	12,725	
Purchases	82,550	
	95,275	
Less: Closing stock	(9,650)	
		85,625
Factory wages		64,750
Prime cost		150,375
Factory overheads		
Rent (W4) (70%)	20,038	
Repairs to buildings (80%)	4,400	
Depreciation – Plant and machinery (W1)	3,650	
– Buildings (80%)	720	
Electricity and power (W2)	12,373	
		41,181
Opening WIP	18,000	
Closing WIP	(21,000)	
		(3,000)
Factory cost of goods produced		188,556

Trading and profit and loss account for the year ended 31 March 19X1

		£	£
Sales			362,720
Less:	Cost of goods sold		
	Opening stock	20,500	
	Transfers from factory	188,556	
		209,056	
Closing stock		(24,500)	
			184,556
Gross profit			178,164
Less:	Selling and distribution expenses		
	Wages	26,920	
	Selling expenses (22,000 + 60% × 240)	22,144	
	Bad and doubtful debts (700 + 354) (W3)	1,054	
	Depreciation of motor vans	4,950	
	Sales manager's commission (W5)	20,516	
			(75,584)
Less:	Administration expenses		
	Wages	24,360	
	Electricity and power (W2)	6,187	
	Rent (30%) (W4)	8,587	
	Repairs to buildings (20%)	1,100	
	Depreciation buildings (20%)	180	
	Sundry (850 + 5,900 + 40% × 240)	6,846	
			(47,260)
Net profit			55,320

Balance sheet as at 31 March 19X1

	Cost £	Depreciation £	£
Fixed assets			
Freehold land and buildings	45,000	3,600	41,400
Plant and machinery	36,500	8,150	28,350
Motor vans	19,800	8,650	11,150
	101,300	20,400	80,900
Current assets			
Stocks– Raw materials		9,650	
– WIP		21,000	
– Finished goods		24,500	
Debtors (W3) (38,270 – 1,914)		36,356	
Cash in hand		45	
		91,551	
Current liabilities			
Bank overdraft		6,320	
Creditors		42,230	
Accruals			
[960 + 240 + 850 + 6,625 (W4) + 20,516 (W5)]		29,191	
		77,741	
			13,810
Net current assets			94,710

Represented by:

	£
Capital @ 1.4.X0	39,390
Profit for the year	55,320
	94,710

Workings

(1) Depreciation
- Land and buildings = 2% x 45,000 = 900
- Plant and machinery = 10% x 36,500 = 3,650
- Motor vehicles = 25% x 19,800 = 4,950

(2) Electricity and power

	£
Per question	17,600
Accruals	960
	18,560
Factory (2/3)	12,373
Admin. (1/3)	6,187

(3) Debtors

	£
Per question	38,970
Less: Bad debt provision	(700)
	38,270

	£
Provision: 5% × 38,270	1,914
Opening provision	1,560
Increase	354

(4) Rent

Charge for the year	=	$22,000 + 3/12 \times 26,500$
	=	$22,000 + 6,625$
	=	$28,625$
Factory (70%)	=	20,038
Admin. (30%)	=	8,587

(5) Sales manager's commission

	£
Gross profit	178,164
Less: Expenses (26,920 + 22,144 + 1,054 + 4,950)	(55,068)
	123,096 (120%)
Commission (20%)	(20,516)
	102,580

Chapter 7

1 Radical Ltd

Balance sheet as at 30 September 19X2

	Note	£	£
Fixed assets			
Tangible assets	1		336,265
Investments	2		22,632
			358,897
Current assets			
Stocks		192,734	
Debtors	3	161,238	
Cash at bank and in hand		45,166	
		399,138	
Creditors: Amounts falling due within one year	4	116,450	
Net current assets			282,688
Total assets less current liabilities			641,585
Creditors: Amounts falling due after more than one year	5		150,000
			491,585

	Note	£	£
Capital and reserves			
Called-up share capital	6		350,000
Share premium account			52,400
Profit and loss account			89,185
			491,585

.... Director

These accounts were approved by the board of directors on ....

Notes to the balance sheet

(1) Tangible fixed assets

	Freehold property £	Motor vehicles £	Total £
Cost			
At 1 October 19X1	105,000	366,345	471,345
Additions	26,000	40,450	66,450
At 30 September 19X2	131,000	406,795	537,795
Accumulated depreciation			
At 1 October 19X1	2,500	112,530	115,030
Charge for year	2,500	84,000	86,500
At 30 September 19X2	5,000	196,530	201,530
Net book value – At 30 September 19X2	126,000	210,265	336,265
– At 1 October 19X1	102,500	253,815	356,315

(2) Fixed asset investments

All investments are listed on the Stock Exchange.

(3) Debtors

	£
Trade debtors (172,062 – 13,420)	158,642
Prepayments and accrued income	2,596
	161,238

(4) Creditors: Amounts falling due within one year

	£
Trade creditors	64,700
Other creditors including taxation and social security	
Corporation tax	26,750
Proposed dividend	25,000
	116,450

(5) Creditors: Amounts falling due after more than one year

	£
Debenture loans	
9½% Loan Stock, repayable 1 October 19Y9	150,000

(6) Called-up share capital

	£
Authorised, issued and fully paid	
1,000,000 ordinary shares of 25p each	250,000
200,000 8% cumulative preference shares of 50p each	100,000
	350,000

Chapter 8

1 Church's Ltd

Profit and loss account for the year ended 31 December 19X0

	Notes	£
Turnover		595,932
Cost of sales		349,996
Gross profit		245,936
Distribution costs (W1)		164,017
Administrative expenses (W1)		43,498
Operating profit	1	38,421
Income from fixed asset investments	4	1,326
Interest payable and similar charges	5	800
Profit on ordinary activities before taxation		38,947
Tax on profit on ordinary activities	6	12,410
Profit on ordinary activities after taxation		26,537
Dividends	7	16,900
Retained profit for the financial year		9,637

Notes to the accounts

(1) Operating profit

Operating profit is stated after charging

	£
Directors' emoluments (13,500 + 13,000 + 858 + 7,500 + 750)	35,608
Auditors' fees	700
Depreciation of tangible fixed assets (5,290 + 520 + 1,000)	6,810

(2) Staff

(a) Aggregate payroll costs (amounts include those in respect of executive directors)

	£
Wages and salaries (62,917 + 7,500)	70,417
Social security costs	4,250
Other pension costs	750
	75,417

(b) The average number of employees working for the company in the financial year was 10.

(3) Income from fixed asset investments

	£
Listed	780
Unlisted	546
	1,326

(4) Interest payable and similar charges

On debenture loan repayable after more than five years	£800

(5) Tax on profit on ordinary activities

UK corporation tax	£12,410

(6) Dividends

	£
Preference: 6½% paid	6,500
Ordinary: 5.2p per share proposed	10,400
	16,900

Workings

(1)

	Distribution costs £	Administrativee xpenses £
Motor expenses	79,842	–
Depreciation	5,290	1,520
Other	39,420	5,746
Wages and salaries	34,715	28,202
Pension to former director's widow	–	750
Superannuation scheme	2,250	2,000
Audit	–	700
Provision for directors' fees	2,500	5,000
Discounts received	–	(420)
	164,017	43,498

(2) Staff costs

	Distribution costs £	Administrative expenses £	£
Wages + salaries			
Per question	34,715	28,202	
Provision for directors' fees	2,500	5,000	
	37,215	33,202	70,417
Social security costs			
Superannuation scheme	2,250	2,000	4,250
Other pension costs			
Director's widow	–	750	750

Chapter 9

1 Claret Ltd

Statement of total recognised gains and losses for the year ended 31 December 19X8

	£'000
Profit for the financial year (1,825 + 250 – 62 + 55)	2,068
Unrealised surplus on revaluation (W1)	40
	2,108
Prior period adjustment (note 1)	(55)
Total gains and losses recognised since last annual report	2,053

Notes to the accounts

(1) **Reconciliation of opening and closing totals of shareholders' funds**

	£'000
Balance 1 January 19X8 (W2)	21,741
Prior period adjustment (note 2)	(55)
As restated	21,686
Profits for the financial year (W3)	2,068
Dividends	(250)
Surplus on revaluation	40
Shares issued (160 × £2.10)	336
Balance 31 December 19X8	23,880

(2) **Prior period adjustment**

The prior period adjustment is in respect of a fundamental error in the valuation of stock. Closing stock and, hence, reserves at 31 December 19X7 were overstated by £55,000.

Workings

(1) Unrealised surplus on revaluation

	£'000	£'000
Revalued amount		430
Original cost	650	
Accumulated depreciation to 31 December 19X8 $(650 \times 8/20)$	(260)	
Net book value at revaluation		(390)
		40

(2) Opening total shareholders' funds

	£'000
Share capital (2,000 × 50p)	1,000
Profit and loss account	20,658
Revaluation reserve	83
	21,741

(3) Profit for financial year

	£'000	£'000
Retained profit		1,825
Add back: Dividend		250
Profit for financial year		2,075
Less: Overstatement of stock		
Opening stock	55	
Less: Closing stock	(62)	
		(7)
		2,068

Chapter 10

1 Ford plc

Accounting policy note

(1) Tangible fixed assets

Interests in buildings are stated at a valuation.

Other tangible fixed assets are stated at cost, together with any incidental expenses of acquisition.

Depreciation is calculated so as to write off the net cost or valuation of tangible fixed assets over their expected useful economic lives. A full year's charge is provided in the year of acquisition. The rates and bases used are as follows:

Buildings	2% pa
Plant and machinery	10% pa
Office equipment and fixtures – on the straight-line basis	20% pa
Motor vehicles – on the reducing-balance method	30% pa

(2) Operating profit

Operating profit is stated after charging:

	£'000
Depreciation of tangible fixed assets	562

(3) Tangible fixed assets

	Freehold land and buildings £'000	Plant and machinery £'000	Motor vehicles £'000	Fixtures, fittings, tools and equipment £'000	Total £'000
Cost or valuation					
At 1 January 19X7	1,440	1,968	449	888	4,745
Additions	500	75	35	22	632
Revaluations	760	–	–	–	760
At 31 December 19X7	2,700	2,043	484	910	6,137
Depreciation					
At 1 January 19X7	144	257	194	583	1,178
Revaluation adjustment	(144)				(144)
Charge for year	60	233	87	182	562
At 31 December 19X7	60	490	281	765	1,596
Net book value					
At 31 December 19X7	2,640	1,553	203	145	4,541
At 1 January 19X7	1,296	1,711	255	305	3,567

(a) Buildings were valued for the purposes of the 19X7 accounts at existing use value. This valuation was made by a firm of independent chartered surveyors. The historical cost of the factory is £1,940,000 and the related depreciation is £183,000 (W).

(b) The company's depreciation policy on motor vehicles has been changed from a rate of 25% pa on cost to a rate of 30% pa on reducing balance in order to give a fairer presentation of the results and of the financial position. The effect of this change is to reduce the depreciation charge for the year by £34,000.

Working

Historical cost depreciation of factory

	£'000
Factory $6/50 \times 1,440$	173
Extension $1/50 \times 500$	10
	183

Chapter 11

1 Newprods Ltd

(a) (i) Pure research expenditure is expenditure incurred on experimental or theoretical work undertaken in order to gain new scientific or technical knowledge for its own sake. Pure research is not primarily directed towards any specific practical aim or application.

(ii) Applied research expenditure is expenditure incurred on an original or critical investigation which has been undertaken in order to gain new scientific or technical knowledge which is directed towards a specific practical aim or objective.

(iii) Development expenditure is expenditure incurred in using scientific or technical knowledge in order to produce new or substantially improved materials, devices, products or services, to install new processes or systems prior to the commencement of commercial applications, or substantially to improve those already produced or installed.

(b) Expenditure on pure and applied research should be written off in the year of expenditure. However, the cost of fixed assets acquired or constructed in order to provide facilities for research and development activities over a number of years should be capitalised and written off over their useful life.

Expenditure on development should be written off in the year of expenditure except in the following circumstances when it may be carried forward:

(i) there is a clearly defined project;

(ii) the related expenditure is separately identifiable;

(iii) the outcome of such a project was assessed with reasonable certainty as to:

- its technical feasibility; and

- its ultimate commercial viability considered in the light of factors such as likely market conditions (including competing products), public opinion, consumer and environmental legislation;

(iv) the aggregate of the deferred development costs, further development costs and related production, selling and administration costs is reasonably expected to be exceeded by related future sales or other revenues; and

(v) adequate resources exist, or are reasonably expected to be available, to enable the project to be completed and to provide any consequential increases in working capital.

The principle behind the above rules is that development expenditure should only be carried forward if the recovery of that expenditure can reasonably be regarded as assured.

(c) *Project 3*

Project 3 may be regarded as development (as defined in SSAP 13) and therefore it may be correct to carry forward a certain amount of the expenditure. However, the cost of producing the new compound is comparable to that of the existing raw material and therefore unless selling prices are increased the expenditure which has been incurred in developing the new compound will not be recovered in future periods.

Assuming that selling prices cannot be increased the expenditure should be shown as follows.

Balance sheet

	£
Fixed assets	
Tangible assets (at cost less depreciation)	9,000

Profit and loss account

	£
Development expenditure written off	11,000
Depreciation	1,000

Project 4

This is also development expenditure. As the yield of the operation is being greatly improved the material costs will obviously decrease and greater profits will be made. Thus the expenditure incurred in development may be recovered in future years. To determine how much of the expenditure may be carried forward it is necessary to calculate whether the aggregate of costs already incurred and future costs will be covered by the saving of material costs which is predicted.

The saving of material costs per annum is £30,000 and the life of the plant is ten years. Therefore, assuming no increases in the costs of the materials the new process will produce a saving of £30,000 per annum for some years. As the costs to date are only £22,000 plus fixed assets cost of £20,000 it seems highly probable that the expenditure will be recovered in future years. It is necessary to assume that the market for the product and its selling price will remain unchanged.

The treatment of the expenditure on Project 4 will therefore be as follows.

Balance sheet

	£
Fixed assets	
Intangible asset: development costs (22,000 + 2,000)	24,000
Tangible assets (20,000 – 2,000)	18,000

A note to the balance sheet should state:

(i) the reasons for capitalising the expenditure; and
(ii) the period over which the costs are being written off.

Note: No charge for development expenditure has been made this year as the commercial production has not yet commenced. The development costs should be amortised over a period coincident with the commercial use of the process.

Project 5

This project should be regarded as development work which is being carried out on behalf of a third party. If there is a firm contract which states that the expenditure is to be fully reimbursed then any such expenditure which has not been reimbursed at the balance sheet date should be included in work in progress.

The treatment would therefore be as follows.

Balance sheet

	£
Fixed assets	
Tangible assets	4,500
Current assets	
Stocks: Work in progress	44,500

Chapter 12

1   S Ltd

(a) (i) Raw materials should be valued at the lower of cost and net realisable value where cost includes all costs in bringing the items to their balance sheet location and conditions.

Both delivery and insurance costs could be included in this definition and so legitimately be added to the valuation.

(ii) The inclusion of these cost elements for the first time would constitute a change in accounting policy and so a prior period adjustment would be required to restate opening stock onto the same basis. There would therefore be no advantageous effect on this year's profit.

(b) (i) SSAP 9 suggests that where overheads are absorbed into production it should be on the basis of a normal level of activity. The costs to be included would be all production overheads, and, at management's discretion, a portion of administrative overheads. Selling overheads should never be included in stock valuation.

(ii) WIP valuation

	£'000
Overheads – variable (300 + 200)	500
– fixed (150 + 240 + 110)	500
	1,000

Normal level of activity   95,000 hours

Absorbed into WIP

$$£1,000,000 \times \frac{500}{95,000} = £5,263$$

Notes

(1) It is assumed that delivery vehicles are used in selling and so depreciation is not absorbed into stock.

(2) Alternatively, only some or possibly none of the administrative expenses might be absorbed. If none, this would give:

$$£(1,000,000 - 240,000) \times \frac{500}{95,000} = £4,000$$

(c) (i) Valuation at cost or net realisable value should be carried out on a product line-by-line basis in accordance with SSAP 9 and the Companies Act 1985. The latter also specifies that the value of assets and liabilities should be determined for individual items not in aggregate. The finance director's statement is therefore incorrect.

(ii) *Obsolete items* must be valued at £500, their net realisable value since this is lower than cost.

New product line. It seems likely from the initial market research that net realisable value will be considerably greater than the cost of £90,000. These items should thus be included at £90,000. If in a later period the launch proves unsuccessful the stock will need to be written down to £1,000 and, if material, may be shown as an exceptional item.

Chapter 15

1 Trunfair Ltd

(1) Uninsured stock loss

The uninsured stock loss totalling £200,000 arising from flood damage occurred after the year-end, and therefore since the condition did not exist at the year-end, the loss would be a non-adjusting event within the definition given in SSAP17. It should be disclosed if it is considered to be of such materiality that its non-disclosure would affect the ability of the users of the financial statements to reach proper understanding of the financial position. The disclosure that would be required would be:

(a) the nature of the event; and

(b) an estimate of the financial effect before taking account of taxation and the taxation implications should be explained where necessary for a proper understanding of the financial position.

(2) Insolvency of a debtor

This is a post balance sheet event within the definition given in SSAP17 *Accounting for post balance sheet events* and would be an adjusting event since it provides additional evidence of a condition existing at the balance sheet date.

The £120,000 should therefore be either provided for as a doubtful debt or, alternatively, written off as a bad debt. (The treatment would depend on the likelihood of any of the debt being recovered.) It may also be necessary to disclose the provision or write-off as an exceptional item in the notes to the accounts.

Chapter 16

1 Lucy Ltd

Task 1

Cash flow statement for Lucy Ltd for the year ended 31 March 1994

	£'000	£'000
Net cash inflow from operating activities		66,000*
Returns on investments and servicing of finance		
Interest paid		(4,500)
Taxation		(35,000)
Capital expenditure		
Payments to acquire fixed assets	(9,500)	
Sale of fixed assets	15,000	
		5,500
Equity dividends paid		(7,500)
Financing activities		
Issue of shares	75,000	
Repayment of loan	(5,000)	
		70,000
Net increase in cash		94,500

* Full credit was also given to students who made the assumption that the net cash flow from operating activities had already been adjusted for the profit on sale of fixed assets. If this were the case, the net increase in cash would be £103,500.

Task 2

Advantages of cash flow accounting

(a) Cash is an easier concept for users to understand than profit.

(b) Survival in business is dependent upon the ability to generate cash and cash flow accounting focuses on this.

(c) Cash flow is less dependent upon accounting policies and this makes inter-company comparison more useful.

(d) Creditors are interested in a company's ability to pay, shareholders may be interested in dividend payments, employees in the ability to pay (and increase) wages, so cash flow accounting is very relevant to the needs of many users of accounts.

Task 3

Differences attributable to:

- Depreciation
- Profit on sale of fixed assets
- Loss on sale of fixed assets
- Changes in stock
- Changes in debtors
- Changes in creditors
- Net cash flows in respect of discontinued activities
- Reorganisation costs

Chapter 17

1 Falcon Ltd

(a) (i) Return on capital employed

19X3	19X2
$\dfrac{53{,}500}{375{,}000} \times 100 = 14.27\%$	$\dfrac{41{,}000}{255{,}000} \times 100 = 16.08\%$

(ii) Profit margin

19X3	19X2
$\dfrac{53{,}500}{525{,}000} \times 100 = 10.19\%$	$\dfrac{41{,}000}{425{,}000} \times 100 = 9.65\%$

(iii) Asset turnover

19X3	19X2
$\dfrac{525{,}000}{375{,}000} = 1.4$	$\dfrac{425{,}000}{255{,}000} = 1.67$

(iv) Current ratio

19X3	19X2
$\dfrac{200{,}000}{80{,}000} = 2.5$	$\dfrac{160{,}000}{50{,}000} = 3.2$

(v) Acid test ratio

19X3	19X2
$\dfrac{80{,}000}{80{,}000} = 1.0$	$\dfrac{60{,}000}{50{,}000} = 1.2$

(vi) Debtor days

19X3	19X2
Average daily sales $\dfrac{525{,}000}{365} = £1{,}438$	$\dfrac{425{,}000}{365} = £1{,}164$
$\dfrac{80{,}000}{1{,}438} = 56$ days	$\dfrac{60{,}000}{1{,}164} = 52$ days

(vii) **Gearing ratio**

19X3

$$\frac{50{,}000}{375{,}000} \times 100 = 13.33\%$$

19X2

$$\frac{50{,}000}{255{,}000} \times 100 = 19.6\%$$

(b) **Comments**

Profitability: The return on capital employed has worsened and this is as a result of less efficient use of assets; the asset turnover has deteriorated, whereas the profit margin has improved. If we look at the assets individually, the debtors' turnover should not have caused any overall reduction of the asset turnover; the major change appears to have occurred in the fixed assets where, at some point during the year, extra capital has been raised for a major investment in fixed assets. If these assets were purchased towards the end of the year, then this would have made the figure for assets at the year-end unrepresentative of the assets used throughout the year. If we take the average of the beginning and year-end assets, the return on capital employed is 16.98%, ie. $\frac{53.5}{\frac{1}{2}(255+375)}$. Therefore, before we can draw any firm conclusions about the performance of the company, we need further information about the purchase of the fixed assets.

Liquidity: The ratios used to measure liquidity have also worsened during the year. This is mostly due to a large increase in the overdraft perhaps to part-finance the purchase of the fixed assets. Once again, it is necessary to establish whether the year-end picture is really representative of the year as a whole before coming to any firm conclusions.

Finance: The gearing ratio has been reduced over the year due entirely to the large amount of share capital raised to finance the purchase of the fixed assets.

Chapter 19

1 Prince plc

Consolidated balance sheet at 31 December 19X4

	£	£
Fixed assets		
Intangible assets: Goodwill		10,000
Tangible assets		132,000
		142,000
Current assets	228,000	
Creditors: Amounts falling due within one year	(131,000)	
Net current assets		97,000
Total assets less current liabilities		239,000
Creditors: Amounts falling due after more than one year		(58,000)
		181,000
Capital and reserves		
Called-up share capital		60,000
Profit and loss account (W4)		121,000
		181,000

Workings

(1) Group structure

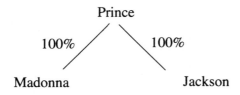

(2) Net assets at acquisition

	Madonna £	Jackson £
Share capital	50,000	30,000
Profit and loss account	4,000	1,000
	54,000	31,000

(3) Goodwill schedule

	Madonna £	Jackson £
Cost of investment	60,000	40,000
Net assets acquired	(54,000)	(31,000)
Goodwill	6,000	9,000
Less: amortisation ($\frac{1}{3}$)	(2,000)	(3,000)
	4,000	6,000

(4) Profit and loss account schedule

	£
P	122,000
M's post-acquisition profit	1,000
J's post-acquisition profit	3,000
	126,000
Less: Goodwill (W3)	(5,000)
	121,000

Chapter 20

1 Heavy plc

Consolidated balance sheet as on 31 March 19X1

	£	£
Fixed assets:		
Intangible assets: Goodwill		2,240
Tangible assets (180 + 40)		220,000
		222,240
Current assets		
Stocks (40 + 32)	72,000	
Cash at bank and in hand (3 + 2.5) (W6)	5,500	
	77,500	
Creditors: Amounts falling due within one year		
Bank loans and overdrafts	6,000	
Trade creditors (41 + 17)	58,000	
Proposed dividends – parent company	10,000	
– minority interests	400	
	74,400	
Net current assets		3,100
Total assets less current liabilities		225,340
Creditors: Amounts falling due after more than one year		
Debenture loans		(50,000)
		175,340
Capital and reserves		
Called-up share capital – £1 ordinary shares		100,000
Share premium account		20,000
Profit and loss account (W5)		42,040
		162,040
Minority interests (W4)		13,300
		175,340

Workings

(1) Group structure

H
|
| 80%
|
S

(2) Net assets of Side Ltd

	Balance sheet date £	Acquisition £
Share capital	10,000	10,000
Share premium	10,000	10,000
Profit and loss		
Per question 48,500		
Dividend proposed (2,000)		
	46,500	38,000
	66,500	58,000

Reserves at acquisition = £48,500 − £10,500

(3) Goodwill

	£
Cost of acquisition	49,200
Share of net assets acquired	
80% × 58,000 (W2)	(46,400)
	2,800
Less: amortisation ($\frac{1}{5}$)	(560)
	2,240

(4) Minority interest

	£
20% × 66,500 (W2)	13,300

(5) Profit and loss

	£
Heavy plc	44,200
Dividend proposed	(10,000)
Dividend receivable (80% × 2,000)	1,600
Side Ltd post-acquisition	6,800
[80% × (46,500 − 38,000) (W2)]	
Goodwill (W3)	(560)
	42,040

(6) Cash in transit

	£	£
Dr Cash at bank	2,500	
Cr Inter-company account		2,500

Chapter 21

1 **Courage Ltd**

Consolidated profit and loss account for the year ended 31 December 19X4

	£
Turnover (3,000 + 900 – 10)	3,890,000
Cost of sales (1,700 + 600 – 10)	(2,290,000)
Gross profit	1,600,000
Distribution costs	(400,000)
Administrative expenses	(696,800)
Operating profit	503,200
Loss on sale of fixed asset investment	(50,000)
Reorganisation costs	(10,000)
Profit on ordinary activities before interest	443,200
Income from other fixed asset investments	10,000
Interest payable and similar charges (3.2 – 1.6)	(1,600)
Profit on ordinary activities before taxation	451,600
Tax on profit on ordinary activities	(199,600)
Profit on ordinary activities after taxation	252,000
Minority interests (W2)	(20,800)
Profit for the financial year attributable to members of Courage Ltd	231,200
Dividends – proposed	(20,000)
Retained profit for the financial year	211,200
Retained profits brought forward (W3)	107,800
Retained profits carried forward	319,000

Workings

(1) Group structure

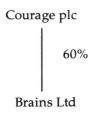

Courage plc

60%

Brains Ltd

(2) Minority interest

		Minority share
	£	£
Profit on ordinary activities after taxation	52,000 x 40%	20,800

335

(3) Retained profits brought forward

	£
Courage Ltd	100,000
Brains Ltd [60% × (25,000 – 12,000)]	7,800
	107,800

CHAPTER 24

Practice Central Assessment

Data and Tasks

This central assessment is in three sections. You are required to attempt EVERY task in EACH section, using the Answer Book provided when instructed to do so.

Note:

A Companies Act 1985 Balance Sheet pro-forma (format 1), a pro-forma profit and loss account (format 1 as supplemented by FRS 3), a pro-forma for journal entries and a pro-forma memorandum are provided in your Answer Book for you to use.

You are advised to spend approximately 55 minutes on Section 1, 90 minutes on Section 2 and 35 minutes on Section 3.

Section 1

This section is in two parts.

PART A

Task 1.1

(i) What is the objective of financial statements?

(ii) Illustrate how this objective is fulfilled by considering the financial statements of one type of profit-making body and one type of public sector or not-for-profit organisation.

Task 1.2

(i) Identify the elements of financial statements.

(ii) Explain how the elements are related in the balance sheet and in the profit and loss account of a profit-making organisation and the relationship between the two financial statements.

(iii) What major difference would you expect to find in the balance sheet of a public sector or not-for-profit organisation when compared with that of a profit-making organisation?

PART B

Data

You have been asked by the directors of Bins Ltd, a distributor of domestic and industrial refuse containers, to analyse the financial statements of a potential supplier. They have identified a company called Gone Ltd as a potential supplier of containers. They have obtained the latest financial statements of the company, in summary form, which are set out below.

Gone Ltd
Summary Profit and Loss Accounts
for the year ended 31 December 19X7

	19X7 £000	19X6 £000
Turnover	1,800	1,300
Cost of sales	1,098	715
Gross profit	702	585
Expenses	504	315
Net profit before interest and tax	198	270

Gone Ltd
Summary Balance Sheets
as at 31 December 19X7

	19X7 £000	19X7 £000	19X6 £000	19X6 £000
Fixed assets		3,463		1,991
Current assets	460		853	
Current liabilities	(383)		(406)	
Net current assets		77		447
Long–term loan		(1,506)		(500)
		2,034		1,938
Share capital		800		800
Revaluation reserve		164		164
Profit and loss account		1,070		974
		2,034		1,938

The industry average ratios are as follows:

	19X7	19X6
Return on capital employed	13.4%	13.0%
Gross profit percentage	44.5%	43.2%
Net profit percentage	23.6%	23.2%
Current ratio	2.0:1	1.9:1
Gearing	36%	34%

Task 1.3

In the Answer Book, prepare a report for the directors recommending whether or not to use Gone Ltd as a supplier for Bins Ltd given the information contained in the financial statements and the industry averages supplied. Your answer should comment on the profitability, liquidity and the level of gearing in the company, and how they have changed over the two years, and compare it with the industry as a whole.

The report should include calculation of the following ratios for the two years:

(i) Return on capital employed
(ii) Gross profit percentage
(iii) Net profit percentage
(iv) Current ratio
(v) Gearing

Section 2

This section is in two parts.

PART A

Data

You have been assigned to assist in the preparation of the financial statements of Deskcover Ltd for the year ended 31 December 19X7. The company is a wholesale distributor of office equipment. You have been provided with the extended trial balance of Deskcover Ltd as at 31 December 19X7 which is set out below.

Deskcover Ltd
Extended Trial Balance 31 September 19X7

DESCRIPTION	Trial balance Debit £000	Trial balance Credit £000	Adjustments Debit £000	Adjustments Credit £000	Profit and Loss Debit £000	Profit and Loss Credit £000	Balance sheet Debit £000	Balance sheet Credit £000
Cash at bank	316						316	
8% debentures		3,400						3,400
Trade debtors	3,386						3,386	
Provision for doubtful debts		125		44				169
Sales		20,469				20,469		
Purchases	12,025				12,025			
Land – cost	1,602						1,602	
Buildings – cost	2,137						2,137	
Fixtures and fittings – cost	1,399						1,399	
Motor vehicles – cost	1,786						1,786	
Office equipment – cost	402						402	
Return inwards	152				152			
Stock	4,502		5,244	5,244	4,502	5,244	5,244	
Accruals				118				118
Prepayments			56				56	
Returns outwards		109				109		
Buildings – accumulated depreciation		413		214				627
Fixtures & Fittings – accumulated depreciation		404		350				754
Motor vehicles – accumulated depreciation		486		417				903
Office equipment – accumulated depreciation		45		68				113
Interim dividend	240				240			
Trade creditors		2,035						2,035
Interest	136				136			
Distribution costs	3,214		542		3,756			
Administration expenses	2,368		613		2,981			
Investment	4,010						4,010	
Share capital		4,000						4,000
Profit and loss account		4,389						4,389
Share premium		1,800						1,800
Profit					2,030			2,030
	37,675	37,675	6,455	6,455	25,822	25,822	20,338	20,338

You have been given the following further information:

- The authorised share capital of the business, all of which has been issued, consists of ordinary shares with a nominal value of £1.

- Depreciation has been calculated on all of the fixed assets of the business and has already been entered on a monthly basis into the distribution expenses and administration costs ledger balances as shown on the extended trial balance.

- The corporation tax charge for the year has been calculated as £726,000.

- The company has paid an interim dividend of 6p per share during the year but has not provided for the proposed final dividend of 8p per share.

- Interest on the 8% debentures has been paid for the first six months of the year only.

Task 2.1

Using the pro–formas provided in the Answer Book and taking into account the further information provided, draft a profit and loss account for the year ended 31 December 19X7 and a balance sheet as at that date.

Notes:

- You must show any **workings** relevant to understanding your calculation of figures appearing in the financial statements.

- You are **not** required to produce journal entries for any necessary adjustments to the figures in the extended trial balance.

- Ignore any effect of these adjustments on the tax charge for the year as given above.

PART B

Data

Following your preparation of the balance sheet and profit and loss account of Deskcover Ltd, you have had a meeting with the directors at which certain other matters were raised. These are set out below:

(1) One of the debtors of Deskcover Ltd has been having cashflow problems. The balance at the end of the year was £186,000. Against this there was a specific provision of £93,000. After the year end, the directors received a letter from the liquidators of the debtor stating that the business had gone into liquidation on 14 January 19X8. The liquidators have stated that there will be no assets available to meet any of the debts of the unsecured creditors.

(2) The investment of £4,010,000 shown in the extended trial balance of Deskcover Ltd represents the cost of acquiring shares in a subsidiary undertaking, Underdesk Ltd. Deskcover Ltd acquired 75% of the ordinary share capital of Underdesk Ltd on 31 December 19X7. The directors have obtained a balance sheet and a profit and loss account fo the company for the last two years that have been prepared for internal purposes. They have not yet received the cashflow statement, which they would like to inspect. Underdesk Ltd's' year end is also 31 December. The net assets of Underdesk Ltd are shown in the balance sheet at their fair values except for the fixed assets, which have a fair value at 31 December 19X7 of £5,761,000.

Underdesk Ltd
Profit and loss account for the year ended 31 December 19X7

	19X7 £000	19X6 £000
Turnover	5,490	4,573
Cost of sales	3,861	3,201
Gross profit	1,629	1,372
Depreciation	672	445
Other expenses	313	297
Profit on the sale of fixed assets	29	13
Operating profit for the year	673	643
Interest paid	156	47
Profit before tax	517	596
Taxation on profit	129	124
Profit after tax	388	472
Ordinary dividend	180	96
Retained profit	208	376

Underdesk Ltd
Balance sheet as at 31 December 19X7

	19X7		19X6	
	£000	£000	£000	£000
Fixed assets		5,461		2,979
Current assets				
Stocks	607		543	
Debtors	481		426	
Cash	–		104	
	1,088		1,073	
Current liabilities				
Trade creditors	(371)		(340)	
Dividends payable	(180)		(96)	
Taxation	(129)		(124)	
Bank overdraft	(89)		–	
	(769)		(560)	
Net current assets		319		513
Long term loan		(1,700)		(520)
		4,080		2,972
Capital and reserves				
Called up share capital		1,400		800
Share premium		400		100
Profit and loss account		2,280		2,072
		4,080		2,972

Further information:

♦ Fixed assets costing £187,000 with accumulated depreciation of £102,000 were sold in 19X7 for £114,000. There were no other disposals in the year.

♦ All sales and purchases were on credit. Other expenses were paid for in cash.

Task 2.2

State whether any adjustment needs to be made to the financial statements of Underdesk Ltd as a result of the liquidation of the debtor. Set out any adjustment required in the form of a journal entry and justify the accounting treatment by reference to applicable accounting standards.

Note:

♦ Narratives are not required for journal entries.

Task 2.3

Provide a reconciliation between cash flows from operating activities and operating profit for the year ended 31 December 19X7 for Underdesk Ltd.

Task 2.4

Using the pro–forma provided in the Answer Book, prepare a cashflow statement for Underdesk Ltd for the year ended 31 December 19X7 in accordance with the requirements of FRS 1 (Revised).

Task 2.5

Calculate the goodwill on consolidation that arose on acquisition of the shares in Underdesk Ltd on 31 December 19X7. Set out the possible accounting treatments of this goodwill in the group accounts of Deskcover Ltd, justifying your answer by reference to applicable accounting standards.

Note:

♦   You are **not** required to produce a consolidated balance sheet for the group.

Section 3

Data

Amanda Blake, John Turner, Sheila Cotman and Fred Reynolds are in partnership together as wholesale distributors of prints of popular paintings. Amanda has produced a draft profit and loss account for the whole partnership for the year ended 31 December 19X7 and has asked you to finalise the partnership accounts. She has given you the following information that is relevant to the year in question:

(1)   Interest on capital is to be paid at a rate of 10% on the balance at the year end on the capital accounts. No interest is paid on the current accounts.

(2)   Cash drawings in the year amounted to:

Amanda	£51,000
John	£38,000
Sheila	£36,000
Fred	£24,000

(3) The partners are entitled to the following salaries per annum:

Amanda	£14,000
John	£11,000
Sheila	£9,000
Fred	£8,000

(4) On 1 January 19X7, the partners admitted Fred Reynolds into the partnership. He paid £45,000 cash into the partnership on that date. The profit–sharing ratios in the old partnership were:

Amanda	4/10
John	3/10
Sheila	3/10

The new profit–sharing ratios are now:

Amanda	4/12
John	3/12
Sheila	3/12
Fred	2/12

On the day that Fred was admitted into the partnership, the goodwill in the partnership was valued at £156,000. No goodwill is to be kept in the accounts of the new partnership. Adjustments for goodwill are to be made in the capital accounts of the partners.

(5) The balances on the current and capital accounts at the beginning of the year, before any adjustments have been made for the admission of Fred into the partnership, were as follows:

Capital accounts:

Amanda	£36,000
John	£31,200
Sheila	£25,200

Current accounts:

Amanda	£4,200
John	£3,600
Sheila	£2,700

(6) The net profit per the accounts given to you by Amanda amounted to £151,800.

Task 3.1

Prepare the partners' capital accounts for the year ended 31 December 19X7 from the information provided above.

Task 3.2

Prepare an appropriation account for the partnership for the year ended 31 December 19X7.

Task 3.3

Prepare the partners' current accounts for the year ended 31 December 19X7.

346

CHAPTER 24

Practice Central Assessment

Answer Book

Task 1.3

REPORT

To: **Date:**

From:

Re:

Task 2.1

Workings

£   £

Task 2.1

Pro–forma Profit and Loss Account
(Format 1 as supplemented by FRS 3)

Turnover
    Continuing operations
    Acquisitions

    Discontinued operations

Cost of sales

Gross profit (or loss)
Distribution costs
Administrative expenses
Operating profit (or loss)
    Continuing operations
    Acquisitions

Discontinued operations

Profit (or loss) on disposal of discontinued operations

Other operating income
Income from shares in group undertakings
Income from participating interests
Income from other fixed asset investments
Other interest receivable and similar income
Amounts written off investments

Profit (or loss) on ordinary activities before interest
Interest payable and similar charges

Profit (or loss) on ordinary activities before taxation
Tax on profit (or loss) on ordinary activities

Profit or (loss) on ordinary activities after taxation
Extaordinary items

Profit (or loss) for the financial year
Dividends

Retained profit for the financial year

Pro–forma Balance Sheet (Format 1)

Fixed assets

    Intangible assets

    Tangible assets

    Investments

                                                    _____

Current assets

    Stocks

    Debtors

    Investments

    Cash at bank and in hand

                                   _____

Creditors: amounts falling due within one year

                                                                                           _____

Net current assets (liabilities)

                                                                                _____

Total assets less current liabilities

Creditors: amount falling due after more than one year

Provisions for liabilities and charges

                                                                                _____

                                                                                _____

Capital and reserves

                                                                                 _____

Task 2.4

**Pro–forma Cash Flow Statement
(in accordance with FRS 1 (Revised))**

 £000

Net cash inflow from operating activities

Returns on investments and servicing of finance

Taxation

Capital expenditure

 ————

Equity dividends paid

 ————

Management of liquid resources

Financing

Increase/(decrease) in cash

 ————

Workings

CHAPTER 24

Practice Central Assessment

Answers

Section 1

PART A

Task 1.1

(i) The objective of financial statements is to 'provide information about the reporting entity's financial performance and financial position that is useful to a wide range of users for assessing the stewardship of management and for making economic decisions'.

(ii) In a profit–making organisation such as a company, financial statements provide information to shareholders to enable them to assess the performance of management, for example in generating profits for the period or in improving the financial position of the company. It may also assist them in deciding whether to continue holding their shares in the business, to acquire more shares or to dispose of all or part of their holding.

In a public sector body like, for example, a local authority, the organisation does not exist to make profits but to provide services to the public. Financial statements may enable payers of council tax to assess the level of spending of the authority in relation to the services provided and to determine whether the services have been provided economically, efficiently and effectively.

In non–for–profit organisations like clubs, for example, the aim is not to make a profit but to achieve the objectives of the club. Financial statements can assist the members of the club to assess how the stewards of the club have used the resources entrusted to them to achieve the club's purposes.

Task 1.2

(i) The elements of financial statements are:

- assets
- liabilities
- ownership interest
- income
- expenditure
- gains
- losses
- contributions from owners
- distributions to owners

(ii) The accounting equation that underlies the balance sheet of an organisation relates the following elements:

$$\text{Assets} - \text{Liabilities} = \text{Ownership interest}$$

In the context of a company, the change in ownership interest in the period is equal to the capital contributed from owners plus gains in the form of revenue and losses in the form of expenses. Revenue less expenses equals profit. Thus the profit and loss account explains how the change in ownership interest arising from sources other than contributions from owners came about (note that some gains or losses are reported only in the statement of total recognised gains and losses and not in the profit and loss account).

(iii) In a profit–making organisation, the ownership interest is referred to as the 'capital' of the business. It is often explained as the amount owing to the owners of the business and includes such things as share capital and undistributed profits earned by the business. In public sector or not–for–profit organisations, the ownership interest is based on the concept of a 'fund'. A fund is established for a particular purpose and the financial statements enable the users to see how the fund has changed in the period and to assist in determining whether the fund has been used for the purposes intended.

Part B

Task 1.3

REPORT

To: Directors of Bins Ltd

From: AAT Student

Date: January 19X8

Re: Analysis of Gone Ltd's financial statements

Introduction

The purpose of the report is to analyse the financial statements of Gone Ltd for 19X6 and 19X7 in order to determine whether to use the company as a supplier. The report will comment on the profitability, liquidity and level of gearing in the company and how this has changed over the two years considered. The ratios of the company will be compared with the industry average.

Calculation of ratios

The following ratios for the companies have been computed:

	19X6	19X7
Return on capital employed	$\frac{270}{2{,}438} = 11.1\%$	$\frac{198}{3{,}540} = 5.6\%$
Gross profit percentage	$\frac{585}{1{,}300} = 45\%$	$\frac{702}{1{,}800} = 39\%$
Net profit percentage	$\frac{270}{1{,}300} = 20.8\%$	$\frac{198}{1{,}800} = 11\%$
Current ratio	$\frac{853}{406} = 2.1$	$\frac{460}{383} = 1.2$
Gearing	$\frac{500}{2{,}438} = 20.5\%$	$\frac{1{,}506}{3{,}540} = 42.5\%$

Page 1/2

Continued

Comment and analysis

From these ratios it is evident that the profitability of Gone Ltd has significantly declined in 19X7. It has a lower return on capital employed in 19X7 and 19X6, which means that it is generating less profit per pound of capital employed that it was in 19X7. The gross profit percentage in 19X6 was higher than in 19X7, which means that the underlying sales have a lower profit margin in 19X7 compared with 19X6. The net profit percentage was also higher in 19X6 as compared with 19X7. This is not just due to the higher gross profit margin but also to tighter control of expenses, as can be seen by the fact that although the gross profit is 6% higher in 19X6 than in 19X7, the net profit percentage is almost 10% higher in 19X6 when compared with 19X7. The company is also significantly less profitable in 19X7 than the average for companies in the industry. Both the return on capital employed and the net profit percentage were less than the industry average in both years, and although the gross profit percentage was higher in 19X6 than the industry average, it has fallen below the industry average in 19X7.

The company's liquidity is also poorer in 19X7 than in 19X6. In 19X6 the company could cover its current liabilities out of current assets 2.1 times, whereas in 19X7 it can cover them only 1.2 times. The industry average is 2.0:1 in 19X7, and so although Gone Ltd had better liquidity than the average in 19X6 (1.9:1), it has now significantly worse liquidity.

Gone Ltd has also higher gearing in 19X7 as compared with 19X6. This means that it has become a more risky operation. It has a higher level of debt than the average of the industry for 19X7. Given the high level of gearing, the company may not find it easy to borrow any more to finance its activities and may have difficulty in meeting interest payments if there is a further downturn in profits.

It would appear that the company has invested substantially in fixed assets this year and financed this with a loan rather than by equity. The expansion has increased the turnover of the business, but this has not resulted in increased profits. It may be that there is a long lead time before the benefits of the investment are to be felt, and perhaps this should be investigated.

Conclusions

Overall, based solely on the information provided in the financial statements of the two companies, it is recommended that you do not use Gone Ltd as a potential supplier. The company has declining profitability and liquidity and a higher level of gearing. Unless it can be established that this trend will be reversed, there is a risk that the company may not be able to continue operations in the long term and hence may not be a secure source of supplies. The industry averages suggest that alternative suppliers may have a stronger financial position and should be considered.

Section 2

Task 2.1

Financial statements for publication:

Deskcover Ltd
Profit and loss account for the year ended 31 December 19X7

	£000
Turnover	
Continuing operations	20,317
Cost of sales	11,174
Gross profit	9,143
Distribution costs	(3,756)
Administrative expenses	(2,981)
Operating profit	
Continuing operations	2,406
Interest payable and similar charges	(272)
Profit (or loss) on ordinary activities before taxation	2,134
Tax on profit (or loss) on ordinary activities	(726)
Profit (or loss) on ordinary activities after taxation	1,408
Dividends	(560)
Retained profit for the financial year	848

Deskcover Ltd
Balance sheet as at 31 December 19X7

	£000	£000
Fixed assets		
Tangible assets		4,929
Investments		4,010
Current assets		
Stocks	5,244	
Debtors	3,273	
Cash at bank and in hand	316	
	8,833	
Creditors: amounts falling due within one year	(3,335)	
Net current assets (liabilities)		5,498
Total assets less current liabilities		14,437
Creditors: amounts falling due after more than one year		(3,400)
		11,037
Capital and reserves		
Called-up share capital		4,000
Share premium		1,800
Profit and loss account		5,237
		11,037

Workings

All figures £000.

1. Sales 20,469 − Returns inwards 152 = 20,317.

2. Calculation of cost of sales

Opening stock	4,502	
Purchases	12,025	
Less Returns outwards	109	
	16,418	
Less Closing stock	5,244	
Cost of sales		11,174

3. Dividends:

Interim dividend	240
Final dividend proposed	320
	560

4. Fixed assets:

	Cost	Acc. Depn.	NBV
Land	1,602	–	1,602
Buildings	2,137	627	1,510
Fixtures and fittings	1,399	754	645
Motor vehicles	1,786	903	883
Office equipment	402	113	289
	7,326	2,397	4,929

5. Debtors:

Trade debtors	3,386	
Less provision for doubtful debts	169	
		3,217
Prepayments		56
		3,273

6. Creditors: amounts falling due within one year

Trade creditors	2,035
Corporation tax payable	726
Dividends payable	320
Accruals (118 + interest 136)	254
	3,335

7. Profit and loss account:

At 1/1/97	4,389
Retained profit for the year	848
At 31/12/97	5,237

Task 2.2

The liquidation of the debtor after the year end would constitute a post balance sheet 'adjusting event' as defined by SSAP 17. An adjusting event is one that 'provides additional evidence of conditions existing at the balance sheet date', namely, evidence about the amount that will be collected from the debtor. As no amount is likely to be received from the debtor, the accounts must be adjusted in the financial statements for the year ended 31 December 19X7. The adjustments required are as follows:

Narration	Debit £	Credit £
Bad debts	186,000	
Debtors		186,000
Provision for doubtful debts	93,000	
Decrease in provision for doubtful debts		93,000

In effect, the full amount of the debt is written off and the provision adjusted to reflect the fact that, as the debt no longer exists, the provision against it is no longer necessary.

Task 2.3

Reconciliation of operating profit to net cash inflow from operating activities.

	£000
Operating profit	673
Depreciation charges	672
Profit on sale of tangible fixed assets	(29)
Increase in stock	(64)
Increase in debtors	(55)
Increase in creditors	31
Net cash inflow from operating activities	1,228

Task 2.4

Cashflow statement of Underdesk Ltd
for the year ended 31 December 19X7

	£000
Net cash inflow from operating activities	1,228
Returns on investments and servicing of finance	
Interest paid	(156)
Taxation	(124)
Capital expenditure	
Payments to acquire tangible fixed assets	(3,239)
Sale of asset	114
	(2,177)
Equity dividends paid	(96)
	(2,273)
Financing	
Loan	1,180
Issue of ordinary share capital	900
Decrease in cash	(193)

Workings

Fixed asset additions (£000):

Opening balance £2,979 − NBV of asset sold £85 − depreciation £672 + additions? = Closing balance £5,461. Therefore, ? = £3,239.

Task 2.5

Goodwill on acquisition:

	Total equity £000	Group share (75%) £000
Share capital	1,400	1,050
Share premium	400	300
Revaluation reserve	300	225
Profit and loss account	2,280	1,710
		3,285
Consideration		4,010
Goodwill on acquisition		725

Under FRS 10, positive goodwill should be capitalised and classified as an asset on the balance sheet. There is a rebuttable presumption that the useful economic life of purchased goodwill is limited and does not exceed 20 years. Where the useful economic life of goodwill is believed to be 20 years or less, the carrying value should be amortised in the profit and loss account on a systematic basis, using the straight-line method unless another method can be demonstrated to be more appropriate, over the estimated useful economic life. If the useful economic life is believed to exceed 20 years but the value is not significant or not capable of future measurement, then it should be amortised over 20 years. If the useful economic life is believed to exceed 20 years and the value is significant and is capable of future measurement, then if the useful economic life can be estimated, it should be amortised over that life, or if it is indefinite then it should not be amortised. In both cases it should be reviewed for impairment each period.

Section 3

Task 3.1

Partners' Capital Accounts

	Amanda £	John £		Amanda £	John £
Goodwill	52,000	39,000	Balance 1/1/X7	36,600	31,200
Balance c/d	47,000	39,000	Goodwill	62,400	46,800
	99,000	78,000		99,000	78,000

	Sheila £	Fred £		Sheila £	Fred £
Goodwill	39,000	26,000	Balance 1/1/X7	25,200	
			Cash		45,000
Balance c/d	33,000	19,000	Goodwill	46,800	
	72,000	45,000		72,000	45,000

Task 3.2

Appropriation Account for the year ended 31 December 19X7

	£	£
Net profit		151,800
Less Partners' salaries		
Amanda	14,000	
John	11,000	
Sheila	9,000	
Fred	8,000	
		(42,000)
Less Interest on capital		
Amanda	4,700	
John	3,900	
Sheila	3,300	
Fred	1,900	
		(13,800)
		96,000
Balance of profits shared		
Amanda 4/12		32,000
John 3/12		24,000
Sheila 3/12		24,000
Fred 2/12		16,000
		96,000

Workings – interest on capital

Amanda	10% x £47,000 = £4,700
John	10% x £39,000 = £3,900
Sheila	10% x £33,000 = £3,300
Fred	10% x £19,000 = £1,900

Task 3.3

Partners' Current Accounts

	Amanda £	John £		Amanda £	John £
Drawings	51,000	38,000	Balance 1/1/97	4,200	3,600
			Interest on capital	4,700	3,900
			Salaries	14,000	11,000
Balance c/d	3,900	4,500	Profit	32,000	24,000
	54,900	42,500		54,900	42,500

	Sheila £	Fred £		Sheila £	Fred £
Drawings	36,000	24,000	Balance 1/1/97	2,700	
			Interest on capital	3,300	1,900
			Salaries	9,000	8,000
Balance c/d	3,000	1,900	Profit	24,000	16,000
	39,000	25,900		39,000	25,900

Unit 10

Drafting Financial Statements

Central Assessment Pack

Technician (NVQ Level 4)

CHAPTER 1

The Accounts of Partnerships and Sole Traders (Questions)

1 Min and Henry

Min and Henry were in partnership sharing profits: Min 2/3, Henry 1/3.

The summarised balance sheet of the partnership at 31 December 19X1 was as follows:

	£	£		£	£
Freehold premises at cost		6,200	Fixed capital accounts		
Plant and machinery			Min	5,000	
at cost	3,200		Henry	4,000	
Less: Dep'n to date	1,400				
		1,800			9,000
			Current accounts		
Stock		3,200	Min	2,600	
Debtors		4,100	Henry	1,800	
Balance at bank		4,500			
					4,400
			Loan account – Min		4,000
			Creditors		2,400
		19,800			19,800

The partners, wishing to retire from the business, have accepted the offer of Moriarty Ltd to acquire the stock and fixed assets at an inclusive price of £14,000.

The purchase consideration was to be satisfied by a cash payment of £3,500 and the allotment by the company to the partners of 4,800 6% preference shares of £1 each valued at par and 12,000 ordinary shares of 25p each.

The debtors realised £3,800 and the creditors were settled for £2,200.

The partners agreed that the following should be the basis of distribution on dissolution of the partnership:

(1)   Min to be allotted preference shares in settlement of her loan, the remaining preference shares being allotted equally between the partners.

(2)   The ordinary shares to be allotted in profit-sharing ratio.

(3)   The balances to be settled in cash.

Tasks

(a) Prepare a realisation account.

(b) Prepare a cash account.

(c) Prepare the partners' capital and current accounts showing the final settlement on dissolution.

2 Alice, Bonny and Clyde (AAT CA J95)

You have been approached by a partnership – Alice, Bonny and Clyde – to prepare their accounts for the year ending 31 October 19X4. You have established that profit available for appropriation is £78,000 for the year and have been given the following information.

(1) Originally only Alice and Bonny were in partnership, sharing profits in a ratio of 2:1. On 1 November 19X3 they admitted the third partner, Clyde. Clyde contributed capital of £10,000 on 1 November 19X3. The new profit-sharing ratio is 3:2:1 to Alice, Bonny and Clyde respectively.

(2) Goodwill was valued at £30,000 on 1 November 19X3 and this must be taken into account when admitting Clyde; goodwill is not to be kept in the accounts. The profit-sharing ratio to be used on elimination of the goodwill is 3:2:1 to Alice, Bonny and Clyde respectively.

(3) Interest on capital is paid at a rate of 10% based on the year-end capital amount. No interest is allowed on the balance of current accounts.

(4) Drawings made for the year ending 31 October 19X4 were as follows:

	£
Alice	38,000
Bonny	19,500
Clyde	15,000

(5) Alice is entitled to a salary of £10,000 per annum and Clyde is entitled to £5,000 per annum.

(6) You have been supplied with the balance sheet of the partnership as at 31 October 19X3.

Balance sheet of Alice and Bonny as at 31 October 19X3

	£	£
Fixed assets		
Motor cars	20,000	
Fixtures and fittings	4,000	
		24,000
Current assets		
Stock	8,000	
Debtors	3,500	
	11,500	
Current liabilities		
Creditors	2,000	
Bank overdraft	3,000	
	5,000	
Net current assets		6,500
Total assets less current liabilities		30,500
Represented by:		
	£	£
Capital accounts		
Alice	14,000	
Bonny	10,000	
		24,000
Current accounts		
Alice	4,000	
Bonny	2,500	
		6,500
		30,500

Task 1

Based on the above information, draw up an appropriation account for the partnership of Alice, Bonny and Clyde for the year ended 31 October 19X4.

Task 2

Prepare the partners' current and capital accounts for the year ended 31 October 19X4 showing clearly the effect of admitting Clyde to the partnership.

3 Tayloriana (AAT CA D95)

Data

You have been approached by Samuel Taylor, a sole trader who runs a small trading company, Tayloriana (distributing catering equipment) for help in producing year-end financial statements. He employs a part-time book-keeper who has produced an extended trial balance for the business as at 31 March 19X5. Samuel is negotiating to enter into an existing partnership, Coleridge & Co, which operates in the same area of activity as his own. The existing partners of Coleridge & Co would like to see the latest profit figures of Samuel's business. You have been asked to assist in the preparation of a profit and loss account for the year ended 31 March 19X5.

The extended trial balance of Tayloriana as at 31 March 19X5 is set out on the following page.

EXTENDED TRIAL BALANCE 31 MARCH 1995

Description	Trial balance Debit £	Trial balance Credit £	Adjustments Debit £	Adjustments Credit £	Profit & loss a/c Debit £	Profit & loss a/c Credit £	Balance sheet Debit £	Balance sheet Credit £
Drawings	21,500						21,500	
Lighting and heating	1,760				1,760			
Purchases	162,430				162,430			
Sales		257,350				257,350		
Sales ledger control account	41,000						41,000	
Fixtures and fittings (cost)	28,000						28,000	
Motor vehicles (cost)	16,500						16,500	
Bad debts	540				540			
Returns outwards		7,460				7,460		
Capital 1/4/X4		44,080						44,080
Stock 1/4/X4	43,700				43,700			
Rent, rates and insurance	8,500		300	150	8,650			
Accumulated depreciation – Fixtures and fittings		12,000		2,800				14,800
Accumulated depreciation – Motor vehicles		6,300		4,100				10,400
Bank charges	320				320			
Cash at bank and in hand	1,800						1,800	
Purchase ledger control account		47,200						47,200
Depreciation – Fixtures and fittings			2,800		2,800			
Depreciation – Motor vehicles			4,100		4,100			
Carriage inwards	1,320				1,320			
Returns inwards	3,350				3,350			
Postage, stationery and telephone	2,910				2,910			
Wages	39,420				39,420			
Carriage outwards	850				850			
Prepayments			150				150	
Accruals				300				300
Discounts allowed	490				490			
Loss for the year						7,830	7,830	
	374,390	374,390	7,350	7,350	272,640	272,640	116,780	116,780

Samuel Taylor has given you the following further information:

(1) Stock has been counted on 31 March 19X5. The cost of the stock calculated on a first in first out basis is £49,300. The selling price of the stock is estimated at £65,450.

(2) After the year-end, one of the debtors, whose year-end balance was £2,500, went into liquidation. The liquidator has stated that there will be no assets available to repay creditors. No provision for this bad debt has been made in the accounts and the balance is still included in year-end debtors.

Task 1

Draft a profit and loss account for Tayloriana for the year ended 31 March 19X5 incorporating any adjustments which may be required as a result of the further information set out above.

Task 2

Explain to Samuel Taylor any adjustments you have made by reference to applicable accounting standards.

Further data

Samuel Taylor has a number of questions about his decision to enter into partnership with Coleridge & Co which he would like your help to answer. He has obtained the latest balance sheet of the partnership. The simplified balance sheet of the partnership Coleridge & Co as at 30 June 19X5 is set out below.

		£
Fixed assets		240,000
Net working capital		120,000
		360,000
Partners' capital accounts:		
Wordsworth	138,000	
Quincey	65,000	
Southey	84,000	
		287,000
Partners' current accounts:		
Wordsworth	35,000	
Quincey	18,000	
Southey	20,000	
		73,000
		360,000

The terms of the proposed entry of Samuel Taylor into the partnership are set out as follows:

(1) On the entry of Samuel Taylor into the partnership, Wordsworth will retire. Samuel will pay £80,000 of capital in cash into the partnership.

(2) Under the existing partnership agreement the three partners share profits in the following ratios:

Wordsworth	5/10
Quincey	3/10
Southey	2/10

When Samuel Taylor joins the partnership the new profit sharing ratio will be:

Quincey	4/10
Southey	3/10
Taylor	3/10

(3) As part of the retirement arrangements the fixed assets of the old partnership will be revalued to £340,000. Goodwill has been estimated at £50,000 and the accounts will be adjusted to reflect this fact on the retirement of Wordsworth. Goodwill is to be eliminated in the books of the new partnership and so no goodwill account will be maintained.

(4) The balance on the capital account of Wordworth is to be transferred to a loan account and will be repaid in two years' time.

Task 3

Make the necessary entries in the capital accounts of the partners to reflect the retirement of Wordsworth and the admission of Samuel Taylor into the partnership of Coleridge & Co in accordance with the provisions set out above, assuming that the entry was made on 30 June 19X5.

Task 4

Samuel Taylor has asked the following questions concerning his proposed entry into the partnership of Coleridge & Co. Provide answers for him.

(a) What is goodwill and why is it necessary to make an adjustment for goodwill on the retirement of a partner?

(b) What are the advantages of conducting business as a partnership rather than as a sole trader? (Name **two** examples.)

4 Jonathan Brown (AAT CA J96)

Data

You have been asked to advise Jonathan Brown, a sole trader, on the accounting treatment of certain transactions which he feels might affect his financial statements for the year ended 31 December 19X5. The matters on which he would like your advice are set out below:

(1) The business paid for an advertising campaign during the year at a cost of £2,800. It is estimated by Jonathan Brown that this will lead to an overall increase in sales of 15%. Half of this increase was achieved in 19X5 and the other half is expected to be achieved in 19X6.

(2) Jonathan Brown took stock costing £500 from the business at the end of the year for his own use. He removed the stock on 31 December 19X5 after the year-end stock count had taken place. No adjustment was made to the stock balance to take account of this action.

(3) During the year a word processor, which had a written down value of £850, was accidentally dropped out of the window during an office party and destroyed. The asset has been written out of the books of the business. The insurance company has refused to meet the cost of the loss. The solicitors of the business are currently pursuing the matter through the courts and say that the company has a reasonable chance of success.

(4) Jonathan Brown has put his own house up as security for a loan made by the bank to his business. The loan was made specifically for the business and not for the personal use of Jonathan Brown.

Task

Advise Jonathan Brown on the accounting treatment of these transactions in his financial statements for the year ended 31 December 19X5. Explain your treatment, where relevant, by reference to accounting concepts and generally accepted accounting principles.

5   Stooge & Co (AAT CA J96)

Data

You have been asked to take over work on finalising the accounts of the partnership of Stooge & Co. An extended trial balance for the year ended 31 March 19X6 has already been produced and is set out below.

EXTENDED TRIAL BALANCE 31 MARCH 1996

Description	Trial balance		Adjustments		Profit & loss a/c		Profit and loss appropriation a/c		Balance sheet	
	Debit £000	Credit £000	Debit £000	Credit £000	Debit £000	Credit £000	Debit £000	Credit £000	Debit £000	Credit £000
Motor vehicles – cost	61								61	
Office equipment – cost	14								14	
Purchases	199				199					
Cash at bank	26								26	
Sales		382				382				
Debtors	79								79	
Stock	28		33	33	28	33			33	
Expenses	36		8	6	38					
Drawings – Curly	30								30	
– Larry	24								24	
– Mo	32								32	
Motor vehicles – accumulated depreciation		20								20
Office equipment – accumulated depreciation		6								6
Creditors		19								19
Accruals				8						8
Current accounts – Curly		6								6
– Larry	4								4	
Capital accounts – Curly		40								40
– Larry		20								20
– Mo		40								40
Prepayments			6						6	
Net profit					150			150		
Partners' salaries – Curly							30			30
– Larry							20			20
– Mo							20			20
Balance of net profit							80			80
	533	533	47	47	415	415	150	150	309	309

You are given the following further information:

(1) Mo was admitted into the partnership on 1 April 19X5. Before he entered the partnership the profit-sharing ratio was as follows:

Curly	6/10
Larry	4/10

After the admission of Mo into the partnership the profit-sharing ratio became:

Curly	5/10
Larry	3/10
Mo	2/10

(2) Goodwill was valued at £60,000 at the time of admission of Mo into the partnership. An adjustment for goodwill should have been made in the accounts of the partnership on the admission of Mo, but this has yet to be done. Although goodwill must be taken into account, no balance of goodwill is to be kept in the final accounts of the partnership.

(3) No adjustment has yet been made for interest on capital. The partnership deed states that interest is to be allowed on the balance of the capital accounts of the partners at the end of the year at a rate of 10%.

Task 1

Prepare an appropriation account for the partnership, starting with the balance of net profit in the profit and loss appropriation account on the extended trial balance.

Task 2

Prepare the partners' current and capital accounts for the year ended 31 March 19X6 from the balances in the extended trial balance, taking into account the further information provided above.

6 Pride and Co (AAT CA D96)

Data

You have been asked by Pride and Co, a partnership, to assist in the preparation of the financial statements for the year ended 31 October 19X6 and to give advice on partnership matters. From you initial discussions with the bookkeeper you have constructed a summarised profit and loss account which is set out below.

Pride and Co
Profit and loss account for the year ended 31 October 19X6

	£
Sales	600,000
Cost of sales	360,000
Gross profit	240,000
Expenses	150,000
Net profit	90,000

You have obtained the following information about the partnership of Pride and Co.

(1) The partners of Pride and Co are Jane, Elizabeth and Lydia. They share profits and losses in the following proportions:

Jane	5/10
Elizabeth	3/10
Lydia	2/10

(2) Jane receives a salary of £15,000, Elizabeth a salary of £10,000 and Lydia a salary of £5,000.

(3) Partners receive interest on their capital accounts of 8% per annum on the balance outstanding at the end of the year. No interest is to be allowed on the balances of current accounts.

(4) The balances on the capital and current accounts at 1 November 19X5 were as follows:

	Capital	Current
	£	£
Jane	25,000	5,700 CR
Elizabeth	22,000	4,200 CR
Lydia	3,000	2,300 DR

There were no injections or withdrawals of capital by the partners during the year to 31 October 19X6.

(5) Jane, in addition to her balance on the capital account, has loaned the partnership £10,000. She is entitled to interest on this loan at a rate of 10% per annum.

(6) The partners' drawings during the year were as follows:

	£
Jane	15,600
Elizabeth	14,700
Lydia	18,900

The partners have been negotiating with Asmah, a sole trader, with a view to admitting her as a partner on 1 November 19X6. If Asmah is admitted into the partnership she will bring into it as her capital contribution the net assets of her business at a fair value of £35,000. She will bring with her the existing customers of her business. Her summarised profit and loss account for the year ended 31 October 19X6 is set out below:

Asmah
Profit and loss account for the year ended 31 October 19X6

	£
Sales	200,000
Cost of sales	110,000
Gross profit	90,000
Expenses	70,000
Net profit	20,000

- If Asmah is admitted into the partnership an adjustment for goodwill, which is currently not shown as an asset in the books of the partnership, is to be made in the books of Pride and Co.

- Goodwill has been valued at £60,000.

- No account for goodwill will be maintained in the books of the new partnership. Any adjustment affecting the partners is to be made in the Capital Accounts of the partners.

- An adjustment will have to be made in order to reflect the fair values of the assets in the existing partnership. The fixed assets of the partnership are currently included in the books of the partnership at a net book value of £88,000. The current market value of the assets is £128,000. Any adjustments affecting the partners is to be made in the capital accounts of the partners.

In the new partnership the profit sharing ratios will be as follows:

Jane	5/12
Elizabeth	3/12
Lydia	2/12
Asmah	2/12

Task 1

Draw up the appropriation account for the partnership of Pride and Co for the year ended 31 October 19X6.

Task 2

Write a report to the existing partners of Pride and Co covering the following matters:

(a) Using appropriate profitability ratios, compare the performance of the existing partnership of Pride and Co with that of Asmah. On the basis of your calculations and any other matters you consider relevant, advise the existing partners on the desirability of admitting Asmah into the partnership.

Note

You can assume that a similar level of sales and expenses will be achieved in the next financial year.

(b) What legal formalities would you recommend as a result of the admission of a new partner into the business?

(c) Show what entries would have to be made in the capital accounts of the partnership if, taking into account your advice, the partnership were to go ahead and admit Asmah into the partnership on 1 November 19X6.

7 Apostles and Co (AAT CA D97)

Data

Georgina Moore, Bob Russell, Jeremy Ward and Louise Dickenson are in partnership together running a wholesale book trading operation called 'Apostles & Co' from a small industrial unit. Georgina keeps the books of the partnership. She has produced a draft profit and loss account for the partnership for the year ended 30 June 19X7, but is not clear how to treat certain items in the year end accounts. She has asked you to assist her in making the necessary adjustments to the profit and loss account and in finalising the partnership accounts. She would also like you to explain some matters to the partners that have arisen out of the transactions during the year.

Georgina supplies you with the following information which is relevant to the year in question.

(i) Bob had removed books, which were purchased at a cost of £1,500 during the year, for use in his own personal library. No adjustment has yet been made for these items.

(ii) One customer who had owed the partnership £5,595 went into liquidation during the year, and the liquidators have said that there is no money available to pay creditors. Georgina estimates that, in addition to this, a provision for doubtful debts of £4,350 is required. A provision for doubtful debts of £1,750 has been brought forward from last year.

(iii) Georgina received the partnership's electricity bill for £1,758, which related to the quarter to 30 June 19X7. She ignored this in preparing her accounts as the bill was received after the year end.

(iv) Interest on capital is to be paid at a rate of 10% on the balance at the year end on the capital accounts. No interest is paid on the current accounts.

(v) Cash drawings in the year amounted to:

Georgina	£13,000
Bob	£11,000
Jeremy	£12,000
Louise	£9,000

(vi) The partners are entitled to the following salaries per annum:

Georgina	£13,000
Bob	£11,000
Jeremy	£10,500
Louise	£8,000

(vii) On 1 July 19X6, the partners admitted Louise Dickenson into the partnership. She paid £35,000 cash into the partnership on that date. The profit sharing ratios in the old partnership were as follows.

Georgina	4/10
Bob	3/10
Jeremy	3/10

The new profit sharing ratios are now as follows.

Georgina	4/12
Bob	3/12
Jeremy	3/12
Louise	2/12

On the day that Louise was admitted into the partnership the goodwill in the partnership was valued at £180,000. No goodwill is to be kept in the accounts of the new partnership. Adjustments for goodwill are to be made in the capital accounts of the partners.

(viii) The balances on the current and capital accounts at the beginning of the year, before any adjustments have been made for the admission of Louise into the partnership, were as follows.

Capital accounts

Georgina	£34,000
Bob	£22,000
Jeremy	£14,000

Current accounts:

Georgina	£6,000
Bob	£4,000
Jeremy	£1,000

(ix) The net profit per the accounts given to you by Georgina amounted to £145,453.

Task 1

Make any adjustments to the ledger balances used in the calculation of the net profit figure that are appropriate given the information provided. Set out your adjustments in the form of journal entries.

Notes

(1) Narratives are not required.

(2) Journals are not required for any of the appropriations of profit.

Task 2

Draft a letter to the partners explaining why you have made the adjustments in Task 1 by reference, where relevant, to accounting concepts, accounting standards or generally accepted accounting principles.

Task 3

Show the new net profit figure taking into account the adjustments made in Task 1.

Task 4

Prepare the partners' capital accounts for the year ended 30 June 19X7 from the information provided.

Task 5

Prepare an appropriation account for the partnership for the year ended 30 June 19X7, starting with your adjusted net profit prepared in Task 3.

Task 6

Prepare the partners' current accounts for the year ended 30 June 19X7 from the information provided and from answers to the above tasks.

CHAPTER 1

The Accounts of Partnerships and Sole Traders (Answers)

1 Min and Henry

(a)

Realisation account

	£	£		£
Freehold premises		6,200	Loan – Min	4,000
Plant and machinery		1,800	Creditors	2,400
Stock		3,200	Moriarty Ltd	14,000
Debtors		4,100	Cash – debtors	3,800
Cash – creditors		2,200		
Preference shares – loan		4,000		
Profit on realisation				
Min (2/3)	1,800			
Henry (1/3)	900			
		2,700		
		24,200		24,200

(b)

Cash account

	£		£	£
Balance b/f	4,500	Creditors		2,200
Debtors	3,800	Partners' accounts		
Moriarty	3,500	Min	5,200	
		Henry	4,400	
				9,600
	11,800			11,800

(c)

Partners' capital and current accounts

	Min £	Henry £		Min £	Henry £
Moriarty Ltd:			Balances b/f		
6% £1 preference shares valued at par (workings)	400	400	Fixed capital accounts	5,000	4,000
			Realisation account	1,800	900
Ordinary shares (working)	3,800	1,900	Current accounts	2,600	1,800
Bank	5,200	4,400			
	9,400	6,700		9,400	6,700

Workings

(1)

Moriarty Ltd

	£		£	£
Realisation account:		Cash		3,500
Purchase consideration	14,000	6% preference shares valued at par		
		Min loan account – 4,000 shares	4,000	
		Partners' accounts – 400 shares each (£400 x 2)	800	
				4,800
				8,300
		Balance in settlement: 12,000 ordinary shares worth £(14,000 – 8,300) = £5,700		
		Min acquires 8,000 shares worth 2/3 x £5,700	3,800	
		Henry acquires 4,000 shares worth 1/3 x £5,700	1,900	
				5,700
	14,000			14,000

(2)

Min loan account

	£		£
Moriarty Ltd	4,000	Balance per question	4,000
	4,000		4,000

Note: A 'buyer's account' for Moriarty Ltd is not compulsory. The individual components of the consideration could be credited directly to the realisation account.

2 Alice, Bonny and Clyde

Task 1

**Profit appropriation account for Alice, Bonny and Clyde
for the year ended 31 October 19X4**

	£	£
Profit available for appropriation		78,000
Less: Salaries		
Alice	10,000	
Clyde	5,000	
		(15,000)
Less: Interest on capital		
Alice	1,900	
Bonny	1,000	
Clyde	500	
		(3,400)
Balance of profits		59,600
Shared 3:2:1		
Alice		29,800
Bonny		19,867
Clyde		9,933
		59,600

Task 2

Capital accounts

	A £	B £		A £	B £
Goodwill	15,000	10,000	b/f	14,000	10,000
c/f	19,000	10,000	Goodwill	20,000	10,000
	34,000	20,000		34,000	20,000

	C £		C £
Goodwill	5,000	1 November 19X3 Bank	10,000
c/f	5,000		
	10,000		10,000

Current accounts

	A £	B £		A £	B £
Drawings	38,000	19,500	b/f	4,000	2,500
c/f	7,700	3,867	Salary	10,000	–
			Capital interest	1,900	1,000
			Profit	29,800	19,867
	45,700	23,367		45,700	23,367

	C £		C £
Drawings	15,000	Salary	5,000
c/f	433	Capital interest	500
		Profit	9,933
	15,433		15,433

Goodwill adjustments were also accepted in the current accounts.

3 Tayloriana

Task 1

Tayloriana
Profit and loss account for the year ended 31 March 19X5

	£	£
Sales	257,350	
Less: Returns inwards	(3,350)	
		254,000
Less: Cost of sales		
Opening stock	43,700	
Purchases	162,430	
Carriage inwards	1,320	
Less: Returns outwards	(7,460)	
	199,990	
Less: Closing stock	(49,300)	
		(150,690)
Gross profit		103,310
Less: Expenses		
Wages	39,420	
Rent, rates and insurance	8,650	
Depreciation – Fixtures and fittings	2,800	
– Motor vehicles	4,100	
Bad debts	3,040	
Bank charges	320	
Lighting and heating	1,760	
Postage, stationery and telephone	2,910	
Carriage outwards	850	
Discounts allowed	490	
		(64,340)
Net profit		38,970

Task 2

(i) *Stock adjustment*

An adjustment must be made for closing stock. Under the matching principle of SSAP 2 costs are to be matched against revenue in the same period. As the revenue from the sale of the stock will not occur until the next period the cost of the stock is carried forward on the balance sheet until the next period. Stock must be valued at the lower of cost and net realisable value in accordance with SSAP 9. As the cost is lower than the net realisable value, being the selling price of £65,450, then the stock must be brought in at £49,300.

(ii) *Bad debts*

The prudence concept of SSAP 2 states that all foreseeable losses must be provided for. As the business will not recover the debt since the liquidator has stated that there are no assets available to repay creditors the business will sustain a loss of £2,500. This must be treated as a bad debt and written off this year against profit. It does not matter that the event, the liquidation of the debtor, occurred after the year-end. Under SSAP 17 this is an example of a post-balance sheet event which is an adjusting event as it provides additional evidence of conditions existing at the balance sheet date.

Task 3

Partners' capital accounts (£'000)

	W	Q	S	T		W	Q	S	T
Goodwill		20	15	15	Balance b/d	138	65	84	
Loan	213				Revaluation	50	30	20	
					Goodwill	25	15	10	
Balance c/d		90	99	65	Cash				80
	213	110	114	80		213	110	114	80

Task 4

(i) Goodwill is defined as the excess of the purchase price of a business over the fair value of the individual assets and liabilities of the business. It arises due to such factors as location, staff expertise, reputation or the ability to earn 'super profits'. In the case of Coleridge & Co goodwill is a genuine asset of the business with a value which could be obtained if the business was sold. In order to give the retiring partner his share of all of the net assets of the business he must be given his share of the asset of goodwill and hence his capital account is credited with the value of this share.

(ii) Advantages of partnership over sole trader:

- more capital
- more expertise with involvement of partners
- stronger market force
- sharing out of management amongst more persons
- economies of scale eg secretarial help.

4 Jonathan Brown

Task

(1) Under the matching principle, costs should be matched against revenues to which they apply. It has been estimated that half of the revenue generated by the advertising will be received in 19X5 and half in 19X6. Applying the matching concept, the business should match half of the cost of the advertising against revenue in 19X5 and half of the cost against revenue in 19X6. This would mean that £1,400 would be treated as deferred expenditure in the financial statements for the year ended 31 December 19X5. However, the prudence concept says that provision should be made for all known liabilities, including expenses. As it is not certain that the revenue will be increased by the amount stated, it would be prudent to write-off all of the advertising expenditure as an expense in 19X5.

(2) The removal of stock from the business came within the period for which the business is reporting. It should be treated as drawings and should be deducted from the capital of the owner in the financial statements for the year ended 31 December 19X5.

(3) The receipt of compensation from the insurance company is contingent upon the outcome of the court case. As such, it would be classified as a contingent asset. As the gain is not certain the prudence principle, which states that profits should not be anticipated, dictates that it should not be accrued for in the financial statements for the year ended 31 December 19X5. It is unclear whether the solicitor's claim of 'reasonable' success renders the gain probable or only possible. If the gain is probable it should be disclosed in a note to the accounts, whereas if it is only possible it should not be disclosed at all.

(4) Putting his house up as security for a loan is a personal transaction between Jonathan Brown and the bank. The house does not belong to the business and so, on the business entity concept, there is no need to disclose this fact in the financial statements of the business.

5 Stooge and Co

Task 1

	£	£
Balance of net profit per extended trial balance		80,000
Less Interest on capital:		
Curly	4,600	
Larry	2,600	
Mo	2,800	
		10,000
Balancing profits		70,000
Profit share		
Curly		35,000
Larry		21,000
Mo		14,000
		70,000

Task 2

Partners' capital accounts

	C	L		C	L
	£	£		£	£
Goodwill	30,000	18,000	Balance per ETB	40,000	20,000
Balance	46,000	26,000	Goodwill	36,000	24,000
	76,000	44,000		76,000	44,000

	M		M
	£		£
Goodwill	12,000	Balance per ETB	40,000
Balance	28,000		
	40,000		40,000

Partners' current accounts

	C	L		C	L
	£	£		£	£
Balance b/d		4,000	Balance b/d	6,000	
Drawings	30,000	24,000	Interest on capital	4,600	2,600
Balance c/d	45,600	15,600	Salary	30,000	20,000
			Profit share	35,000	21,000
	75,600	43,600		75,600	43,600

	M		M
	£		£
Drawings	32,000	Salary	20,000
		Interest on capital	2,800
Balance c/d	4,800	Profit share	14,000
	36,800		36,800

6 Pride & Co

Task 1

Appropriation account for the year ended 31 October 19X6

	£	£
Net profit		90,000
Less Interest on loan		1,000
		89,000
Adjusted net profit		
Less Partners' salaries		
Jane	15,000	
Elizabeth	10,000	
Lydia	5,000	
		30,000
Less: Interest on capital		
Jane	2,000	
Elizabeth	1,760	
Lydia	240	
		4,000
		55,000
Balance of profits shared		
Jane 5/10		27,500
Elizabeth 3/10		16,500
Lydia 2/10		11,000
		55,000

Workings – interest on capital

Jane   8% x £25,000 = £2,000
Elizabeth 8% x £22,000 = £1,760
Lydia   8% x £3,000 = £240

Task 2

Report

To Partners of Pride & Co **Date** 5 December 19X6
From AAT Student
Re Admission of Asmah to the partnership

In answer to your queries as set out in your memorandum of 31 October 19X6 I set out my reply as follows.

(a) Pride & Co has the following profitability ratios (all figures in £000):

Gross profit % $\dfrac{240}{600} = 40\%$

Net profit % $\dfrac{90}{600} = 15\%$

Expenses/sales $\dfrac{150}{600} = 25\%$

Asmah has the following profitability ratios (all figures in £000):

Gross profit % $\dfrac{90}{200} = 45\%$

Net profit % $\dfrac{20}{200} = 10\%$

Expenses/sales $\dfrac{70}{200} = 35\%$

It is clear that although Asmah has a more profitable underlying business as is shown by the higher gross profit figure, because her expenses use up a greater proportion of the income than in Pride & Co, as shown by the expenses/sales ratio, she has a lower net profit ratio and hence, overall, a less profitable business. The combined business would have the following ratios:

Gross profit % $\dfrac{240+90}{600+200} = \dfrac{330}{800} = 41\%$

Net profit % $\dfrac{90+20}{600+200} = \dfrac{110}{800} = 14\%$

Expenses/sales $\dfrac{150+70}{600+200} = \dfrac{220}{800} = 28\%$

Although the gross profit percentage in the combined business would increase, the overall net profit percentage would fall because of the higher percentage of expenses to sales. On this basis one might advise caution about admitting Asmah into the partnership. However, if economies of scale could be achieved by combining the two businesses, or if the expenses of Asmah's operation could be reduced, then given the greater profitability of Asmah's underlying operation, the combination may well prove a good thing for the existing partnership.

(b) As the admission of a new partner effectively dissolves the old partnership and creates a new partnership, a new partnership agreement is required. It should include details of the capital contributed by each partner, the profit sharing ratios, the rate of interest on capital and the salaries to be paid to the partners. All of these have already been agreed except for the salaries to be paid to the partners which have now to be determined.

(c) Adjustments required on entry of Asmah to the partnership.

Partners' capital accounts

	£000					£000			
	J	E	L	A		J	E	L	A
Goodwill	25	15	10	10	Balance b/d	25	22	3	
					Reval	20	12	8	
Balance					Goodwill	30	18	12	
c/d	50	37	13	25	Net assets				35
	75	52	23	35		75	52	23	35

I hope that this is satisfactory for your purposes.

Regards

AAT Student

7 Apostles and Co

Task 1

	£	£
DR Current account – Bob	1,500	
CR Purchases		1,500
DR Bad debts	5,595	
CR Debtors		5,595
DR Increase in provision for doubtful debts	2,600	
CR Provision for doubtful debts		2,600
DR Electricity	1,758	
CR Accruals		1,758

Task 2

> AAT Student
> Address
>
> 4 December 19X7
>
> Dear Partners,
>
> In respect of your questions about the adjustments to the draft accounts I set out the following answers.
>
> 1 The books that Bob removed for his own personal use which had cost £1,500 are treated as drawings from the partnership. Under the business entity concept personal transactions must be kept separate from business transactions. As the purchases of books were, in effect, for personal use I have deducted the books taken from the purchases to show only the purchases for the business in the profit and loss account.
>
> 2 The fact that the customer owing £5,595 has gone into liquidation during the year and there is no money available for creditors means that the partnership has sustained a loss. The prudence concept says that losses must be recognized as soon as they are known. The debtor balance can no longer be collected and so the debt must be written off as we know that we have now sustained a loss.
>
> The fact that we know that we will not collect all of the amount owing by the other debtors means that we are also aware that a loss will be sustained by the business. Therefore, under the prudence concept again, we must recognize this loss now. Because we do not know the specific debtors that will go bad we need to set up a provision for doubtful debts. As there is already a provision of £1,750 from last year we only need to increase the provision by £2,600 to make it up to the required level of £4,350.
>
> 3 Although the electricity bill was not received until after the year end the electricity expense relates to the year ended 30 June 19X7. Under the matching concept we need to match all expenses of generating income against the income in the same period. Given that the electricity cost relates to the year ended 30 June 19X7 we need to match it against income for that year and hence we need to adjust the electricity cost to include this amount and set up an accrual for £1,758.
>
> I hope that this answers your questions about the adjustments to the draft accounts. If you have any further queries do not hesitate to contact me.
>
> Yours sincerely
>
> AAT Student

Task 3

	£	£
Net profit per draft accounts		145,453
Adjustments:		
add Drawings	1,500	
deduct Bad debts	(5,595)	
Increase in provision for doubtful debts	(2,600)	
Electricity accrual	(1,758)	
		(8,453)
Adjusted net profit		137,000

Task 4

Partners' Capital Accounts

	Georgina £	Bob £		Georgina £	Bob £
Goodwill	60,000	45,000	Balance 1/7/X6	34,000	22,000
Balance c/d	46,000	31,000	Goodwill	72,000	54,000
	106,000	76,000		106,000	76,000

	Jeremy £	Louise £		Jeremy £	Louise £
Goodwill	45,000	30,000	Balance 1/7/X6	14,000	
			Cash		35,000
Balance c/d	23,000	5,000	Goodwill	54,000	
	68,000	35,000		68,000	35,000

Task 5

Apostles and Company
Appropriation account for the year ended 30 June 19X7

			£	£
Adjusted net profit				137,000
Less	Partners' salaries			
	Georgina		13,000	
	Bob		11,000	
	Jeremy		10,500	
	Louise		8,000	
				42,500
Less	Interest on capital			
	Georgina	10% x £46,000	4,600	
	Bob	10% x £31,000	3,100	
	Jeremy	10% x £23,000	2,300	
	Louise	10% x £5,000	500	
				10,500
				84,000
Balance of profits shared				
	Georgina	4/12		28,000
	Bob	3/12		21,000
	Jeremy	3/12		21,000
	Louise	2/12		14,000
				84,000

Task 6

Partners' current accounts

	Georgina £	Bob £		Georgina £	Bob £
Drawings	13,000	12,500	Balance 1/7/X6	6,000	4,000
			Interest on capital	4,600	3,100
			Salaries	13,000	11,000
Balance c/d	38,600	26,600	Profit	28,000	21,000
	51,600	39,100		51,600	39,100

	Jeremy £	Louise £		Jeremy £	Louise £
Drawings	12,000	9,000	Balance 1/7/X6	1,000	-
			Interest on capital	2,300	500
			Salaries	10,500	8,000
Balance c/d	22,800	13,500	Profit	21,000	14,000
	34,800	22,500		34,800	22,500

394

CHAPTER 2

Manufacturing Accounts (Questions)

1 Nadia Ltd

The following trial balance was prepared by Nadia Ltd, clock manufacturers, on 31 August 19X6.

	£	£
Share capital		
400,000 ordinary shares of 25p each fully paid		100,000
50,000 10% cumulative preference shares of £1 each fully paid		50,000
Share premium account		20,000
Profit and loss account, 31 August 19X5		116,490
Leasehold property at cost	75,000	
Amortisation of leasehold property, 31 August 19X6		16,500
Plant and machinery at cost	163,750	
Accumulated depreciation, 31 August 19X6		42,123
Fixtures and fittings at cost	28,000	
Accumulated depreciation, 31 August 19X6		15,200
Motor vehicles at cost	124,600	
Accumulated depreciation, 31 August 19X6		75,480
8% debentures		100,000
Debtors/Creditors	379,500	398,100
Bank overdraft		73,600
Stock of raw materials, 31 August 19X5	119,400	
Purchases of raw materials	965,750	
Carriage inwards (raw materials)	12,600	
Manufacturing wages	235,800	
Manufacturing overheads	126,750	
Cash	2,510	
Work in progress, 31 August 19X5	74,680	
Sales		1,745,740
Administrative expenses	168,240	
Selling and distribution expenses	141,970	
Property amortisation	1,500	
Depreciation of plant and machinery	24,563	
Depreciation of fixture and fittings	2,800	
Depreciation of motor vehicles	12,280	
Provision for doubtful debts, 31 August 19X5		15,960
Stock of finished goods, 31 August 19X5	109,500	
	2,769,193	2,769,193

You discover the following information:

(1) Stocks at 31 August 19X6:

	£
Raw materials	123,300
Work in progress	81,740
Finished goods	114,600

(2) Provision is to be made for a full year's interest on the debentures.

(3) Bad debts amounting to £2,800 are to be written off and the provision for doubtful debts increased to £18,970.

(4) Prepayments on 31 August 19X6 were as follows: rent £2,600, delivery vehicle licences £450 and accruals expenses on that date were: electricity and power £3,980, insurance £1,740, and repairs £2,790.

(5) The leasehold property is held on a 50 year lease.

(6) Expenses are to be allocated as follows:

	Factory	Selling and distribution	Administration
Rent and insurance	5/8	1/8	2/8
Electricity and power	12/15	1/15	2/15
Repairs	6/10	3/10	1/10
Property amortisation	5/8	1/8	2/8

(7) Provision is to be made for taxation of £16,490 and proposed dividends of £20,000.

Tasks

(a) Prepare the manufacturing account for the year ended 31 August 19X6.

(b) Prepare the profit and loss account for the year ended 31 August 19X6 and a balance sheet as at that date in a form suitable for publication using Format 1 in accordance with the Companies Act 1985 as supplemented by FRS3 *Reporting financial performance*.

(You are *not* required to prepare a statement of total recognised gains and losses or the reconciliation of movements in shareholders' funds required under FRS3.)

CHAPTER 2

Manufacturing Accounts (Answers)

1 Nadia Ltd

Manufacturing account for the year ended 31 August 19X6

	£	£
Opening stock of raw materials	119,400	
Purchases	965,750	
	1,085,150	
Less: Closing stock of raw materials	(123,300)	
	961,850	
Carriage inwards	12,600	
Direct materials		974,450
Direct labour		235,800
Prime cost		1,210,250
Overhead expenses (W1)	132,007	
Depreciation of plant and machinery	24,563	
		156,570
Add: Opening work in progress	74,680	
Less: Closing work in progress	(81,740)	
		(7,060)
Factory cost of goods produced		1,359,760
Add: Opening stock of finished goods	109,500	
Less Closing stock of finished goods	(114,600)	
		(5,100)
Cost of sales		1,354,660

Profit and loss account for the year ended 31 August 19X6

	£
Turnover	1,745,740
Cost of sales	(1,354,660)
Gross profit	391,080
Distribution costs (W1)	(154,983)
Administrative expenses (W1)	(177,820)
Operating profit	58,277
Interest payable and similar charges (100,000 x 8%)	(8,000)
Profit on ordinary activities before taxation	50,277
Tax on profit on ordinary activities	(16,490)
Profit on ordinary activities after taxation	33,787
Proposed dividends	(20,000)
Retained profit for the year	13,787
Retained profit brought forward	116,490
Retained profit carried forward	130,277

All operations are continuing.

Chapter 2 Manufacturing Accounts (Answers)

Balance sheet at 31 August 19X6

	£	£
Fixed assets (W1)		
Leasehold property		58,500
Plant and machinery (121,627 + 49,120)		170,747
Fixtures, fittings, tools and equipment		12,800
		242,047
Current assets		
Stocks (123,300 + 81,740 + 114,600)	319,640	
Debtors (379,500 – 2,800 – 18,970 + 2,600 +450)	360,780	
Cash at bank and in hand	2,510	
	682,930	
Creditors: Amounts falling due within one year (W2)	(524,700)	
Net current assets		158,230
Total assets less current liaiblities		400,277
Creditors: Amounts falling due after more than one year		
8% debentures		(100,000)
		300,277
Capital and reserves		
Called–up share capital		
Preference shares of £1 each fully paid		50,000
Ordinary shares of 25p each fully paid		100,000
Share premium account		20,000
Profit and loss account		130,277
		300,277

Workings

(1) **Expense allocation**

	Manufacturing	Selling and distribution	Administration
	£	£	£
Per trial balance	126,750	141,970	168,240
Bad debts			
Written off			2,800
Change in provision			
(18,970 – 15,960)			3,010
Prepayments:			
Rent £2,600 (5:1:2)	(1,625)	(325)	(650)
Licences	–	(450)	–
Accruals			
Electricity £3,980 (12:1:2)	3,184	265	531
Insurance £1,740 (5:1:2)	1,087	218	435
Repairs £2,790 (6:3:1)	1,674	837	279
Property amortisation (5:1:2)	937	188	375
Depreciation			
Fixtures			2,800
Vehicles		12,280	
	132,007	154,983	177,820

(2) **Creditors: Amounts falling due within one year**

	£
Trade creditors per trial balance	398,100
Bank overdraft	73,600
Debenture interest (8% x 100,000)	8,000
Accruals	
Electricity	3,980
Insurance	1,740
Repairs	2,790
Taxation	16,490
Dividends	20,000
	524,700

CHAPTER 3

Limited Company Accounts (Questions)

1 Franco Ltd (AAT CA J95)

Data

You have been asked to prepare the financial statements of Franco Ltd (a company which distributes confectionery) for the year ending 31 March 19X5. A book-keeper at the company has prepared an extended trial balance for the year ending 31 March 19X5; this includes the normal year-end adjustments. You have been asked to review the trial balance in the light of some further information which may be relevant to the accounts and to make any adjustments necessary before they are published.

The extended trial balance of Franco Ltd is set out on pages 403 and 404.

The following further information is provided.

(1)   The corporation tax charge for the year has been agreed at £110,000.

(2)   Motor expenses of £10,000 and wages of £2,000 have been wrongly included in the general expenses figure in the trial balance. Of the remaining general expenses, £100,000 should be classified as administrative, the balance being distribution expenses.

(3)   The amount representing share capital and reserves in the extended trial balance consists of 400,000 50p ordinary shares and 50,000 £1 (8%) preference shares. The directors have just declared the final dividend for the ordinary shares and this has not yet been entered into the accounts. The preference dividend also needs to be provided for. The total (ordinary and preference) dividend for the year amounts to £72,000.

(4)   Interest due on the long-term loan for the year needs to be provided for; it is charged at 10% per annum.

(5)   An audit fee of £9,000 needs to be provided for.

(6)   Included in the total salaries figure is £98,000 of directors' emoluments. £68,000 of directors' emoluments should be classed as administrative expenses, the remainder being distribution. £104,000 of salaries and wages (excluding directors' emoluments) should be classed as administrative expenses, the remainder being distribution expenses.

(7)   Rates and light and heat should be split equally between administration and distribution expenses.

(8)   £27,000 of motor expenses are to be classed as distribution, the remainder as administration expenses.

(9) The depreciation charges should be classed as follows:

	Administration £	Distribution £
Buildings	3,000	1,000
Fixtures and fittings	4,000	1,000
Motor vehicles	2,000	8,000
Office	1,000	–

(10) The insurance payment should be split in the ratio of 75/25 between administration and distribution expenses respectively.

Chapter 3 Limited Company Accounts (Questions)

Franco Ltd – Extended trial balance 31 March 19X5

	Trial balance Debit £000	Trial balance Credit £000	Adjustments Debit £000	Adjustments Credit £000	Profit & loss a/c Debit £000	Profit & loss a/c Credit £000	Balance sheet Debit £000	Balance sheet Credit £000
Turnover		2,470				2,470		
Purchases	1,000				1,000			
Salaries and wages	400				400			
Motor expenses	27				27			
Rates	25			5	20			
Light and heat	32		4		36			
Carriage inwards	14				14			
Advertising	95				95			
Stock	215		225	225	215	225	225	
Trade debtors	450						450	
Provision for doubtful debts		6		3				9
Increase in provision for doubtful debts			3		3			
Cash in hand	1						1	
Cash at bank	6						6	
Trade creditors		170						170
Land (cost)	375						375	
Buildings (cost)	200						200	
Fixtures and fittings (cost)	35						35	
Motor vehicles (cost)	94						94	
Office equipment (cost)	20						20	
Buildings – accumulated depreciation		20		4				24
Fixtures and fittings – accumulated depreciation		18		5				23
Motor vehicles – accumulated depreciation		54		10				64
Office equipment – accumulated depreciation		4		1				5
c/f	2,989	2,742	232	253	1,810	2,695	1,406	295

	Trial balance		Adjustments		Profit & loss a/c		Balance sheet	
	Debit £000	Credit £000	Debit £000	Credit £000	Debit £000	Credit £000	Debit £000	Credit £000
b/f	2,989	2,742	232	253	1,810	2,695	1,406	295
Depreciation – Buildings			4		4			
Depreciation – Fixtures and fittings			5		5			
Depreciation – Motor vehicles			10		10			
Depreciation – Office equipment			1		1			
Returns inwards	10				10			
Interim dividend	30				30			
Returns outwards		5				5		
General expenses	135				135			
Insurance	13			1	12			
Profit and loss account		160						160
Accruals				4				4
Prepayments			6				6	
Share capital – Ordinary shares		200						200
– Preference shares		50						50
Long–term loan		20						20
Profit					683			683
	3,177	3,177	258	258	2,700	2,700	1,412	1,412

Tasks

(a) Make any adjustments you feel necessary to the balances in the extended trial balance as a result of the matters set out in the further information provided. Set out your adjustments in the form of journal entries. (Ignore any effect of these adjustments on the tax charge for the year.)

(b) Draft a profit and loss account for the year ended 31 March 19X5 and a balance sheet as at that date in a form suitable for publication using Format I in accordance with the Companies Act as supplemented by FRS3 *Reporting financial performance*. (You are *not* required to prepare a statement of total recognised gains and losses or the reconciliation of movements in shareholders' funds required under FRS3.)

2 Lawnderer Ltd (AAT CA D95)

Data

You have been asked to assist the directors of Lawnderer Ltd, a company that markets and distributes lawnmowers and other garden machinery, in the preparation of the financial statements for the year ended 30 September 19X5. The company employs a book-keeper who is competent in some areas of financial accounting but has gaps in his knowledge which you are required to fill. He has already prepared the extended trial balance which is set out on the following pages.

EXTENDED TRIAL BALANCE 30 SEPTEMBER 19X5

Folio	Description	Trial balance Debit £000	Trial balance Credit £000	Adjustments Debit £000	Adjustments Credit £000	Profit & loss a/c Debit £000	Profit & loss a/c Credit £000	Balance sheet Debit £000	Balance sheet Credit £000
	Depreciation – Land and buildings			18		18			
	– Fixtures and fittings			72		72			
	– Motor vehicles			298		298			
	– Office equipment			24		24			
	Goodwill	360						360	
	Accruals				102				102
	Dividends	120				120			
	Interest on debentures	153				153			
	Net sales		22,129				22,129		
	Trade debtors	2,603						2,603	
	Prepayments			43				43	
	Bank overdraft		362						362
	Cash in hand	3						3	
	Purchases	14,112				14,112			
	Stock 1/10/94	3,625				3,625			
	Stock 30/9/95			4,572	4,572		4,572	4,572	
	Profit and loss account 1/10/94							134	
	Provision for doubtful debts		78						78
	Trade creditors		2,967						2,967
	Distribution costs	4,028		37	25	4,040			
	9% Debentures		3,400						3,400
	Administration expenses	1,736		65	18	1,783			
	Accumulated depreciation – Land and buildings		83		18				101
	– Fixtures and fittings		214		72				286
	– Motor vehicles		644		298				942
	– Office equipment		83		24				107
	Land and buildings (cost)	1,875						1,875	
	Fixtures and fittings (cost)	576						576	
	Motor vehicles (cost)	1,691						1,691	
	Office equipment (cost)	244						244	
	Called up share capital		1,000						1,000
	Share premium		300						300
	Profit					2,456			2,456
		31,260	31,260	5,129	5,129	26,701	26,701	12,101	12,101

The following further information is provided by the book-keeper:

(1) The company disposed of motor vehicles during the year. The cost of the vehicles of £491,000 and the accumulated depreciation of £368,000 are still included in the figures in the trial balance. The sale proceeds of £187,000 were credited to the sales account.

(2) Salesmen's commission of £52,000 relating to sales in the year has not been paid or charged as an expense in the figures in the trial balance.

(3) Interest on the 9% debentures has been included in the trial balance only for the first six months of the year.

(4) The tax charge for the year has been calculated at £843,000.

(5) A final dividend of 5 pence per share has yet to be provided for. The authorised and issued share capital of the company consists of shares with a nominal value of 25p.

(6) Goodwill is being written off on a straight-line basis over a period of 10 years, but no amortisation has yet been charged in the trial balance.

(7) The doubtful debts provision in the trial balance has not yet been adjusted for this year. The total doubtful debts provision required has been calculated at £115,000.

The directors of the company have also had a meeting with you regarding the possible treatment of certain future expenditure in the financial statements of the company. They have told you that the company has been approached by an inventor who has an idea to develop a revolutionary new lawnmower. The project looks technically feasible and preliminary marketing studies suggest a significant market for the product. Cost and revenue projections suggest that future profits should adequately cover the cost of development and have a beneficial effect on the future profitability of the company. The only problem the directors foresee is how to finance the operation to completion given the high level of borrowing already in the company. Their other concern is the effect that the expenditure on developing the new product will have on future profits, given that it will take some time between commencing the project and commercial production.

The directors have also asked you, at the same meeting, about the contents of the Directors' Report.

Task 1

(a) Make any adjustments you feel to be necessary to the balances in the extended trial balance as a result of the matters set out in the further information given by the book-keeper above. Set out your adjustments in the form of journal entries (narratives are not required).

(b) Calculate the new retained profit which would result from these adjustments being made.

(Ignore any effect of these adjustments on the tax charge for the year as given above.)

Task 2

Draft a balance sheet for the year ended 30 September 19X5, in a form suitable for publication, using Format 1 in accordance with the Companies Act 1985 and supplemented by FRS3 (no statement of recognised gains and losses or reconciliation of movement in shareholders' funds are required).

Task 3

Answer the following questions of the directors arising out of the further information given to you by them.

(a) How would the costs of developing the new lawnmower be reflected in the future results of the company?

(b) What is 'gearing'? Would Lawnderer Ltd be considered to be a highly geared company and, if so, how might this affect the decision of a potential lender to lend money to the company?

Task 4

The directors are aware that a Directors' Report has to be produced with the financial statements. State **four** things that must appear in the Directors' Report, with a brief explanation of their nature.

3 Dowango Ltd (AAT CA J96)

Data

You have been assigned to assist in the preparation of the financial statements of Dowango Ltd for the year ended 31 March 19X6. The company is a cash and carry operation that trades from a large warehouse on an industrial estate. You have been provided with the extended trial balance of Dowango Ltd on 31 March 19X6 which is set out on the following page.

Chapter 3 Limited Company Accounts (Questions)

EXTENDED TRIAL BALANCE 31 MARCH 19X6

Description	Trial balance Debit £000	Trial balance Credit £000	Adjustments Debit £000	Adjustments Credit £000	Profit & loss a/c Debit £000	Profit & loss a/c Credit £000	Balance sheet Debit £000	Balance sheet Credit £000
Land – cost	431						431	
Buildings – cost	512						512	
Fixtures and fittings – cost	389						389	
Motor vehicles – cost	341						341	
Office equipment – cost	105						105	
Buildings – accumulated depreciation		184						184
Fixtures and fittings – accumulated depreciation		181						181
Motor vehicles – accumulated depreciation		204						204
Office equipment – accumulated depreciation		56						56
Stock	298		365	365	298	365	365	
Investment	64						64	
Debtors	619						619	
Provision for doubtful debts		27						27
Prepayments			21				21	
Cash in hand	3						3	
Cash at bank		157						157
Creditors		331						331
Accruals				41				41
Sales		5,391				5,391		
Purchases	2,988				2,988			
Returns inwards	39				39			
Returns outwards		31				31		
Carriage inwards	20				20			
Distribution expenses	1,092		23	11	1,104			
Administrative costs	701		18	10	709			
Interest charges	15				15			
Interim dividend	20				20			
Share capital		500						500
Profit and loss account		275						275
Long term loan		300						300
Profit					594			594
	7,637	7,637	427	427	5,787	5,787	2,850	2,850

You have been given the following further information:

(1) The authorised and issued share capital of the business consists of ordinary shares with a nominal value of £1.

(2) The company has paid an interim dividend of 4p per share during the year but has not provided for the final dividend of 6p per share.

(3) Depreciation has been calculated on all of the fixed assets of the business and has already been entered on a monthly basis into the distribution expenses and administration costs ledger balances as shown on the extended trial balance.

(4) The tax charge for the year has been calculated as £211,000.

(5) Interest on the long-term loan has been paid for six months of the year. No adjustment has been made for the interest due for the final six months of the year. Interest is charged on the loan at a rate of 10% per annum.

(6) An advertising campaign was undertaken during the year at a cost of £19,000. No invoices have yet been received for this campaign and no adjustment for this expense has been made in the extended trial balance.

(7) The investments consist of shares in a retail company that were purchased with a view to resale at a profit. Dowango Ltd owns 2% of the share capital of the company. At the end of the year a valuation of the shares was obtained with a view to selling the shares in the forthcoming year. The shares were valued at £56,000.

Task 1

Make any adjustments you feel to be necessary to the balances in the extended trial balance as a result of the matters set out in the further information above. Set out your adjustments in the form of journal entries. Narratives are not required.

(Ignore any effect of these adjustments on the tax charge for the year as given above).

Task 2

Draft a profit and loss account for the year ended 31 March 19X6 and a balance sheet as at that date using Format 1 in accordance with the Companies Act 1985 as supplemented by FRS 3 *Reporting Financial Performance*.

(You are **NOT** required to prepare a statement of total recognised gains and losses or the reconciliation of movements in shareholders' funds required under FRS 3).

Task 3

The directors of Dowango Ltd have asked to have a meeting with you. They wish to ask the bank for a further long-term loan to make some future investments. They have sent you the following letter with some questions they would like you to answer.

DOWANGO LTD

Dear AAT student

In preparation for discussions about a possible loan to Dowango Ltd, the bank has asked to see the latest financial statements of Dowango Ltd. We wish to ensure that the financial statements show the company in the best light. In particular, we wish to ensure that the assets of the business are shown at their proper value. We would like to discuss with you the following issues:

(1) The fixed assets of our company are undervalued. We have received a professional valuation of the land and buildings which shows that they are worth more than is stated in our financial statements. The land has a current market value of £641,000 and the buildings are valued at £558,000.

(2) The investments are recorded in our trial balance at cost. We realise that the market value of the investment is less than the cost, but since we have not yet sold it, we have not made a loss on it and so we should continue to show it at cost.

(3) Stocks are recorded in our balance sheet at cost. Most of our stock is worth more than this as we could sell it for more than we paid for it. Only a few items would sell for less than we paid for them. We have worked out the real value of our stock as follows.

	Cost £000	Sales price £000
Undervalued items	340	460
Overvalued items	25	15
Total	365	475

We have set out a number of questions we would like answered at our meeting in an appendix to this letter. We would also like you to advise us at that meeting on the profitability and return on capital of the two companies targeted for takeover (whose financial statements we have already sent to you) and on the reporting implications if we purchase one of the companies.

Yours sincerely

The directors

Appendix

(a) (i) Can we show the land and buildings at valuation rather than cost?

(ii) If we did so, how would the valuation of land and buildings be reflected in the financial statements?

(iii) Would revaluing the land and buildings have any effect upon the gearing ratio of the company and would this assist us in our attempt to get a loan from the bank?

(iv) What effect would a revaluation have upon the future results of the company?

(b) Can we continue to show the investments at cost?

(c) What is the best value for stock that we can show in our balance sheet in the light of the information we have given you about sales price?

Required

Write a memo to the directors answering these questions, which relate to the financial statements of Dowango Ltd. Explain your answers, where relevant, by reference to company law, accounting concepts and applicable financial reporting and accounting standards.

4 Primavera Fashions Limited (AAT CA J97)

Data

You have been assigned to assist in the preparation of the financial statements of Primavera Fashions Limited for the year ended 31 March 19X7. The company is a trading company which distributes fashion clothing. It has one subsidiary undertaking and one associated company.

Primavera Fashions Limited recently engaged a financial accountant to manage a team of book-keepers. The book-keepers produced a correct extended trial balance of the company and gave it to the accountant so that he could draft the year end financial statements.

The book-keeping staff have reported that he appeared to have some difficulty with the task and, after several days, apparently gave up and has not been seen since. He left behind him a balance sheet and some pages of workings which appear to contain a number of errors.

There is to he a meeting of the Board next week at which the financial statements will be approved. You have been brought in to assist in the production of a corrected balance sheet and to advise the directors on matters concerning the year end accounts. The uncorrected balance sheet, the workings left by the financial accountant and the correct extended trial balance of Primavera Fashions Limited on 31 March 19X7 are set out below.

Primavera
Extended trial balance as at March 19X7

	Trial Balance Debit £'000	Trial Balance Credit £'000	Adjustments Debit £'000	Adjustments Credit £'000	Profit and loss a/c Debit £'000	Profit and loss a/c Credit £'000	Balance sheet Debit £'000	Balance sheet Credit £'000
Profit and loss account		2,819						2,819
Land – cost	525						525	
Buildings – cost	1,000						1,000	
Fixtures and fittings – cost	1,170						1,170	
Motor vehicles – cost	1,520						1,520	
Office equipment	350						350	
Sales		12,604				12,604		
Buildings – accumulated depreciation		170		50				220
Fixtures and fittings – accumulated depreciation		229		117				346
Motor vehicles – accumulated depreciation		203		380				583
Office equipment – accumulated depreciation		73		70				143
Stock	1,097		1,178	1,178	1,097	1,178	1,178	
Interest charges	153				153			
Goodwill	128						128	
Trade debtors	857						857	
Purchases	7,604				7,604			
Interim dividend	160				160			
Investments	2,924						2,924	
Cash at bank	152						152	
Distribution costs	1,444		68	17	1,495			
Administrative expenses	1,441		36	20	1,457			
Depreciation – buildings			50		50			
Depreciation – fixtures and fittings			117		117			
Depreciation – motor vehicles			380		380			
Depreciation – office equipment			70		70			
Share capital		1,000						1,000
Provision for doubtful debts		61						61
Trade creditors		483						483
Sub-total c/f	20,525	17,642	1,899	1,832	12,583	13,782	9,804	5,655

	Trial Balance		Adjustments		Profit and loss a/c		Balance sheet	
	Debit £'000	Credit £'000	Debit £'000	Credit £'000	Debit £'000	Credit £'000	Debit £'000	Credit £'000
Sub-totals b/f	20,525	17,642	1,899	1,832	12,583	13,782	9,804	5,655
Accruals		23		104				104
Dividends from subsidiary undertaking			37			23	37	
Prepayments		10				10		
Dividends from associated company		1,500						1,500
10% Debentures		800						800
Share premium		550						550
Revaluation reserve					1,232			1,232
Profit								
	20,525	20,525	1,936	1,936	13,815	13,815	9,841	9,841

Primavera Fashions Limited
Balance sheet as at 31 March 19X7

	£'000	£'000
Fixed assets		
Intangible assets		128
Tangible assets		3,948
Investments		2,924
		7,000
Current assets		
Stocks	1,097	
Debtors	924	
Cash at bank and in hand	152	
	2,173	
Creditors: amounts falling due within one year	2,486	
Net current assets (liabilities)		(313)
Total assets less current liabilities		6,687
Creditors: amounts falling due after more than one year		800
		5,887
Capital and reserves		
Called up share capital		1,000
Revaluation reserve		550
Profit and loss account		4,051
		5,601

Workings

(W1) *Fixed assets*

	Cost	Accumulated depreciation	NBV
	£'000	£'000	£'000
Land	525	–	525
Buildings	1,000	50	950
Fixtures and fittings	1,170	117	1,053
Motor vehicles	1,520	380	1,140
Office equipment	350	70	280
	4,565	617	3,948

(W2) *Debtors*

	£'000	£'000
Trade debtors	857	
plus Accruals	104	
		961
less Prepayments		(37)
		924

(W3) *Creditors (amounts falling due within one year)*

	£'000
Trade creditors	483
Corporation tax payable	382
Dividends payable	60
Provision for doubtful debts	61
10% Debentures	1,500
	2,486

(W4) *Creditors (amounts falling due after more than one year)*

	£'000
Share premium	800

(W5) *Profit and loss account*

	£'000
At 1/4/X6	2,819
Retained profit for the year	1,232
At 31/3/X7	4,051

You have also received the following additional information to assist you in your task.

(a) The share capital consists of ordinary shares with a nominal value of 25 pence. The company has paid an interim dividend during the year and the directors have recommended a final dividend of 6 pence per share, which has not been provided for in the extended trial balance.

(b) The tax charge for the year has been estimated at £382,000.

(c) The investments shown on the extended trial balance relate to long-term investment in the shares of one subsidiary undertaking and one associated company.

Task

Redraft the company balance sheet for Primavera Fashions Limited as at 31 March 19X7. Make any changes that you feel to he necessary to the balance sheet and workings provided by the financial accountant using the information contained in the extended trial balance for the year ended 31 March 19X7 and the additional information provided above.

Note

You are **not** required to produce a profit and loss account.

CHAPTER 3

Limited Company Accounts (Answers)

1 Franco Ltd

(a)

				£	£
(1)		Dr	Tax charge (appropriation account)	110,000	
		Cr	Tax payable		110,000

Being provision of tax charge for the year

(2)	Dr	Motor expenses	10,000	
	Dr	Salaries and wages	2,000	
	Cr	General expenses		12,000

Being a correction of a misclassification of expenses

(3)	Dr	Final dividend	38,000	
	Dr	Preference dividend	4,000	
	Cr	Dividends proposed		42,000

Being provision of ordinary and preference dividends payable

(4)	Dr	Loan interest	2,000	
	Cr	Interest payable		2,000

Being provision of debenture interest payable

(5)	Dr	Audit fees	9,000	
	Cr	Accruals		9,000

Being provision for audit fees

(b) **Financial statements for publication**

Franco Ltd
Profit and loss account for the year ended 31 March 19X5

	£'000	£'000
Turnover		
Continuing operations		2,460
Cost of sales		(999)
Gross profit		1,461
Distribution expenses	416	
Administrative costs	341	
		(757)
Operating profit – Continuing operations		704
Interest payable and similar charges		(2)
Profit on ordinary activities before taxation		702
Tax on profit on ordinary activities		(110)
Profit on ordinary activities after tax		592
Dividends		(72)
Retained profit for the year		520

Franco Ltd
Balance sheet as at 31 March 19X5

	£'000	£'000
Fixed assets		
Tangible assets		608,000
Current assets		
Stocks	225,000	
Debtors	447,000	
Cash in hand and at bank	7,000	
	679,000	
Creditors: Amount falling due within one year	337,000	
Net current assets		342,000
Total assets less current liabilities		950,000
Creditors: Amount falling due after more than one year		
Debentures		20,000
		930,000
Capital and reserves		
Called–up share capital		250,000
Profit and loss account		680,000
		930,000

Chapter 3 Limited Company Accounts (Answers)

Workings

(1) Turnover £2,470,000 less £10,000 returns = £2,460,000

(2) Cost of sales

	£'000
Opening stock	215
Purchases	1,000
Plus carriage inwards	14
Less: Returns outwards	5
	1,224
Less: Closing stock	225
Cost of sales	999

(3) Costs

	Administrative	Distribution
	£'000	£'000
Audit fee	9,000	–
Rates	10,000	10,000
Provision for bad debts	3,000	–
Light and heat	18,000	18,000
Motor expenses	10,000	27,000
Insurance	9,000	3,000
Advertising	–	95,000
Directors' salaries	68,000	30,000
Salaries and wages (£400 + 2 – 98)	104,000	200,000
Depreciation		
Buildings	3,000	1,000
Fixtures and fittings	4,000	1,000
Motor vehicles	2,000	8,000
Office equipment	1,000	–
General expenses	100,000	23,000
Total	341,000	416,000

The provision for bad debts charge was also accepted if it was included as a distribution expense.

(4) Tangible assets

	Cost £	Acc dep £	NBV £
Land	375,000	–	375,000
Buildings	200,000	24,000	176,000
Fixtures and fittings	35,000	23,000	12,000
Motor vehicles	94,000	64,000	30,000
Office equipment	20,000	5,000	15,000
Total	724,000	116,000	608,000

(5)

	£
Debtors	450,000
Less: Provision	(9,000)
Plus prepayments	6,000
	447,000

(6)

	£	£
Creditors		170,000
Tax		110,000
Accruals		
Audit fee	9,000	
Light and heat	4,000	
Interest	2,000	
		15,000
Dividends payable		42,000
Total		337,000

(7) Called–up share capital and reserves

	£	£
OSC		200,000
PSC		50,000
Profit and loss account		
b/f	160,000	
in year	520,000	
c/f		680,000
Total		930,000

2 Lawnderer Ltd

Task 1

(a)

				£'000	£'000
(1)	Dr		Sales	187	
	Dr		Motor vehicles: acc. depn.	368	
	Cr		Motor vehicles: cost		491
	Cr		P & L profit on disposal		64
(2)	Dr		Distribution costs	52	
	Cr		Accruals		52
(3)	Dr		Interest charge	153	
	Cr		Accruals		153
(4)	Dr		Tax charge	843	
	Cr		Corporation tax payable		843
(5)	Dr		Dividends	200	
	Cr		Dividends payable		200
(6)	Dr		P & L amortisation of goodwill	36	
	Cr		Goodwill		36
(7)	Dr		Increase in provision for doubtful debts (P & L)	37	
	Cr		Provision for doubtful debts		37

(b) Calculation of new retained profit:

	£'000
Original profit per trial balance	2,456
+ profit on disposal of fixed assets	64
− adjustment to sales	(187)
− accrual of commission	(52)
− interest accrual	(153)
− tax charge	(843)
− final dividend	(200)
− amortisation of goodwill	(36)
− increase in provision for doubtful debts	(37)
New profit	1,012

Task 2

Lawnderer Ltd
Balance sheet as at 30 September 19X5

	£	£
Fixed assets		
Intangible assets	324	
Tangible assets	2,827	
		3,151
Current assets		
Stocks	4,572	
Debtors	2,531	
Cash at bank and in hand	3	
	7,106	
Creditors: amounts falling due within one year	(4,679)	
Net current assets		2,427
Total assets *less* current liabilities		5,578
Creditors: amounts falling due after more than one year		(3,400)
		2,178
Capital and reserves		
Called up share capital		1,000
Share premium		300
Profit and loss account		878
		2,178

Workings

(1) *Fixed assets*

Tangible fixed assets

	Land and buildings £'000	Fixtures and fittings £'000	Motor vehicles £'000	Office equipment £'000	Total £'000
Cost 1/10/X4	1,875	576	1,691	244	
Disposals	–	–	(491)	–	
	1,875	576	1,200	244	3,895
Accumulated depreciation 1/10/X4	101	286	942	107	
Disposals	–	–	(368)	–	
	101	286	574	107	1,068
					2,827

(2) *Debtors*

Debtors are made up as follows:

	£'000	£'000
Trade debtors	2,603	
Less: Provision for doubtful debts	(115)	
		2,488
Prepayments		43
		2,531

(3) *Creditors: amounts falling due within one year*

This is made up of:

	£'000
Bank overdraft	362
Trade creditors	2,967
Corporation tax payable	843
Dividends payable	200
Accruals	307
	4,679

Task 3

(a) The costs of developing the new lawnmower may qualify as development costs. For this to be so, the company must establish all of the following criteria:

(i) there must be a clearly defined project,

(ii) the project must be technically feasible and commercially viable,

(iii) the future profit from the project must be sufficient to cover the development costs,

(iv) the company must have adequate resources to complete this project.

The project fulfils all of the criteria except possibly (iv) above. If the company can convince the bank of the viability of the project and borrow the finance or, if the shareholders would be willing to invest more capital, then the project may have the necessary resources.

If the criteria are met then the costs of the development may be capitalised and carried forward in the balance sheet until such time as the project commences commercial production. The costs will then be amortised against future profits. The effect of this is that the costs will not affect profits until production commences and sales are made.

(b) The gearing of a company represents the proportion of debt finance to the total capital of the business. It is often calculated by the ratio:

$$\frac{\text{Debt}}{\text{Total capital}}$$

In Lawnderer Ltd the gearing is calculated as:

$$\frac{3,400}{5,578} = 61\%$$

A gearing ratio over 50% is often thought of as high in the British context, although it depends on the sector in which the company is operating.

A high level of gearing will concern lenders as it can lead to doubt about the ability of a company to meet interest payments in times of falling profits and to repay the debt when it becomes due. As a result the lender may decide that the company is a high risk borrower and may decline to lend money.

Task 4

Contents of Directors' Report

Fair review of development of the business
Principal activities of the company
Proposed dividends
Names of directors holding office during the period
Significant contracts
Directors' interests in shares or debentures
Details of acquisition of own shares
Significant differences between book and market value of land and buildings
Likely future developments
Political and charitable donations
Employee involvement and consultation
Employment of disabled persons
Research and development expenditure
Post balance sheet events
Creditor payment policy

3 Dowango Ltd

Task 1

			£'000	£'000
(1)	Dr	Final dividend	30	
	Cr	Dividends payable		30
(2)	Dr	Tax charge	211	
	Cr	Corporation tax payable		211
(3)	Dr	Interest charges	15	
	Cr	Interest payable		15
(4)	Dr	Distribution expenses	19	
	Cr	Accruals		19
(5)	Dr	Amounts written off investments	8	
	Cr	Investments		8

Task 2

Financial statements for publication

Dowango Ltd
Profit and loss account for the year ended 31 March 19X6

	£'000
Turnover	
Continuing operations	5,352
Cost of sales	(2,910)
Gross profit	2,442
Distribution costs	(1,123)
Administrative expenses	(709)
Operating profit	
Continuing operations	610
Amounts written off investments	(8)
Interest payable and similar charges	(30)
Profit (or loss) on ordinary activities before taxation	572
Tax on profit (or loss) on ordinary activities	(211)
Profit or (loss) on ordinary activities after taxation	361
Dividends	(50)
Retained profit for the financial year	311

Dowango Ltd
Balance sheet as at 31 March 19X6

	£'000	£'000
Fixed assets		
Tangible assets		1,153
Current assets		
Investments	56	
Stocks	365	
Debtors	613	
Cash at bank and in hand	3	
	1,037	
Creditors: amounts falling due within one year	(804)	
Net current assets		233
Total assets less current liabilities		1,386
Creditors: amounts falling due after more than one year		(300)
		1,086
Capital and reserves		
Called up share capital		500
Profit and loss account		586
		1,086

Workings

(1) *Sales* (5,391) – Returns inwards (39) = 5,352

	£'000
(2) *Cost of sales:*	
Opening stock	298
Purchases	2,988
plus Carriage inwards	20
less Returns outwards	(31)
	3,275
less Closing stock	(365)
Cost of sales	2,910

	£'000
(3) *Dividends:*	
Interim dividend	20
Final dividend proposed	30
	50

(4) *Fixed assets*

	Cost £'000	Acc Depn £'000	NBV £'000
Fixed assets			
Land	431	–	431
Buildings	512	184	328
Fixtures and fittings	389	181	208
Motor vehicles	341	204	137
Office equipment	105	56	49
	1,778	625	1,153

(5) *Debtors*

	£'000
Trade debtors	619
Less Provision for doubtful debts	(27)
	592
Prepayments	21
	613

(6) *Creditors: amounts falling due within one year*

	£'000
Bank overdraft	157
Trade creditors	331
Corporation tax payable	211
Dividends payable	30
Accruals (41 + 19 + interest 15)	75
	804

(7) *Profit and loss account*

	£'000
At 1/4/X5	275
Retained profit for the year	311
At 31/3/X6	586

Task 3

(a) (i) The Companies Act 1985 states that historical cost principles constitute the normal basis for preparing financial statements. However, alternative bases are allowed for revaluation of assets.

(ii) If the alternative basis was used the land and buildings would be shown in the balance sheet at their valuation of land £641,000 and buildings £558,000. The difference between NBV and valuation (land: £641,000 – £431,000 = £210,000; buildings: £558,000 – £238,000 = £230,000 giving a total revaluation of £440,000) would be credited to a 'revaluation reserve' which would form part of the capital and reserves of the company.

(iii) Gearing before and after revaluation would be as follows:

	Before	After
Gearing ratio	$\frac{300}{1,386} = 22\%$	$\frac{300}{1,826} = 16\%$

The lower gearing would make the company look less risky from the point of view of the bank and thus they may be more willing to lend the company the money to finance the acquisition. However, since the gearing is already fairly low, it may not make too much difference to the bank's attitude.

(iv) Future results would be affected because depreciation on the buildings would be calculated on the revalued amount and not on the basis of the original cost.

(b) The investment is a current asset, as it was purchased for resale, and, in accordance with the concept of prudence, should be shown at the lower of purchase price and net realisable value. The prudence concept says that profits should not be anticipated but foreseeable losses provided for. As we can foresee a loss on the sale of the investment it should be shown at its realisable value of £56,000.

(c) SSAP 9 states that stocks should be shown at the lower of cost and net realisable value (NRV). NRV is the expected selling price less any costs of getting them into a saleable condition and selling costs. If NRV is less than cost then, given the prudence concept that requires losses to be provided for as soon as they become probable, the stock should be reduced to NRV. The comparison of cost and NRV should be done for separate items of stock or groups of similar items and not on the total of all stocks. Applying this policy would lead us to value the undervalued items at cost of £340,000 and the overvalued items at the sale price of £15,000. The effect of this is to reduce the value of stock overall from the £365,000 in the accounts to £355,000.

4 Primavera Fashions Ltd

Task 1

Corrected version

Primavera Fashions Limited
Balance sheet as at 31 March 19X7

	£'000	£'000
Fixed assets		
Intangible assets		128
Tangible assets		3,273
Investments		2,924
		6,325
Current assets		
Stocks	1,178	
Debtors	833	
Cash at bank	152	
	2,163	
Creditors: amounts failing due within one year	1,209	
Net current assets		954
Total assets less current liabilities		7,279
Creditors: amounts falling due after more than one year		1,500
		5,779
Capital and reserves		
Called up share capital		1,000
Share premium		800
Revaluation reserve		550
Profit and loss account		3,429
		5,779

Workings

		Cost £'000	Accumulated depreciation £'000	NBV £'000
1	**Fixed assets:**			
	Land	525	-	525
	Buildings	1,000	220	780
	Fixtures and fittings	1,170	346	824
	Motor vehicles	1,520	583	937
	Office equipment	350	143	207
		4,565	1,292	3,273

		£'000
2	**Debtors:**	
	Trade debtors	857
	less provision for doubtful debts	(61)
		796
	Prepayments	37
		833
3	**Creditors: amounts falling due within one year:**	
	Trade creditors	483
	Corporation tax payable	382
	Dividends payable	240
	Accruals	104
		1,209
4	**Creditors: amounts falling due after more than one year:**	
	10% Debentures	1,500
5	**Profit and loss account**	
	At 1/4/X6	2,819
	Retained profit per ETB	1,232
	less final dividend	(240)
	less corporation tax charge	(382)
	At 31/3/X7	3,429

CHAPTER 4
Reporting Financial Performance (Questions)

1 Leonard plc

Leonard plc incurs considerable R&D expenditure. Its accounting policy to date has been to carry forward development expenditure where the criteria for this are met. The draft accounts for the year ended 30 June 19X3 reflect this policy and show the following:

	19X3 £000
Profit after tax	4,712
Dividends	(2,500)
Retained profit for the financial year	2,212
Profit and loss account brought forward	23,950
	26,162

The directors have now decided to change the accounting policy to one of immediate write-off of all development expenditure as it is incurred.

The net book value of development costs included in intangible fixed assets has been as follows:

	£
At 30 June 19X2	450,000
At 30 June 19X3	180,000

Amortisation of, and expenditure on, development has been as follows:

	Amortisation £	Expenditure £
Year ended 30 June 19X3	870,000	600,000

Task

Show how the change in accounting policy will be reflected in the profit and loss account and statement of reserves for the year ended 30 June 19X3.

2 Fitou Ltd

The draft profit and loss account of Fitou Ltd for the year ended 31 December 19X8 is set out below:

	19X8 £000
Profit on ordinary activities before taxation	3,657
Tax on profit on ordinary activities	(474)
Profit on ordinary activities after taxation	3,183
Dividends	(100)
Retained profit for the financial year	3,083

You are provided with the following additional information:

(1) On 1 January 19X8 an asset which cost £156,000 on 1 January 19X5 and on which there was £46,800 accumulated depreciation was revalued to £175,000.

Depreciation for the year was based on this revalued amount and the asset's remaining useful economic life of seven years.

(2) The company bought a freehold building on 1 January 19X7 for £750,000. The property satisfies the definition in SSAP19 and is treated as an investment property. Its current market value is £825,000, and was £800,000 at 31 December 19X7.

Tasks

Prepare the following extracts from the financial statements of Fitou Ltd as at 31 December 19X8:

(a) statement of total recognised gains and losses;
(b) note of historical cost profits and losses.

3 Nimbus plc

Nimbus plc is preparing its accounts for the year ended 30 April 19X2.

At 30 April 19X1, there were credit balances on the share premium account of £1,825,000, the revaluation reserve of £3,925,000 and the profit and loss account of £2,575,000. The company issued share capital of two million ordinary shares of £1 each.

During the year to 30 April 19X2 the following transactions occurred:

(1) One million shares of £1 each were issued for cash of £3,755,000.

(2) A factory property that had been revalued from £500,000 to £1,310,000 in 19X0 was sold for £2,525,000.

(3) A warehouse property was revalued from £1,000,000 to £1,540,000.

A prior period adjustment of £1,350,000 was required which had arisen from a change in accounting policy that had overstated the previous year's profit.

The profit and loss account for the year ended 30 April 19X2 showed a profit attributable to members of the company of £920,000 and a dividend of £675,000.

Tasks

(a) Draft a statement of total recognised gains and losses and a reconciliation of movements in shareholders' funds for Nimbus plc for the year ending 30 April 19X2.

(b) Explain briefly:

   (i) the purpose of the statement of total recognised gains and losses; and

   (ii) why gains and losses should not be recognised twice; illustrate with reference to Nimbus plc.

CHAPTER 4

Reporting Financial Performance (Answers)

1 Leonard plc

Profit and loss account
Year ended 30 June 19X3 (extract)

	£'000
Profit after tax (W1)	4,982
Dividends	(2,500)
Retained profit for the financial year	2,482

Statement of reserves

	Profit and loss account £'000
At 30 June 19X2	
As previously stated	23,950
Prior–year adjustment (W2)	(450)
As restated	23,500
Retained profit for the financial year (2,212 + 270)	2,482
At 30 June 19X3 [26,162 − 180 (W3)]	25,982

Note: The prior–year adjustment arises due to a change of accounting policy from capitalisation of development costs to immediate write–off of expenditure as incurred.

Workings

(1) Profit after tax

	£'000
As previously	4,712
Add back amortisation	870
Deduct expenditure in year	(600)
As restated	4,982

(2) Prior–year adjustment (in balance sheet at 30 June 19X2)

Adjustment is the elimination of the £450,000 asset. This gives the figure for the PYA in the statement of reserves, ie adjustment in opening balances for current year.

(3) Balance sheet at 30 June 19X3

Adjustment is £180,000 asset to be eliminated.

2 Fitou Ltd

(a) Statement of total recognised gains and losses for year ended 31 December 19X8

	£'000
Profit for the financial year	3,183
Unrealised surplus on revaluation (W1)	91
Total recognised gains and losses relating to the year	3,274

(b) Note of historical cost profits and losses

	£'000
Reported profit on ordinary activities before taxation	3,657
Difference between an historical cost depreciation charge and the actual charge calculated on the revalued amount (W2)	9
	3,666
Historical cost profit for the period retained after taxation, minority interests, extraordinary items and dividends (W3)	3,092

Workings

(1) *Revaluation surpluses*

	£'000	£'000
Asset revalued in year		
Revalued amount		175.0
NBV at revaluation (156 – 46.8)		(109.2)
		65.8
Investment property		
Valuation at end of year	825	
Valuation at start of year	(800)	
		25.0
		90.8

(2) *Difference between historical cost depreciation charge and the actual charge calculated on the revalued amount*

	£'000
Depreciation on revalued amount (175/7)	25.0
Historical cost depreciation (156 – 46.8)/7	(15.6)
	9.4

(3) *Historical cost retained profit*

	£'000
Profit for financial year	3,183
Depreciation adjustment (W2)	9
Dividends	(100)
	3,092

3 Nimbus plc

(a) Statement of total recognised gains and losses

	£'000
Profit attributable to members of the company	920
Unrealised surplus on revaluation of warehouse	540
Total recognised gains and losses for the year	1,460
Prior period adjustment	(1,350)
Total gains and losses recognised since last annual report	110

Reconciliation of movements in shareholders' funds

	£'000	£'000
Profit for the financial year		920
Dividends		(675)
		245
Other recognised gains and losses relating to the year		540
New share capital subscribed		3,755
Net addition to shareholders' funds		4,540
Opening shareholders' funds (W)	10,325	
Less: prior period adjustment	(1,350)	
		8,975
Closing shareholders' funds		13,515

Working

	Share capital £'000	Share premium £'000	Revaluation reserve £'000	Profit & loss £'000	Total £'000
Opening balances	2,000	1,825	3,925	2,575	10,325
Prior period adjustment				(1,350)	(1,350)
Share issue	1,000	2,755			3,755
Profit for year				245	245
Surplus on revaluation			540		540
Transfer of realised profit			(810)	810	–
Closing balances	3,000	4,580	3,655	2,280	13,515

(b) (i) The purpose of the statement of total recognised gains and losses is to highlight changes that have been recognised in the financial statements other than those resulting from capital payments or repayments.

If a company follows the historic cost convention the balance on the profit and loss account for the year represents the movement in net assets. However, where fixed assets are carried at a valuation, there are other gains and losses which do not pass through the profit and loss account. The statement will highlight these movements.

(ii) The statement of total recognised gains and losses shows the extent to which shareholders' funds have changed due to gains and losses recognised in a period. Once a gain or loss has been recognised in the statement, it would not be appropriate to recognise it for a second time in a subsequent statement.

The factory was revalued in 19X0 from £500,000 to £1,310,000 and a surplus would have been recognised in 19X0 of £810,000.

The profit on disposal can be recognised in the year ended 30 April 19X2 but must be calculated by comparing the net sale proceeds of £2,525,000 with the net carrying amount based on the revalued net book value.

CHAPTER 5

Fixed Assets: Tangible Assets (Questions)

1 Fixed asset examples

On 1 January 19X1, Tiger Ltd buys a fixed asset for £120,000, which has an estimated useful economic life of 20 years with no residual value. Tiger Ltd depreciates its fixed assets on a straight-line basis with a full year's charge in the year of acquisition and none in the year of disposal. Tiger Ltd's year-end is 31 December.

On 31 December 19X3, the asset will be included in the balance sheet as follows:

	£
Fixed assets at cost	120,000
Accumulated depreciation [3 × (120,000 ÷ 20)]	(18,000)
	102,000

Tasks

Show how the following would be dealt with, considering each separately:

(a) On 1 January 19X4, the remaining useful economic life is revised to 15 years, but the net book value is still considered to be recoverable in full.

Calculate the revised depreciation charge.

(b) On 1 January 19X4, the remaining useful economic life is revised to 10 years and the recoverable amount is considered to be only £50,000.

Show how the impairment would be recorded and calculate the revised depreciation charge.

(c) On 1 January 19X4, the asset is revalued to £136,000. The total useful economic life remains unchanged.

(i) Show the journal to record the revaluation.

(ii) Calculate the revised depreciation charge and show how it would be accounted for.

(iii) On 1 January 19X7, the asset is sold for £127,000. Calculate the profit or loss on disposal.

439

2 Toronto plc

Your client, Toronto plc, owns a large number of material items of plant and equipment. An item of plant which was purchased several years ago for £200,000 and which was being depreciated over ten years is now thought to have a useful life of a further 16 years.

Task

Answer the following question asked by the finance director of Toronto plc.

'Surely making a change in the annual depreciation charge is against the accounting conventions of prudence and consistency?'

3 Monet Ltd

Monet Ltd has purchased items of fixed plant costing £282,000. The company's depreciation policy on such plant is to write off the cost evenly over ten years. In due course, the company received a regional development grant of 20%.

The company has also received a government grant in respect of its proposed job creation programme amounting to £58,000. It estimates that the expenditure relating to this will be incurred over the next two years.

Mr Constable, the company accountant, proposes to take the whole of both the grants to the credit of the profit and loss account in the year in which they are received.

Task

State the advice which you would give to Mr Constable regarding the possible methods of accounting for the regional development grant received, showing the appropriate workings and the correct treatment in respect of the job creation grant.

CHAPTER 5

Fixed Assets: Tangible Assets (Answers)

1 Fixed asset examples

(a) Revised charge $= \dfrac{\text{NBV at revision} - \text{Residual value}}{\text{Revised remaining life}}$

$= \dfrac{£102,000}{15}$

$= £6,800$ per annum

(b) Write down to recoverable amount:

1.1.X4		£	£
Dr	Profit and loss account for year £(102,000 − 50,000)	52,000	
	Cr Accumulated depreciation		52,000

Revised annual charge from 19X4 onwards = £5,000 per annum (£50,000 ÷ 10)

(c) (i) To record the revaluation on 1.1.X4:

		£	£
Dr	Fixed assets cost/valuation £(136,000 − 120,000)	16,000	
Dr	Accumulated depreciation	18,000	
	Cr Revaluation reserve £(136,000 − 102,000)		34,000

(ii) Annual depreciation from 19X4 onwards:

		£	£
Dr	P&L depreciation expense £(136,000 ÷ 17)	8,000	
	Cr Accumulated depreciation		8,000

(iii) At 1 January 19X7, balances relating to the asset will be as follows:

	£
Fixed asset at valuation	136,000
Accumulated depreciation	(24,000)
	112,000
Revaluation reserve	34,000

Profit on disposal, shown in profit and loss account for the year (separately below operating profit if material):

	£
Proceeds	127,000
Less: Net book value at date of disposal	(112,000)
Profit on disposal	15,000

2 Toronto plc

The overall aim of the depreciation charge is to match revenue with expense. This means apportioning the cost less any residual value over the life of the assets as fairly as possible.

The accounting policy adopted is to depreciate on a straight–line basis over the useful life of the asset. To change the period over which an asset is depreciated (because it is recognised that its useful economic life is greater than hitherto thought) does not constitute a change of that accounting policy, but only a change in the estimate of the useful economic life. Hence, merely by changing the estimate, the company is still consistently applying its accounting policy. If the change made a significant difference to the company's results, it should be referred to in a note.

The doctrine of prudence should only be applied where it is uncertain what the outcome of a set of circumstances will be. In this case, there is little uncertainty and the usual overriding of the matching concept by the prudence concept will not apply.

3 Monet Ltd

Mr Constable's treatment of crediting the full amount of the grants to profit and loss account is not appropriate for either of the two grants.

In respect of the regional development grant, SSAP4 *Accounting for government grants* puts forward two alternative treatments.

(1) To reduce the cost of the acquired fixed asset by the amount of the grant, and to charge annual depreciation on the reduced amount (but see note below re CA 1985).

	£
Cost of fixed asset	282,000
Less: Grant received (20%)	(56,400)
Net cost	225,600

The company will depreciate the net cost of £225,600 evenly over ten years, ie provide annual depreciation of £22,560.

At the end of the first year, the net book value of the fixed asset will be £(225,600 – 22,560) = £203,040.

(2) To treat the grant as a deferred credit, a portion of which is transferred to revenue annually. The fixed asset is recorded at its full cost, and the full cost is depreciated.

	£
Cost of fixed asset	282,000

The company will depreciate the full cost of £282,000 evenly over ten years, ie provide annual depreciation of £28,200.

The grant will be treated as a deferred credit and credited to revenue over the expected useful life of the asset.

	£
Accruals and deferred income	56,400

This amount will be credited to profit and loss account evenly over ten years (matching the depreciation charge) ie £5,640 per annum.

At the end of the first year the net book value of the fixed asset will be £(282,000 − 28,200) = £253,800, and the deferred credit will be £(56,400 − 5,640) = £50,760.

Note that the two methods have exactly the same effect on profit and net assets.

However, SSAP4 does note that the first of these alternatives may be a contravention of CA 1985 with regard to the valuation of fixed assets.

The advice to Mr Constable would be to adopt the second of the two treatments allowed.

In respect of the job creation grant, although this is a revenue–based grant SSAP4 still dictates that such a grant should be credited to profit and loss in the period in which the related expenditure is charged.

Thus, of the £58,000, £29,000 should be credited in each of the two periods in which the programme is expected to be carried out. Any amount not yet credited would be included under the heading 'Accruals and deferred income' in the balance sheet. SSAP4 gives guidance on exactly how to match such grants with the related expenditure.

CHAPTER 6
Fixed Assets: Intangible Assets (Questions)

1 Tishoo Ltd

Tishoo Ltd, a pharmaceuticals company, has developed a new drug for treating the common cold. The latest tests show a 90% success rate in curing colds within 24 hours. The tests have also shown that the only side effect is a slight drowsiness. The company intends to commence commercial production of the drug on 1 January 19X8.

The drug has taken five years to develop and the company had carried forward development expenditure in respect of it amounting to £1,300,000 at 31 December 19X6. Development costs incurred during the current period to 31 December 19X7 were £400,000.

The company forecasts sales of the drug as follows:

	£
19X8	1,500,000
19X9	1,700,000
19Y0	1,900,000

The directors are of the opinion that it will take its competitors at least another three years to bring a similar drug onto the market.

Tasks

Answer the following questions which the directors of the company have asked. Justify your answers, where appropriate, by reference to FRSs and/or SSAPs.

(a) Under what circumstances can development expenditure be carried forward to future periods?

(b) How should Tishoo Ltd account for development expenditure in its financial statements for the year ended 31 December 19X7 and 31 December 19X8? Show how the development expenditure would be presented in the balance sheet insofar as the information allows.

2 Crosby plc

You are the financial accountant of Crosby plc. You have received a memorandum from the chairman who is anxious to discuss certain matters relating to the parent company accounts for the year ended 31 January 19X9.

The points he raises are as follows:

(1) On 31 January 19X9 the company bought out a local partnership, Young & Co, for £150,000 cash. The book value of the net assets of the firm at the date of purchase was £112,500.

The chairman feels that in reality these were worth only £100,000 as stock values were over-stated.

(2) He feels that Crosby plc's balance sheet does not reflect the real worth of the company and wishes to include goodwill of £175,000.

He has reached this figure by looking at the land and buildings figure in the balance sheet which shows all assets at original cost. He feels that they are now worth £100,000 more than this. The extra £75,000 consists of the amount necessary to take the net assets up to his estimate of the value of the business.

Task

Write a memorandum to the chairman defining goodwill in simple terms and indicating how the above items should be treated in the company's financial statements at 31 January 19X9. You are not required at this stage to decide which option to use where a choice exists. The chairman simply requires initial information about the various possibilities.

CHAPTER 6
Fixed Assets: Intangible Assets (Answers)

1 Tishoo Ltd

(a) Development expenditure may be carried forward under SSAP13 and matched against future revenues generated by the new or improved product if:

(i) there is a clearly defined project; and

(ii) the related expenditure is separately identifiable; and

(iii) the outcome of the project has been assessed with reasonable certainty as to

- its technical feasibility; and

- its ultimate commercial viability considered in the light of such as likely market conditions (including competing products, public opinion, consumer and environmental legislation); and

(iv) if further development costs are to be incurred on the same project the aggregate of such costs together with related production, selling and administration costs are reasonably expected to be exceeded by related future revenues; and

(v) adequate resources exist, or are reasonably expected to be available, to enable the project to be completed and provide any consequential increases in working capital.

It appears that expenditure relating to the new drug meets these criteria.

(b) (i) The deferred development expenditure would be included under the heading 'Fixed assets – Intangible assets' in the balance sheet and the movement in the balance over the year would be shown in a note to the financial statements.

Extract from balance sheet at 31 December 19X7

	£'000
Fixed assets	
Intangible assets	1,700

Intangible assets – Development costs	
Cost	
At 1 January 19X7	1,300
Additions	400
At 31 December 19X7	1,700
Net book value	
At 31 December 19X7	1,700
At 1 January 19X7	1,300

(ii) At the end of 19X8 the company would have commenced commercial production of the drug and would therefore amortise the development expenditure in line with the revenues generated. The amortisation for 19X8 would be calculated as follows.

Estimated revenue

	£
19X8	1,500,000
19X9	1,700,000
19Y0	1,900,000
Total revenue	5,100,000

Amortisation for 19X8

$$£1,700,000 \times \frac{1,500,000}{5,100,000} = £500,000$$

Extract from balance sheet at 31 December 19X8

	£'000
Fixed assets	
Intangible assets	1,200

Intangible assets – Development costs	£'000
Cost at 1 January 19X8 and 31 December 19X8	1,700
Amortisation	£'000
At 1 January 19X8	Nil
Charge for the year	500
At 31 December 19X8	500
Net book value	
At 31 December 19X8	1,200
At 1 January 19X8	1,700

2 Crosby plc

MEMORANDUM

To: The Chairman   Date:

From: The Financial Accountant

Re: Company financial statements for the year ended 31 January 19X9

In reply to your memo of 29 January 19X9 the following points can be made:

Goodwill is an accounting term used to explain the difference between what a business is worth in total and what its adjusted balance sheet would say it was worth.

In other words, even if the balance sheet were to be adjusted to reflect the fair values of all the business's assets and liabilities, that does not tell you what price the owner of that business might be prepared to sell it for, nor what a purchaser might be prepared to pay.

This reflects the fact that the price to be paid depends on many more factors than the existing assets and liabilities of a business, notably its expected future profitability.

The accounting profession has standardised treatment for goodwill in **FRS 10**. I will use this to explain the accounting consequences of the other issues you raised.

(i) **Purchase of Young & Co**

By buying out the partnership we have taken over ownership of its assets and agreed to settle its liabilities.

Therefore we must bring the net assets into our accounts at 31 January 19X9 at what we think they are worth, £100,000. We will therefore have to recognise the fair value of the stock.

As we spent £150,000 to obtain these existing assets we have effectively paid £50,000 for another asset – goodwill.

FRS 10 requires that purchased goodwill is included in the balance sheet and treated as an intangible fixed asset. It should be amortised through the profit and loss account over its useful economic life. There is a rebuttable presumption that the useful economic life of goodwill is 20 years or less. However, goodwill may be amortised over a longer period, or treated as having an indefinite useful economic life (and therefore not amortised), provided that:

- the durability of the acquired business can be demonstrated and justifies estimating the useful economic life to exceed 20 years; and

- the goodwill is capable of continued measurement; and

- impairment reviews are carried out at the end of each reporting period.

The Companies Act 1985 requires that all fixed assets are depreciated over their useful economic lives. Non-amortisation of goodwill can only be justified if that treatment is necessary in order to give a true and fair view of the company's results and state of affairs. If the 'true and fair view override' is invoked, additional disclosures must be made in the financial statements.

(ii) **Value shown by Crosby plc balance sheet**

As mentioned previously, goodwill represents the difference between the fair value of the assets and what the company as a whole is worth.

In your opinion, the present balance sheet total is £175,000 lower than the existing value of the net assets.

This £175,000 consists of two components:

(a) the revaluation of the land and buildings of £100,000; and

(b) your opinion on the real worth of business over the value of the individual assets (an additional £75,000).

We cannot simply insert a goodwill figure of £175,000 for this as company law and accounting practice does not allow us to account for non-purchased or inherent goodwill. Goodwill can appear in the accounts of a purchaser only when a business has been bought, since it is only evidenced by a market transaction that its cost can be determined. The opinion of one person, however well-researched the figure may be, is too subjective to be prudently included in the accounts.

We are, however, allowed to recognised the £100,000 increase in the value of land and buildings. This can be included by taking the £100,000 to a revaluation reserve.

The other £75,000 of your estimated increase cannot be accounted for unless you can identify it to specific assets. If this can be done we can consider whether accounting rules allow them to be revalued.

CHAPTER 7

Stocks and Long–term Contracts (Question)

1 Stocks and small company exemptions (AAT CA J95)

You have been asked by the directors of the company to prepare a short report covering the following:

(1) Stock is valued at the lower of cost and net realisable value in the accounts in accordance with SSAP9. The directors would like you to explain how cost and net realisable value are derived.

(2) The directors have heard of the filing exemptions available to small companies and they would like you to explain what these exemptions are.

Task

Write a report which covers the required points.

CHAPTER 7

Stocks and Long–term Contracts (Answer)

1 Stocks and small company exemptions

[**Tutorial note:** The answer to point (2) below is considerably more detailed than might be expected in the examination. To achieve maximum marks, a student would be expected to outline the major points given below rather than discuss them in detail.]

Report

To: Directors of Franco Ltd

From: A Student

Re: Stock valuation and small company exemptions   Date: 22/06/X5

(1) SSAP 9 defines cost as that expenditure which has been incurred in the normal course of business in bring the product or service to its present location and condition. Thus cost should include such costs of conversion (for example, direct costs and production overheads) as are appropriate to the location and condition.

Net realisable value should be taken as the actual or estimated selling price (net of trade but before settlement discounts) less all further costs to completion and all costs to be incurred in marketing, selling and distribution.

(2) A company qualifies as a small company in a particular financial year if, for the current and previous financial year, it satisfies at least two of the following conditions.

- The turnover for the year does not exceed £2.8 million (where a financial year is shorter or longer than 12 months, this figure must be proportionally adjusted).

- The balance sheet total (ie total assets before the deduction of current and long–term liabilities) does not exceed £1.4 million.

- The average number of employees during the year does not exceed 50.

Certain companies may never qualify for small company exemptions, namely public limited companies, banking and insurance companies, companies which are authorised persons under the Financial Services Act 1986 and companies which are members of a group containing any of these excepted companies.

Small companies are not required to file either a profit and loss account or a directors' report. No details need be filed of the emoluments of directors. The notes to the financial statements are limited and need only cover the following matters:

- accounting policies
- share capital (including the allotment of shares)
- long–term creditors, including any security given by the company
- basis of foreign currency translation
- the aggregate amount of debtors falling due after more than one year
- fixed assets.

CHAPTER 8

Accounting for Leases and Hire Purchase Contracts (Question)

1 Montreal Ltd

The directors of Montreal Ltd are currently investigating the possibility of acquiring fixed assets by means of lease contracts.

Tasks

Answer the following questions which the directors of the company have asked. Justify your answers, where appropriate, by reference to accounting concepts, FRSs and SSAPs.

(a) What is the difference between a finance lease and an operating lease?

(b) Why is it necessary to include an asset acquired under a finance lease in fixed assets? Surely this is incorrect if we do not actually own the asset?

CHAPTER 8

Accounting for Leases and Hire Purchase Contracts (Answer)

1 Montreal Ltd

(a) A lease is a finance lease if it transfers substantially all the risks and rewards of ownership of an asset from a lessor to a lessee. Where there is no such transfer the lease is an operating lease.

A finance lease is similar in substance to the ownership of an asset, financed by a loan repayable in instalments over the period of the lease. The lessee normally has sole use of the asset and is responsible for its maintenance, repair and insurance, even though legal title to the asset remains with the lessor. An operating lease, on the other hand, is the short term hire of an asset.

(b) SSAP21 recognises the accounting principle of commercial substance over legal form with respect to finance leases.

The legal title to the asset remains with the lessor throughout a lease. However, application of legal form would mean that neither the asset nor the obligation to make payments would be recognised in the balance sheet. This could distort the true and fair view given by the balance sheet.

The definition of a finance lease centres on the transfer of the risks and rewards of ownership being passed to the lessee. The commercial substance of a finance lease is therefore the acquisition of an asset through a long-term loan.

Accordingly, SSAP21 requires that assets acquired under finance leases are capitalised in the balance sheet and the obligations to repay are shown within creditors.

CHAPTER 9

Post Balance Sheet Events, Provisions and Contingencies (Questions)

1 Three matters (AAT CA J95)

The directors of Franco Ltd have drawn your attention to three matters and requested your advice on how these should be treated:

(1) An issue of shares was made on 10 April 19X5. Fifty thousand 50p ordinary shares were issued at a premium of 25p.

(2) A debtor owing £30,000 to Franco Ltd on 31 March 19X5 went into liquidation on 3 April 19X5. The £30,000 is still unpaid and it is unclear whether any monies will be received.

(3) The company is awaiting the outcome of a legal suit; an independent lawyer has assessed that it is probable that the company will gain £25,000 from it.

Task

Write a memo to the directors of Franco Ltd outlining the required treatment for *each* of the three events.

2 Window-dressing (AAT CA J95)

Financial statements should be prepared on the basis of conditions which exist at the balance sheet date. The term *window-dressing* is used to describe a situation where transactions have been undertaken just before the balance sheet date and will be reversed after that date, simply to improve the appearance of the position of the company at the year-end.

Tasks

(a) Give *two* examples of how window-dressing might be used to improve the cash balance in the balance sheet.

(b) Explain how SSAP17 *Post balance sheet events* requires window-dressing to be dealt with.

CHAPTER 9

Post Balance Sheet Events, Provisions and Contingencies (Answers)

1 Three matters

To: Directors, Franco Ltd   Date:

From: A Student

Re: Treatment of accounting matters

(1) The issue of shares is a post balance sheet event (as defined by SSAP17 *Accounting for post balance sheet events*) but, as it does not affect conditions at the balance sheet date, the amounts in the financial statements should not be changed (ie it is non–adjusting). The issue should only be disclosed if it is considered to be of such materiality that non–disclosure would be misleading.

(2) The debtor owed £30,000 at the year–end so the subsequent liquidation does provide further evidence of conditions at the balance sheet date. As the amount is likely to be considered to be material, the financial statements should be adjusted.

(3) This is a contingent asset and its treatment will depend upon its likelihood of realisation. It has been assessed as being a probable gain and should, therefore, be disclosed by way of a note to the financial statements to comply with FRS 12 *Provisions, contingent liabilities and contingent assets*. The financial statements should disclose a brief description of the nature of the contingent asset at the balance sheet date and an estimate of its financial effect.

Should you require further assistance with these matters, please do not hesitate to contact me.

With regards

A Student

A Student

2 Window–dressing

(a) Examples could include: delaying posting cheques to creditors until after the year–end and selling assets before the year–end, with the intention of repurchasing them immediately after the year–end. Both actions would improve the appearance of the cash/bank balance.

(b) SSAP17 requires the disclosure of a post balance sheet event which is the reversal or maturity after the year–end of a transaction entered into before the year–end, the substance of which was primarily to alter the appearance of the company's balance sheet.

CHAPTER 10

Cash Flow Statements (Questions)

1 George Ltd (AAT CA J95)

Data

You have been given the following information about George Ltd for the year ending 31 March 19X5, with comparative figures for the year ending 31 March 19X4:

George Ltd
Profit and loss account for the year ended 31 March 19X5

	19X5		19X4	
	£000	£000	£000	£000
Turnover		2,500		1,775
Opening stock	200		100	
Purchases	1,500		1,000	
Closing stock	(210)		(200)	
Cost of sales		1,490		900
Gross profit		1,010		875
Depreciation		275		250
Other expenses		500		425
Profit on sale of fixed asset		2		–
Operating profit for the year		237		200
Interest paid		20		35
Profit before tax		217		165
Taxation on profit		25		21
Profit after tax		192		144
Proposed dividends		35		30
Retained profit		157		114

George Ltd
Balance sheet as at 31 March 19X5

	19X5 £000	19X5 £000	19X4 £000	19X4 £000
Fixed assets		330		500
Current assets				
Stocks	210		200	
Debtors	390		250	
Cash	–		10	
	600		460	
Current liabilities				
Trade creditors	150		160	
Dividends payable	35		30	
Taxation	25		21	
Bank overdraft	199		–	
	409		211	
Net current assets		191		249
		521		749
Debentures		–		500
Long–term loan		200		100
		321		149
Capital and reserves				
Called–up share capital		40		25
Profit and loss account		281		124
		321		149

Further information

(1) In May 19X4 an asset was sold which originally cost £10,000 and was purchased when the company was started up two years ago. A new asset was bought for £110,000 in June 19X4. Fixed assets are depreciated at 25% of cost. The policy is to charge a full year's depreciation in the year of purchase and none in the year of sale.

(2) Loan interest is charged at 10% per annum. The long-term loan was increased on 1 April 19X4.

(3) The 5% debentures were redeemed on 1 April 19X4.

(4) Sales and purchases were on credit. All other expenses, including interest due, were paid in cash.

(5) On 1 October 19X4 there was a new issue of shares. Fifteen thousand ordinary £1 shares were issued at par.

Task 1

Prepare a cash flow statement for the period.

Task 2

Prepare a reconciliation between cash flows from operating activities and operating profit.

2 Cashedin Ltd (AAT CA D95)

The book-keeper of Cashedin Ltd has asked for your assistance in producing a cash flow statement for the company for the year ended 30 September 19X5 in accordance with FRS 1. He has derived the information which is required to be included in the cash flow statement, but is not sure of the format in which it should be presented. The information is set out below:

	£000
Operating profit before tax	24
Depreciation charge for the year	318
Proceeds from sale of fixed assets	132
Issue of shares for cash	150
Cash received from new loan	200
Purchase of fixed assets for cash	358
Interest paid	218
Taxation paid	75
Dividends paid	280
Increase in stocks	251
Increase in debtors	152
Increase in creditors	165
Decrease in cash	345

Task 1

Using the information provided by the book-keeper given above, prepare a cash flow statement for Cashedin Ltd for the year ended 30 September 19X5 in accordance with the requirements of FRS 1. Show clearly your reconciliation between operating profit and net cash inflow from operating activities.

3 Poised Ltd

You have been asked to assist in the production of a reconciliation between cash flows from operating activities and operating profit for the year ended 31 July 19X6 for Poised Ltd. The financial statements of the company drafted for internal purposes are set out below, along with some further information relating to the reporting year.

Poised Ltd
Profit and loss account for the year ended 31 July 19X6

	£'000	19X6 £'000
Turnover		12,482
Opening stock	2,138	
Purchases	8,530	
Closing stock	(2,473)	
Cost of sales		8,195
Gross profit		4,287
Depreciation		1,347
Other expenses		841
Operating profit for the year		2,099
Interest paid		392
Profit before tax		1,707
Ordinary dividend		360
Retained profit		785

Poised Ltd
Balance sheet as at 31 July 19X6

	19X5 £000	19X6 £000
Fixed assets	6,867	6,739
Current assets		
Stocks	2,473	2,138
Trade debtors	1,872	1,653
Cash	1,853	149
	6,198	3,940
Current liabilities		
Trade creditors	1,579	1,238
Dividends payable	240	265
Taxation	562	477
	2,381	1,980
Net current assets	3,817	1,960
Long-term loan	4,200	3,800
	6,484	4,899

	19X5 £000	19X6 £000
Capital and reserves		
Called up share capital	3,000	2,500
Share premium	400	100
Profit and loss account	3,084	2,299
	6,484	4,899

Further information:

(1) No fixed assets were sold during the year.
(2) All sales and purchases were on credit. Other expenses were paid for in cash.

Task 1

Provide a reconciliation between cash flows from operating activities and operating profit for the year ended 31 July 19X6.

Note You are NOT required to prepare a cash flow statement.

4 Hegel Limited (AAT CA D97)

Data

Due to the success of a board game 'The Absolute', McTaggart Limited is thinking of expanding its operations. It has identified another company, Hegel Limited, which also distributes board games, as a possible target for takeover. The directors have obtained a set of financial statements of the company for the last two years; these have been prepared for internal purposes. Hegel Limited's year-end is 30 September. The directors have established that if they had purchased 80% of the ordinary share capital of Hegel Limited at 30 September 19X7 they would have had to pay £3,300,000. The net assets of Hegel Limited are shown in the balance sheet at their fair values, except for the fixed assets which have a fair value at 30 September 19X7 of £6,672,000.

The directors have a number of questions relating to the company and to the possible takeover which they would like you to answer. The financial statements for Hegel Limited are set below.

Hegel Limited
Profit and loss account for the year ended 30 September 19X7

	19X7 £'000	19X7 £'000	19X6 £'000	19X6 £'000
Turnover		6,995		3,853
Opening stock	681		432	
Purchases	4,245		2,561	
Closing stock	(729)		(681)	
Cost of sales		4,197		2,312
Gross profit		2,798		1,541
Depreciation		971		311
Other expenses		593		415
Profit on the sale of fixed assets		20		-
Operating profit for the year		1,254		815
Interest paid		302		28
Profit before tax		952		787
Taxation on profit		333		276
Profit after tax		619		511
Ordinary dividend		144		120
Retained profit		475		391

Hegel Limited
Balance sheet as at 30 September 19X7

	19X7 £'000	19X6 £'000
Fixed assets	6,472	2,075
Current assets		
Stocks	729	681
Debtors	574	469
Cash	-	320
	1,303	1,470
Current liabilities		
Trade creditors	340	424
Dividends payable	144	120
Taxation	333	276
Bank overdraft	158	-
	975	820
Net current assets	328	650
Long-term loan	3,350	350
	3,450	2,375
Capital and reserves		
Called up share capital	1,200	1,000
Share premium	400	-
Profit and loss account	1,850	1,375
	3,450	2,375

Further information:

♦ Fixed assets costing £156,000 with accumulated depreciation of £83,000 were sold in 19X7 for £93,000.

♦ All sales and purchases were on credit. Other expenses were paid for in cash.

Task 1

Provide a reconciliation between cash flows from operating activities and operating profit for the year ended 30 September 19X7.

Task 2

Prepare a cash flow statement for Hegel Limited, for the year ended 30 September 19X7 in accordance with the requirements of FRS 1 (Revised).

Task 3

Calculate the goodwill on consolidation that would have arisen on acquisition if McTaggart Limited had purchased 80% of the shares in Hegel Limited on 30 September 19X7.

Note

(1) You are **not** required to produce a consolidated balance sheet for the group.

Task 4

Prepare a report for the directors of McTaggart Limited which covers the relevant calculations and questions set out below.

(a) Calculate the current and quick ratios (also known as the 'acid test') of Hegel Limited for the two years. Using this information and that provided in the cash flow statement, state how the liquidity of Hegel Limited has changed from 19X6 to 19X7.

(b) Calculate the gearing ratio for Hegel Limited for 19X6 and 19X7 and comment on the results. Explain whether the level of borrowings in Hegel Limited would have any impact on the level of gearing in the group accounts of McTaggart Limited.

Note

(1) You are *not* required to calculate the gearing ratio of the group.

CHAPTER 10
Cash Flow Statements (Answers)

1 George Ltd

Task 1

Cash flow statement of George Ltd for the year ending 31 March 19X5

	£'000
Net cash inflow from operating activities	350
Returns on investments and servicing of finance	
Interest paid	(20)
Taxation	(21)
Capital expenditure	
Payments to acquire tangible fixed asset	(110)
Sale of tangible fixed asset	7
Equity dividends paid	(30)
Net cash inflow before financing	176
Financing	
Redemption of debentures	(500)
Increase in long–term loan	100
Issue of share capital	15
Decrease in cash	(209)

Task 2

	£'000
Operating profit	237
Depreciation	275
Profit on sale of tangible fixed asset	(2)
Increase in stocks	(10)
Increase in debtors	(140)
Decrease in creditors	(10)
Net cash inflow from operating activities	350

2 Cashedin Ltd

Cash flow statement of Cashedin Ltd for the year ended 30 September 19X5

	£'000
Net cash inflow from operating activities	104
Returns on investments and servicing of finance:	
Interest paid	(218)
Taxation	(75)
Investing activities:	
Payments to acquire tangible fixed assets	(358)
Sale of assets	132
Equity dividends paid	(280)
Net cash outflow before financing	(695)
Financing:	
Loan	200
Issue of ordinary share capital	150
Decrease in cash	(345)

Reconciliation between cash flows from operating activities and operating profit:

	£'000
Operating profit	24
Depreciation charges	318
Increase in stock	(251)
Increase in debtors	(152)
Increase in creditors	165
Net cash inflow from operating activities	104

3 Poised Ltd

Reconciliation between the cash flows from operating activities and the operating profit:

	£'000
Operating profit	2,099
Depreciation charges	1,347
Increase in stock	(335)
Increase in debtors	(219)
Increase in creditors	341
Net cash inflow from operating activities	3,233

4 Hegel Ltd

Task 1

Reconciliation of operating profit to net cash inflow from operating activities

	£'000
Operating profit	1,254
Depreciation charges	971
Profit on sale of tangible fixed assets	(20)
Increase in stock	(48)
Increase in debtors	(105)
Decrease in creditors	(84)
Net cash inflow from operating activities	1,968

Task 2

Cashflow statement of Hegel Limited for the year ended 30 September 19X7

	£'000
Net cash inflow from operating activities	1,968
Returns on investments and servicing of finance	
Interest paid	(302)
Taxation	(276)
Capital expenditure	
Payments to acquire tangible fixed assets	(5,441)
Sale of asset	93
	(3,958)
Equity dividends paid	(120)
	(4,078)
Financing	
Loan	3,000
Issue of ordinary share capital	600
Decrease in cash	(478)

You could also have analysed items in notes rather than on the face of the statement.

Workings

Fixed asset additions

	£'000
Opening balance	2,075
NBV of asset sold	(73)
Depreciation	(971)
Additions (balancing figure)	5,441
Closing balance	6,472

Task 3

Goodwill on acquisition:

	Total equity £'000	Group share (80%) £'000
Share capital	1,200	960
Share premium	400	320
Revaluation reserve	200	160
Profit and loss account	1,850	1,480
		2,920
Consideration		3,300
Goodwill on acquisition		380

Task 4

REPORT

To: Directors of McTaggart Limited

From: AAT Student

Re: Questions about the takeover of Hegel Limited

Date: 4 December 19X7

Following your recent enquiry requesting answers to various questions concerning the takeover of Hegel Ltd by McTaggart, I set out the following answers:

(a) The liquidity of Hegel Ltd had deteriorated over the past year. The cash flow statement shows that there were large purchases of fixed assets (£5,441,000). These were partly funded by a loan of £3,000,000 and an issue of shares for £600,000. The deficit was made up from profits, by the utilisation of existing cash balances and by an overdraft of £158,000. Cash balances have, in consequence, reduced by £478,000 in the year.

The deterioration in the liquidity position can also be seen by the worsening of the current and quick ratios:

	19X7	19X6
Current ratio	$\dfrac{1{,}303}{975} = 1.3$	$\dfrac{1{,}470}{820} = 1.8$
Quick ratio	$\dfrac{574}{975} = 0.6$	$\dfrac{789}{820} = 1.0$

From a fairly safe position in 19X6 the current ratio and the quick ratio have both fallen in 19X7. In 19X6 the company could almost meet its current liabilities out of its current assets, but in 19X7 there is a considerable shortfall. This suggests that if the deficit cannot be made up out of profits a cash injection may be required in the event of a takeover.

(b)

	19X7	19X6
Gearing ratio	$\dfrac{3{,}350}{3{,}350 + 3{,}450} = 49\%$	$\dfrac{350}{350 + 2{,}375} = 13\%$

From a low level of gearing in 19X6 Hegel Limited has increased its borrowing until the business is just about equally funded by debt as by equity. The increased gearing will mean that more of the profits of the company will be swallowed up in interest payments and in the event of a downturn in profits it may not be possible to sustain payment of this level of interest out of profits. As a result of the increased borrowing the company is a more risky investment and may need cash support in the event of a takeover.

As the borrowings of Hegel Limited are added to the borrowings of McTaggart Limited in the group balance sheet a relatively high level of borrowing in Hegel Limited will increase the gearing ratio of the group itself and hence make the group itself appear to be a riskier investment.

AAT Student

CHAPTER 11

Interpretation of Accounts (Questions)

1 Rita Ltd

You are presented with the following information relating to Rita Ltd:

Profit and loss accounts for the year to 31 March 19X0 and 31 March 19X1

	19X0 £000	19X1 £000
Sales (all credit)	15,000	20,000
Less: Cost of goods sold		
Opening stock	1,200	1,500
Purchases (all credit)	7,800	18,700
	9,000	20,200
Less: Closing stock	(1,500)	(7,200)
	7,500	13,000
Gross profit	7,500	7,000
Less: Expenses	(6,000)	(6,900)
Net profit	1,500	100
Taxation	(450)	(20)
	1,050	80
Dividends	(800)	–
Retained profit for the year	250	80

Balance sheets at 31 March 19X0 and 31 March 19X1

	19X0 £000	19X1 £000
Fixed assets at cost	5,000	5,500
Less: Accumulated depreciation	1,500	1,820
	3,500	3,680
Current assets		
Stock at cost	1,500	7,200
Trade debtors	4,500	9,000
Cash at bank	500	50
	6,500	16,250
Current liabilities		
Trade creditors	(2,500)	(8,500)
Taxation	(450)	(20)
Proposed dividend	(800)	–
Bank overdraft	–	(3,080)
	(3,750)	(11,600)
	6,250	8,330
Capital and reserves		
Ordinary shares of £1 each	5,000	5,000
Profit and loss account	1,250	1,330
	6,250	6,330
Long-term loans – 15% debenture stock (issued on 1 April 19X0)	–	2,000
	6,250	8,330

Tasks

(a) Calculate the following accounting ratios being careful to detail the formula adopted in the preparation of each ratio:

    (i)   gross profit margin
    (ii)   acid test (or quick or liquid)
    (iii) trade debtor collection period (in days)
    (iv) trade creditor payment period (in days)
    (v)   gearing

(b) From the information provided, outline clearly *five* possible reasons why Rita Ltd has an overdrawn bank account balance as at 31 March 19X1.

You need not necessarily confine your reasons to the ratios calculated above.

2 A & B (AAT CA J96)

Data

The directors of Dowango Ltd have asked to have a meeting with you. They are intending to ask the bank for a long-term loan to enable them to purchase a company which has retail outlets. The directors have identified two possible companies to take over and they intend to purchase the whole of the share capital of one of the two targeted companies. The directors have obtained the latest financial statements of the two companies, in summary form. The financial statements are set out below:

Summary profit and loss accounts

	Company A £000	Company B £000
Turnover	800	2,100
Cost of sales	440	1,050
Gross profit	360	1,050
Expenses	160	630
Net profit before interest and tax	200	420

Summary balance sheets

	Company A £000	Company B £000
Fixed assets	620	1,640
Net current assets	380	1,160
Long-term loan	(400)	(1,100)
	600	1,700
Share capital and reserves	600	1,700

Task 1

Advise the directors as to which of the two companies targeted for takeover is the more profitable and which one provides the higher return on capital. Your answer should include calculation of the following ratios:

(i) return on capital employed;
(ii) net profit margin;
(iii) asset turnover.

You should also calculate and comment on at least **one** further ratio of your choice, for which you have sufficient information, which would be relevant to determining which of the companies is more profitable or provides the greater return on capital.

Task 2

Advise the directors as to whether Dowango Ltd would have any further reporting requirements in the future as a result of the purchase of shares in one of the companies targeted for takeover.

3 Botticelli Ltd

Data

Botticelli Limited is a trading company that sells carpets to retail outlets. The shareholders of Botticelli Limited have some questions about the profitability and liquidity of the company and about how cash flows from operating activities can be reconciled to operating profit. The profit and loss account and balance sheet produced for internal purposes are set out below.

Botticelli Limited
Profit and loss account for the year ended 31 December 19X6

	19X6 £'000	19X6 £'000	19X5 £'000	19X5 £'000
Turnover		2,963		1,736
Opening stock	341		201	
Purchases	1,712		1,097	
Closing stock	(419)		(341)	
Cost of sales		1,634		957
Gross profit		1,329		779
Depreciation		247		103
Other expenses		588		334
Profit on the sale of fixed assets		15		-
Operating profit for the year		509		342
Interest paid		78		26
Profit before tax		431		316
Taxation on profit		138		111
Profit after tax		293		205
Ordinary dividend		48		22
Retained profit		245		183

Botticelli Limited
Balance sheet as at 31 December 19X6

	19X6 £'000	19X5 £'000
Fixed assets	2,800	1,013
Current assets		
Stocks	419	341
Debtors	444	381
Cash	-	202
	863	924
Current liabilities		
Trade creditors	322	197
Dividends payable	48	41
Taxation	158	103
Bank overdraft	194	-
	722	341
Net current assets	141	583
Total assets less current liabilities	2,941	1,596
Long-term loan	970	320
	1,971	1,276
Capital and reserves		
Called up share capital	400	200
Share premium	250	-
Profit and loss account	1,321	1,076
	1,971	1,276

Task 1

Prepare a report to the shareholders about the profitability and liquidity of Botticelli Limited for the two years 19X5 and 19X6. Your report should include:

(a) calculation of the following ratios for the two years:

- return on capital employed;
- gross profit ratio;
- net profit ratio;
- current ratio;
- quick ratio (also called acid test);

(b) comments on the changes in the ratios from 19X5 to 19X6.

Task 2

Prepare a reconciliation between cash flows from operating activities and operating profit for the year end 31 December 19X6.

CHAPTER 11

Interpretation of Accounts (Answers)

1 Rita Ltd

			19X0	19X1

(a) (i) Gross profit margin

$$\frac{\text{Gross profit}}{\text{Sales}} \times 100 \qquad \frac{7,500}{15,000} \times 100\% \qquad \frac{7,000}{20,000} \times 100\%$$

$$= 50\% \qquad = 35\%$$

(ii) Acid test ratio

$$\frac{\text{Current assets} - \text{Stocks}}{\text{Current liabilities}} \qquad \frac{6,500 - 1,500}{3,750} \qquad \frac{16,250 - 7,200}{11,600}$$

$$= 1.33 \qquad = 0.78$$

(iii) Trade debtor collection period

$$\frac{\text{Trade debtors}}{\text{Sales per day}} \qquad \frac{4,500}{15,000 / 365} \qquad \frac{9,000}{20,000 / 365}$$

$$= 110 \text{ days} \qquad = 164 \text{ days}$$

(iv) Trade creditor payment period

$$\frac{\text{Trade creditors}}{\text{Purchases per day}} \qquad \frac{2,500}{7,800 / 365} \qquad \frac{8,500}{18,700 / 365}$$

$$= 117 \text{ days} \qquad = 166 \text{ days}$$

(v) Gearing

$$\frac{\text{Prior charge capital}}{\text{Total capital}} \times 100\% \qquad \frac{-}{6,250} \times 100\% \qquad \frac{2,000}{8,330} \times 100\%$$

$$= 0\% \qquad = 24\%$$

An alternative (and equally acceptable) gearing ratio would be obtained by defining gearing with a denominator of equity capital only. Then we would have the following.

Gearing

$$\frac{\text{Prior charge capital}}{\text{Ordinary shareholders' funds}} \times 100\% \qquad \frac{-}{6,250} \times 100\% \qquad \frac{2,000}{6,330} \times 100\%$$

$$= 0\% \qquad = 32\%$$

(b) The bank overdraft as at 31 March 19X1 has arisen for the following reasons:

 (i) Trade debtors are being collected more slowly. The average trade debtor collection period has increased from 110 days in 19X0 to 164 days in 19X1, so the inflow of cash after sales on credit is being delayed.

 (ii) The introduction of gearing into the capital structure means that debenture interest is payable for the first time.

 (iii) Fixed assets costing £500,000 have been acquired in the year. Since there is no sundry creditor in the 31 March 19X1 balance sheet it appears that these fixed assets were bought for cash.

 (iv) The stock level at 31 March 19X1 is substantially higher than at 31 March 19X0. Stock turnover figures can be calculated to illustrate the increased investment in stocks:

	19X0	19X1
Stock turnover = $\dfrac{\text{Cost of sales}}{\text{Stocks}}$	$\dfrac{7{,}500}{1{,}500} = 5.0$	$\dfrac{13{,}000}{7{,}200} = 1.8$

 (v) The declining gross profitability of sales means that less cash has flowed into the business per pound of sales in 19X1 than in 19X0.

2 A & B

Task 1

	Company A	Company B
Return on capital employed	$\dfrac{200}{1{,}000} = 20\%$	$\dfrac{420}{2{,}800} = 15\%$
Net profit margin	$\dfrac{200}{800} = 25\%$	$\dfrac{420}{2{,}100} = 20\%$
Asset turnover	$\dfrac{800}{1{,}000} = 0.8$	$\dfrac{2{,}100}{2{,}800} = 0.75$
Other possible ratios:		
Gross profit margin	$\dfrac{360}{800} = 45\%$	$\dfrac{1{,}050}{2{,}100} = 50\%$
Expenses: Sales	$\dfrac{160}{800} = 20\%$	$\dfrac{630}{2{,}100} = 30\%$

From the calculations we can see that Company A has both the highest return on capital employed and also the highest profit margin and asset turnover. It would, therefore, be the better company to target for takeover. However, the gross profit margin for Company B is, in fact, higher suggesting that the underlying business is more profitable. It is only because of the expenses of Company B in relation to sales that it has a lower net profit margin. If Company B could be made more efficient in terms of expenses and utilisation of assets by the introduction of a new management team on takeover, then, given the more profitable underlying business, it might be worth considering as a target for takeover.

Task 2

As a result of the takeover, Dowango Ltd would become a parent undertaking, given that it would own more than 50% of the voting rights in the subsidiary undertaking. Under FRS2 consolidated accounts would be required in addition to the accounts required for the individual companies.

3   Botticelli Ltd

Report

To: Shareholders of Botticelli Ltd   Date: June 19X7

From: AAT Student

Re: **Profitability and liquidity of Botticelli Ltd**

In answer to your questions about the profitability and liquidity of Botticelli Ltd for 19X5 and 19X6 I set out the following points:

The relevant ratios are as follows:

	19X6	19X5
Return on capital employed	$\frac{509}{2,941} = 17.3\%$	$\frac{342}{1,596} = 21.4\%$
Gross profit	$\frac{1,329}{2,963} = 44.9\%$	$\frac{779}{1,736} = 44.9\%$
Net profit	$\frac{509}{2,963} = 17.2\%$	$\frac{342}{1,736} = 19.7\%$
Current ratio	$\frac{863}{722} = 1.2:1$	$\frac{924}{341} = 2.7:1$
Quick ratio (acid test)	$\frac{444}{722} = 0.6:1$	$\frac{583}{341} = 1.7:1$

As you can see, the return on capital employed has fallen from 19X5 to 19X6. This means that less profit is being generated from the capital employed in the company in 19X6 than in 19X5. The expansion of activities as shown by increased investment in fixed assets in 19X6 has not yet generated a comparable increase in profits, but this may be due to the time lag between investment and the generation of profits from the new investment, so may not indicate that the increased investment has been a failure.

The gross profit percentage has remained constant over the two years, indicating that selling margins have been maintained. The increased level of sales has not been achieved at the expense of profit margins.

Page 1/2

> The net profit percentage has fallen in 19X6 from its level in 19X5. This is largely due to the increased depreciation charges as a result of the expansion mentioned above. Again, this may change once the profits from the expansion are fully felt in the results of the company.
>
> In conclusion, it is too early to tell whether the decrease in profitability in the company as shown by the return on capital employed and the net profit percentage will continue in the future, or whether we will see a return to former levels as the profits from the new investment have their full impact.
>
> The liquidity of the company has deteriorated in 19X6 from 19X5. The current ratio and quick ratio in 19X5 show that the company could easily pay its current liabilities out of current assets. This is not the case in 19X6 with the deterioration of the cash position. This appears to be a result of the expansion of fixed assets which have not been fully funded by long term capital injections, but have been paid for by utilising cash balances and an overdraft. Unless the profits from the expansion can make up the shortfall next year or further loans are received, the company may be facing a liquidity crisis.
>
> Page 2/2

Task 2.2

Reconciliation between the cash flows from operating activities and the operating profit.

	£'000
Operating profit	509
Depreciation charges	247
Profit on sale of tangible fixed assets	(15)
Increase in stock	(78)
Increase in debtors	(63)
Increase in creditors	125
Net cash inflow from operating activities	725

CHAPTER 12

Group Accounts – Consolidated Balance Sheet (Questions)

1 Edinburgh Ltd

The following are the draft balance sheets of Edinburgh Ltd and its subsidiary Glasgow Ltd as at 31 December 19X5:

Edinburgh Ltd

	£	£
Fixed assets		
Tangible assets		157,000
Investments		70,000
Current assets		
Stocks	73,200	
Debtors	82,100	
Glasgow Ltd current account	14,700	
Cash at bank and in hand	8,000	
	178,000	
Creditors: Amounts falling due within one year		
Trade creditors	123,000	
Net current assets		55,000
Total assets less current liabilities		282,000
Capital and reserves		
Called-up share capital (£1 shares)		250,000
Profit and loss account		32,000
		282,000

Glasgow Ltd

	£	£
Fixed assets: Tangible assets		82,000
Current assets		
Stocks	35,200	
Debtors	46,900	
Cash at bank and in hand	25,150	
	107,250	
Creditors: Amounts falling due within one year		
Trade creditors	50,000	
Edinburgh Ltd current account	8,000	
	58,000	
Net current assets		49,250
Total assets less current liabilities		131,250
Creditors: Amounts falling due after more than one year		
6% debentures		20,000
		111,250
Capital and reserves		
Called-up share capital (£1 shares)		50,000
Share premium account		6,250
Revaluation reserve		15,000
Profit and loss account		40,000
		111,250

Notes

(1) Edinburgh Ltd acquired 40,000 shares in Glasgow Ltd on 1 January 19X4 for a cost of £53,000 when the balance on Glasgow Ltd's reserves were:

	£
Share premium account	6,250
Revaluation reserve	–
Profit and loss account	10,000

Edinburgh Ltd also acquired £12,000 of Glasgow Ltd's debentures at par on the same date.

(2) Both Edinburgh Ltd and Glasgow Ltd wish to declare a £2,000 dividend.

(3) The current account difference is due to cash in transit.

(4) Goodwill arising on consolidation is amortised through the profit and loss account over 5 years.

Task

Prepare the consolidated balance sheet as at 31 December 19X5 of Edinburgh Ltd.

2 Close Ltd

The summarised balance sheets of Close Ltd and Steele Ltd as at 31 December 19X2 were as follows:

	Close Ltd £	Steele Ltd £
Fixed assets		
Tangible assets	110,000	58,200
Investments	75,000	–
Current assets		
Stocks	18,000	12,000
Debtors	62,700	21,100
Investments	–	2,500
Cash at bank	10,000	3,000
Current account – Close Ltd	–	3,200
	275,700	100,000
Called-up share capital: Ordinary shares of £1 each	120,000	60,000
Share premium account	18,000	–
Revaluation reserve on 1 January 19X2	23,000	16,000
Profit and loss account on 1 January 19X2	61,000	8,000
Profit for 19X2	16,000	5,000
Trade creditors	35,000	11,000
Current account – Steele Ltd	2,700	–
	275,700	100,000

The following information is relevant:

(1) On 31 December 19X1, Close Ltd acquired 48,000 shares in Steele Ltd for £75,000 cash.

(2) The stock of Close Ltd includes £4,000 goods from Steele Ltd invoiced to Close Ltd at cost plus 25%.

(3) A cheque for £500 from Close Ltd to Steele Ltd, sent before 31 December 19X2, was not received by the latter company until January 19X3.

(4) Goodwill arising on acquisition is amortised through the profit and loss account over 5 years.

Task

Prepare the consolidated balance sheet of Close Ltd and its subsidiary Steele Ltd as at 31 December 19X2.

3 Thomas and James (AAT CA D96)

You have been asked to assist in the preparation of the consolidated accounts of the Thomas Group. Set out below are the balance sheets of Thomas Ltd and James Ltd for the year ended 30 September 19X6:

Balance sheet as at 30 September 19X6

	Thomas Ltd £000	James Ltd £000
Fixed assets	13,022	3,410
Investment in James Ltd	3,760	–
Current assets		
Stocks	6,682	2,020
Debtors	5,526	852
Cash	273	58
	12,481	2,930
Current liabilities		
Trade creditors	3,987	507
Taxation	834	173
	4,821	680
Net current assets	7,660	2,250
Total assets less current liabilities	24,442	5,660
Long-term loan	8,000	1,500
	16,442	4,160
Capital and reserves		
Called up share capital	5,000	1,000
Share premium	2,500	400
Profit and loss account	8,942	2,760
	16,442	4,160

You have been given the following further information:

(1) The share capital of both Thomas Ltd and James Ltd consists of ordinary shares of £1 each. There have been no changes to the balances during the year.

(2) Thomas Ltd acquired 800,000 shares in James Ltd on 30 September 19X5 at a cost of £3,760,000.

(3) At 30 September 19X5 the balance on the profit and loss account of James Ltd was £2,000,000.

(4) The fair value of the fixed assets of James Ltd at 30 September 19X5 was £3,910,000. The revaluation has not been reflected in the books of James Ltd.

(5) Goodwill arising on consolidation is to be amortised through the profit and loss account over four years.

Task

Prepare a consolidated balance sheet for Thomas Ltd and its subsidiary undertaking as at 30 September 19X6.

4 Spring Ltd (AAT CA J97)

Data

The directors of Primavera Fashions Limited have asked you to prepare some answers to certain questions they have relating to the year end financial statements that are due to be considered at next week's meeting of the Board.

The directors are uncertain as to how the balance on the share premium account arose and how it can be used.

The directors have just learned that one of their trade debtors has gone into liquidation owing them £24,000. The liquidator has informed them that it is likely that there will be no assets available to pay off creditors and they wonder whether this will have any effect on the financial statements for the year ended 31 March 19X7.

The directors are also uncertain as to the accounting treatment of their investment in shares of an associated company, Spring Limited. Primavera Fashions Limited purchased a 35% interest in the company for £400,000 in April 19X5 when the total net assets of the company amounted to £800,000. (There was no goodwill shown in the associated company's own balance sheet.) Since acquisition Spring Limited has made profits amounting to £200,000 and, as at 31 March 19X7, the total net assets of the company amounted to £1,000,000. Goodwill acquisition is amortised through the profit and loss account over four years, with a full year's charge in the year of acquisition.

Task

Reply to the following questions from the directors. Where appropriate justify your answers by reference to company law, accounting concepts and applicable financial reporting and accounting standards.

(a) (i) How did the balance on the 'share premium' arise?

    (ii) Can it be used to pay dividends to the shareholders?

    (iii) Give one use of the share premium account.

(b) Will the fact that the debtor went into liquidation after the end of the financial year have any impact upon the financial statements for the year ended 31 March 19X7?

(c) (i) At what amount will the investment in Spring Limited be shown in the group balance sheet as at 31 March 19X7?

    (ii) Show how the total investment in Spring Limited will be analysed in the notes to the group financial statements.

5   Edward Limited (AAT CA J98)

On 1 March 19X8 Solu Limited bought 75% of the share capital of Edward Limited for £200,000. The share capital and reserves of Edward Limited at that date were as follows:

	£
Ordinary share capital	100,000
Share premium account	50,000
Profit and loss account	25,000

The fixed assets of Edward Limited were included in the balance sheet at a net book value of £70,000 but a valuation on 31 March 19X8 valued them at £95,000.

Task 1

The directors understand that Edward Limited is now a subsidiary undertaking of Solu Limited but they would like to have the definition of a subsidiary undertaking clarified. Define in simple terms a subsidiary undertaking account to FRS 2 *Accounting for subsidiary undertakings* and the Companies Act.

Task 2

Calculate the minority interest in the Solu Group as at 31 March 19X8.

CHAPTER 12

Group Accounts – Consolidated Balance Sheet (Answers)

1 Edinburgh Ltd

Consolidated balance sheet at 31 December 19X5

	£	£
Fixed assets		
Tangible assets		239,000
Investments (70,000 – 53,000 – 12,000)		5,000
		244,000
Current assets		
Stocks	108,400	
Debtors – trade debtors	129,000	
Cash at bank and in hand (8,000 + 25,150 + 6,700)	39,850	
	277,250	
Creditors: Amounts falling due within one year		
Trade creditors	173,000	
Proposed dividend – parent company	2,000	
– minority interests	400	
	175,400	
Net current assets		101,850
Total assets less current liabilities		345,850
Creditors: Amounts falling due after more than one year		
6% Debenture loan (20,000 – 12,000)		8,000
		337,850
Capital and reserves		
Called-up share capital – £1 ordinary shares, fully paid		250,000
Revaluation reserve (W6)		12,000
Profit and loss account (W5)		54,000
		316,000
Minority interests (W4)		21,850
		337,850

Workings

(1) Group structure

```
    Edinburgh
        |
       80%
        |
    Glasgow
```

(2) Net assets of Glasgow

	Balance sheet date		Acquisition
	£	£	£
Share capital		50,000	50,000
Share premium		6,250	6,250
Revaluation reserve		15,000	–
Profit and loss account			
Per question	40,000		10,000
Less: Dividend	(2,000)		
	———		
		38,000	
		———	———
		109,250	66,250
		———	———

(3) Goodwill

	£
Cost of shares	53,000
Net assets required [80% x 66,250) (W2)]	(53,000)
	———
	–
	———

(4) Minority interest   [(20% x 109,250) (W2)]   21,850

(5) Profit and loss account

	£
Edinburgh Ltd	32,000
Proposed dividend	(2,000)
Dividend receivable from Glasgow	1,600
Glasgow Ltd [80% x (38,000 – 10,000) (W2)]	22,400
	———
	54,000
	———

(6) Revaluation reserve

	£
Glasgow Ltd [80% x 15,000 (W2)]	12,000

2 Close Ltd

Consolidated balance sheet at 31 December 19X2

	£	£
Fixed assets:		
Intangible assets: goodwill (W3)		6,240
Tangible assets		168,200
		174,440
Current assets		
Stocks (18,000 + 12,000 – 800)	29,200	
Debtors	83,800	
Investments	2,500	
Cash at bank and in hand (10,000 + 3,000 + 500)	13,500	
	129,000	
Creditors: Amounts falling due within one year	(46,000)	
Net current assets		83,000
Total assets less current liabilities		257,440
Capital and reserves		
Called–up share capital – £1 ordinary shares, fully paid		120,000
Share premium account		18,000
Revaluation reserve		23,000
Profit and loss account (W5)		78,800
		239,800
Minority interests (W4)		17,640
		257,440

Workings

(1) Group structure

Close Ltd

80%

Steele Ltd

(2) Net assets of Steele Ltd

	Balance sheet date	Acquisition
	£	£
Share capital	60,000	60,000
Revaluation reserve	16,000	16,000
Profit and loss account	13,000	8,000
	89,000	84,000

(3) Goodwill

	£
Cost of shares	75,000
Net assets acquired [80% x 84,000 (W2)]	67,200
	7,800
Less: amortisation ($\frac{1}{5}$)	(1,560)
	6,240

(4) Minority interest [20% x 89,000 (W2)]   £ 17,800

Less: unrealised profit on stock [(4,000 x $\frac{25}{125}$) x 20%]   160

    17,640

(5) Profit and loss account

	£
Close Ltd	77,000
Less: Unrealised profit on stock [(4,000 x $\frac{25}{125}$) x 80%]	(640)
Steele Ltd [80% x (13,000 – 8,000) (W2)]	4,000
Less: Goodwill amortised	(1,500)
	78,800

3 Thomas and James

Thomas Ltd
Consolidated balance sheet as at 30 September 19X6

	£000	£000
Fixed assets:		
Intangible assets: goodwill		480
Tangible assets		16,932
		17,412
Current assets		
Stocks	8,702	
Debtors	6,378	
Cash	331	
	15,411	
Current liabilities		
Trade creditors	4,494	
Taxation	1,007	
	5,501	
Net current assets		9,910
Total assets less current liabilities		27,322
Long–term loan		9,500
		17,822
Capital and reserves		
Called up share capital		5,000
Share premium		2,500
Profit and loss account		9,390
		16,890
Minority interest		932
		17,822

Workings

(i) Thomas Ltd holding in James Ltd:

$$\frac{800,000}{1,000,000} = 80\%$$

Minority interest:

$$\frac{200,000}{1,000,000} = 20\%$$

(ii) Revaluation of assets in James Ltd to fair value at date of acquisition:

DR Fixed assets   £500,000
CR Revaluation reserve   £500,000

(**Note**: the assumption made here is that the book value of James Ltd fixed assets at 30 September 19X5 was not significantly different from that at 30 September 19X6 (that is, there were no significant additions or disposals). Full credit is given for alternative assumptions.)

(iii) Calculation of goodwill arising on consolidation and minority interest.

	Total equity £'000	(Attributable to Thomas Ltd) At acquisition £'000	Since acquisition £'000	Minority interest £'000
Share capital	1,000	800		200
Share premium	400	320		80
Revaluation reserve	500	400		100
P&L:				
– at acquisition	2,000	1,600		400
– since acquisition	760		608	152
	4,660	3,120	608	932
Consideration		3,760		
Goodwill arising on consolidation		640		
P&L account Thomas Ltd			8,942	
Less goodwill amortised ($\frac{1}{4}$)		160	160	
		480	9,390	

4 Spring Ltd

(a) (i) The share premium account balance arose when shares were issued at an amount in excess of their nominal value. The share capital account would be credited with the nominal value of the shares issued and the share premium account would be credited with the difference between the nominal value of the shares and the issue price.

(ii) The share premium account is a non-distributable reserve and so dividends cannot be paid out of this reserve.

(iii) The Companies Act allows the share premium account to be used for:

- bonus share issues
- writing off preliminary expenses
- writing off the expenses of, or the commission paid or discount allowed on, any issue of shares or debentures
- providing for the premium payable on redemption of debentures.

(b) The liquidation of the debtor after the year end would constitute a post balance sheet 'adjusting event' as defined by SSAP 17. An adjusting event is one that 'provides additional evidence of conditions existing at the balance sheet date', namely, evidence about the amount that will be collected from the debtor. As no amount is likely to be received from the debtor the account must be adjusted and the £24,000 balance on the debtor's account must be written off as a bad debt in the financial statements for the year ended 31 March 19X7.

(c) (i) The investment in Spring Limited will be shown in the group balance sheet as a long term investment at £470,000.

(ii) The note to the accounts will disclose the following:

	£
Group share of net assets of Spring Limited	350,000
Goodwill (see workings)	30,000
	380,000

Workings

	£
Cost of investment	400,000
Group share of net assets of Spring Limited at acquisition (35% x £800,000)	280,000
Goodwill	120,000
Less: amortisation (3/4)	(90,000)
	30,000

5 Edward Ltd

Task 1

An undertaking is a subsidiary of a parent if any of the following apply:

♦ the parent holds a majority of voting rights in the undertaking;

♦ the parent is a member of the undertaking and has the right to appoint/remove directors holding the majority of voting rights;

♦ the parent has the right to exercise dominant influence over the undertaking by virtue of the Memorandum/Articles or a control contract;

♦ the parent is a member of the undertaking and controls alone, or by agreement with other shareholders, the majority of voting rights;

♦ the parent has a participating interest in the undertaking but exercises dominant control or is managed on a unified basis with the undertaking;

♦ a parent is also treated as the parent of the subsidiary undertakings of its subsidiary.

Task 2

Description	Edward Ltd Total £	Minority interest (25%) £
Ordinary share capital	100,000	25,000
Share premium account	50,000	12,500
Profit and loss account	25,000	6,250
Revaluation reserve (W1)	25,000	6,250
Total minority interest		50,000

Workings

1   Revaluation reserve

	£
Balance sheet valuation	70,000
Current value	95,000
Credit to revaluation reserve	25,000

CHAPTER 13

Group Accounts – Consolidated Profit and Loss Account (Questions)

1 Zen plc

Profit and loss statements for Zen plc and its subsidiary Xerxes Ltd for the year ended 31 December 19X0

	Zen plc £'000	Xerxes Ltd £'000
Turnover	3,200	2,560
Cost of sales	(2,200)	(1,480)
Gross profit	1,000	1,080
Administrative expenses	(400)	(80)
Distribution costs	(280)	(180)
	320	820
Investment income	160	–
	480	820
Taxation	(280)	(420)
	200	400
Dividend	(96)	(200)
Retained profit for year	104	200
Retained profit brought forward	1,200	1,120
Retained profit carried forward	1,304	1,320

(1) Zen plc paid £1.5m on 31 December 19W6 for 80% of Xerxes Ltd's share capital of £800,000. The balance on Xerxes Ltd's profit and loss account was £600,000 at that time. Goodwill on acquisition had been fully amortised through the profit and loss account at 1 January 19X0.

(2) Zen plc made sales to Xerxes Ltd which were worth a total of £600,000 during the year. Not all of the goods had been resold by the year-end. The profit element included in Xerxes Ltd's closing stock was £30,000.

(3) The figure for investment income in Zen plc's profit statement comprises the holding company's share of the subsidiary's total dividend for the year.

Tasks

(a) Prepare a consolidated profit and loss account for the year ended 31 December 19X0 for the Zen group.

(b) Explain your treatment of the inter-company sales and closing stock figures in (2) above.

2 Y plc and Z Ltd

The following profit statements have been prepared for Y plc and its subsidiary Z Ltd for the year ended 30 September 19X2:

	Y plc		Z Ltd	
	£'000	£'000	£'000	£'000
Sales		700		300
Opening stock	20		11	
Purchases	310		190	
	330		201	
Closing stock	24		15	
		306		186
Gross profit		394		114
Selling expenses	27		19	
Administration costs	15		14	
		42		33
Profit before tax		352		81
Taxation		92		26
Profit after tax		260		55
Dividends		100		35
Retained profit for the year		160		20
Retained profit brought forward		460		320
Retained profits carried forward		620		340

Notes

(1) Y plc acquired 60% of the share capital of Z Ltd in 19X7, when the balance on Z Ltd's profit and loss account was £120,000. Z Ltd had ordinary share capital of £300,000 at that time and the balance on Z Ltd's share premium account was £260,000. Y plc paid £550,000 for its investment in Z Ltd. The goodwill on consolidation had been fully amortised through the profit and loss account at 1 October 19X1.

(2) Y plc made sales of £30,000 to Z Ltd during the year. These goods originally cost Y plc £20,000. All but 10% of these goods had been resold by Z Ltd by 30 September 19X2.

Task

Prepare a consolidated profit and loss account for the Y group for the year ended 30 September 19X2.

CHAPTER 13

Group Accounts – Consolidated Profit and Loss Account (Answers)

1 Zen plc

(a)

**Consolidated profit and loss account
for the year ended 31 December 19X0**

	£'000
Turnover (3,200 + 2,560 – 600)	5,160
Cost of sales (2,200 + 1,480 – 600 + 30)	(3,110)
Gross profit	2,050
Distribution costs (280 + 180)	(460)
Administrative expenses (400 + 80)	(480)
Profit on ordinary activities before taxation	1,110
Tax on profit on ordinary activities (280 + 420)	(700)
Profit on ordinary activities after taxation	410
Minority interests (20% x 400)	(80)
Profit for the financial year	330
Dividends	(96)
Retained profit for the year	234
Retained profit brought forward (W1)	1,236
Retained profits carried forward (W2)	1,470

(b) A consolidated profit and loss account is prepared on the basis that the group is just one entity. Consolidated sales must therefore represent sales to third parties outside the group. All inter–company sales are therefore excluded from sales (in the selling company's accounts) and purchases (in the buying company's accounts) before the consolidation takes place to calculate the combined sales and cost of sales.

Without adjustment the closing stock figure for an inter–company purchased item not yet sold outside of the group will be stated at cost; ie inclusive of any profit recorded by the selling company. This profit has not yet been realised by an external sale, so must be eliminated so that closing stock is stated at cost to the group.

Workings

		£'000	£'000
(1)	Retained profit brought forward		
	Z plc		1,200
	X Ltd: Share of post–acquisition profits		
	[80% x (1,120 – 600)]		416
	Less: Goodwill amortised		
	Cost	1,500	
	Net assets acquired [80% x (800 + 600)]	(1,120)	
			(380)
			1,236

		£'000	£'000
(2)	Retained profits carried forward (proof)		
	Z plc		1,304
	X Ltd: Share of post–acquisition profits		
	[80% x (1,320 – 600)]		576
	Less: Goodwill amortised		
	Cost	1,500	
	Net assets required [80% x (800 + 600)]	(1,120)	
			(380)
	Provision for unrealised profit		(30)
			1,470

2 Y plc and Z Ltd

Consolidated profit and loss account for the year ended 30 September 19X2

	£'000
Turnover (700 + 300 − 30 (W1))	970
Cost of sales (306 + 186 − 30 + 1 (W1))	(463)
Gross profit	507
Distribution costs (27 + 19)	(46)
Administration expenses (15 + 14)	(29)
Profit on ordinary activities before taxation	432
Taxation (92 + 26)	(118)
Profit on ordinary activities after taxation	314
Minority interest (40% x 55)	(22)
Profits attributable to the group	292
Dividends	(100)
Retained for the financial year	192
Retained profits brought forward (W3)	438
Retained profits carried forward (W4)	630

Workings

(1) *Unrealised profit on stock*

	£'000
Inter–company sales	30
Original cost	(20)
Profit	10
Unrealised (10%)	1

Eliminate £30,000 from turnover and purchases, reduce closing stock by £1,000 therefore reduce cost of sales by £29,000.

(2) *Goodwill*

	£'000	£'000
Cost of investment		550
Less: net assets acquired:		
Share capital	300	
Share premium	260	
Profit and loss account	120	
	680	
Group share (60%)		(408)
		142

(3) *Retained profit brought forward*

	£'000
Y plc	460
Z Ltd post–acquisition share only [60% x (320 – 120)]	120
Less: Goodwill amortised (W2)	(142)
	438

(4) *Retained profit carried forward*

Y plc	620
Divided receivable from Z (60% x 35)	21
Z Ltd post–acquisition share only [60% x (340 – 120)]	132
Less: Goodwill amortised (W2)	(142)
Less: Unrealised profit on stock (W1)	(1)
	630

CHAPTER 14

Group Accounts – Legal and Professional Requirements (Questions)

1 Group financial statements

Explain why a parent company must produce group financial statements and the concept that underlies consolidated accounts.

2 Advantages and disadvantages

Discuss the advantages and disadvantages of preparing consolidated accounts for a company and its subsidiaries.

3 Paulo plc

Paulo plc has made two investments in the year ended 31 December 19X4. On 1 January 19X4, it acquired the following shares:

	Cost £	Shares acquired
Matty Ltd (issued share capital 50,000 £1 shares)	60,000	30,000
Josie Ltd (issued share capital 30,000 £1 shares)	40,000	14,000

The holding of shares in Matty Ltd gives Paulo plc the right to appoint a majority of the Board of Directors of that company.

Josie Ltd has two classes of shares. Class A shares carry 2 votes each and there are 20,000 of these. Class B shares carry one vote each and there are 10,000 of these. Paulo acquired Class A shares only.

Task

On the basis of the information above, discuss the principles involved in determining how Matty Ltd and Josie Ltd should be included in the group accounts.

CHAPTER 14

Group Accounts – Legal and Professional Requirements (Answers)

1 Group financial statements

The requirement to prepare group accounts comes from the Companies Act 1985 which states that a company should prepare group accounts in the form of consolidated accounts if it has one or more subsidiaries at the year–end. This requirement is based on the idea that where a holding company has control, accounting for the investment at cost does not give a true and fair view of the state of affairs of the company and its underlying investments.

Consolidated accounts are based on the single entity concept, ie treating the group as a single entity (as opposed to a number of separate companies). Consolidated accounts therefore show the assets and liabilities, income and expenses of the group as a whole.

2 Advantages and disadvantages

The advantages of preparing consolidated accounts for a company and its subsidiaries include the following:

- Consolidated accounts show a true and fair view of the whole group's business activities, reflecting the fact that all the group companies are subject to the control of the parent company and its directors. This reflects commercial substance rather than legal form.

- All group assets and liabilities are brought into the accounts and assets and liabilities inflated through intra–group transactions are eliminated.

The potential disadvantages of preparing consolidated accounts include the following:

- The cost and time for preparing the relevant information.

- Consolidation of subsidiaries will often necessitate the creation of goodwill in the consolidated accounts. The calculation of goodwill can be a subjective exercise, involving the estimation of the fair value of the separable net assets acquired. The goodwill will either have to be written off through reserves, often significantly reducing shareholders' funds potentially distorting gearing measures/investor perceptions; or will be capitalised and written off through the profit and loss account over an appropriate period, reducing profit on ordinary activities each year.

- Unsophisticated investors may misinterpret consolidated accounts as representing the legal accounts of a single company.

- Reflection of the whole group's assets and results as a 'single entity' may detract from the needs of investors to determine the assets and results of individual segments of the business.

3 Paulo plc

S258 of the Companies Act 1985 defines a subsidiary undertaking. The definition would apply to the two investments as follows.

(a) **Matty Ltd**

A company will be a subsidiary of another company where either the holding company has a majority of the voting rights in that company or where the holding company has the right to appoint or remove a majority of its directors. There is no information given as to the level of voting rights held.

Paulo plc's right to appoint a majority of the directors does not of itself make Matty Ltd a subsidiary. Paulo plc must have the right to appoint directors who carry a majority of the voting rights at general meetings.

From the information given, it would appear that Matty is *prima facie* a subsidiary due to the size of the shareholding and the control of the directors. However, there is no conclusive evidence.

(b) **Josie Ltd**

Although Paulo plc only owns 47% of Josie Ltd's total share capital, Paulo plc controls 56% of the voting rights. Thus Josie Ltd would fall within the definition of a subsidiary company as outlined above.

CHAPTER 15

Mock Central Assessment

Questions

This central assessment is in THREE sections. You are reminded that competence must he achieved each section. You should therefore attempt and aim to complete every task in each section, using the Answer Book provided.

All workings should be shown in the Answer Book section.

A proforma for journal entries and a proforma profit and loss account (Companies Act format 1 as supplemented by FRS 3) are provided in your Answer Book for your use.

You are advised to spend approximately 55 minutes on Section 1, 70 minutes on Section 2 and 55 minutes on Section 3.

Section 1

This section is in two parts.

PART A

Task 1.1

State one type of profit-making and one type of public sector or not-for-profit organisation.

For each type of organisation:

(a) give one example of an external user of the financial statements; and

(b) describe one type of decision which would be made by the users with the assistance of the financial statements of the organisation.

Task 1.2

The accounting equation is often expressed as.

$$\text{Assets} - \text{liabilities} = \text{Ownership interest}$$

(a) Explain what each of the terms 'assets', 'liabilities' and 'ownership interest' means.

(b) Identify, in general terms only, the balances that would appear in the 'ownership interest' section of the balance sheet of one profit-making and one public sector or not-for-profit organisation.

PART B

Data

Bimbridge Hospitals Trust has just lost its supplier of bandages. The company that has been supplying it for the last five years has gone into liquidation. The Trust is concerned to select a new supplier which it can rely on to supply it with its needs for the foreseeable future. You have been asked by the Trust managers to analyse the financial statements of a potential supplier of bandages. You have obtained the latest financial statements of the company, in summary form, which are set out below.

Patch Limited
Summary Profit and Loss Accounts for the years ended 30 September 19X8 and 19X7

	19X8	19X7
	£'000	£'000
Turnover	2,300	2,100
Cost of sales	1,035	945
Gross profit	1,265	1,155
Expenses	713	693
Net profit before interest and tax	552	462

Patch Limited
Summary Balance Sheets as at 30 September 19X8 and 19X7

	19X8		19X7	
	£'000	£'000	£'000	£'000
Fixed assets		4,764		5,418
Current assets				
Stocks	522		419	
Debtors	406		356	
Cash	117		62	
	1,045		837	
Current liabilities				
Trade creditors	305		254	
Taxation	170		211	
	475		465	
Net current assets		570		372
Long-term loan		(1,654)		(2,490)
		3,680		3,300
Share capital		1,100		1,000
Share premium		282		227
Profit and loss account		2,298		2,073
		3,680		3,300

You have also obtained the relevant industry average ratios which are as follows.

	19X8	19X7
Return on capital employed	9.6%	9.4%
Net profit percentage	21.4%	21.3%
Quick ratio/acid test	1.0: 1	0.9:1
Gearing (Debt/Capital employed)	36%	37%

Task 1.3

In the Answer Book, prepare a report for the managers of Bimbridge Hospitals Trust recommending whether or not to use Patch Limited as a supplier of bandages. Use the information contained in the financial statements of Patch Limited and the industry averages supplied.

Your answer should:

♦ comment on the company's profitability, liquidity and financial position;

♦ consider how the company has changed over the two years;

♦ include a comparison with the industry as a whole.

The report should include calculation of the following ratios for the two years.

(i) Return on capital employed;

(ii) Net profit percentage;

(iii) Quick ratio/acid test;

(iv) Gearing.

Section 2

This section is in two parts.

PART A

Data

You have been asked to assist in the preparation of the financial statements of Fun Limited for the year ended 30 September 19X8. The company is a distributor of children's games. You have been provided with the extended trial balance of Fun Limited as at 30 September 19X8 which is set out below.

Fun Limited
Extended trial balance as at 30 September 19X8

Description	Trial balance		Adjustments		Profit and Loss		Balance sheet	
	£'000	£'000	£'000	£'000	£'000	£'000	£'000	£'000
Trade debtors	2,863						2,863	
Bank overdraft		316						316
Interest	300				300			
Profit and loss account		3,811						3,811
Provision for doubtful debts		114						114
Distribution costs	2,055		614		2,669			
Administration expenses	1,684		358		2,042			
Returns inwards	232				232			
Sales		14,595				14,595		
Land – cost	2,293						2,293	
Buildings – cost	2,857						2,857	
Fixtures and fittings – cost	1,245						1,245	
Motor vehicles – cost	2,524						2,524	
Office equipment – cost	872						872	
Stock	1,893		2,041	2,041	1,893	2,041	2,041	
Purchases	6,671				6,671			
Interim dividend	480				480			
Trade creditors		804						804
Buildings – accumulated depreciation		261		51				312
Fixtures and fittings – accumulated depreciation		309		124				433
Motor vehicles – accumulated depreciation		573		603				1,176
Office equipment – accumulated depreciation		184		81				265
Prepayments	63						63	
Carriage inwards	87				87			
Returns outwards		146				146		
Accruals				113				113
Investments	2,244						2,244	
Loan		3,600						3,600
Ordinary share capital		2,000						2,000
Share premium		1,300						1,300
Revaluation reserve		350						350
Profit					2,408			2,408
Total	28,363	28,363	3,013	3,013	16,782	16,782	17,002	17,002

You have been given the following further information.

- The share capital of the business consists of ordinary shares with a nominal value of 25 pence.

- The company has paid an interim dividend of 6 pence per share this year and is proposing a final dividend of 10 pence per share.

- Depreciation has been calculated on all of the fixed assets of the business and has already been entered into the distribution costs and administrative expenses ledger balances as shown on the extended trial balance.

- The corporation tax charge for the year has been calculated as £972,000.

- Interest on the loan has been paid for the first eleven months of the year only, but no interest has been paid or charged for the final month of the year. The loan carries a rate of interest of 8% per annum of the balance outstanding on the loan.

Answer Tasks 2.1-2.5 in the Answer Book provided.

Task 2.1

In the Answer Book, make any additional adjustments you feel to be necessary to the balances in the extended trial balance as a result of the matters set out in the further information above. Using the proforma provided, set out your adjustments in the form of journal entries.

Note:

- Narratives and dates are not required.
- Ignore any effect of these adjustments on the tax charge for the year as given above.

Task 2.2

Using the proforma profit and loss account in the Answer Book, and taking account of any adjustments made in Task 2.1, draft a profit and loss account for the year ended 30 September 19X8 using Format 1 in accordance with the Companies Act 1985 as supplemented by FRS 3 *Reporting Financial Performance*. You are **not** required to produce notes to the accounts.

Data

The directors are interested in expanding operations next year. They wish to be clear about the constituents of the equity on the balance sheet and on the impact that leasing equipment, rather than purchasing equipment, might have on the company's balance sheet. They would like you to attend the next meeting of the Board.

Task 2.3

Prepare notes to bring to the Board meeting dealing with the following matters.

(a) How the balances on the share premium and the revaluation reserve arose

(b) The recommendation of one of the directors is to lease the assets as he says that this means that the asset can be kept off the balance sheet. Comment on this recommendation.

PART B

Data

The directors of Fun Limited have a number of questions relating to the financial statements of their recently acquired subsidiary undertaking, Games Limited. Fun Limited acquired 75% of the ordinary share capital of Games Limited on 30 September 19X8 for £2,244,000. The fair value of the fixed assets in Games Limited as at 30 September 19X8 was £2,045,000. The directors have provided you with the balance sheet of Games Limited as at 30 September 19X8 along with some further information.

Games Limited
Balance sheet as at 30 September 19X8

	19X8 £'000	19X7 £'000
Fixed assets	1,845	1,615
Current assets		
Stocks	918	873
Trade debtors	751	607
Cash	23	87
	1,692	1,567
Current liabilities		
Trade creditors	583	512
Dividends payable	52	48
Taxation	62	54
	697	614
Net current assets	995	953
Long-term loan	560	420
	2,280	2,148
Capital and reserves		
Called up share capital	1,000	1,000
Share premium	100	100
Profit and loss account	1,180	1,048
	2,280	2,148

Further information

♦ No fixed assets were sold during the year. The depreciation charge for the year amounted to £277,000.

♦ All sales and purchases were on credit. Other expenses were paid for in cash.

♦ The profit on ordinary activities before taxation was £246,000. Interest of £56,000 was charged in the year.

Task 2.4

Provide a reconciliation between cash flows from operating activities and operating profit for Games Limited for the year ended 30 September 19X8. You are **not** required to prepare a cash flow statement.

Task 2.5

Prepare notes to take to the Board meeting to answer the following questions of the directors.

(a) What figure for the minority interest would appear in the consolidated balance sheet of Fun Limited as at 30 September 19X8?

(b) Where in the balance sheet would the minority interest be disclosed?

(c) What is a 'minority interest'?

Section 3

Data

Jack Locke, Jane Berkeley and Sreela Hume were in partnership together selling and distributing scientific equipment. On 1 October 19X7 they admitted Bhatti Ayer into the partnership. You have been asked to finalise the partnership accounts for the year ended 30 September 19X8 and to make the entries necessary to account for the admission of Bhatti into the partnership. You have been given the following information.

(i) On 1 October 19X7 Bhatti paid £50,000 into the partnership. The profit-sharing ratios in the old partnership were:

Jack	5/12
Jane	4/12
Sreela	3/12

The new profit-sharing ratios are now:

Jack	5/15
Jane	4/15
Sreela	3/15
Bhatti	3/15

On the day that Bhatti was admitted into the partnership, the goodwill in the partnership was valued at £180,000. No goodwill is to be kept in the accounts of the new partnership. Adjustments for goodwill are to he made in the capital accounts of the partners.

(ii) Jack has produced a set of accounts which shows a profit of £164,100 for the year ended 30 September 19X8.

On further enquiry you discover that one of the debtors, who had owed the business £12,500, had gone into liquidation during the year ended 30 September 19X8 and the liquidators have said that there are no funds available to meet creditor balances. No adjustment has yet been made for this item.

An invoice for £4,200 was received on 13 November 19X8 relating to delivery costs of equipment sold to customers during the year to 30 September 19X8. It had not been included in the accounts as it had been received after the year end.

(iii) Interest on capital is to he paid at a rate of 10% on the balance at the year end on the capital accounts. No interest is paid on the current accounts.

(iv) Cash drawings in the year amounted to:

Jack	£48,200
Jane	£39,300
Sreela	£29,800
Bhatti	£25,400

(v) The partners are entitled to the following salaries per annum:

Jack	£15,000
Jane	£12,000
Srecla	£8,000
Bhatti	£8,000

(vi) The balances on the current and capital accounts at the beginning of the year, before any adjustments had been made for the admission of Bhatti into the partnership, were as follows.

	Capital accounts	Current accounts
Jack	£37,000	£5,300
Jane	£31,000	£4,200
Sreela	£26,000	£3,100

Answer Tasks 3.1-3.5 in the Answer Book provided.

Task 3.1

Produce a statement adjusting the profit figure given to you by Jack, taking into account the matters set out above and calculate the net profit figure for appropriation. You do **not** need to set out your adjustments in the form of journal entries.

Task 3.2

Justify any adjustments made to the profit figure in Task 3.1 by referring, where relevant, to accounting concepts.

Task 3.3

Prepare the partners' capital accounts for the year ended 30 September 19X8.

Task 3.4

Prepare an appropriation account for the partnership for the year ended 30 September 19X8.

Task 3.5

Prepare the partners' current accounts for the year ended 30 September 19X8.

CHAPTER 15

Mock Central Assessment

Answer Book

Task 1.1

Task 1.2

Task 1.3

Task 2.1

Proforma Journal Entries

	Debit	Credit
	£	£

Task 2.2

Proforma Profit and Loss Account
(Format 1 as supplemented by FRS 3)

Turnover

    Continuing operations

        Acquisitions

    Discontinued operations

Cost of sales

Gross profit (or loss)

Distribution costs

Administrative expenses

Operating profit (or loss)

      Continuing operations

      Acquisitions

Discontinued operations

Profit (or loss) on disposal of discontinued operations

Other operating income

Income from shares in group undertakings

Income from participating interests

Income from other fixed asset investments

Other interest receivable and similar income

Amounts written off investments

Profit (or loss) on ordinary activities before interest

Interest payable and similar charges

Profit (or loss) on ordinary activities before taxation

Tax on profit (or loss) on ordinary activities

Profit (or loss) on ordinary activities after taxation

Extraordinary items

Profit (or loss) for the financial year

Dividends

Retained profit for the financial year

Workings for Task 2.2

Task 2.3

Task 2.4

Task 2.5

Task 3.1

Task 3.2

Task 3.3

Task 3.4

Task 3.5

CHAPTER 15

Mock Central Assessment

Answers

Section 1

PART A

Task 1.1

(a) The organisations and their users are as follows.

Profit-making organisations

Type of organisation	Example of user
Companies	Shareholders
Partnerships	Bank
Sole traders	Creditors

Public sector/not-for-profit organisations:

Type of organisation	Example of user
Local authorities	Council taxpayers
National Health Service Trusts	Department of Health
Charities	People making donations
Clubs	Members

Other reasonable types of organisation and users are also acceptable.

(b) The types of decision may be as follows.

Profit-making organisations:

User	Example of decisions
Shareholders	To sell or buy more shares
	To assess stewardship of managers
Bank	To decide whether to grant a loan
Creditors	To decide whether to supply goods or services

Public sector/not-for-profit organisations:

User	Example of decisions
Council taxpayers	To decide whether the local authority has given value for money
Department of Health	To decide whether the trust has been efficiently run by the managers
People making donations	To decide whether donations have been effectively used
Members	To decide if the officers have run the club efficiently

Other reasonable examples of decisions are acceptable.

Task 1.2

(a) 'Assets' are rights or other access to future economic benefits controlled by an entity as a result of past transactions or events.

'Liabilities' are obligations of an entity to transfer economic benefits as a result of past transactions or events.

'Ownership interest' is the residual amount found by deducting all of the entity's liabilities from all of the entity's assets.

(b) In the ownership interest section of the balance sheet of a profit-making organisation capital balances would appear. These can include amounts paid in by owners (such as share capital in the case of companies) plus reserves which are owed to owners (such as the balances in the profit and loss account). In a public sector or not-for-profit organisation fund balances would appear in the ownership interest section of the balance sheet. These are amounts which have been allocated to certain purposes of the organisation.

Part B

Task 1.3

Report

To: Managers of Bimbridge Hospitals Trust   Date: 3 December 19X8

From: AAT Student

Subject: Analysis of Patch Limited's financial statements

Introduction

The purpose of this report is to analyse the financial statements of Patch Limited for 19X8 and 19X7 to determine whether to use the company as a supplier.

Calculation of ratios

The following ratios for the company have been computed.

	Patch Limited 19X8	Industry average 19X8	Patch Limited 19X7	Industry average 19X8
Return on capital employed	$\frac{552}{5,334} = 10.3\%$	9.6%	$\frac{462}{5,790} = 8.0\%$	9.4%
Net profit percentage	$\frac{552}{2,300} = 24\%$	21.4%	$\frac{462}{2,100} = 22\%$	21.3%
Quick ratio/acid test	$\frac{523}{475} = 1.1:1$	1.0:1	$\frac{418}{465} = 0.9:1$	0.9:1
Gearing				
Debt/capital employed	$\frac{1,654}{5,334} = 31\%$	36.0%	$\frac{2,490}{5,790} = 43\%$	37.0%
or				
Debt/equity	$\frac{1,654}{3,680} = 45\%$		$\frac{2,490}{3,300} = 75\%$	

Comment and analysis

The overall profitability of the company has improved from 19X7 to 19X8. The return on capital employed has increased from 8% in 19X7 to 10.3% in 19X8. This means that the company is generating more profit from the available capital employed in 19X8 as compared with 19X7. The company was below average for the industry in 19X7, but has performed better than the average in 19X8. The net profit percentage has also improved. It increased from 22% in 19X7 to 24% in 19X8. This means that the company is generating more profit from sales in 19X8 than in the previous year. In both years the company had a higher than average net profit percentage when compared against the industry average. From these ratios it would seem that the company is relatively more profitable in 19X8 as compared with 19X7 and that it now performs better than the average of the industry. This suggests that its long-term prospects for success are higher than the average of the industry.

Page 1/2

The liquidity of the company has also improved in the year. The quick ratio shows how many current assets, excluding stock, there are to meet the current liabilities and is often thought of as a better indicator of liquidity than the current ratio. The quick ratio in Patch Limited has improved from 19X7 to 19X8. It has gone up from 0.9:1 to 1.1:1. This means that in 19X8 there were more than enough quick assets to meet current liabilities. Again, the quick ratio of Patch Limited is better than the industry average in 19X8, and matched it in 19X7. We can conclude that Patch Limited is more liquid than the average of the industry in 19X8.

There has been a considerable decline in the gearing of the company in 19X8 as compared with 19X7. In 19X7 the gearing ratio was 43% and this has fallen to 31% in 19X8. This means that the percentage of debt funding to equity funding has declined between the two years. High gearing ratios are often thought of as increasing the risk of the company in that, in times of profit decline, it becomes increasingly difficult for highly geared companies to meet interest payments on debt, and in extreme cases the company could be forced into liquidation. The gearing ratio of Patch Limited was above the industry average in 19X7, making it relatively more risky, in this respect, than the average of companies in the industry. However, the ratio in 19X8 is considerably less than the industry average and hence may now be considered less risky than the average. There is thus less of a risk from gearing in doing business with the company than the average of companies in the sector.

Conclusions

Overall, based solely on the information provided in the financial statements of the company, it is recommended that you use Patch Limited as a supplier. The company has increasing profitability and liquidity and a lower level of gearing in 19X8 than in 19X7. It also compares favourably with other companies in the same industry and seems to present a lower risk than the average of the sector.

Section 2

PART A

Task 2.1

Journal entries

		£'000	£'000
(1)	DR Final dividend	800	
	CR Dividends payable		800
(2)	DR Tax charge	972	
	CR Corporation tax payable		972
(3)	DR Interest charges	24	
	CR Interest payable		24

Task 2.2

Fun Limited
Profit and Loss Account for the year ended 30 September 19X8

	£'000
Turnover	
Continuing operations (W1)	14,363
Cost of sales (W2)	6,464
Gross profit	7,899
Distribution costs	2,669
Administrative expenses	2,042
Operating profit	
Continuing operations	3,188
Interest payable and similar charges	324
Profit on ordinary activities before taxation	2,864
Tax on profit on ordinary activities	972
Profit for the financial year	1,892
Dividends (W3)	1,280
Retained profit for the financial year	612

Workings

All figures £000.

1. Sales 14,595 – Returns inwards 232 = 14,363

2. *Calculation of cost of sales.*

		£
	Opening stock	1,893
	Purchases	6,671
	plus Carriage inwards	87
	less Returns outwards	(146)
		8,505
	less Closing stock	2,041
	Cost of sales	6,464

3. *Dividends:*

	£
Interim dividend	480
Final dividend proposed	800
	1,280

Task 2.3

Notes

(a) The balance on the share premium arose when shares were issued at more than their nominal value. For example, if a share with a nominal value of £1.00 was issued for £1.50 then the accounting entries would be as follows.

	£	£
DR Cash	1.50	
CR Share capital		1.00
CR Share premium		0.50

The revaluation reserve represents the excess of the valuation of an asset over its net book value. If the fixed assets had a net book value of £500,000 and their market value was established by a valuation as £700,000 then the (simplified) entry would be as follows.

	£	£
DR Fixed assets	200,000	
CR Revaluation reserve		200,000

(b) The accounting for the leased asset would depend upon whether the lease was a finance lease or an operating lease. SSAP 21 defines a finance lease as a lease which transfers substantially all the risks and rewards of ownership of an asset to the lessee. An operating lease is a lease other than a finance lease.

A finance lease should be recorded in the balance sheet of Fun Limited as an asset and as an obligation to pay future rentals. The amount recorded should be the present value of the minimum lease payments derived by discounting them at the interest rate implicit in the lease. If the asset was leased on an operating lease it would not be shown on the balance sheet of the lessee, but on the balance sheet of the lessor. The obligation to pay future rentals would not be shown as a liability on the balance sheet of the lessee.

Part B

Task 2.4

Reconciliation between the cash flows from operating activities and the operating profit is as follows.

	£'000
Operating profit	302
Depreciation charges	277
Increase in stock	(45)
Increase in debtors	(144)
Increase in creditors	71
Net cash inflow from operating activities	461

Working

	£'000
Profit on ordinary activities before taxation	246
plus Interest charges	56
Operating profit	302

Task 2.5

Notes

(a) Calculation of minority interest.

	Total equity £'000	Minority interest £'000
Share capital	1,000	250
Share premium	100	25
Revaluation reserve (W1)	200	50
Profit and loss at acquisition	1,180	295
	2,480	620

Working (W1)

Revaluation of assets in Games Limited to fair value at date of acquisition:

DR Fixed assets	£200,000
CR Revaluation reserve	£200,000

(b) The minority interest should be shown as a separate item in the capital and reserves part of the balance sheet following the capital and reserves balances attributable to the group.

(c) A minority interest is defined by FRS 2 as the interest in a subsidiary undertaking included in the consolidation that is attributable to the shares held by persons other than the parent undertaking and its subsidiary undertakings.

Section 3

Task 3.1

	£
Profit per Jack	164,100
Bad debt written off	(12,500)
Accrual for delivery costs	(4,200)
Adjusted profit for appropriation	147,400

Task 3.2

(a) The liquidation of the debtor during the year and the lack of funds to pay off the debt to the partnership means that the business has sustained a loss. The prudence concept says that all losses must be provided for as soon as they are known. As the business is aware that a loss has been sustained it must be provided for immediately and the bad debt of £12,500 be written off in the year to 30 September 19X8.

(b) The invoice for £4,200 representing delivery costs for sales made during the year to 30 September 19X8 must be included in this year's accounts even though the invoice was not received until after the year end. The accrual or matching concept states that all costs must be matched against the income which they helped to generate. As the income was recorded in the year the costs of delivery must be matched against this income and recorded in the year to 30 September 19X8.

Task 3.3

Partners' capital accounts

	Jack	Jane		Jack	Jane
	£	£		£	£
Goodwill 1/10/X7	60,000	48,000	Balance 1/10/X7	37,000	31,000
Balance c/d 30/9/X8	52,000	43,000	Goodwill 1/10/X7	75,000	60,000
	112,000	91,000		112,000	91,000

	Sreela	Bhatti		Sreela	Bhatti
	£	£		£	£
Goodwill 1/10/X7	36,000	36,000	Balance 1/10/X7	26,000	
Balance c/d 30/9/X8	35,000	14,000	Cash 1/10/X7		50,000
			Goodwill 1/10/X7	45,000	
	71,000	50,000		71,000	50,000

Task 3.4

Jack, Jane, Sreela and Bhatti
Appropriation account for the year ended
30 September 19X8

		£	£
Net profit			147,400
Less	Partners' salaries		
	Jack	15,000	
	Jane	12,000	
	Sreela	8,000	
	Bhatti	8,000	
			43,000
Less	Interest on capital		
	Jack	5,200	
	Jane	4,300	
	Srecla	3,500	
	Bhatti	1,400	
			14,400
			90,000
Balance of profits shared			
	Jane 5/15		30,000
	Jane 4/15		24,000
	Sreela 3/15		18,000
	Bhatti 3/15		18,000
			90,000

Working – Interest on capital

Jack	10% x £52,000	= £5,200
Jane	10% x £43,000	= £4,300
Sreela	10% x £35,000	= £3,500
Bhatti	10% x £14,000	= £1,400

Task 3.5

Partners' current accounts

	Jack £	Jane £		Jack £	Jane £
Drawings 30/9/X8	48,200	39,300	Balance 1/10/X7	5,300	4,200
Balance c/d 30/9/X8	7,300	5,200	Interest on capital 30/9/X8	5,200	4,300
			Salaries 30/9/X8	15,000	12,000
			Profit 30/9/X8	30,000	24,000
	55,500	44,500		55,500	44,500

	Sreela £	Bhatti £		Sreela £	Bhatti £
Drawings 30/9/X8	29,800	25,400	Balance 1/10/X7	3,100	–
Balance c/d 30/9/X8	2,800	2,000	Interest on capital 30/9/X8	3,500	1,400
			Salaries 30/9/X8	8,000	8,000
			Profit 30/9/X8	18,000	18,000
	32,600	27,400		32,600	27,400

Index

Accounting bases	10
Accounting concepts	9
Accounting policies	11
Accounting records	80
Accounting standards	3
Accounts of small and medium-sized companies	115
Accruals concept	10
Acquisition accounting	298
Acquisitions	121
Administrative expenses	73
Admission of new partners	54
Alternative valuation rules	3
Annual accounts	80
Appropriation of profit	47
ASB	3
ASC	3
Assets	16
Associates	290,296
Auditors' report	81
Authorised share capital	75
Balance sheet disclosures	97
Balance sheet formats	93,94
Balance sheet	1
Best practice	42
Bonus issues	77
Calculating ratios	214
Cancellation of intra-group balances	258
Capital and reserves	103
Capital instruments	79
Cash flow statements	1,195
Companies Act 1985	2
Companies Act 1989	3
Compliance with accounting standards	112
Conceptual framework	9
Confidentiality	6
Consistency concept	10
Consolidated balance sheet	239,255
Consolidated profit and loss account	252,275
Contingencies	190
Continuing operations	121
Control and ownership distinction	244
Corporation tax	73,181
Credit sale	177
Current assets	31,100
Current liabilities	31
Debentures	79
Deferred tax	184
Depreciation	139
Directors' emoluments	109
Directors' report	80,112
Disclosure of accounting policies	112
Discontinued operations	121
Dissolution of partnership	63
Distribution costs	72
Dividends	73,263
Exceptional items	123
Exemption from requirement to prepare group accounts	288
Exemptions for small and medium-sized companies	116
Exemptions for small companies	117
Extended trial balance	35
Extraordinary and exceptional items	111,125
Factory cost	85
Fair values	266
Finance lease	178
Financial statements	1
Fixed assets	31,97,137,153
Foreign currency translation	229
Formats	2
FRRP	4
FRS1 Cash Flow Statements	199
FRS2 Accounting for Subsidiary Undertakings	287,289
FRS3 Reporting Financial Performance	121
FRS5 Reporting the Substance of Transactions	233
FRS8 Related Party Transactions	235
FRS9 Associates and Joint Ventures	297
FRS10 Goodwill and Intangible Assets	157
FRS11 Impairment of Fixed Assets and Goodwill	162
FRS12 Provisions and Contingencies	190
FRS14 Earnings per share	113
FRS15 Tangible Fixed Assets	137
FRSs	3
FRSSE	117
Fundamental accounting concepts	10
Fundamental accounting principles	2
Funds	26
Gains	17
Gearing ratios	217
Going concern	10
Goodwill on consolidation	245,247
Goodwill	157,162,283
Group accounts - legal and professional requirements	287

Index

Group accounts 237

Hire purchase contracts 177,179
Historical cost accounting 3
Historical cost profits and losses 129
Historical cost 13

Impairment 162
Incorporation 22
Intangible assets 153
Interpretation of accounts 213
Interpreting a cash flow statement 206
Interpreting ratios 218
Intra-group trading 281
Issued share capital 75

Journal entries 32

Leases 177
Liabilities 17,101
Limited company accounts 71
Limited companies 22
Limited liability 22
Liquidity ratios 216
Long-term contract work in progress 170
Losses 17

Management accounts 5
Manufacturing accounts 85
Materiality 12,16
Merger accounting 298
Minority interests 290

Net assets working 251
Non-aggregation principle 11
Non-profit making entities 24

Objective of financial statements 14
Operating lease 178,179
Ordinary shares 75
Ownership interest 17

Parent definition 288
Partnership 22
Partnership accounts 45
Partnership agreement 46
Partnership changes 49
Partnership goodwill 50
Pension costs 231
Post balance sheet events 187
Preference shares 75
Preparing final accounts 27
Prime cost 85
Prior-period adjustments 125
Profit and loss account 1
Profit and loss account disclosures 108
Profit and loss account formats 108
Profitability ratios 215

Proforma balance sheet 30
Proforma cash flow statement 199
Proforma company balance sheet 74
Proforma company profit and loss account 72
Proforma consolidated profit and loss account 276
Proforma consolidation workings 270
Proforma manufacturing account 86
Proforma profit and loss account 29
Provision for unrealised profit 281
Provisions 101,190
Prudence concept 10

Ratio analysis 213,218
Realisation account 65
Realisation 13
Reconciliation of movements in shareholders'
    funds and statement of reserves 130
Related party transactions 234
Research and development expenditure 153
Reserves 76
Retirement of partners 59
Revaluation of fixed assets 142
Revaluation of partnership assets 52
Rights issues 78

Separate legal personality 22
Share capital 74
Share premium account 76
Single entity concept 238
Sole trader accounts 29
Sole trader 21
SSAPs 3
SSAP2 Disclosure of Accounting Policies ... 2,10
SSAP4 Accounting for Government Grants. 148
SSAP5 Accounting for VAT 183
SSAP9 Stocks and Long-Term Contracts 167
SSAP13 Accounting for Research and
    Development 153
SSAP17 Accounting for Post Balance Sheet
    Events 187
SSAP19 Accounting for Investment
    Properties 146
SSAP20 Foreign Currency Translation 229
SSAP24 Accounting for Pension Costs 231
SSAP25 Segmental Reporting 224
Standard setting process 4
Statement of financial performance 25
Statement of group reserves 284
Statement of Principles 13
Statement of total recognised gains and losses 127
Stock 167
Subsidiary 288
Substance of transactions 233
Substance over form 12
Summary financial statements 117

Tangible assets 137
Taxation in company accounts 181

True and fair concept 12
Types of business organisation 21
Types of company 80
Types of standard 5

UITF 4
Unrealised intra-group profit 265
Users of accounts 41

VAT 183

STUDY PACK REVIEW FORM

We hope that you have found this Study Pack stimulating and useful and that you now feel confident and well-prepared for your Central Assessment in Unit 10.

We would be grateful if you could take a few moments to complete the questionnaire below, so we can assess how well our material meets the needs of students. There's a prize for four lucky students who fill in one of these forms from across the AAT range and are lucky enough to be selected!

	Excellent	Adequate	Poor
Depth and breadth of technical coverage			
Appropriateness of coverage to Central Assessment once completed			
Presentation			
Level of accuracy			

Did you spot any errors or ambiguities? Please let us have the details below.

Thank you for your feedback.

Please return this form to:

AAT review forms
Profex Publishing
1 High Street
Maidenhead
Berkshire SL6 1JN

Or e-mail your comments to: profex@clara.co.uk